The Teachings of Modern Orthodox Christianity
on Law, Politics, and Human Nature

The Teachings of Modern Orthodox Christianity

❖ ON LAW, POLITICS, AND HUMAN NATURE ❖

EDITED BY

John Witte Jr. and Frank S. Alexander

INTRODUCTION BY

Paul Valliere

COLUMBIA UNIVERSITY PRESS   NEW YORK

Columbia University Press
Publishers Since 1893
New York   Chichester, West Sussex
Copyright © 2007 Columbia University Press
All rights reserved

Library of Congress Cataloging-in-Publication Data

The Teachings of modern Orthodox Christianity on law, politics, and human nature /
edited by John Witte, Jr. and Frank S. Alexander ; introduction by Paul Valliere.
p.   cm.
Includes index.
ISBN 978-0-231-14264-9 (cloth : alk. paper) — ISBN 978-0-231-14265-6 (pbk.)
1. Orthodox Eastern Church—Doctrines.   I. Witte, John, 1959–
II. Alexander, Frank S., 1952–   III. Title.

BX320.3.T43   2007
261.8088'2819—dc22   2007002064

Columbia University Press books are printed on permanent and durable acid-free paper.
This book was printed on paper with recycled content.

Printed in the United States of America

c 10 9 8 7 6 5 4 3 2 1
p 10 9 8 7 6 5 4 3 2 1

References to Internet Web sites (URLs) were accurate at the time of writing. Neither the
volume editors nor the authors nor Columbia University Press is responsible for URLs
that may have expired or changed since the manuscript was prepared.

BUT WHAT IS government itself, but the greatest of all reflections on human nature? If men were angels, no government would be necessary. If angels were to govern men, neither external nor internal controls on government would be necessary. In framing a government which is to be administered by men over men, the great difficulty lies in this: you must first enable the government to control the governed; and in the next place oblige it to control itself. A dependence on the people is, no doubt, the primary control on the government; but experience has taught mankind the necessity of auxiliary precautions.

—*James Madison, Federalist Paper No. 51*

Contents

Original Source Materials

3. Vladimir Nikolaievich Lossky (1903–1958)

Commentary

MIKHAIL M. KULAKOV 172

Original Source Materials

4. Mother Maria Skobtsova (1891–1945)

Commentary

MICHAEL PLEKON 233

Original Source Materials

5. Dumitru Stăniloae (1903–1993)

Commentary

LUCIAN TURCESCU 295

Original Source Materials

Foreword

THIS VOLUME IS part and product of a major new project on Christian Jurisprudence undertaken by our Center for the Study of Law and Religion at Emory University. We first published this work as a two-volume cloth edition designed to provide a comparative analysis of modern Catholic, Protestant, and Orthodox Christian teachings on law, politics, and human nature. One volume provided an illustrative collection of primary texts written by a score of Christian scholars and activists who led the main movements in Catholicism, Protestantism, and Orthodoxy in the later nineteenth and twentieth centuries. A second cloth volume provided a collection of fresh essays that analyzed the theology and jurisprudence of these modern Christian leaders. The introductions to these volumes and the opening and closing essays to the second volume sought to situate these Catholic, Protestant, and Orthodox Christian contributions in the broader context of law, politics, and society, and to compare and contrast them with one another and with various secular legal and political philosophies. We have been most gratified by the generous reception of the first edition, and the glowing reviews it has occasioned. The volumes seem to have struck a real nerve in Christian and non-Christian circles alike, and have opened whole new areas of teaching and research for our readers. Indeed, our project on Christian jurisprudence has commissioned two dozen new volumes to amplify some of the themes set forth therein.

This three-volume edition offers a leaner and more denominationally specific presentation of the same modern Christian teachings on law, politics, and society. Each volume now focuses specifically on Catholic, Protestant, or Orthodox teachings with a short introduction to provide broader comparative and ecumenical perspective. Each volume also couples analytical essays on the selected modern Christian scholars with those scholars' original source materials. We have presented the material in this form not because we have given up on ecumenism but because we have given thought to pedagogy. We are eager to have these volumes read and used not only by scholars and church leaders but also by students, novitiates, and catechumens in churches, colleges, graduate schools, law schools, seminaries, divinity schools, Sunday schools, and various learned societies. For most such classrooms, the cloth volumes are too wide in sweep, too weighty in tone, and too hard on the wallet. Hence this more accessible and economical edition—updated and corrected a bit for even more ready use.

We express anew our warmest thanks to our friends at Columbia University Press, notably Wendy Lochner and Christine Mortlock, for lending so generously of their time and talents. We express our profound gratitude for the generous support of our project on Christian jurisprudence by our friends at The Pew Charitable Trusts, Inc., particularly Rebecca Rimel and Susan Billington Harper; our friends at the Lilly Endowment, Inc., notably Craig Dykstra; and our friends at the Alonzo L. McDonald Family Foundation, notably Alonzo, Peter, and Suzie McDonald, and Robert Pool. Finally, we express our warmest appreciation to our colleague Linda King for her expert work on the production of this volume and its companions.

—John Witte Jr. and Frank S. Alexander, Emory University

Acknowledgments

THIS VOLUME AND its companions are products of a three-year project of the Center for the Study of Law and Religion at Emory University, parts of a broader effort of The Pew Charitable Trusts and the University of Notre Dame to stimulate and support new scholarship on the place of Christianity in various fields of academic specialty. Armed with a major grant from Pew, Notre Dame Provost Nathan O. Hatch and his colleagues have assembled ten groups of scholars in the fields of law, philosophy, literature, economics, and other subjects who have an interest in the scholarly place of Christianity in their particular discipline. Each group of specialists has been asked to address the general theme of "Christianity and the nature of the person" from the perspective of its particular discipline and to produce a major new study that speaks to this theme in a manner edifying both to scholars in other fields and to peers of all faiths in its own field.

We have been privileged to lead the team on law. We wish to thank the immensely talented group of contributors to this volume and to the companion volumes on the Protestant and Catholic traditions. We give special thanks to Professor Paul Valliere, who gave valuable advice on the shape of this volume, and who contributed such a brilliant introduction.

On behalf of our colleagues in the Center for the Study of Law and Religion, we express our deep gratitude to our friends at The Pew Charitable Trusts for their generous support of this project, particularly Pew's President Rebecca Rimel, and Program officers Dr. Luis Lugo, Dr. Susan Billington Harper, and Dr. Diane Winston. We also express our gratitude to our friends at the University of Notre Dame, particularly then-Provost Dr. Nathan O. Hatch, who now serves as President of Wake Forest University.

We wish to thank Dr. Craig Dykstra and his colleagues at the Lilly Endowment, Inc. in Indianapolis for their generous grant in support of John

Witte's project on "Law, Religion, and the Protestant Tradition," which has provided him with release time to work on this and other book projects.

We wish to recognize and thank several of our colleagues in the Center for the Study of Law and Religion for their exceptional work on the administration of this project and the production of the original two volumes. We are particularly grateful to Ms. Linda King for masterminding the administration of the project, for coordinating the three conferences that it occasioned, and for working so expertly and assiduously on the production of the resulting manuscripts. We express our gratitude to Ms. Anita Mann, Ms. Amy Wheeler, Ms. Eliza Ellison, and Ms. Janice Wiggins for sharing so generously of their administrative expertise.

Finally, we would like to thank Wendy Lochner and her colleagues at Columbia University Press for taking on these volumes and working so efficiently and effectively to ensure their timely production. And we appreciate the very helpful criticisms and suggestions of the three anonymous outside reviewers of an earlier version of this manuscript.

This volume is dedicated to the students of the Center for the Study of Law and Religion at Emory University, past, present, and future.

—John Witte Jr. and Frank S. Alexander, Emory University

Contributors

FRANK S. ALEXANDER, J.D. (Harvard), M.T.S. (Harvard), is professor of law; Founding Director, Center for the Study of Law and Religion; and Director of the Project on Affordable Housing and Community Development at Emory University.

VIGEN GUROIAN, LOYOLA COLLEGE, PH.D. (Drew), is professor of theology at Loyola College.

MIKHAIL KULAKOV, D.PHIL. (Christ Church, Oxford), M.A. (Andrews University), is associate professor of political studies and philosophy, Columbia Union College.

MICHAEL PLEKON, PH.D. (Rutgers), M.A. (Rutgers), is professor of sociology and Coordinator of the Religion and Culture Program at Baruch College, City University of New York.

LUCIAN TURCESCU, PH.D. (St. Michael's College, University of Toronto), M.T. (Bucharest University), is associate professor in the Theological Studies Department at Concordia University, Montreal, and President of the Canadian Society of Patristic Studies.

PAUL VALLIERE, PH.D. (Columbia), M.A. (Columbia), is professor of religion and McGregor Professor of the Humanities at Butler University.

JOHN WITTE JR., J.D. (Harvard), is Jonas Robitscher Professor of Law and Director of the Center for the Study of Law and Religion at Emory University.

Introduction

THE CONTEXT

The better the society, the less law there will be. In Heaven there will be no law, and the lion will lie down with the lamb. . . . In Hell there will be nothing but law, and due process will be meticulously observed.

SO REMARKED THE eminent legal scholar Grant Gilmore in closing his 1974 lecture series at Yale Law School, later published as *The Ages of American Law*. Gilmore crafted this catchy couplet to capture the pessimistic view of law, politics, and society made popular by the American jurist and Supreme Court Justice Oliver Wendell Holmes Jr. (1841–1935). Contrary to the conventional portrait of Holmes as the sage and sartorial "Yankee from Olympus,"[1] Gilmore saw him as a "harsh and cruel" man, chastened and charred by the savagery of the American Civil War and the gluttony of the industrial revolution. These experiences, Gilmore argued, had made Holmes "a bitter and lifelong pessimist who saw in the course of human life nothing but a continuing struggle in which the rich and powerful impose their will on the poor and the weak."[2] The cruel excesses of the Bolshevik Revolution, World War I, and the Great Depression in the first third of the twentieth century only confirmed Holmes in his pessimism that human life was "without values."[3]

This bleak view of human nature shaped Holmes's bleak view of law, politics, and society. He regarded law principally as a barrier against human depravity—a means to check the worst instincts of the proverbial "bad man" against his worst instincts and to make him pay dearly if he yielded to temptation.[4] Holmes also regarded law as a buffer against human suffering—a means to protect the vulnerable against the worst exploitation by corporations, churches, and Congress. For him, there was no higher law in heaven to guide the law below. There was no path of legal virtue up which a man should go. The "path of the law" cut a horizontal line between human sanctity and depravity. Law served to keep society and its members from sliding into the abyss of hell, but it could do nothing to guide its members in their ascent to heaven.

Holmes was the "high priest" of a new "age of faith" in American law, Gilmore wrote with intended irony, that replaced an earlier era dominated by the church and the clergy.[5] The confession of this new age of faith was that America was a land "ruled by laws, not by men." Its catechism was the new case law method of the law school classroom. Its canon was the new concordance of legal codes, amply augmented by New Deal legislation. Its church was the common law court where the rituals of judicial formalism and due process would yield legal truth. Its church council was the Supreme Court, which now issued opinions with as much dogmatic confidence as the divines of Nicaea, Augsburg, and Trent.

This new age of faith in American law was in part the product of a new faith in the positivist theory of knowledge that swept over America in the later nineteenth and twentieth centuries, eclipsing earlier theories that gave religion and the church a more prominent place in the law. The turn to positivism proceeded in two stages. The first stage was scientific. Inspired by the successes of the early modern scientific revolution—from Copernicus to Newton—eighteenth-century European and nineteenth-century American jurists set out to create a method of law that was every bit as scientific and rigorous as that of the new mathematics and the new physics. This was not merely an exercise in professional rivalry. It was an earnest attempt to show that law had an autonomous place in the cadre of positive sciences, that it could not and should not be subsumed by theology, politics, philosophy, or economics. In testimony to this claim, jurists in this period poured forth a staggering number of new legal codes, new constitutions, new legal encyclopedias, dictionaries, textbooks, and other legal syntheses that still grace, and bow, the shelves of our law libraries.[6]

The second stage of the positivist turn in law was philosophical. A new movement—known variously as legal positivism, legal formalism, and analytical jurisprudence—sought to reduce the subject matter of law to its most essential core. If physics could be reduced to "matter in motion" and biology to "survival of the fittest," then surely law and legal study could be reduced to a core subject as well. The formula was produced in the mid-nineteenth century, most famously by John Austin in England and Christopher Columbus Langdell in America: Law is simply the concrete rules and procedures posited by the sovereign and enforced by the courts. Many other institutions and practices might be normative and important for social coherence and political concordance, but they are not law. They are the subjects of theology, ethics, economics, politics, psychology, sociology, anthropology, and other humane disciplines. They stand beyond the province of jurisprudence properly determined.[7]

This positivist theory of law, which swept over American universities from the 1890s onward, rendered legal study increasingly narrow and insular. Law was simply the sovereign's rules. Legal study was simply the analysis of those rules and their application in particular cases. Why the rules were posited, whether their positing was for good or ill, how they affected society, politics, or morality were not relevant questions for legal study. By the early twentieth century, it was rather common to read in legal textbooks that law is an autonomous science; that its doctrines, language, and methods are self-sufficient; and that its study is self-contained.[8] It was rather common to think that law has the engines of change within itself, that through its own design and dynamic, law marches teleologically through time "from trespass to case to negligence, from contract to quasi-contract to implied warranty."[9]

Holmes was an early champion of this positivist theory of law and legal development. He rebuked more traditional views with a series of famous aphorisms that are still often quoted today. Against those who insisted that the legal tradition was more than simply a product of pragmatic evolution, he wrote: "The life of the law is not logic but experience."[10] Against those who appealed to a higher natural law to guide the positive law of the state, he cracked: "There is no such brooding omnipresence in the sky."[11] Against those who argued for a more principled jurisprudence, he retorted: "General principles do not decide concrete cases."[12] Against those who insisted that law needed basic moral premises to be cogent, he mused: "I should be glad if we could get rid of the whole moral phraseology which I think has tended to distort the law. In fact even in the domain of morals I think that it would be a gain, at least for the educated, to get rid of the word and notion [of] Sin."[13]

Despite its new prominence, American legal positivism had ample detractors. Already in the 1920s and 1930s, sociologists of law argued that the nature and purpose of law and politics cannot be understood without reference to the spirit of a people and their times—a *Volksgeist und Zeitgeist*, as their German counterparts put it. The legal realist movement of the 1930s and 1940s used the new insights of psychology and anthropology to cast doubt on the immutability and ineluctability of judicial reasoning. The revived natural law movement of the 1940s and 1950s saw in the horrors of Hitler's Holocaust and Stalin's gulags the perils of constructing a legal system without transcendent checks and balances. The international human rights movement of the 1950s and 1960s pressed the law to address more directly the sources and sanctions of civil, political, social, cultural, and economic rights. Marxist, feminist, and neo-Kantian movements in the 1960s and 1970s used linguistic and structural critiques to expose the fallacies and false equalities of legal and political doctrines. Watergate and other political scandals in the 1970s and 1980s highlighted the need for a more comprehensive understanding of legal ethics and political accountability.

By the early 1970s, the confluence of these and other movements had exposed the limitations of a positivist definition of law standing alone. Leading jurists of the day—Lon Fuller, Jerome Hall, Karl Llewellyn, Harold Berman, and others—were pressing for a broader understanding and definition of law.[14] Of course, they said in concurrence with legal positivists, law consists of rules—the black letter rules of contracts, torts, property, corporations, and sundry other familiar subjects. Of course, law draws to itself a distinctive legal science, an "artificial reason," as Sir Edward Coke once put it.[15] But law is much more than the rules of the state and how we apply and analyze them. Law is also the social activity by which certain norms are formulated by legitimate authorities and actualized by people subject to those authorities. The process of legal formulation involves legislating, adjudicating, administering, and other conduct by legitimate officials. The process of legal actualization involves obeying, negotiating, litigating, and other conduct by legal subjects. Law is a set of rules, plus the social and political processes of formulating, enforcing, and responding to those rules.[16] Numerous other institutions besides the state are involved. The rules, customs, and processes of churches, colleges, corporations, clubs, charities, and other nonstate associations are just as much part of a society's legal system as those of the state. Numerous other norms besides legal rules are involved. Order and obedience, authority and liberty are exercised out of a complex blend of concerns and conditions—class, gender, persuasion, piety, charisma, clemency, courage, moderation, temperance, force, faith, and more.

Legal positivism could not, by itself, come to terms with law understood in this broader sense. In the last third of the twentieth century, American jurists thus began to (re)turn with increasing alacrity to the methods and insights of other disciplines to enhance their formulations. This was the birthing process of the modern movement of interdisciplinary legal study. The movement was born to enhance the province and purview of legal study, to refigure the roots and routes of legal analysis, and to render more holistic and realistic our appreciation of law in community, in context, in concert with politics, social sciences, and other disciplines.[17] In the 1970s, a number of interdisciplinary approaches began to enter the mainstream of American legal education—combining legal study with the study of philosophy, economics, medicine, politics, and sociology. In the 1980s and 1990s, new interdisciplinary legal approaches appeared in rapid succession—the study of law coupled with the study of anthropology, literature, environmental science, urban studies, women's studies, gay-lesbian studies, and African American studies. And, importantly for our purposes, in these last two decades, the study of law was also recombined with the study of religion, including Christianity.

THE CONTENT

In this context, it is no surprise that, until recently, modern Western Christian teachings on law, politics, and society have been largely lost on the academy.[18] To be sure, medieval and early modern Christian influences on the Western legal tradition were recognized. And the valuable contributions of a few Christian lights of the twentieth century—Reinhold Niebuhr, Jacques Maritain, and Martin Luther King Jr. especially—have long been closely studied. But the prevailing assumption of most scholars has been that, for good or ill, the historical contributions of Christianity to our understanding of law, politics, and society were gradually eclipsed in the modern period. Outside of specialty discussions of natural law and church-state relations, it has been widely assumed, modern Christianity has had little constructive or original to say.

The premise of this volume and its two companions is that modern Christianity did have a great deal to say about law, politics, and society, and its teachings can still have a salutary influence today, in the West and well beyond. Many branches of modern Christianity did become theologically anemic, ethically compromised, and jurisprudentially barren. But in each generation, we submit, strong schools of Christian legal, political, and social teaching remained, each grounded in a rich and nuanced Christian theology—including a theology of human nature or, more technically, a theological anthropology. Not surprisingly, given the prominence of legal positivism, most of the best such teaching happened outside of the legal profession—in seminaries and church councils, among philosophers and ethicists, on soapboxes and in prison cells, in intellectual isolation if not outright exile. But by word, by deed, and by declaration, modern Christians addressed the cardinal issues of law, politics, and society, drawing on a rich theology of human nature.

These three volumes sample these teachings and map their insights for the most pressing issues of our day. Such issues include topics familiar to scholars of law, politics, and society whatever their persuasion: the nature and purpose of law and authority, the mandate and limits of rule and obedience, the rights and duties of officials and subjects, the care and nurture of the needy and innocent, the rights and wrongs of war and violence, the separation and cooperation of church and state, and the sources and sanctions of legal reasoning. Such issues also include questions more specifically Christian in accent but no less important for our understanding of law, politics, and society: Are people fundamentally good or evil? Is human dignity essentially rational or relational? Is law inherently coercive or liberating? Is law a stairway to heaven or a fence against hell? Did government predate or postdate the fall into sin? Should authorities only proscribe vices or also prescribe virtues? Is the state a divine or a popular sovereign? Are social institutions fundamentally hierarchical or egalitarian in internal structure and external relations? Are they rooted in creation or custom, covenant or contract? What is justice, and what must a Christian do in its absence?

Together these volumes address the lives, writing, and thought of twenty leading modern Catholic, Protestant, and Orthodox Christians who addressed just these types of questions: modern theologians, philosophers, ethicists, jurists, statesmen, and churchmen who spoke to many issues of law, politics, and society on the strength of their theological anthropology— or spoke to one or two issues with particular acuity and originality. They are introduced by analytical essays followed by a set of illustrative selections from their main writings.

Permit us a few words about how we have selected and arranged the figures included in these volumes. First, the focus is on *modern* Christian teachings on law, politics, society, and human nature. "Modern," "modernism," and "modernity" are highly contested labels these days— not least within Christian churches, where the terms have often been associated with dangerous liberal tendencies. We are using the word "modern" nontechnically. We are focused principally on twentieth-century Christianity, reaching back into the later nineteenth century to understand movements that culminated more recently. The time period in question includes the Reconstruction era after the American Civil War, the later industrial revolution, the Bolshevik Revolution and the emergence of socialism, two world wars, the Holocaust and the Stalinist purges, the modern human rights revolution, the Great Depression and the rise of the Western welfare state, the technological revolution, and the emergence of globalization. These modern moments and movements had monumental, and sometimes devastating, effects on modern Christianity.

Many of these twentieth-century movements were continuous with earlier movements that are often also described as "modern." Among these are the Glorious Revolution of England (1689), the American Revolution (1776), and the French Revolution (1789). Important also was the scientific revolution in the seventeenth and eighteenth centuries and the later rise of what Max Weber called technical rationality and the bureaucratization of the state and society. Most important of all was the eighteenth- and nineteenth-century Enlightenment in Europe and North America, with its new secular theology of individualism, rationalism, and nationalism that often challenged core Christian beliefs. To Enlightenment exponents, the individual was no longer viewed primarily as a sinner seeking salvation in the life hereafter. Every individual was created equal in virtue and dignity, vested with inherent rights of life, liberty, and property, and capable of choosing his or her own means and measures of happiness. Reason was no longer the handmaiden of revelation, rational disputation was no longer subordinate to homiletic declaration. The rational process, conducted privately by each person and collectively in the open marketplace of ideas, was considered a sufficient source of private morality and public law. The nation-state was no longer identified with a national church or a divinely blessed covenant people. It was to be glorified in its own right. Its constitutions and laws were sacred texts reflecting the morals and mores of the collective national culture. Its officials were secular priests, representing the sovereignty and will of the people.

The introductions address some of the earlier phases of the modern age, but not all of them, and not with a depth that will satisfy specialists. It would require a set of volumes considerably heftier than these to take full account of these earlier modern movements and their impact on Christian teachings on law, politics, and society. The later modern period is less known, and it is the period with which these volumes are principally occupied.

Second, we have deliberately used the term "teachings," rather than "theories," "theologies," or other formal labels, to describe what modern Christianity has offered to law, politics, and society. In part, this is to underscore that the call to "teach" is what all Christians, despite their vast denominational differences, have in common. Christ's last words to his disciples, after all, were, "Go ye, therefore, and make disciples of all nations . . . *teaching* them to observe all that I have commanded you."[19] In part this is to recognize that "social teachings," "political teachings," "moral teachings," and "legal teachings" have become terms of art in current scholarship. Particularly in the Catholic and Protestant worlds, "social teaching" has become shorthand for a fantastic range of speculation on issues of law, politics, society, and morality.[20] And, in part, we use "teachings" to underscore that modern Christians have contributed to our understanding of law, politics, and society by word and by deed, by books and by speeches, by brilliant writings and by sacrificial acts. It would be foolish to dismiss the novel teachings of Susan B. Anthony or Dorothy Day just because they had thin resumes. It would be equally foolish not to draw lessons from the martyrdom of Mother Maria, Dietrich Bonhoeffer, or Martin Luther King Jr. just because they left their papers in disarray.

Third, we have divided the twenty figures covered in these three volumes into Catholic, Protestant, and Orthodox Christian groups, while recognizing that some were more ecumenically minded than others. We have included an introduction to each tradition to contextualize and connect the studies of the individuals that are included and have arranged the chapters more or less chronologically for each tradition, assigning varying word limits and selections for each figure in accordance with their relative importance for the themes of these volumes.

Fourth, with respect to the Catholic tradition, we have blended episcopal and lay voices from both sides of the Atlantic. Leo XIII, John XXIII, and John Paul II offered the most original and enduring contributions among modern popes, though Pope Pius XII was important as well. Leo XIII led the revival and reconstruction of the thought of the thirteenth-century sage Thomas Aquinas. He applied this "neo-Thomism," as it was called, to the formulation of several of the Catholic Church's core "social teachings," not least a theory of social institutions that would later ripen into subsidiarity doctrine, and a theory of labor that would later form the backbone of the church's stand for social, cultural, and economic rights. John XXIII was the architect of the Second Vatican Council (1962–65), with its transforming vision of religious liberty, human dignity, and democracy, and its deliberate agenda to modernize the Catholic Church's political platforms and social teachings. John Paul II, who faced the ravages of both the Nazi occupation and the Communist takeover of his native Poland, was a fierce champion of democratization and human rights in the first years of his pontificate, as well as an active sponsor of rapprochement among Catholics, Protestants, and Jews and of revitalization of the church's canon law. In his last years, he also became an equally fierce critic of the growing secularization of society, liberalization of theology, and exploitation of human nature. These latter concerns have drawn the church's leadership to new (and sometimes controversial) interpretations of its earlier "social teachings."

The French philosopher Jacques Maritain and the American theologian John Courtney Murray were among the most original and influential of the many European and American Catholic writers in the mid-twentieth century. Maritain combined neo-Thomism and French existentialism into an intricate new theory of natural law, natural rights, human dignity, equality, and fraternity, which inspired the Universal Declaration of Human Rights (1948). Murray combined neo-Thomism and American democratic theory into a powerful new argument for natural law, human dignity, religious liberty, church-state relations, and social organization. Both theories were initially controversial. Maritain was blistered by his reviewers; Murray was censored for a time by the church. But they and the many scholars they influenced laid much of the foundation for the Second Vatican Council's declaration on human dignity and religious freedom and the church's emerging global advocacy of human rights and democratization.

American political activist Dorothy Day and Latin American liberation theologian Gustavo Gutiérrez represent important new strains of social and political critique and activism within modern Catholicism. Day defied state and church authorities alike in her relentless crusade to protect the rights of workers and the poor and to protest warfare, grounding her work in a robust theology of personalism. Gutiérrez combined some of the teachings of Vatican II and Marxism into a searing critique of global capitalism and its devastating impact on the poor and on the underdeveloped world. Both Day and Gutiérrez adduced the Bible above all to press for a preferential option for the poor, the needy, and the vulnerable. Both figures have been controversial and both drew episcopal censure, but they have helped to illustrate, if not inspire, many new forms of social and political activism among Catholics worldwide.

Fifth, the Protestant tradition, with its hundreds of independent denominations that share only the Bible as their common authority, does not lend itself to easy illustration. We present Abraham Kuyper and Karl Barth as two strong and independent voices who addressed, and sometimes defined, many of the main themes of law, politics, society, and human nature that have occupied many modern Protestants. Kuyper, though not so well known today, was something like the Protestant Leo XIII of his day. He called for a return to the cardinal teachings of the sixteenth-century Protestant Reformation and developed a comprehensive Reformed theory of human nature and human knowledge. He also developed an important new "sphere sovereignty" theory of liberty, democracy, and social institutions, which would become a Protestant analogue, if not answer, to Catholic subsidiarity theory.

If Kuyper was the Leo of modern Protestantism, Barth was its Maritain. This brilliant Swiss theologian produced the most comprehensive Protestant dogmatic system of the twentieth century, centered on the Bible and on Christ. Many theories of law, politics, and society were embedded in his massive writings, not least his famous critique of theories of natural law and natural rights, the source of a strong antinaturalist and antirights tendency among many later Protestants. Most memorable was Barth's leadership in crafting the Barmen Declaration of 1934, which denounced the emerging laws and policies of Adolf Hitler and the German Nazi Party.

German theologian Dietrich Bonhoeffer knew firsthand about Nazi belligerence: he was killed in a concentration camp for conspiring to assassinate Hitler. Bonhoeffer's decision to join the plot had required a complex rethinking of his own Lutheran tradition of political ethics and Christian discipleship, and of the proper relations of the church and its members to a world that had abandoned reason and religion in pursuit of tribalism and totalitarianism. Bonhoeffer's American contemporary Reinhold Niebuhr saw some of these same lusts for power and self-interest in modern states and corporations. Building on the classic Protestant doctrine of total depravity, Niebuhr developed an applied theology of Christian realism that prized democratic government, but with strong checks and balances; that protected human rights, but informed by moral duties; and that championed racial equality and economic justice.

We have included Susan B. Anthony, a freethinking Quaker, as an early exemplar of an important tendency of modern American Protestants to counsel legal disobedience and legal reform simultaneously on selected issues. Today, these Protestant political preoccupations include abortion, same-sex marriage, faith-based initiatives, and religion in public schools. For Anthony, the cardinal issue was women's rights. Using basic biblical texts as her guide, she worked relentlessly to effect many legal reforms in Congress and the states, not least passage of the Nineteenth Amendment to the Constitution, the world's first modern constitutional guarantee of a woman's right to vote.

Martin Luther King Jr. and William Stringfellow later led comparable movements for racial and economic justice, although they grounded their advocacy more deeply in traditional biblical warrants and allied themselves more closely with the church. King was "America's Amos" who used pulpit, pamphlet, and political platform alike to lead America to greater racial justice, including passage of the Civil Rights Act of 1964. When he faced political opposition and repression, King also developed a novel theology of nonviolent resistance to authority. William Stringfellow spent much of his career representing the interests of the poor and needy in Harlem as well as those who protested America's war policy, appearing in several sensational cases. He grounded his work in a novel Protestant theory of law and gospel. The Mennonite theologian John Howard Yoder likewise pressed for social and economic justice and democratic virtues, on the strength of a classic Anabaptist biblicism and pacifism coupled with a new appreciation for natural law, human rights, and democratization.

Sixth, we have thought it imperative to devote one of these three volumes to the Eastern Orthodox tradition. Many leading Orthodox lights dealt with fundamental questions of law, politics, society, and human nature with novel insight, often giving distinct readings and renderings of the biblical, apostolic, and patristic sources. Moreover, the Orthodox Church has immense spiritual resources and experiences whose implications are only now beginning to be seen. These resources lie, in part, in Orthodox worship—the passion of the liturgy, the pathos of the icons, the power of spiritual silence. They lie, in part, in Orthodox church life—the distinct balancing of hierarchy and congregationalism through autocephaly, of uniform worship and liturgical freedom through alternative vernacular rites, of community and individuality through a trinitarian communalism, centered on the parish, the extended family, and the wise grandmother, the *babushka*. And these spiritual resources lie, in part, in the massive martyrdom of millions of Orthodox faithful in the twentieth century—whether suffered by Russian Orthodox under the Communist Party, Greek and Armenian Orthodox under Turkish and Iranian radicals, Middle Eastern Copts at the hands of religious extremists, North African Orthodox under all manner of fascist autocrats and tribal strongmen.[21]

These deep spiritual resources of the Orthodox Church have no exact parallels in modern Catholicism and Protestantism, and most of their implications for law, politics, and society have still to be drawn out. It would be wise to hear what an ancient church, newly charred and chastened by decades of oppression and martyrdom, considers essential to the regime of human rights. It would be enlightening to watch how ancient Orthodox communities, still largely centered on the parish and the family, reconstruct Christian theories of society. It would be instructive to hear how a tradition that still celebrates spiritual silence as its highest virtue recasts the meaning of freedom of speech and expression. And it would be illuminating to feel how a people that has long cherished and celebrated the role of the woman—the wizened babushka of the home, the faithful remnant in the parish pews, the living icon of the Dormition of the Mother of God—elaborates the meaning of gender equality.

To illustrate the potential of some of these resources and the rich theological anthropologies that Orthodoxy has already produced, we have selected three key Russian Orthodox scholars—Soloviev, Berdyaev, and Lossky. Each interacted with several Western Christian thinkers. Each challenged the (increasingly compromised) Russian Orthodox authorities of their day, while channeling the best theology and jurisprudence of their tradition into fundamentally new directions. Vladimir Soloviev, a philosopher, was the first modern Russian to work out an intricate Orthodox philosophy of law that grounded law and political order in morality and anchored morality directly in a Christian theology of salvation. Soloviev also challenged the traditional Orthodox theology of theocracy, which tied church, state, and nation into an organic whole and laid some of the foundations for a new theory of social pluralism. Nicholas Berdyaev, a theologian, worked out a complex new theology of human nature anchored in an ethic of creation, redemption, and law. He also crafted an original theory of human dignity and salvation that he tied to the Orthodox doctrine of theosis. Vladimir Lossky, a philosopher, drew from several earlier church fathers and mystics a brilliant new theory of human dignity, freedom, and discipline anchored in the Orthodox doctrine of the Trinity. He also challenged the politically compromised church and its socially anemic members to reclaim both their freedoms and their duties to discharge divinely appointed tasks. The Romanian theologian Dumitru Stăniloae drew from some of the same predecessors a comparable theory of the meaning of human freedom and sinfulness and the symphony of natural and supernatural sources of law and authority. Unlike Lossky, he supported Romanian ethnic nationalism and had little say to about the political compromises of the Romanian Orthodox Church during the period of Communism.

We have also included a chapter on the Russian nun and social reformer Mother Maria Skobtsova, whose thought and example evoke images of both Dorothy Day and Dietrich Bonhoeffer. Maria, who was exiled in Paris, worked tirelessly in the hostels feeding the poor and needy, while developing a rich theology of incarnational living and sacramental care and a harsh critique of some of the reclusive tendencies of many monastics. Her work during the Nazi occupation of Paris brought her to the attention of the Gestapo, which condemned her to death in a concentration camp.

The biographies of some of these twenty figures are as edifying as their writings, and the chapters that follow spend time recounting them.

Fifteen of these people served, at least for a time, as university professors of theology, philosophy, ethics, history, or law. Ten served in traditional church offices: three as popes (Leo XIII, John XXIII, and John
Paul II), five as pastors (Gutiérrez, Barth, Bonhoeffer, Niebuhr, and
King), two as monastics (Maria and Murray). Two served in political
office—Kuyper as the prime minister of the Netherlands, Maritain as
France's ambassador to the Vatican. One served as a lawyer (Stringfellow). One was active as a political advisor (Niebuhr). Eight were stirred
to radical social or political activism (Gutiérrez, Day, Barth, Bonhoeffer,
Niebuhr, King, Stringfellow, and Maria). Four were censured by church
authorities (Anthony, Day, Murray, and Gutiérrez). Three were exiled
from their homeland (Berdyaev, Lossky, and Maria). Two were removed
from their professorships (Bonhoeffer and Stăniloae). Nine were indicted
or imprisoned by state authorities (Anthony, Day, Bonhoeffer, King,
Stringfellow, Soloviev, Berdyaev, Maria, and Stăniloae). One faced brutal
and lengthy political imprisonment (Stăniloae). Two were murdered in
concentration camps (Bonhoeffer and Maria). One fell to an assassin's
bullet (King).

The diversity of these biographies underscores an important criterion
of selection that we have used in assembling these three volumes. The
twenty figures included herein are intended to be points on a large canvas,
not entries on an exhaustive roll of modern Christian teachers of law,
society, and politics. We present them as illustrations of different venues,
vectors, and visions of what a Christian understanding of law, politics,
and society entails. Some of these figures were lone voices. Others attracted huge throngs of allies and disciples, many of whom make no appearance in these pages. Moreover, we have not included some who are
still alive and well today—including several authors in these volumes—
whose work will likely shape Christian teachings on law, politics, and society in the twenty-first century.

Many readers will thus look in vain for some of their favorite authors.
Missing from the collection are some who did or do speak to some issues
of law, politics, and society with a distinctly Christian understanding of
human nature: Hans Urs von Balthasar, John Finnis, Joseph Fuchs, Mary
Ann Glendon, Germain Grisez, Etienne Gilson, Bernard Lonergan, Karl
Rahner, Heinrich Rommen, Thomas Schaeffer, and Yves Simon, among
Catholics; Emil Brunner, Herman Dooyeweerd, Johannes Heckel, Carl
Henry, Karl Holl, Wolfgang Huber, Richard Niebuhr, Oliver O'Donovan,
Wolfhart Pannenberg, Paul Ramsey, Walter Rauschenbusch, and Rudolph
Sohm, among Protestants; John Erickson, Pavel Florensky, Georges Floro-
vsky, John Meyendorff, and Christoph Yannaras, among Orthodox. Every

reader will have a list of favorites beyond those represented here. The greatest compliment that could be made to this book is that it stimulates the production of many more and better studies of the scores of other modern Christian thinkers who deserve analysis.

THE CHALLENGE

This last point invites a few final reflections on some of the main challenges that remain—beyond the formidable task of filling in the vast canvas of modern Christian teachings on law, politics, society, and human nature.

One challenge is to trace the roots of these modern Christian teachings back to the earlier modern period of the seventeenth through early nineteenth centuries. Scholars have written a great deal about patristic, scholastic, early Protestant, and post-Tridentine Catholic contributions to law, politics, and society. But many of the best accounts stop in 1625. That was the year the father of international law, Hugo Grotius, uttered the impious hypothesis that law, politics, and society would continue even if "we should concede that which cannot be conceded without the utmost wickedness, that there is no God, or that the affairs of men are of no concern to him."[22] While many subsequent writers conceded Grotius's hypothesis and embarked on the great secular projects of the Enlightenment, many great Christian writers did not. They have been forgotten to all but specialists. Their thinking on law, politics, and society needs to be retrieved, restudied, and reconstructed for our day.

A second challenge is to make these modern Christian teachings on law, politics, and society more concrete. In centuries past, the Catholic, Protestant, and Orthodox traditions all produced massive codes of canon law and church discipline that covered many areas of private and public life. They instituted sophisticated tribunals for the equitable enforcement of these laws and produced massive works of political theology and theological jurisprudence, with ample handholds in catechisms, creeds, and confessional books, to guide the faithful. Some of that sophisticated legal and political work continues today. Modern Christian ethicists still take up some of the old questions. Some Christian jurists have contributed to the current discussion of human rights, family law, and church-state relations. But the legal structure and sophistication of the modern Christian church as a whole is a pale shadow of what went before. It needs to be restored lest the church lose its capacity for Christian self-rule and its members lose their capacity to serve as responsible Christian "prophets, priests, and kings."

A third challenge is for modern Catholic, Protestant, and Orthodox Christians to develop a rigorous ecumenical understanding of law, politics, and society. This is a daunting task. Only in the past three decades, with the collapse of Communism and the rise of globalization, have these three ancient warring sects begun to come together and to understand one another. It will take many generations to work out the great theological disputes over the nature of the Trinity or the doctrine of justification by faith. But there is more confluence than conflict in Catholic, Protestant, and Orthodox understandings of law, politics, and society, especially if they are viewed in long and responsible historical perspective. Scholars from these three great Christian traditions need to join together to work out a comprehensive new ecumenical "concordance of discordant canons" that incorporates the best of these traditions, is earnest about its ecumenism, and is honest about the greatest points of tension. Few studies would do more both to spur the great project of Christian ecumenism and to drive modern churches to get their legal houses in order.

A final, and perhaps the greatest, challenge will be to join the principally Western Christian story of law, politics, and society told in these volumes with comparable stories that are told in the rest of the Christian world. Over the past two centuries, Christianity has become very much a world religion, claiming nearly two billion souls. Strong new capitals and captains of Christianity now stand in the south and the east—in Latin America and sub-Saharan Africa, in Eastern Europe and the Russian theater, in Korea, China, the Indian subcontinent, and beyond. In some of these new zones of Christianity, the Western Christian classics, including the works of some of the figures represented here, are still being read and studied. But rich new indigenous forms and norms of law, politics, and society are emerging, premised on very different Christian understandings of theology and anthropology. It would take a special kind of cultural arrogance for Western and non-Western Christians to refuse to learn from each other.

NOTES

1. Catherine Drinker Bowen, *Yankee from Olympus: Justice Holmes and His Family* (Boston: Little, Brown, 1944).
2. Grant Gilmore, *Ages of American Law* (New Haven, Conn.: Yale University Press, 1977), 48–56, 110, 147n12.
3. Albert W. Alschuler, *Life Without Values: The Life, Work and Legacy of Justice Holmes* (Chicago: University of Chicago Press, 2000).

4. Oliver Wendell Holmes Jr., *Collected Legal Papers* (New York: Harcourt, Brace and Howe, 1920), 170.

5. Gilmore, *Ages of American Law*, 41–67.

6. I. Bernard Cohen, *Revolution in Science* (Cambridge, Mass.: Harvard University Press, 1985); Donald R. Kelly, *The Human Measure: Social Thought in the Western Legal Tradition* (Cambridge, Mass.: Harvard University Press, 1990).

7. See especially John Austin, *The Province of Jurisprudence Determined, Being the First of a Series of Lectures on Jurisprudence, or, The Philosophy of Positive Law*, 2nd ed., 3 vols. (London: John Murray, 1861–63); Christopher Columbus Langdell, *A Selection of Cases on the Law of Contracts*, 2nd ed. (Boston: Little, Brown, 1879), preface; Langdell, "Harvard Celebration Speeches," *Law Quarterly Review* 3 (1887): 123.

8. See, e.g., John Wigmore, "Nova Methodus Discendae Docendaeque Jurisprudentiae," *Harvard Law Review* 30 (1917): 812; Holmes, *Collected Legal Papers*, 139, 231; Robert Stevens, *Law School: Legal Education in America from the 1850s to the 1980s* (Chapel Hill: University of North Carolina Press, 1983).

9. Barbara Shapiro, "Law and Science in Seventeenth-Century England," *Stanford Law Review* 21 (1969): 724, 728.

10. Oliver Wendell Holmes Jr., *The Common Law* (Boston: Little, Brown, 1881), 1.

11. *S. Pac. Co. v. Jensen*, 244 U.S. 205, 222 (1917) (Holmes, J. dissenting); see also Michael H. Hoffheimer, *Justice Holmes and the Natural Law* (New York: Garland, 1992).

12. *Lochner v. New York*, 198 U.S. 45, 76 (1905).

13. Letter to Sir Frederick Pollock (May 30, 1927) in *Holmes-Pollock Letters: The Correspondence of Mr. Justice Holmes and Sir Frederick Pollock, 1874–1932*, ed. Mark DeWolfe Howe, 2 vols. (Cambridge, Mass.: Harvard University Press, 1941), 2:200.

14. See especially Karl Llewellyn, *Jurisprudence* (Chicago: University of Chicago Press, 1962); Lon L. Fuller, *The Morality of Law*, rev. ed. (New Haven, Conn.: Yale University Press, 1964); Jerome Hall, *Studies in Jurisprudence and Criminal Theory* (New York: Oceana Publishers, 1958); Hall, *Foundations of Jurisprudence* (Indianapolis: Bobbs-Merrill, 1973); Harold J. Berman, *The Interaction of Law and Religion* (Nashville, Tenn.: Abingdon Press, 1974).

15. Anthony Lewis, "Sir Edward Coke (1552–1633): His Theory of 'Artificial Reason' as a Context for Modern Basic Legal Theory," *Law Quarterly Review* 84 (1968): 330.

16. See Harold J. Berman, *Law and Revolution: The Formation of the Western Legal Tradition* (Cambridge, Mass.: Harvard University Press, 1983), 4–5; Jerome Hall, *Comparative Law and Social Theory* (Baton Rouge: Louisiana State University Press, 1963), 78–82.

17. See, e.g., Richard A. Posner, "The Present Situation in Legal Scholarship," *Yale Law Journal* 90 (1981): 1113; Robert C. Clark, "The Interdisciplinary Study of Legal Education," *Yale Law Journal* 90 (1981): 1238; Symposium, "American Legal Scholarship: Directions and Dilemmas," *Journal of Legal Education* 33 (1983): 403.

18. For a notable recent exception, see Michael W. McConnell, Robert F. Cochran Jr., and Angela C. Carmella, eds., *Christian Perspectives on Legal Thought* (New Haven, Conn.: Yale University Press, 2000).

19. Matthew 28:20.

20. See, e.g., Ernst Troeltsch, *The Social Teachings of the Christian Churches*, trans. Olive Wyon, 2 vols. (Chicago: University of Chicago Press, 1981), and review of later literature in John Witte Jr., *Law and Protestantism: The Legal Teachings of the Lutheran Reformation* (New York: Cambridge University Press, 2002).

21. See James H. Billington, "Orthodox Christianity and the Russian Transformation," in *Proselytism and Orthodoxy in Russia: The New War for Souls*, ed. John Witte Jr. and Michael Bourdeaux (Maryknoll, N.Y.: Orbis Books, 1999), 51; Billington, "The Case for Orthodoxy," *The New Republic* (May 30, 1994), 24.

22. Hugo Grotius, *De Iure Belli ac Pacis* (1625), Prolegomena, 11, discussed in Oliver O'Donovan and Joan Lockwood O'Donovan, *From Irenaeus to Grotius: Christian Political Thought, 100–1625* (Grand Rapids, Mich.: Eerdmans, 1999); Brian Tierney, *The Idea of Natural Rights: Studies on Natural Rights, Natural Law, and Church Law, 1150–1625* (Atlanta: Scholars Press, 1997).

Introduction to the Modern Orthodox Tradition

PAUL VALLIERE

In her study of the Orthodox Church in the Byzantine Empire, Joan Hussey begins with a caveat: "In the present state of our knowledge a book on the Byzantine Church must necessarily be in the nature of an interim report since much pioneer work remains to be done."[1] The same must be said about the attempt to present the "teachings" of modern Orthodoxy concerning law, society, and politics. While the historical sources for the study of modern Orthodox social ethics stand closer to us in time than those on which Byzantinists must rely, our level of knowledge about the subject is not markedly higher.

There are at least two reasons for this. The first is the catastrophe of the Russian Revolution (1917), which ruined the largest, richest, and best-educated Orthodox church in the world. The destruction wrought by Communism in Russia and elsewhere made civilized discourse on church and society in the Orthodox East extremely difficult for most of the twentieth century. The second is misleading stereotypes of Orthodoxy. The perception of Orthodoxy in the West has been deeply affected by a Christian "orientalism" that alternates between a condescending, essentially imperialist view of Orthodoxy as a backward form of Christianity and a romantic view of it as preserving mystical values from which a putatively rationalistic Western Christianity has fallen away.[2] Both stereotypes, though opposed, promote the notion that Orthodox theology is not fundamentally concerned with law, society, and politics. In fact, Orthodoxy has been wrestling with issues of modern legal, political, and social order for almost three hundred years, and a large body of primary source material for the study of the subject is at hand, albeit underexplored.

Orthodoxy's meeting with modernity began in Russia during the reign of Peter the Great (1682–1725), and by the late eighteenth century this encounter was having a significant impact throughout the Orthodox world. In the nineteenth century, as Russia emerged as one of the most dynamic cultural centers of world civilization and as smaller Orthodox nations won their independence from the Ottoman Empire, a broad modern-style discourse about church and society was cultivated through a number of channels: new educational institutions, arts and letters, secular and theological journalism, scholarship, politics, secular and ecclesiastical courts, and other venues. In short, there is a historical record—the annals of what might be called the Orthodox Enlightenment—against which to check our generalizations about the teachings of modern Orthodoxy on law, society, and politics. Because this record has been so little investigated, however, checking it is an arduous procedure. Hence the caveat about an "interim report."

In the following pages, the views of five modern Orthodox thinkers on issues of law, society, and politics are presented—Vladimir Soloviev, Nicholas Berdyaev, Vladimir Lossky, Mother Maria Skobtsova, and Dumitru Stăniloae. It cannot be stressed strongly enough that all five of these thinkers were *modern*; that is to say, they wrestled with the situation of Orthodoxy in the expansive global civilization produced by the scientific and political revolutions of the Enlightenment. As Orthodox thinkers, all five also drew on patristic sources, that is to say, the writings of the church fathers.[3] However, it is not always possible to make a neat distinction between patristic and modern elements in their thought. The patristic corpus is variegated. Interpreters find different elements of significance in it, depending on the issues they wish to pursue. There is no reason to suppose that all elements drawn from the patristic tradition by modern Orthodox thinkers will be consistent with each other. On the contrary, one should expect to find differences of opinion, tensions, even contradictions.

Modern historical scholarship on patristics is another variable. To their credit, modern Orthodox thinkers have always paid close attention to historical research on the ancient and medieval church. Some, such as Vladimir Lossky, were patristic or medieval scholars in their own right. Like all scholarly disciplines, however, patristics evolves. New facts are discovered, new hypotheses are introduced, old views are revised. As a result, the scholarly consensus keeps shifting. What is deemed patristic at one point in time might be viewed otherwise at a later time; and of course the later view, too, is susceptible to revision. This is a perfectly natural state of affairs, but it is often forgotten by theologians who accuse their predecessors of betraying the church fathers without taking into account what the scholarship of an earlier day had to say about those same fathers. In short, the patristic connection in modern Orthodox theology is itself a modern, not just a traditional, factor; it is a complicating, not just a clarifying, factor.

This point bears directly on the relations between the thinkers presented in this volume. Their collective labors span about a century—from Vladimir Soloviev's first book (*The Crisis of Western Philosophy*, 1874) to Dumitru Stăniloae's magnum opus (*Orthodox Dogmatic Theology*, 1978). The most important historical event affecting Orthodox theology in this period was the Russian Revolution of 1917 and its long, sad aftermath. The most significant theological shift occurred a bit later, however, with the rise of the neopatristic theology of Father Georges Florovsky and Vladimir Lossky. The key books signaling the neopatristic turn were Florovsky's *The Paths of Russian Theology*, published in Russian in 1937, and Lossky's *The Mystical Theology of the Eastern Church*, published in French in 1944.[4] Florovsky and Lossky sharply rejected the religious-philosophical approach to theology practiced by Soloviev and those whom he inspired, such as Nicholas Berdyaev, Sergei Bulgakov, Pavel Florensky, and Lev Karsavin. As Florovsky and Lossky saw it, Soloviev and his heirs were bad expositors of the mind of Orthodoxy because of the heavy dose of nineteenth-century German idealism and other modern tendencies in their thought. The antidote was to return to the church fathers, hence the name neopatristic. By the middle of the twentieth century, Florovsky and Lossky's approach had won the day, and it has dominated the Orthodox theological scene ever since. Its long life is due in no small measure to a brilliant second generation, such as Father John Meyendorff and Bishop Kallistos Ware, who quietly set aside the polemical spirit of the founders and developed the positive features of the neopatristic approach.

When reading the neopatristic theologians, however, one should not accept their initial assumption at face value—namely, that they returned to the church fathers while their rivals served other masters. To take this view is to ignore the fact that the fathers are not monolithic. Vladimir Soloviev was well versed in patristics as it was practiced in his time. Sergei Bulgakov was even better schooled, thanks to advances in the discipline that he followed carefully. The fact that neither Soloviev nor Bulgakov viewed the fathers in neopatristic terms does not mean that they failed to take the patristic heritage seriously, as their neopatristic critics subsequently alleged. It is true that Soloviev and Bulgakov were subject also to other intellectual and spiritual influences, but so were the neopatristic theologians. Neopatristic theology was not a unique or isolated phenomenon in modern theology. It was the Orthodox manifestation of the pan-European, pan-confessional rebellion against liberalism and modernism that reshaped the theological scene following World War I. It is no accident that Roman Catholic neo-Thomism, Protestant neo-orthodoxy, and Orthodox neopatristic theology bear similar names. The three streams had much in common, and mutual influences abounded. Secular influences, such as existentialism and cultural pessimism, also had an impact on all three.

An area of concern which neopatristic theology did not share with the other movements in twentieth-century theology is the one with which this volume is chiefly concerned, namely, law, society, and politics. Neo-Thomism, with which most modern Roman Catholic thinkers were connected in one way or another, is inconceivable without its legal, social, and political agenda. Protestant neo-orthodoxy, however we understand its original motivation, inspired the ethical and political genius of Dietrich Bonhoeffer. Its American counterpart produced Reinhold Niebuhr. The Orthodox neopatristic movement, by contrast, did not inspire much work on law, society, or politics.[5] Some would explain this apparent anomaly by observing that the construction of ethical systems reflects the West's "scholastic" approach to theology, that is, the interpretation and application of mysteries of faith by means of discursive reasoning. The procedure is supposedly alien to Orthodoxy, which prefers to set theology in a liturgical and mystical context. Orthodox theologians, so the argument goes, do not seek general principles but focus on personal experience.[6]

Whatever the merits of this explanation, it must be qualified in at least two respects. First, it is not true that Orthodox thinkers have always steered clear of systematic reflection on law, politics, and human nature. Many modern Orthodox thinkers, including (in this volume) Vladimir Soloviev and Nicholas Berdyaev, have engaged in just such a project. To assume that this separates them from "genuine" Orthodox theology is to grant the neopatristic case without investigating it. Presumably it is better to examine what Soloviev and Berdyaev actually had to say before passing judgment on them.

Second, one must not fail to connect the neopatristic movement with the peculiar circumstances produced by the devastation of the Orthodox world in the twentieth century. Neither neo-Thomism nor Protestant neo-orthodoxy developed in exile or in emigration. Both were products of a well-patronized theological establishment. Even the martyred Dietrich Bonhoeffer was no exception: he ended his career in the catacombs, but he certainly did not begin it there. Orthodox theologians, after the Russian Revolution in 1917, and again after World War II ended in 1945, found themselves in a completely different situation. Almost all of the social and institutional networks for the support of theology in the historic Orthodox lands lay in ruins. Orthodox theology was cultivated for the most part in small communities of émigrés and Western converts without access to a large natural audience. Except in Greece, Orthodox theologians worked in contexts where they had virtually no access to social or political power and bore no responsibility for its management. It is no wonder that they regarded theological reflection on law, society, and politics to be disconnected from reality—scholastic in the pejorative sense.

Neopatristic writers occasionally did concede that the legal, social, and political dimensions of human life can be theologized. Bishop Kallistos Ware, for example, pointed to the implications of trinitarian dogma for social philosophy:

> The doctrine of the Trinity is not merely a theme for abstract speculation by specialists; it has practical and indeed revolutionary consequences for our understanding of human personhood and society. The human person is made in the image of God, that is to say, of God the Trinity, and the doctrine of the Trinity affirms that God is not just a monad, the One loving himself, but a triad of divine persons loving each other. Formed in the trinitarian image, the human person is thus created for relationship, sharing, and reciprocity. Cut off from others, isolated, unloving and unloved, no one is a true person, but only a bare individual. Our human vocation is therefore to reproduce on earth at every level, in the church and in society, the movement of mutual love that exists from all eternity within God the Trinity. In the words of the Russian thinker Nikolai Fedorov (c. 1828–1903), "Our social program is the dogma of the Trinity."[7]

Clearly this is an insight that could inspire a major work on Christian law, society, and politics. Indeed, it has done so—in Leonardo Boff's *Trinity and Society*.[8] Yet one looks in vain for a neopatristic Orthodox contribution to match that of this Brazilian Catholic liberation theologian.[9] It is telling that the arresting summation of Bishop Kallistos's case—"our social program is the doctrine of the Trinity"—is taken from Fedorov, one of the Russian religious philosophers whom the first generation of neopatristic theologians excoriated as misguided modernists.

PHILOKALIA AND PHILOSOPHY

Two streams of thought have been especially important in shaping the discourse about human nature and human destiny in modern Orthodoxy. They may be called the *philokalic* and the *philosophic*. The first, issuing from a revival of contemplative monasticism, reenergized and popularized the patristic concept of *theosis* (deification). The second took shape in nineteenth-century Russian philosophy. Its guiding ideas were wholeness and *sobornost* (fellowship, togetherness, spiritual unity).

After declining in the seventeenth and eighteenth centuries, Orthodox contemplative monasticism began to revive in the later eighteenth century. The vehicle of the revival was an anthology of patristic and medieval mystical-ascetical texts known as the *Philokalia*. The pioneers in the dissemination of this material were the Greek monks Makarios of Corinth and Nikodemos of the Holy Mountain, whose *Philokalia* was published in Venice in 1782, and the Russian monk Paisy Velichkovsky, who directed a Slavonic edition at about the same time. In the nineteenth century, Russian and other vernacular translations began to be made.[10]

The spiritual practices associated with the *Philokalia* are usually called hesychasm, from the Greek word *hesychia*, meaning quietness. These practices include quiet sitting, contemplative prayer, and the Jesus Prayer. The last consists of the words "Lord Jesus Christ, Son of God, have mercy on me a sinner," repeated as a mantra in fulfillment of the Apostle Paul's counsel to "pray without ceasing" (1 Thess. 5:17). These practices were traditionally cultivated by a monastic elite. With the wider vernacular dissemination of philokalic literature in modern times, a certain democratization of hesychasm occurred as laypeople, including some intellectuals, began assimilating the material and applying it in new ways. The prestige of monks as confessors and spiritual directors, a relationship that could be conducted by correspondence as well as in person, also widened the appreciation for hesychasm. Dostoevsky's celebrated portrait of Russian monasticism in *The Brothers Karamazov* (1878–80), based on the author's pilgrimage to Optina Hermitage, a center of the hesychast revival in Russia, is an early example of this democratization.

The aspiration of hesychast piety is *theosis* (deification), an idea containing both an anthropological and an eschatological dimension. Anthropologically, theosis is related to Orthodoxy's traditionally strong affirmation of the enduring, substantial reality of the image of God in human beings. Unlike Catholic theology, which came to distinguish sharply between nature and grace, Orthodox theology prefers to see nature and grace as forever connected because created nature is always and every-where dependent on the power of God.[11] Even in their fallen state, humans possess a divine beauty because their very being is irradiated by the ener-gies (grace) of God. Human beings are potentially "gods." The realization of this potential is eschatological. In Orthodoxy, however, eschatological does not mean "far off." Orthodoxy inclines to a realized eschatology; that is to say, it proclaims the kingdom of God as something that can be seen and experienced *already*. Many features of Orthodox practice reinforce this view, such as the all-engulfing sacramentalism of the liturgy, the icons that mystically host the glorified beings who already live in the king-dom, and the veneration of the saints. Realized eschatology means that theosis has already begun and that its effects can be perceived and assimi-lated in a holy life.

The idiom of theosis sometimes strikes Western Christians as an invita-tion to idolatry. In fact, it is a Greek way of stating a truth about eternal life: since only God is eternal, all who are granted eternal life must in some way partake of the divine life. Eternalization implies deification. That there is a danger of idolatrous misunderstanding here has always been clear to Or-thodox theologians, who guard against it by distinguishing between the "essence" and the "energies" of God. Not even the saints in glory partake of the essence of God; they are eternalized by the divine energies, God's gra-cious, indwelling, transfiguring presence in them. These energies are fully divine, however, not an intermediate, subdivine reality (which, if it existed, would indeed be the stuff of idolatry).

Theosis may also be understood as a way of speaking about sanctifica-tion, the being-made-holy of the redeemed. This interpretation makes the concept relatively easy for Roman Catholics to appreciate, since Ro-man Catholics, like Orthodox, have an optimistic view of the possibilities of growth in holiness, a view warranting the canonization and veneration of saints. Protestants have greater difficulty with the concept because of their ambivalence about sanctification as such. Protestantism sees the essence of the gospel as consisting in God's gracious, unprompted justifi-cation of the sinner. The issue of whether and to what extent justified sin-ners can achieve personal holiness has been a divisive issue for Protestants ever since the sixteenth-century Protestant Reformation. Martin Luther and many after him held that justified sinners are holy only by imputa-tion: God in his mercy chooses to regard the justified as holy by imputing to them the holiness of Christ, which they themselves cannot approxi-mate, much less achieve. Ulrich Zwingli and John Calvin believed that justified sinners are regenerated in a more concrete way, being empow-ered by God's grace to live a holier life than the unredeemed. Because the template of a righteous and holy life is found in the divine law revealed in scripture, these theologians sometimes referred to the cultivation of holiness as "the third use of the law."[12] While such a pointed appeal to law in the context of sanctification would strike Orthodox as strange and somehow unevangelical, one may nevertheless draw an analogy between the third use of the law and monasticism. The zealous pursuit of theosis in Orthodoxy has always been closely connected with the ascetical life. In modern times this connection has been loosened a bit by the democratization of piety mentioned above, but traditionally the pursuit of theosis was a project that belonged to contemplative monks. To the extent that monasticism involves a structured, closely regulated lifestyle constituting a kind of polity or "republic" of its own, its connection with theosis is in some ways comparable to the third use of the law.

The primary social and political legacy of hesychasm has been quietism, as the name suggests. In cases where the threshold of political advocacy was crossed, the results were usually conservative, ranging from conventional acceptance of the status quo to reactionary forms of expression. For more constructive approaches to Christian legal, social, and political thought, one must turn to philosophic Orthodoxy.

Modern Orthodox religious philosophy emerged in Russia in the second quarter of the nineteenth century. It began as an effort to make sense of Russia's anomalous status in Europe after the end of the Napoleonic wars. Militarily, Russia had become one of the arbiters of European destiny. Yet Russia was not European in the sense that its Western neighbors were. Russia's political tradition (autocracy), socioeconomic system (peasant communalism), and religious affiliation (Orthodoxy) set it apart from the West. In the 1820s and 1830s, Russian intellectuals began a debate about Russia's destiny that would last until the revolution. What was Russia called to be and to do in the modern world? The answers turned largely on the assessment of Russia's Eastern Christian heritage. Those who lamented Russia's affiliation with "miserable, despised Byzantium" (as Pyotr Yakovlevich Chaadaev put it) imagined a future in which Russia would be fully integrated into Western European civilization. They were called Westernizers. Those who preached loyalty to Russian tradition, opining that Orthodoxy held the solution to the problems of modernity, were called Slavophiles.

The most important thinkers of the first generation of Slavophiles were Ivan Kireevsky (1806–56) and Aleksei Khomiakov (1804–60).[13] Both were well acquainted with Western thought. They had studied in Germany and were indebted in particular to the German Romantic tradition, especially the philosophy of Friedrich W. J. Schelling. Like their Romantic mentors, the Slavophiles rejected the materialism, liberalism, and egoistic individualism of the Enlightenment. They believed that such trends, if left unchecked, would cause people to devour each other just as the leaders of French Revolution had devoured each other. The alternative to this evil prospect lay in rediscovering the wholeness of life, the reality of spiritual things, and the ethics of Christian love. Kireevsky elaborated a philosophy of "wholeness" embracing both reason and faith, with faith leading reason to the experience of God. Khomiakov elaborated a social philosophy based on Christian love, the socio-ethical counterpart to the wholeness cultivated by Kireevsky in the noetic sphere. His model for the good society was the loving communion of the church at prayer, a fellowship uniting each with all and all with God. The neologism *sobornost* was subsequently devised to express this vision in a resonant word.[14] Both Kireevsky and Khomiakov contrasted external or political freedom with inner or spiritual freedom: spiritual freedom opens people to fellowship with their neighbors and with God; liberal individualism isolates people and enslaves them to selfish passions.

The political legacy of the early Slavophiles was conservative without being reactionary. In fact, Slavophilism had reformist implications to the extent that its vision of what an ideal Orthodox society should look like was obviously at odds with the Russia that actually existed in their day. This dissonance did not escape the notice of the censors, who prevented the publication of most of Kireevsky and Khomiakov's writings during their lifetime. It would be wrong to cast the Slavophiles as dissidents, however. Their discontent did not impel them to political activism, which they distrusted. Nor did they look to law as a means of solving social and political problems. On the contrary, they viewed "juridicalism" as the quintessential expression of Western rationalism, the very opposite of *sobornost*. Slavophile antilegalism, inspired as much by Western Romantic philosophers as by evangelical conscience, contributed to what has been called "the tradition of the censure of law" in Russia.[15] The antilegalism of Aleksandr Solzhenitsyn is a more recent example of the same phenomenon.[16]

In the next generation the Slavophile tradition grew more complicated. The towering figure of Russian religious philosophy, Vladimir Soloviev (1853–1900), had one foot in the Slavophile tradition. His philosophy of "integral knowledge" picked up where Kireevsky's had left off, and his Christian social philosophy developed some of Khomiakov's insights. But Soloviev was also interested in the reconciliation of Orthodoxy with

European liberalism, a project that led him far from the Slavophile path. Soloviev's philosophy inspired the flowering of interest in religion among Russian intellectuals at the turn of the twentieth century and contributed to the emergence of an indigenous Russian liberalism.[17]

Later Slavophiles became increasingly nationalistic. Slavophilism encouraged the development of Russian nationalism to the extent that it celebrated the differences between Russia and Europe. For Kireevsky and Khomiakov, the affirmation of difference was not an end in itself but a means of promoting the universal Christian faith, which according to them was better preserved in Orthodoxy than in Catholicism or Protestantism. For many nationalists, by contrast, difference was the end, and Orthodoxy was a means of promoting it.

The philokalic and philosophic streams of modern Orthodox thought were not completely isolated from each other. Beginning with Kireevsky, religious philosophers took an interest in philokalic sources. Conversely, the appropriation of philokalic values by artists and intellectuals always involved some sort of philosophical mediation. Dostoevsky's pilgrimage to Optina Hermitage in the company of the philosopher Vladimir Soloviev is the perfect symbol of such mediation.

Scholarly studies of hesychasm in the twentieth century, of which John Meyendorff's *A Study of Gregory Palamas* (1959) was the most influential, furthered the democratization of hesychast spirituality and made an important contribution to neopatristic theology in particular.[18] The philosophical mediation of hesychasm, while much less prominent than historical-theological appropriations of the subject, also continues.[19]

CHURCH AND STATE IN THE ORTHODOX TRADITION

For a long time, Western scholars persisted in characterizing the system of church-state relations in the Christian East as "caesaropapism." The term denotes "the rigid control of matters spiritual and ecclesiastical by the temporal ruler."[20] Although the stereotype of a docile, politically apathetic Orthodox Church still flourishes in the popular imagination, scholars have for some time agreed that the concept of caesaropapism is flawed.[21] The most obvious problem is that it construes Orthodoxy in Western terms by assuming that the Orthodox Church has a "pope" of some kind, that is to say, a central executive authority. Since the Orthodox Church does not possess such an authority yet has been closely linked to the state for most of its history, the political ruler was seen as "pope." That the Christian church can avoid papalism without becoming Protestant was not considered.

Another problem with the concept of caesaropapism is that it does not fit the facts of the church-state relationship in the Christian East, especially in the Byzantine period for which it was invented. While the Byzantine emperors, beginning with Emperor Constantine in the fourth century, were active and sometimes aggressive participants in the affairs of the church, relations between secular rulers and Orthodox bishops were often stormy, with many leading churchmen suffering deposition, exile, or worse in the defense of dogmatic and canonical positions that they deemed non-negotiable. Almost all of the great heresies of the patristic period—Arian, Monophysite, Monothelite, Iconoclast—enjoyed extensive imperial patronage, yet none of them prevailed in the long run. Even Justinian in the sixth century, who came closer than any Byzantine emperor to mastering the church, failed to achieve his most crucial objective in ecclesiastical affairs, which was the reconciliation of Orthodoxy and monophysitism.[22] Justinian's interest in this issue was political and strategic. By his time monophysitism had become the majority view among the Christians of Syria and Egypt, and Justinian feared for the loyalty of these important Eastern provinces. The Islamic conquest a century later proved the emperor's fears to be well founded, and it is certainly legitimate to wonder whether a more moderate stance in the monophysite controversy might not have served the Orthodox Church better than the one it took. What is not legitimate is to characterize the Byzantine church as a passive tool in the hands of Justinian or any other caesar. On the issues it deemed crucial, the Orthodox Church followed its own lights.

The concept that Orthodox thinkers have traditionally used to describe the right relationship between church and state is "harmony" (Greek *symphonia*). The idea is that church and state are two parts of an ensemble whose conductor is Christ. The two entities are distinct, for without distinction there can be no harmony; but they complement and support each other in the larger whole, which is a godly Christian society. Justinian's epitome of the ideal in his sixth *Novella* is famous:

> There are two greatest gifts which God, in his love for man, has granted from on high: the priesthood and the imperial dignity. The first serves divine things, the second directs and administers human affairs; both, however, proceed from the same origin and adorn the life of mankind. Hence, nothing should be such a source of care to the emperors as the dignity of the priests, since it is for the welfare [of the empire] that they constantly implore

God. For if the priesthood is in every way free from blame and possesses access to God, and if the emperors administer equitably and judiciously the state entrusted to their care, general harmony will result, and whatever is beneficial will be bestowed upon the human race.[23]

The most striking feature of this ideal is the positive, theocentric view of the state: the state, like the church, receives its mandate directly from God. It is not subordinate to the church any more than the church is subordinate to the state. Church and state do not occupy higher and lower points in a great chain of being. Each is divinely gifted with its own being and vocation. The gifts are distinct, but the sacred body politic is one. The powerful theological paradigm of the Incarnation underlies this conception. "In the thought of Justinian, the 'symphony' between 'divine things' and 'human affairs' was based upon the Incarnation, which united the divine and human natures, so that the person of Christ is the unique source of the two—the civil and ecclesiastical hierarchies."[24] In a word, the state is as "Christic" as the church, albeit in a different sphere.

Symphonia helps us appreciate many idioms of Orthodoxy. When Orthodox Christians honor certain rulers, such as Constantine the Great or Vladimir of Kiev, as "equals of the apostles" (*isapostoloi*), Western Christians tend to take offense. Secular rulers as apostles? Is this not caesaropapism? Viewed in terms of symphonia, however, the usage makes more sense. When Prince Vladimir of Kiev made the decision to invite missionaries from Byzantium to evangelize and baptize his people, he was accomplishing a divine mission, using the charisma of rulership bestowed upon him by God to cause the gospel to be preached in his heathen land. As the first of his princely line to exercise power in this way, Vladimir was "like" an apostle. His power was political and spiritual at the same time; his decision to invite the missionaries was a creative act, a fresh actualization of the spirit-guided charisma of right government. The "palladian" display of icons during sieges and military campaigns is another example of symphonia. When General Kutuzov and his army prayed before an icon of the Mother of God in the field at Borodino in 1812, they were engaging in a public as well as a personal act, affirming the divine source of the state as well as of the church.[25]

While appreciating the logic of symphonia, however, one must keep two facts in mind. First, symphonia was the ideal, not the reality, of church-state relations in the East. It was constantly proclaimed but seldom realized. Second, conditions for the realization of the ideal, at least in its original sense, have not existed in the Orthodox world for some time. Symphonia assumes the existence of a Christian empire or at least a

Christian state. In fact, after the fall of the Byzantine Empire in 1453, most Orthodox Christians except for the Russians lived in Muslim states. After 1917 most Russians lived in an atheist state. Today, most Orthodox Christians live in secular states. Symphonia has become problematic in a way that cannot be mitigated by the banal observation that ideals always fall short in practice.

To the extent that symphonia persists as an ideal in the Orthodox world—and the extent to which it persists demands investigation—the reason is probably the majority status of the Orthodox community in the populations of most of the post-Ottoman and post-Soviet successor states. The locus of symphonia has simply shifted from ruler to society. This fits in with the general democratization of political charisma in modern times: traditionally the prince or emperor was the "earthly god," in modern times the state or society assumes the role. Because the majority of the population in historic Orthodox countries still identifies with Orthodoxy at least nominally, it is possible to dream of effecting symphonia on the social and cultural, if not the political, plane. The Orthodox Church's claims to special status in postcommunist states are a reflection of this mentality, the expression of an ingrained sense of religious establishment that has survived the political disestablishment of Orthodoxy.[26] In theological terms, of course, populist symphonia is suspect. Symphonia depends on charisma, and charisma is conferred on persons, not abstract entities. While it might be possible, given the logic of symphonia, to appreciate evaluations of Constantine or Vladimir of Kiev as "equal of the apostles," it is a stretch to extend the honor to a society or nation. The emotional appeal of such theologized populism is nevertheless considerable in modern Orthodoxy.

The political challenge for Orthodoxy in modern times is to find a resonant alternative to symphonia as traditionally conceived. The thinkers represented in this volume all wrestled with this challenge in one way or another. Of the five, Vladimir Soloviev took the most traditional approach in that he continued to think in terms of an organic Christian society in which the disparate elements of spiritual, social, and political life are harmoniously interconnected. As we shall see, Soloviev's way of conceiving symphonia was quite modern; nevertheless, he stood firmly in the historic tradition of Orthodox social and political thought. The fact that he still lived in an Orthodox empire had much to do with this.

The neosymphonic approach was also adopted by most of the Russian Orthodox religious philosophers inspired by Soloviev, including Sergei Bulgakov.[27] Nicholas Berdyaev was more radical, however. While inspired by Soloviev, Berdyaev was also a great admirer of nineteenth-century

Westerners such as Friedrich Nietzsche, Søren Kierkegaard, and other fountainheads of the individualist and anarchist orientation that eventually came to be called existentialism. Berdyaev's "philosophy of freedom" left no room for organicism of any kind. Unlike many existentialists, however, Berdyaev remained loyal to the Solovievian tradition of social Christianity. Mother Maria Skobtsova, who was close to Bulgakov and Berdyaev, also promoted an Orthodox social gospel, and in the best possible way: by living it.

Neopatristic thinkers broke with symphonia in an even more radical way than Berdyaev: they stopped looking for an Orthodox legal, social, and political doctrine. They did not address issues of law, society, and politics in any of their major works. In part this was a reaction to their special social and political circumstances, which have already been noted. But there was another factor. Lossky, Florovsky, and other first-generation neopatristic thinkers embraced a rigorously mystical and apophatic view of theology that effectively discouraged the theological interpretation of legal, social, and political questions.[28] Mystical or apophatic theology is an effective means of contemplating the mystery of God as experienced in the depths of personal being. It is not a useful tool for fashioning a theory of the state, evaluating a system of positive law, forging an interpretation of history, or other tasks normally involved in the construction of a social and political ethic.

Not all theologians who contributed to the neopatristic movement were as radical as Florovsky and Lossky. Dumitru Stăniloae, for example, was shaped by the *Gândirea* circle in Romania between the world wars, a religious-philosophical movement strongly resembling Russian Slavophilism in its blending of Orthodoxy with national and cultural values. The effects can be detected in the more organic character of his theology.[29] In the Communist era, of course, the search for Orthodox legal, social, and political thought came to a halt in Romania as it did elsewhere. Only in recent years, with the emergence of free if struggling civil societies in the Christian East, has the search resumed, and it is too early to predict where it will lead. Orthodox nationalism, Christian socialism, neosymphonism, quietism, and some sort of accommodation between Orthodoxy and liberalism are all possible outcomes.

ORTHODOXY AND LAW

The fourth-century Constantinian settlement that regularized the status of the Christian church in the Roman Empire did not involve a legal revolution. On the contrary, the Roman legal system was a key element of the new arrangement. To be sure, the system was incorporated into symphonia. But the law did not depend on symphonia. One might even argue that it was the other way around, since symphonia necessarily involves an extra-ecclesiastical element: the imperial dignity as well as the priesthood, in Justinian's words. The Western medieval ideal of the supreme pontiff as the supreme lawgiver, or at least as the supreme arbiter of law in Christian society, was alien to Byzantium from the beginning. The emperor was the supreme lawgiver, a vocation conferred on him by God without priestly mediation and put into practice by his respect for the Roman legal tradition. When Eusebius of Caesarea, Constantine's apologist and the architect of symphonia, "developed the notion of a human viceroy dispensing Divine justice on earth in God's name,"[30] he was Christianizing the Roman imperial office. But the justice the emperor dispensed was defined first of all by Roman law. Over time Christian ethical teachings had an impact on the law, especially in the areas of marriage, sexuality, inheritance, the treatment of women and children, capital punishment, and of course religion. Although significant, however, the impact fell short of being revolutionary.[31] Some of the differences between Orthodox and Catholic ethical norms, such as the Orthodox Church's toleration of divorce, are traceable to the fact that for a thousand years the Orthodox Church had to accommodate itself to the preexisting Roman legal system. The Western church had a freer hand to legislate as it saw fit because of the fifth-century collapse of imperial authority in the West.

The Orthodox Church's legal competence widened in the twilight centuries of Byzantium (1204–1453), initiating a metamorphosis that was completed in the Ottoman period when the sultan recognized the Orthodox Church as the judicial authority over his Christian subjects. Roman law still figured in the system to the extent that bits and pieces of it had long been incorporated into the "nomocanons" which guided the Church in matters of civil and ecclesiastical law. Nomocanons were concise reference works assembled in the Byzantine period to facilitate the judicial tasks of bishops and the ecclesiastical dealings of imperial bureaucrats. The distinctive feature of the books was the conflation of ecclesiastical and imperial legislation. Imperial laws (*nomoi*) and church canons dealing with related issues appeared side by side, carrying equal weight and supposedly harmonizing with each other. The continued use of such instruments by the Orthodox Church during the Turkish period was a powerful statement of loyalty to the Byzantine heritage, but it did not and could not replicate the Byzantine legal order. In Byzantium, law was crafted by the imperial authority, not by the church; and the study of law flourished as an independent discipline with its own specialists and schools. All of this passed away with the collapse of the empire. The system patronized by the Turks may be called an ecclesiocracy. It left no room for an autonomous legal order.

The influence of Roman law in the Slavic lands converted to Orthodoxy during the Byzantine period is a complicated question.[32] Nomocanons were part of the cultural and ecclesiastical legacy transmitted to the converts. In Slavonic translation, these "pilot books"— *kormchie knigi*, as they were called—had an impact on the legislative monuments with which medieval Slavic princes occasionally adorned their "little Byzantiums."[33] But as has often been noted, the Byzantines were selective in what they shared with the "barbarians." They focused on religion rather than culture, on Christianization rather than Hellenization. The missionary strategy of evangelizing the Slavs in their own language rather than the imperial language reinforced this selectivity by withholding the tool that would have given the Slavs direct access to the Byzantine cultural tradition. Roman legal science was not transmitted to the Slavs any more than classical Greek poetry was. Even if it had been, the effects would have been minimized by the Mongol conquest of Russia and the Ottoman conquest of the South Slavs in the thirteenth and fourteenth centuries. By the time the Russians regained their independence and began building a great Orthodox empire in the north, Byzantium was no more. The Russians fashioned their polity from a variety of sources including nomocanons, Slavic customary law, and Mongol administrative practices. The state that emerged was emphatically Orthodox, and its ruler proudly claimed the Byzantine imperial titles of *tsar* (caesar) and autocrat. But Russian Byzantinism was one-sided: it replicated Roman autocracy without Roman law. The political reforms of Peter the Great did nothing to correct this deficiency.[34]

Orthodox canon law survived the fall of Byzantium, of course, and shaped personal life and civil society both in Muscovy and in the ecclesiocratic system of the Ottoman Empire.[35] But Orthodox canon law was a conservative discipline. It did not stimulate jurisprudence as the study of Roman Catholic canon law did in the West. The dynamism of Roman Catholic canon law depended on two conditions that did not exist in the East: a complex ("feudal") web of competing secular and ecclesiastical jurisdictions requiring regulation, and the existence of a supreme legislator in the church, namely the Pope of Rome, whose decrees were a constant source of new law ("reform") for the church. Like the Protestants of a later age, the Orthodox regarded the growth of law in the Western church as a hypertrophy, a violation of the spirit of the gospel. But Protestant and Orthodox criticisms of Roman legalism were differently motivated. The Protestants were interested in reforming the church, a concept for which they were ironically indebted to the authority structure against which they rebelled, namely, the reforming papacy of the Middle Ages. The Orthodox rejected papalism on grounds of tradition, a standard quite different from reform.

The traditional character of Orthodox canon law is reflected in the organization of the canonical collections and in the fact that one must speak of collections in the plural. The Orthodox Church does not possess a "Code of Canon Law."[36] It preserves a number of esteemed collections and commentaries, some medieval, some more recent. The drive to forge a "Concordance of Discordant Canons," as Gratian did around 1140 for medieval Catholicism, never caught on in Orthodoxy, probably because of the recognition that such an enterprise would end up making new laws, hence in some sense "reforming" the church. Orthodox canonists do not relish such a prospect, preferring to regard themselves as faithful transmitters of that which they have received from the ancients. The outlook is reflected in the tripartite organization of Orthodox canonical collections: apostolic canons come first, the canons of the ecumenical councils and other important synods stand next, and selected chapters from the writings of the church fathers round out the collection. Apostles, councils, and fathers—in that order—are treasured as prototypes of the unbroken practice of the church, not as raw material to be manipulated by legal rationality.

The strength of the Orthodox approach to canon law is the sense of limits brought to the subject by respect for tradition, in spiritual terms a kind of humility. Orthodoxy, like other forms of Christianity, has had its share of power-hungry prelates, but they have not found it easy to use canon law to justify their rapaciousness. The dictatorial legalism of the Roman papacy at its worst is absent from Orthodoxy. Unfortunately, another kind of legalism has not been absent: that which springs from an exaggerated and excessively literal dependence on the past, "the tendency to freeze history," as Meyendorff has characterized it.[37] One might call it paleocracy. Modern Orthodox theologians attempt to mitigate this type of legalism by distinguishing between tradition and traditions, that is to say, between the inalterable essentials of Orthodoxy and the many historically relative customs that not only can but in some circumstances must be changed in order to preserve the core values of tradition. The distinction is an important one, but it is not itself traditional, at least not in its strong form. An invention of modern theologians beginning with John Henry Newman, the distinction would have seemed strange to Orthodox churchmen of an earlier age. The history of Orthodoxy is full of conflicts over small points of practice that were deemed inalterable because they were traditional.

The most tragic case was the Russian Orthodox schism of the seventeenth century, when Old Believers separated from the Patriarchal church as a result of minute changes in prayer books and ritual practices. The defection probably commanded the loyalty, active or tacit, of the majority of Russian Orthodox Christians at the time. There are many other examples. A bitter dispute over the appropriate day (Saturday or Sunday) for memorial services for the departed embroiled the Greek church for many decades in the eighteenth century. In our day, Old Calendrists and New Calendrists battle each other in many Orthodox jurisdictions. If disputes of this kind were the work of an obscurantist fringe, as is sometimes thought, they could be ignored. In fact, they reflect the power of the paleocratic mentality in Orthodoxy. When Russian Orthodox Old Believers accepted torture and death rather than change (for example) the number of fingers they used to make the sign of the cross, they were not manifesting willful hearts as their detractors charged. They were abiding by a pattern which they honestly believed to be apostolic—and reasonably so, in that the apostles and saints were shown crossing themselves in just such a way on the icons that festooned their churches, images that were regarded as absolutely faithful copies of their prototypes.

The same attitude sometimes appears in learned theology. When one of the greatest Orthodox canonists of modern times, Nikodemos of the Holy Mountain (1749–1809), in his celebrated collection and commentary known as the *Pedalion* (The Pilot), emphatically defended the authenticity of all eighty-five Apostolic Canons against the Roman Catholic count of fifty—an old dispute—he was doing more than excoriating "Latin heretics." As he saw it, he was standing up for the actual practice of the apostles of Christ. That the Apostolic Canons is a fourth or fifth century composition, that the Roman count also dates from antiquity, and that even some Byzantine authorities doubted whether the Apostolic Canons issued from the hands of the apostles—these considerations were trumped by the force of a long-standing tradition. The eighty-five Apostolic Canons appeared in all Orthodox collections of canons since formal compendia began to be made in Byzantium in the ninth century. It was inconceivable to Nikodemos that the tradition of the church in this matter could be anything other than what it claimed to be, namely, apostolic.[38]

The Orthodox canonical tradition did not always lead the church to defend the status quo. In some historical contexts, appeal to the canons had reformist implications, especially where the Orthodox Church was forced by an oppressive political regime to violate its canonical structure. In these situations the appeal to restore canonical order was in effect a demand for political reform and greater latitude for civil society.

Orthodox resistance to the Petrine ecclesiastical settlement in the Russian Empire had this character. In his zeal to make Russia a European power, Peter the Great reconstructed the Muscovite polity along the lines of Western European absolutism. In the process he imposed a radically untraditional constitution on the Russian Orthodox Church.[39] The patriarchate of Moscow and the conciliar institutions of the church were suspended and replaced by a small synod of bishops chaired by a lay bureaucrat, or oberprocurator, responsible solely to the emperor. Every aspect of church life was brought under government supervision. Even the sanctity of confession was violated as priests were charged with certain police functions. The bishops of the Holy Synod were not at liberty to assemble without the permission of the oberprocurator. The episcopate as a whole never assembled, not once during the entire synodal period (1721–1917).

There was much dissatisfaction with this patently uncanonical system of church government among learned Russian Orthodox, although state censorship limited public expression of dissent. Unfortunately, no one ever found a way to change the system from within. The Great Reforms of the 1860s, which abolished serfdom, created a modern judicial system, put a system of local government in place, and reformed the army, ignored the church. A promising conciliar movement in 1905–1906 enjoyed widespread support but failed to convene a council because the tsar's government withheld permission.[40] The council did not assemble until 1917, after the imperial regime had fallen and the Bolsheviks were literally at the door. The Local Council of 1917 restored the patriarchate and cast off the other oppressive features of the synodal regime, but its resolutions soon became moot as the young Soviet regime set about forcibly dismantling the Orthodox Church.

Following World War II, when the Soviet government allowed the Orthodox Church to reconstitute itself within strict limits and under state supervision, the appeal to canonical order again emerged as a vehicle for dissent. Soviet laws on religion had suppressed almost all of the canonical structures that protect the autonomy of the church, such as conciliar government and the clerical presidency of parish councils. The criticism of this legislation was the point of the celebrated letters to the patriarch and the Soviet president by Fathers Eshliman and Yakunin in 1965, one of the opening salvos of the Soviet human rights movement.[41] Meanwhile the quiet but forceful example of Father Aleksandr Men, a Moscow priest with a gift for ministry to intellectuals, showed that a profound Orthodox ministry to society was possible (if rare) in spite of the suppression of canonical order by the Soviet regime.[42] Canonical order was restored by the *glasnost*-era Council of 1988, two years before Soviet legislation on religion was officially changed.

Of course, some disturbances of canonical order come from within the church. A contemporary example is the "canonical chaos" that obtains in the Orthodox diaspora.[43] Nothing is more basic to canonical order in Orthodoxy than the unity of the local church: one city, one bishop, one church. Yet nothing is more characteristic of the Orthodox diaspora than the maze of overlapping and competing ecclesiastical jurisdictions operating in the same space. In most places this antisystem is the result of the movement of populations in modern times. Relocated ethnic groups wish to maintain their ties with the mother church and introduce its hierarchy abroad. Understandable as these loyalties are, their effect has been to undercut the unity and mission of Orthodoxy. In America, for example, most non-Orthodox regard the various Orthodox bodies as completely different churches. The extent to which these bodies agree on doctrine, liturgy, and discipline is rarely appreciated. Divisions of a more serious kind, springing from internecine conflict, are also a problem. In Estonia, Ukraine, and elsewhere, bitter divisions and jurisdictional disputes bedevil the life of the church.

What makes these internal lapses of canonical order especially demoralizing is that the Orthodox Church today has the freedom to correct them but, so far, cannot seem to do so. Aside from vested interests, the problem is the absence of central authority. Interjurisdictional coordination is difficult in Orthodoxy because no one in particular is responsible for it. Not even the Ecumenical Patriarch (the Patriarch of Constantinople) has this authority; indeed, he is often one of the parties in need of coordination. The national and regional churches that constitute the Orthodox communion are "autocephalous," that is to say, administratively and judicially independent of each other. The unity of Orthodoxy is expressed through fidelity to a common tradition and in conciliar gatherings. When Orthodox bishops come into conflict with each other, only a council can restore order. In the case of conflicts between autocephalous churches, this means a worldwide or general council. But there is a problem here: for all its famed *sobornost*, the Orthodox Church has not actually held a worldwide council since the year 787—not exactly a recent precedent. In effect, worldwide Orthodoxy finds itself in the situation that the Roman Catholic Church would be in if, while professing the ideal of a papal monarchy, it lacked an actual papacy.

The gap between the theory and practice of *sobornost* is a manifestation of a general problem in the Orthodox canonical tradition, namely, the tendency to cherish mystically authenticated concepts without doing much to effectuate them. The distinguished Orthodox canonist John Erickson has written of the need "to rediscover the implications of communion for community, lest our much-vaunted [Orthodox] 'spirituality' and 'mystical theology' degenerate into dilettantish escapism."[44] His plea, delivered in 1982, is as relevant as ever today.

ORTHODOXY AND DEMOCRACY

The overarching challenge for Orthodox thought on law, politics, and society in the twenty-first century is to clarify the role the church should play in the construction of a democratic civil society. The church has a huge stake in the matter. No responsible party wishes to repeat the catastrophes of the Communist era, and most Orthodox leaders today recognize that a stable democratic order is the surest safeguard against doing so. The situation is nevertheless unprecedented. The large majority of Orthodox have little if any experience of democracy. Moreover, like other churches that relied on state establishment, the Orthodox Church has inherited a low degree of popular participation in its institutions and programs. In *The Russian Question at the End of the Twentieth Century*, Aleksandr Solzhenitsyn lamented "our ingrained and wretched Russian tradition: we refuse to learn how to organize *from below*, and are inclined to wait for instructions from a monarch, a leader, a spiritual or political authority."[45] This is not just a Russian question. It applies to state and church in most parts of the Orthodox world today.

The Orthodox thinkers treated in this volume offer various resources on the issue of Orthodoxy and democracy without providing anything like a blueprint of the solution. The latter is too much to expect, given the enormous changes that have taken place in the social and political circumstances of Orthodoxy in recent years. The gap between the world that our five Orthodox thinkers knew and the present situation of their faith tradition is greater than in the case of the Protestant or Roman Catholic figures treated in the companion volumes. Of the five, the one who thought the most systematically about the role of Orthodoxy in civil society is the farthest removed from us in time: Vladimir Soloviev. The apparent irony is dispelled when one considers that Soloviev was the only one of the five who completely predated the Communist upheaval. A modern-style civil society was emerging in Russia in Soloviev's day, however unevenly, and his social and political philosophy contributed to it.

The other Orthodox thinkers presented here endured the political traumas of twentieth-century Europe in one way or another, including the lengthy political imprisonment suffered by Dumitru Stăniloae and martyrdom in a Nazi death camp in the case of Mother Maria Skobtsova. Yet there is a brighter side to the picture in that Berdyaev, Lossky, and Mother Maria also experienced democracy by virtue of their many years of residence in France. During their lifetimes, they did not have the opportunity to share their experience with those living on historically Orthodox soil, but their example has fresh relevance for their coreligionists who wrestle with the issue of Orthodoxy and democracy today.

There is evidence that contemporary Orthodox leaders recognize the need for greater attention to problems of law, society, and politics in the postcommunist environment. A good example is the detailed outline of Christian social teachings, "Bases of the Social Concept of the Russian Orthodox Church," that the episcopate of the Russian Orthodox Church (Moscow Patriarchate) adopted at a council in 2000.[46] The document contains specific teachings on topics as various as church-state relations, Orthodoxy and secular law, economic justice, criminal law, bioethics, environmental ethics, sexual ethics, religion and science, and international relations. The 125-page compendium represents a striking innovation in Orthodox practice, bearing greater resemblance to a papal encyclical or a report by a national Roman Catholic bishops' conference than to any traditional Orthodox form of expression. Some of the positions incorporated in it, such as the theological defense of civil disobedience in certain circumstances, are virtually unprecedented in Orthodox legal, social, and political thought.

The cultivation of *sobornost* also bears on the practice of Orthodoxy in a democracy. To be sure, a church council is not a democratic assembly. Yet it is an assembly, and the virtues and skills that sustain it are transferable. These include the practice of shared responsibility, an understanding of due process, techniques of discussion, debate, and decision making, and above all the experience of participating in decisions about matters that affect one's life. For this reason one may claim that conciliar practice and democracy, though not the same thing, can reinforce and enrich each other. This connection also works in the negative: oligarchy in the state and oligarchy in the church reinforce each other.

The issue of initiative and participation pertains to other sectors of Orthodox church life besides councils, such as liturgy and parish life. The great liturgies of the Christian East are the glory of Orthodoxy, but as currently practiced in most parts of the Orthodox world they discourage broad participation in worship. Liturgical reforms are needed to address this problem, but few churchmen are willing to touch the issue because of the explosive potential of Orthodox legalism. Priests who have experimented with new forms have been marginalized and sometimes vilified. Although fears that reform could land Orthodoxy in a state of liturgical confusion comparable to that of post–Vatican II Catholicism are by no means groundless, criticism of Western pathologies cannot compensate for absence of renewal in the East. As for the Orthodox parish, its renewal is closely connected with liturgical reform. There are other challenges as well, such as the need for a theology of the laity in Orthodoxy.[47]

Admittedly, one should not abuse the theme of Orthodoxy and democracy by implying that the primary vocation of the Orthodox Church is to build democracy. For the sake of its distinctive mission, the church must keep its distance from the powers of this world, including the democratic powers of this world. The distance is healthy not just for the church but for the democratic state because it keeps prophetically open the issue of how the Christian love-ethic relates to the ethics of democracy. This profound question has not yet been adequately clarified anywhere. Democracy is still a relatively new phenomenon in world history, and neither its grandeur nor its pitfalls have been sufficiently probed. The transcendent love which Orthodoxy serves—the "acosmic love" that so impressed Max Weber in the heroes of Dostoevsky and Tolstoy[48]—has not figured conspicuously in the ethics of democracy. Yet Orthodox Christians are clearly called to witness to this "more excellent way" (1 Cor. 12:31).

And witnesses there have been. Surely the most enduring legacy of twentieth-century Orthodoxy will be the veneration of the martyrs and confessors who suffered for their faith at the hands of the Communist state—a state, let it be remembered, that called itself "social-democratic." No discussion of justice, law, and society in modern Christianity can pass over this historical record in silence. A life-giving resource for the church, the blood of the new martyrs is a thundering stream of judgment on the powers of the modern world, including the democratic powers. It will not do to object that Communism was not "true" democracy. Of course it was not; but neither was it unconnected with modern democratic ideas. The ethicist will do better to follow Reinhold Niebuhr at this point and recognize the threat of the demonic in all social and political ideologies.

As the Orthodox churches that suffered under Communism investigate the historical record, a new martyrology is emerging. The process is most advanced in the Russian Orthodox Church. At the Council of 2000, no fewer than 1,149 new Russian saints were canonized, most of them martyrs of the Communist period. The number alone is an indication of how long it will take to assimilate the meaning of what happened to the Orthodox Church in the twentieth century.

The report of the investigative commission that recommended the canonizations to the Council of 2000 is a document without much rhetorical embellishment, and therein lies its eloquence.[49] The record speaks for itself. The "throng" (*sonm*) of the martyred embraces all canonical stations of the church: metropolitan bishops, archbishops, bishops, archimandrites, archpriests, hegumens, priests (the largest group), hieromonks, protodeacons, deacons, monks and nuns, novices, and laypersons. Presented by diocese and distinguished by canonical rank, the martyrs are listed alphabetically by their first name, a reminder of the ultimate significance of the individual person—and of personal responsibility—in the kingdom of God. Also included among the canonized are forty-six individuals who are "not yet revealed to the world by name, but known to God."

The council also resolved "to canonize as passion-bearers, in the throng of new martyrs and confessors of Russia, the Imperial Family: Emperor Nicholas II, Empress Aleksandra, the Tsarevich Aleksy, and the grand princesses Olga, Tatiana, Maria, and Anastasia." "Passion-bearers" (*strastoterptsy*) is a term traditionally applied to princes who manifested Christian virtues while suffering at the hands of their political enemies. But the princely connection was less important to the authors of the report than the national connection: "Through the sufferings of the Imperial Family in their captivity, borne with meekness, patience and humility, and in their martyr's death in Yekaterinburg on the night of July 4 (17), 1918, the light of the faith of Christ which overcomes evil was made manifest, just as it shone in the life and death of the millions of Orthodox Christians who endured persecution for Christ in the twentieth century."

In time, the annals of the new martyrs will become part of the sacred story of every diocese in Orthodoxy. Icons of the new saints have been prepared, and more will follow. The cloud of witnesses to a more excellent way will shine as a perpetual reminder of the glory of the kingdom of God and the limits of all earthly polities.

Yet the critique of democracy, important as it is, cannot be the first order of business in twenty-first century Orthodoxy. More important for the church's present welfare is the task of measuring up to the challenges facing it in a democratic society, including the need for a more positive understanding of law. In rising to this occasion, Orthodoxy will discover more about itself than it has known before and more about the gospel than it has known before. A new challenge is at hand. In the Communist era Orthodox Christians died for their faith. In the world after Communism they must learn to live for it.

NOTES

1. J. M. Hussey, *The Orthodox Church in the Byzantine Empire* (Oxford: Clarendon Press, 1986), 1.
2. The insights of Edward Said's concept of "orientalism" have long been assimilated by scholars of Islam and non-Western religions. The concept is also relevant to the study of Orthodox Christianity, although this has rarely been recognized.
3. The branch of theology concerned with the writings of the "fathers" of the ancient and medieval church is usually called patristics. The fathers did not occupy any one station or office in the church. Some were bishops, some presbyters (priests), some monks, some scholars. Because they were male, the discipline devoted to studying their writings is accurately named. However, inasmuch as the role of women in the ancient church was enormous, albeit traditionally ignored, the pursuit of "matristics" is sure to grow in the coming years and provide a corrective to one-sided attention to the fathers.

    The major languages of patristic literature are Greek, Latin, and Syriac. The literature falls into three historical periods: the early period, when Christianity was a persecuted faith (first to early fourth centuries); the classical period, when Christianity became the established religion of the Roman Empire and codified its fundamental doctrines at the first ecumenical councils (fourth through sixth centuries); and the medieval period, when the Greek-speaking (Byzantine) East and the Latin-speaking West gradually uncoupled (seventh through fifteenth centuries). Before the twentieth century, Western patristic scholarship focused almost exclusively on the first two periods, ignoring Byzantine (but not medieval Latin) theology. Since the early twentieth century, Byzantine theology has received attention. Some of its greatest minds—Maximus the Confessor (ca. 580–662), Symeon the New Theologian (949–1022), and Gregory Palamas (1296–1359), among others—have begun to be appreciated beyond the boundaries of Orthodoxy and have also become much better known in the Orthodox world. In general it is fair to say that interest in the Greek and Syrian fathers of all three patristic periods is growing steadily. The early Byzantine theologians Gregory of Nazianzus (Gregory the Theologian, ca. 329–390), Basil of Caesarea (Basil the Great, 330–379), and Gregory of Nyssa (331/40–ca. 395)—called the Cappadocians after the name of their native province in Asia Minor—are especially prominent reference points in contemporary theological discussions.

    The standard handbook to patristic literature of the early and classical periods is Johannes Quasten, *Patrology*, 4 vols. (Westminster, Md.: Christian Classics, 1990). Another useful tool is *Dictionary of Early Christian Literature*, ed. Siegmar Döpp and Wilhelm Geerlings, trans. Matthew O'Connell (New York: Crossroad, 2000). For a survey of early patristic theology by a contemporary Orthodox scholar, see John Behr, *The Way to Nicaea: The Formation of Christian Theology*, vol. 1 (Crestwood, N.Y.: St. Vladimir's Seminary Press, 2001). A magnificent introduction to the world of the Cappadocians is provided by John McGuckin, *Saint Gregory of Nazianzus: An Intellectual Biography* (Crestwood, N.Y.: St. Vladimir's Seminary Press, 2001). The best introduction to Byzantine theology in English is John Meyendorff, *Byzantine Theology: Historical Trends and Doctrinal Themes* (New York: Fordham University Press, 1974). Good monographs also exist on individual theologians: for example, Aidan Nichols, *Byzantine Gospel: Maximus the Confessor in Modern Scholarship* (Edinburgh: T & T Clark, 1993); John Meyendorff, *A Study of Gregory Palamas*, trans. George Lawrence, 2d ed. (Crestwood, N.Y.: St. Vladimir's Seminary Press, 1974); and Hilarion Alfeyev, *St. Symeon the New Theologian and Orthodox Tradition* (Oxford: Oxford University Press, 2000).

Some of the most readable English-language editions of patristic writings are found in the Paulist Press series "Classics of Western Spirituality," which includes a fair sampling of Eastern Christian works. ("Western" in the series title refers collectively to Jewish, Christian, and Islamic traditions, not to Western as opposed to Eastern Christianity.) Standard collections of the fathers in English include two continuing series, "Ancient Christian Writers: The Works of the Fathers in Translation," now published by the Catholic University of America Press, and "The Fathers of the Church: A New Translation," now published by the Paulist Press. Still useful, although extremely antiquated, are two nineteenth-century collections: *The Ante-Nicene Fathers: Translations of the Fathers down to A.D. 325*, ed. Alexander Roberts and James Donaldson, 10 vols., and *A Select Library of the Nicene and Post-Nicene Fathers of the Christian Church*, ed. Philip Schaff and Henry Wace, 28 vols., repr. ed. (Grand Rapids, Mich.: Eerdmans, 1978–79).

4. Lossky's book had a considerable impact in the English-speaking world thanks to a relatively early translation: Vladimir Lossky, *The Mystical Theology of the Eastern Church* (Cambridge: James Clarke, 1957). Florovsky's long and difficult book was translated much later: Georges Florovsky, *The Ways of Russian Theology*, part 1, trans. Robert L. Nichols, *The Collected Works of Georges Florovsky*, vol. 5 (Belmont, Mass.: Nordland, 1979); part 2, *The Collected Works of George Florovsky*, vol. 6 (Vaduz, Liechtenstein: Büchervertriebsanstalt, 1987). The best introduction to Florovsky's thought is not *The Ways of Russian Theology* but the elegant, pithy essays on a wide variety of patristic topics in *The Collected Works of Georges Florovsky*, 14 vols. (Belmont, Mass.: Nordland, 1972–89).

5. The pioneering work in Orthodox ethics by Stanley Harakas, Vigen Guroian, and other American scholars is not primarily neopatristic in inspiration. It owes more to the sustained dialogue between creative Orthodox

ethicists and the interconfessional discipline of Christian ethics as practiced in North America. The Greek theologian Christos Yannaras comes
closer to being an ethicist of neopatristic inspiration. See his *The Freedom
of Morality*, trans. Elizabeth Briere with a foreword by Bishop Kallistos of
Diokleia (Crestwood, N.Y.: St. Vladimir's Seminary Press, 1984). For a fine
example of the American contribution, see Vigen Guroian, *Incarnate Love:
Essays in Orthodox Ethics*, 2d ed. (Notre Dame, Ind.: University of Notre
Dame Press, 2002).

6. "Actually, one can hardly find, in the entire religious literature of Byzantium,
any systematic treatment of Christian ethics, or behavior, but rather innumer-
able examples of moral exegesis of Scripture, and ascetical treatises on prayer
and spirituality. This implies that Byzantine ethics were eminently 'theological ethics.' The basic affirmation that *every* man, whether Christian or not, is
created according to the image of God and therefore called to divine communion and 'deification,' was of course recognized, but no attempt was ever made
to build 'secular' ethics for man 'in general.'" Meyendorff, *Byzantine Theology*,
226.

7. Kallistos Ware, "Eastern Christianity," *The Encyclopedia of Religion*, ed. Mircea Eliade (New York: Free Press, 1987), 4:571.

8. Leonardo Boff, *Trinity and Society*, trans. Paul Burns (Maryknoll, N.Y.: Orbis
Books, 1988).

9. Michael Aksionov Meerson's *The Trinity of Love in Modern Russian Theology:
The Love Paradigm and the Retrieval of Western Medieval Love Mysticism in
Modern Russian Trinitarian Thought (from Solovyov to Bulgakov)* (Quincy,
Ill.: Franciscan Press, 1998) is an important contribution to a widened trinitar-
ianism in Orthodox theology. Although this book has ethical implications, it
is not primarily an essay in ethics; neither can the author be called a neopatristic theologian.

10. Makarios and Nikodemos's work is available in English: *The Philokalia: The
Complete Text, compiled by St Nikodimos of the Holy Mountain and St.
Makarios of Corinth*, trans. G.E.H. Palmer, Philip Sherrard and Kallistos
Ware, 3 vols. (London: Faber and Faber, 1979–84). Dumitru Stăniloae pro-
duced a twelve-volume Romanian *Philokalia* (1946–91). See chapter 5, this
volume.

11. "The view of man prevailing in the Christian East is based upon the notion of
'participation' in God. Man has been created not as an autonomous or self-sufficient being; his very *nature* is truly itself only inasmuch as it exists 'in God'
or 'in grace.' Grace, therefore, gives man his 'natural' development. This basic
presupposition explains why the terms 'nature' and 'grace,' when used by Byzantine authors, have a meaning quite different from the Western usage; rather
than being in direct opposition, the terms 'nature' and 'grace' express a dynamic, living, and necessary relationship between God and man, different by
their *natures*, but in *communion* with each other through God's energy, or
grace." Meyendorff, *Byzantine Theology*, 138.

12. The first two uses are the civil use of the law as a means of preserving public order and the theological use of the law as a means of convicting sinners of unrighteousness, thereby awakening in them a hunger for redemption.

13. The best introduction to Slavophilism is Andrzej Walicki, *The Slavophile Controversy: History of a Conservative Utopia in Nineteenth-Century Russian Thought*, trans. Hilda Andrews-Rusiecka (Notre Dame, Ind.: University of Notre Dame Press, 1989). The best collection of Slavophile writings in English is *On Spiritual Unity: A Slavophile Reader*, trans. and ed. Boris Jakim and Robert Bird (Hudson, N.Y.: Lindisfarne Books, 1998).

14. *Sobornost* comes from the Slavic root meaning "gather." So, for example, the noun *sobor* means "church council" and also "cathedral" (where the people gather for liturgy). The adjective *sobornyi* translates "catholic" in the Nicene Creed: "one holy, catholic and apostolic Church." Community, fellowship, conciliarity, catholicity, cathedral-feeling—all these meanings resound in the term *sobornost*. In recent decades the word has begun an international career, appearing, for example, in *Webster's Third New International Dictionary* (1981).

15. Andrzej Walicki, *Legal Philosophies of Russian Liberalism* (Oxford: Clarendon Press, 1987), 9–104.

16. For a fine discussion, see Harold J. Berman, "The Weightier Matters of the Law: A Response to Solzhenitsyn," in *Faith and Order: The Reconciliation of Law and Religion* (Atlanta, Ga.: Scholars Press, 1993), 381–392.

17. On the liberalism of Soloviev and some of the thinkers inspired by him, see Walicki, *Legal Philosophies of Russian Liberalism*; and the classic Russian work of 1902, *Problems of Idealism: Essays in Russian Social Philosophy*, trans. and ed. Randall A. Poole (New Haven, Conn.: Yale University Press, 2003).

18. See note 3 above.

19. Sergei Horuzhy, a mathematical physicist, has elaborated a philosophy of "energetism" based, as he claims, on hesychasm. See Sergei Khoruzhii, *K fenomenologii askezy* (Moscow: Izdatel'stvo gumanitarnoi literatury, 1998) and *O starom i o novom* (St. Petersburg: Aleteiia, 2000). For a related essay in English see Sergei S. Horuzhy, "Neo-Patristic Synthesis and Russian Philosophy," *St. Vladimir's Theological Quarterly* 44 (2000): 309–328.

20. John W. Barker, *Justinian and the Later Roman Empire* (Madison: University of Wisconsin Press, 1966), 97.

21. The essential essay on the subject is Deno J. Geanakoplos, "Church and State in the Byzantine Empire: A Reconsideration of the Problem of Caesaropapism," in id., *Byzantine East and Latin West: Two Worlds of Christendom in Middle Ages and Renaissance, Studies in Ecclesiastical and Cultural History* (New York: Harper & Row, 1966), 55–83.

22. Monophysitism, literally "one-nature-ism," is the view that humanity and divinity were so integrally united in Christ that one may speak of "one incarnate nature of God the Word." The Orthodox doctrine, confirmed at the Council of

Chalcedon in 451, is that, in Christ, two distinct natures (divine and human) were united without confusion or division in one Person. The Chalcedonians rejected monophysitism because they believed it compromised the humanity of Christ. The monophysites rejected Chalcedon because they believed it compromised the fullness of the incarnation. Orthodox, Roman Catholic, and Protestant churches are Chalcedonian. Coptic, Syrian, Armenian, and Ethiopian churches are non-Chalcedonian. The popularity of monophysitism in the Eastern provinces of the Byzantine Empire owed much to regional resentment against the political and cultural hegemonism of Constantinople.

23. Quoted by Meyendorff, *Byzantine Theology*, 213.

24. Ibid., 213–214. Meyendorff views this civil-political application of incarnational theology as misguided because it assumed "that the ideal humanity which was manifested, through the Incarnation, in the person of Jesus Christ could also find an adequate manifestation in the Roman Empire." But this is the assessment of a theologian reflecting on the fall of the two great Orthodox empires in world history, the Byzantine and the Russian. The vast majority of Orthodox Christians until quite recently shared Justinian's view that the Orthodox state was as much a divine institution as the Orthodox Church.

25. On the "palladian" qualities of icons, see Hussey, *The Orthodox Church in the Byzantine Empire*, 31–32; Judith Herrin, *The Formation of Christendom* (Princeton, N.J.: Princeton University Press, 1987), 307–308, 314–315; and Leo Tolstoy, *War and Peace*, book 3, chap. 2.

26. Orthodox appeals to the state to help resist proselytism by other Christian groups are a good example. See John Witte Jr. and Michael Bourdeaux, eds., *Proselytism and Orthodoxy in Russia: The New War for Souls* (Maryknoll, N.Y.: Orbis Books, 1999).

27. English-language discussion of Bulgakov's thought has flourished in recent years. See Judith Deutsch Kornblatt and Richard F. Gustafson, eds., *Russian Religious Thought* (Madison: University of Wisconsin Press, 1996), 135–192; Catherine Evtuhov, *The Cross and the Sickle: Sergei Bulgakov and the Fate of Russian Religious Philosophy* (Ithaca, N.Y.: Cornell University Press, 1997); Rowan Williams, ed., *Sergii Bulgakov: Towards a Russian Political Theology* (Edinburgh: T & T Clark, 1999); Paul Valliere, *Modern Russian Theology: Bukharev, Soloviev, Bulgakov* (Grand Rapids, Mich.: Eerdmans, 2000), 227–371; and the pioneering study by Philip Max Walters, "The Development of the Political and Religious Philosophy of Sergei Bulgakov, 1895–1922: A Struggle for Transcendence" (Ph.D. diss., London School of Economics and Political Science, 1978).

28. "Apophatic" comes from a Greek word meaning "negative." In theology it refers to discourse about the divine in terms of what God is not (e.g., God is not finite, not mortal, not human, not comprehensible, not reducible to the measure of this world or of any world, and so on), as opposed to positive or "kataphatic" statements about God (e.g., God is good, just, loving, wise, and so on).

The aim of apophatic discourse is to induce the mind to confess the radical transcendence and mystery of God.

29. The contrast is developed by Silviu Eugen Rogobete, "Mystical Existentialism or Communitarian Participation? Vladimir Lossky and Dumitru Staniloae," in *Dumitru Staniloae: Tradition and Modernity in Theology*, ed. Lucian Turcescu (Iasi, Romania: Center for Romanian Studies, 2002), 167–206. On *Gândirea* (*Thought*, the name of a journal), see Keith Hitchins, "*Gândirea*: Nationalism in a Spiritual Guise," *Social Change in Romania, 1860–1940: A Debate on Development in a European Nation*, ed. Kenneth Jowitt (Berkeley: Institute of International Studies, University of California, 1978).

30. Herrin, *The Formation of Christendom*, 38.

31. Stephen Runciman, *Byzantine Civilization* (London: Edward Arnold, 1959), 75–76. For a concise presentation of Justinian's legislation, including its Christian elements, see Percy Neville Ure, *Justinian and his Age* (Harmondsworth, England: Penguin, 1951), 139–167.

32. For an introduction to the issues and the literature see Ia. N. Shchapov, *Vizantiiskoe i iuzhnoslavianskoe pravovoe nasledie na Rusi v XI–XIIIvv* (Moscow: Izdatel'stvo Nauka, 1978).

33. The phrase is from John Meyendorff, *Living Tradition: Orthodox Witness in the Contemporary World* (Crestwood, N.Y.: St. Vladimir's Seminary Press, 1978), 195.

34. "In Russia, unlike the West, no rising class of jurists, specially trained in rational law, had prepared the way for eighteenth-century absolutist rule and modernization. Therefore Russian absolutism adopted the ethos of rational legislation and the policy of the *état bien policé*, while preserving many features of a traditional patriarchal autocracy, and did not have to concern itself with an organized legal profession. The institution of the Bar only appeared in Russia with the judicial reforms of 1864." Walicki, *Legal Philosophies of Russian Liberalism*, 15. See also Marc Raeff, *The Well-Ordered Police State: Social and Institutional Change Through Law in the Germanies and Russia, 1600–1800* (London, 1983).

35. For an introduction to Orthodox canon law and some of its applications, see the essays by John H. Erickson, *The Challenge of Our Past: Studies in Orthodox Canon Law and Church History* (Crestwood, N.Y.: St. Vladimir's Seminary Press, 1991); and "*Oikonomia* in Byzantine Canon Law," in *Law, Church and Society: Essays in Honor of Stephan Kuttner*, ed. K. Pennington and R. Somerville (Philadelphia: University of Pennsylvania Press, 1977), 225–236.

36. A unitary "code" of canon law as opposed to a "corpus" of officially recognized sources is a recent development even in Roman Catholicism. The first *Codex iuris canonici* was promulgated in 1917. A new code was issued in 1983.

37. *Byzantine Theology*, 54, 225.

38. For an introduction to Nikodemos, see *Nicodemos of the Holy Mountain: A Handbook of Spiritual Counsel*, trans. Peter A. Chamberas (New York: Paulist Press, 1989); and the penetrating critique by John H. Erickson, "On the Cusp

of Modernity: The Canonical Hermeneutic of St. Nikodemos the Haghiorite (1748–1809)," *St. Vladimir's Theological Quarterly* 42 (1998): 45–66. The *Pedalion* is available in a not altogether satisfactory English edition: *The Rudder*, trans. D. Cummings (Chicago: Orthodox Christian Educational Society, 1957).

39. The standard account in English is James Cracraft, *The Church Reform of Peter the Great* (Stanford, Calif.: Stanford University Press, 1971). See also *The Spiritual Regulation of Peter the Great*, trans. and ed. Alexander V. Muller (Seattle: University of Washington Press, 1972).

40. Many changes in the regulation of the church, some of them constructive, were made in the nineteenth century, but they cannot be said to add up to a reform of the synodal system, much less of the church itself. For a detailed account, see Gregory L. Freeze, *The Parish Clergy in Nineteenth-Century Russia: Crisis, Reform, Counter-Reform* (Princeton, N.J.: Princeton University Press, 1983). The standard work on the conciliar movement of 1905–6 is James W. Cunningham, *A Vanquished Hope: The Movement for Church Renewal in Russia, 1905–1906* (Crestwood, N.Y.: St. Vladimir's Seminary Press, 1981).

41. For a complete English translation see "Documents: Appeals for Religious Freedom in Russia," *St. Vladimir's Seminary Quarterly* 10 (1966): 67–111. For a detailed discussion of Orthodox dissent during the Soviet period, see Jane Ellis, *The Russian Orthodox Church: A Contemporary History* (Bloomington: Indiana University Press, 1986), 285–454. See also Paul Valliere, "Russian Orthodoxy and Human Rights," in *Religious Diversity and Human Rights*, ed. Irene Bloom, J. Paul Martin, and Wayne L. Proudfoot (New York: Columbia University Press, 1996), 278–312.

42. For an introduction, see *Christianity for the Twenty-first Century: The Prophetic Writings of Alexander Men*, ed. Elizabeth Roberts and Ann Shukman (New York: Continuum, 1996).

43. The phrase is from John Meyendorff, *Living Tradition*, 105.

44. Erickson, *The Challenge of Our Past*, 20.

45. *The Russian Question at the End of the Twentieth Century*, trans. Yermolai Solzhenitsyn (New York: Farrar, Straus & Giroux, 1995), 98.

46. "Osnovy sotsial'noi kontseptsii russkoi pravoslavnoi tserkvi" (Bases of the Social Concept of the Russian Orthodox Church). The document, with English translation, can be found at the website of the Moscow Patriarchate, http://www.russian-orthodox-church.org.ru.

47. On this issue, see *Religion, State & Society* 27, no. 1 (March 1999), the record of a conference on "Reflection on the Laity: a Focus for Christian Dialogue Between East and West" sponsored by Keston College and the University of Leeds.

48. Max Weber, "Politics as a Vocation," in *From Max Weber: Essays in Sociology*, trans. H.H. Gerth and C. Wright Mills (New York: Oxford University Press, 1970–72), 126.

49. "Deianie iubileinogo osviashchennogo arkhiereiskogo sobora russkoi pravoslavnoi tserkvi o sobornom proslavlenii novomuchenikov i ispovednikov rossiiskikh XX veka." See also the report of the chair of the canonization commission, "Doklad mitropolita krutitskogo i kolomenskogo Iuvenaliia, predsedatelia sinodal'noi komissii po kanonizatsii sviatykh, na arkhiereiskom sobore," and the summary of the proceedings, "Proslavlenie sviatykh na iubileinom arkhiereiskom sobore." The documents can be found at the website of the Moscow Patriarchate, http://www.russian-orthodox-church.org.ru.

{ CHAPTER 1 }

Vladimir Soloviev (1853–1900)

COMMENTARY

PAUL VALLIERE

The systematic study of law, one of the central concerns of Western Christian civilization since the Middle Ages, has not enjoyed comparable centrality in the Christian East. The Byzantine legal tradition, described in the preceding introduction, perished with the fall of the Byzantine Empire (1453). Since then, the catalyst for the development of legal thought in the Orthodox East has been contact with the West. The dynamic, often aggressive, projection of Western influence into the Orthodox world in modern times forced Eastern Christians to take an interest in Western civilization whether they wished to or not. Among the many subjects demanding attention, Western legalism—civil, political, and ecclesiastical—was particularly difficult for Orthodox people to appreciate because of the absence of analogous structures in their own living tradition.

Orthodox reflection on modern legalism began in Russia, not because the Russians were better prepared to think about law than the other Orthodox peoples, but because Russia was the first Orthodox country to attempt to remake itself into a state and society of the modern type. The reforms of Peter the Great and Catherine the Great in the eighteenth century stimulated profound reflection on the foundations of civil society. During the "Moscow Spring" of 1809–12, the statesman and jurist Mikhail Speransky—the son of an Orthodox village priest—convinced Tsar Alexander I to contemplate an extensive reform of the Russian Empire along legal lines. Napoleon's invasion in 1812 put an end to this project, but Russian legal science continued to develop. Speransky devoted the second half of his career to preparing the first systematic code of law in the history of Russia. The first edition of this massive work was published in 1832. Later in the century Timofei Granovsky (1813–55) and Boris Chicherin (1828–1903) laid the foundations of Russian legal philosophy. As part of the Great Reforms of the 1860s, a new judicial system was set up, jury trial was introduced, and a Russian bar was created. The rule of law appeared to have begun in Russia.

What had not begun was the reconciliation of the fledgling Russian legal tradition with the Orthodox Christian tradition, which commanded the religious loyalty of the large majority of the population of the Russian Empire. Aleksei Khomiakov (1804–60), Ivan Kireevsky (1806–56), and the other early Slavophiles who created modern Russian Orthodox religious philosophy viewed legal rationality as the quintessential manifestation of cold-hearted, ultimately atheistic Western rationalism. Against it they preached an Orthodox Christian ethic of love and community. Later in the century the novelist Leo Tolstoy propounded a similar view along humanist rather than Orthodox lines. Unfortunately, Orthodox hierarchs and church theologians had little to say on the subject. The close, not to say confining, bonds that tied the Orthodox Church to the imperial state meant that church leaders had much less freedom to address the issues of the day than lay theologians. Many Russians were thus left with the impression that they had to choose between the Orthodox moral and spiritual tradition on one hand and modern legalism on the other, between Christian love and human rights. The most brilliant Orthodox jurists, such as Speransky, certainly did not view the case in such stark terms. But they were specialists. They did not deal directly with the religious and theological implications of their subject.

The breakthrough came with Vladimir Soloviev (1853–1900). Soloviev was the first modern Orthodox thinker who both regarded law in a positive light and set out to relate it to the grand themes of Orthodox theology. He applied himself to the project in a variety of venues for more than twenty years, assigning it a central place in his magnum opus, *The Justification of the Good* (1897). No other modern Orthodox thinker has yet matched his contribution to the discussion of law, society, and human nature from an Orthodox perspective.

SOLOVIEV'S LIFE AND WORK

Vladimir Sergeevich Soloviev was born in Moscow in 1853 to a prominent academic family.[1] His father, Sergei Mikhailovich, descended from a long line of Orthodox priests, and was a professor of history at Moscow University. His mother, Poliksena Vladimirovna, came from a military family of Polish and Ukrainian extraction.

Vladimir matriculated at Moscow University in 1869 after receiving an excellent classical education. Somewhat unexpectedly, he chose to study the natural sciences, although he eventually completed his degree in the faculty of history and philology. Soloviev's false start in the sciences is sometimes attributed to a youthful passion for philosophical materialism, the doctrine of choice for young intellectuals in Russia in the 1860s. But one should reckon also with a young man's need to put some distance between himself and his famous father. Sergei Soloviev (1820–79) was the most prominent Russian historian of his generation. His massive *History of Russia from Ancient Times* remains one of the most impressive monuments of Russian intellectual culture.[2] When Vladimir matriculated at Moscow University, Sergei was dean of the faculty of history and philology. In 1871 he became rector of the university.

Vladimir discovered where his genius lay thanks to the mentoring of Pamfil Danilovich Yurkevich (1827–74), a professor of philosophy. Yurkevich had been at Moscow University since 1861, but his roots lay in the Orthodox theological schools where he trained and taught for many years. Yurkevich is remembered for seminal essays in philosophical anthropology in which he criticized modern materialist conceptions of human nature from a biblical perspective emphasizing the wholeness and moral consciousness of human beings—what the Bible calls the "heart."[3]

After graduation in 1873 Soloviev elected to spend a postgraduate year at Moscow Theological Academy, one of four graduate schools of theology operated by the Russian Orthodox Church. This was an unusual step for an aspiring academic to take at the time and attests to Soloviev's unconventional personality as well as to his religious interests. In 1874 Soloviev returned to the university to defend his master's thesis and first book, *The Crisis of Western Philosophy*. The following year he began teaching at his alma mater but soon departed for a year's study in London. There he did research on mysticism and gnosticism in the British Museum and mixed with the local spiritualist community. The spiritualists left him cold, but in the museum he had a mystical vision of Divine Wisdom (Sophia). Sophia directed him to travel to Egypt, promising to reveal herself again there—which she did, although not until Soloviev nearly lost his life at the hands of hostile Bedouin on a walk in the desert near the pyramids.

In 1876 Soloviev resumed teaching at Moscow University only to resign before the end of the academic year and move to St. Petersburg. It was becoming obvious that Soloviev was a man who disliked established paths. Restless, impulsive, visionary, he gravitated to a peripatetic lifestyle. He would have made a fine bohemian were it not for his extraordinary work ethic. He finished his second book, *The Philosophical Principles of Integral Knowledge* in 1877, began *Lectures on Divine Humanity* in the same year, and defended his doctoral dissertation, which became *The*

Critique of Abstract Principles, in 1880. The author of four books in six years was twenty-seven years old.[4]

SOLOVIEV'S SLAVOPHILISM

In Petersburg Soloviev lectured in both academic and popular venues, presenting himself as a young Slavophile. Slavophilism and its antagonist, Westernism, were vehicles of the culture wars of nineteenth-century Russia, the century-long debate over Russia's destiny in the modern world. The debate concerned the features of Russian civilization that distinguished it from the West: Orthodox Christianity, political autocracy, and a tradition of communalism in economic and social life. The Westernizers believed that Russia should set aside its traditional value system and integrate itself into modern European civilization. The Slavophiles affirmed Russian distinctiveness. Differences of opinion existed within as well as between the two points of view. In Westernism there was a split between evolutionists and revolutionists. In Slavophilism, the affirmation of Russian particularity at times inspired isolationism (Russia should keep away from the West), at other times militancy (Russia has a mission to the West). Soloviev was a missionary Slavophile, believing that Russia had a message the world needed to hear.

The message was the advent of a new, modern cultural synthesis combining the best values of the European Enlightenment with the deepest truths of Christianity. The idea had been advanced in Russia in the previous generation by Ivan Kireevsky, who in turn was indebted to German Romanticism, especially the philosophy of Schelling.[5] Kireevsky had studied in Berlin and Munich and carefully followed developments in European philosophy. Thanks to his Orthodox wife and the proximity of his estate to Optina Hermitage, he also paid close attention to the revival of monastic spirituality in Russia. His hope, stated in an essay "On the Possibility and Necessity of New Principles in Philosophy" (1854), was that "Orthodox enlightenment should master the whole intellectual development of the contemporary world, so that, having enriched itself with secular wisdom, Christian truth may the more fully and solemnly demonstrate its prevalence over the relative truths of human reason."[6]

Kireevsky's quest for wholeness of life through the synthesis of reason with religion was Soloviev's point of departure. In *The Crisis of Western Philosophy (Against the Positivists)* he argued that the analytic and materialistic approaches to philosophy were spiritual dead-ends showing the need for new principles in philosophy. In *The Philosophical Principles of Integral*

Knowledge he stated the case for wholeness in more positive terms. In *The Critique of Abstract Principles* he masterfully recapitulated both his critique of Western philosophy and the case for wholeness, lending a militant spirit to his program by calling for its realization in a "free theocracy."

In *Lectures on Divine Humanity* Soloviev focused on the theological substance of his vision, what he called *bogochelovechestvo*. The term is translated into English as Godmanhood, divine humanity or humanity of God. The concept is a thematization of the Orthodox Christian doctrine of the incarnation. For Orthodox theology, God's becoming-human accomplishes not just the moral transformation of humanity (Christ "for" us) but also an ontological transformation (Christ "in" us). Thanks to God's assumption of human nature, human nature can be raised from glory to glory to the point of assimilation to divine nature, or *theosis* (deification). Theosis is an eschatological state, but the process is already underway and can be seen in the radiant lives of the saints. Soloviev gave this conceptuality a historical-prophetic application: the divine-human union in the incarnation points the way to the cultural synthesis of the future by offering the world a better moral and spiritual ideal than the "godless human individual" of modern Western civilization or the "inhuman God" of Islam. Orthodox Russia, poised between West and East, has the providential mission of proclaiming the good news of "divine humanity."[7]

One of the Petersburg intellectuals to whom Soloviev's prophetism appealed was the novelist Feodor Dostoevsky (1821–81). Although Dostoevsky was much older than Soloviev, the two men became friends, as evidenced by the fact that Dostoevsky invited Soloviev to accompany him on his pilgrimage to Optina Hermitage in 1878 following the death of the novelist's three year-old son Alyosha.[8] The excursion occupies a special place in Russian literary history because the community at Optina was the model for Dostoevsky's portrait of Russian monasticism in *The Brothers Karamazov* (1878–80). Not surprisingly, critics have looked for Soloviev's portrait as well, and indeed *The Brothers Karamazov* portrays a brilliant young philosopher in Ivan Karamazov.

While it would be a mistake to equate Soloviev and Ivan Karamazov— Soloviev's optimistic, believing personality bears no resemblance to Ivan's tortured soul—there is definitely a link between the two on the level of ideas. During the Karamazov family's visit to the monastery, Ivan becomes involved in a conversation about the scope of the jurisdiction of ecclesiastical courts, a subject on which he has published a controversial article. Ivan's thesis is that the modern secular state, because it has severed its connection with the church, cannot deal with crime and punishment in spiritual terms and so administers justice in a mechanical and utilitarian manner. Incapable of fostering repentance and amendment of life, the state can only repress the criminal. The criminal reacts by construing his relationship to society in equally utilitarian terms, at times even regarding his crime as a justifiable act of rebellion against an oppressive social order. If Russia is to avoid this outcome, Ivan argues, the state must reaffirm and expand the role of the church in society and in the legal system in particular. "Ultramontanism!" exclaims Mr. Miusov, a Westernizer horrified by the theocratic implications of Ivan's logic. But the monks are stirred to enthusiasm: "It will be! It will be!"[9] As we shall see, in *The Critique of Abstract Principles* Soloviev advocated an ideal much like Ivan's, envisioning a theocracy of love inspired and sanctified by the church.

The reference to ultramontanism interjects a comparison between Orthodoxy and Roman Catholicism. The comparison is taken further by one of the monks, Father Paisy, who criticizes Roman Catholicism for making the church into a kind of state, whereas Orthodoxy envisions the transformation of the state by the spirit of the church. The indictment of Roman Catholicism for juridicalizing the gospel is also a theme in the most famous chapter of *The Brothers Karamazov*, "The Grand Inquisitor." Soloviev repeated the charge in his *Lectures on Divine Humanity*.[10] The contrast between the supposedly harsh, legalistic Western church and the loving, all-embracing Eastern church was a cherished stereotype in Slavophilism.

UNIVERSALISM AND ECUMENISM

Soloviev's theocratism underwent a significant change in the 1880s. The decade began with a crisis. On March 1, 1881, Tsar Alexander II was assassinated in Petersburg by populist revolutionaries. As Russians reeled in horror and confusion, Soloviev delivered a public lecture in which he called on the new tsar, Alexander III, to deal with his father's assassins in the spirit of Christian love by refusing to condemn them to death. The revolutionaries had acted as death-dealers, but a Christian monarch should not. Unfortunately for Soloviev, the tsar and his government were not impressed by this interpretation of theocracy and forced the young philosopher to resign from the university. The incident was important because it caused Soloviev to reassess his understanding of theocracy. He did not question the ideal, but he began to question some of the forms in which he had been preaching it, especially the facile association of Orthodox Christianity with the Russian way of life. He also began saying positive things about Western civilization, including Roman Catholicism. His Slavophile friends soon closed their journals to him.

Soloviev pressed his case for a more cosmopolitan understanding of theocracy by taking a critical look at how the Russian Orthodox community related to its non-Russian and non-Orthodox neighbors inside and outside the Russian Empire. In *The National Question in Russia*, a collection of essays written between 1883 and 1891, Soloviev criticized Russian national egoism and the oppression of ethnic and religious minorities.[11] He also stepped forward as a strong advocate of religious liberty, which in 1889 he called "the good which [Russia] needs first of all."[12] In "The Development of Dogma and the Question of Church Union" (1886) he examined Orthodoxy's relations with the Roman Catholic Church, arguing that there were no insuperable obstacles to reunion. The essay makes a passionate case for what would eventually be called ecumenism.

The ecumenical cause occupied much of Soloviev's time in the later 1880s. In 1886 he spent three months in Zagreb, Croatia, for discussions with two other nineteenth-century prophets of the idea, Bishop Josip Juraj Strossmayer of Bosnia and Canon Franko Racki of the South Slav Academy. In 1888 he lived most of the year in France in dialogue with Catholics and other Christians and arranged for the publication of *La Russie et l'Eglise universelle* (1889). Through Bishop Strossmayer, Soloviev's vision of a reunited Christendom was shared with Pope Leo XIII. "Bella idea," the pontiff reportedly replied, "ma fuor d'un miracolo è cosa impossibile"—a good idea, but without a miracle it's impossible.[13]

THE JEWS AND THE "CHRISTIAN QUESTION"

A new relationship between Christians and Jews also figured in Soloviev's theocratic program. Here the issue went beyond minority rights. To Soloviev, the Jews were exactly who they claimed to be: the chosen people, the theocratic people par excellence, "the axis of universal history."[14] He regarded the Hebrew Bible, with its detailed account of the collaboration of prophets, priests, and kings in the history of Israel, as the constitution of theocracy. When he designed *The History and Future of Theocracy*, a three-volume study of the theocratic idea in human history, he assigned the first volume to ancient Israel.[15] To enhance his competence in the subject matter he studied Hebrew with the help of Faivel B. Gets, a Jewish intellectual who became one of his closest friends. Gets also introduced Soloviev to the study of rabbinic texts.

Soloviev reflected on the meaning of Judaism in several essays including "The Jews and the Christian Question" (1884) and "The Talmud and Recent Polemics in Austria and Germany" (1886).[16] The point of "The Jews and the Christian Question" is adumbrated in the title. Breaking with the nearly universal assumption by nineteenth-century Christians that there was a Jewish Question in Europe, Soloviev argued that the so-called Jewish Question was in fact a Christian Question, that is to say, a question about how Christians treat the Jews:

> The Jews have always and everywhere regarded Christianity and behaved towards it in accordance with the precepts of their religion, in conformity with their faith and their law. The Jews have always treated us in the Jewish way; we Christians, on the contrary, have not learned to this day to adopt a Christian attitude to the Jews. They have never transgressed their religious law in relation to us; we, on the other hand, have always broken the commandments of the Christian religion in relation to them.[17]

What Soloviev meant is that the Jews, whose law constitutes them as a people set apart by a special religio-historical vocation, have obeyed their law by preserving their identity apart from Christianity; while Christians, whose Lord calls them to an ethic of universal love, have repeatedly violated this ethic in their relations with Jews. Since the group in need of repentance and change of life is the Christians, not the Jews, one should speak of a Christian Question rather than a Jewish Question.

In his essay on the Talmud, Soloviev promoted a positive attitude toward Jewish law against anti-Semitic denigration of it. He pointed out that, while Christians tend to make a sharp distinction between Christianity and Judaism, most Christians have never even read, much less studied, the Jewish law. If they did so, they would discover that Jewish and Christian ethical teachings are basically the same. What Christianity has to offer is not a new ethic but the redemptive humanity of God in Christ. This is a truth that the Jews need to receive, but they should not be expected to receive it until Christians do a better job of showing how Christian doctrine can transform life. The enduring paganism of supposedly Christian societies and the sectarian divisions in the church itself present a sorry spectacle to law-abiding Jews. "As we see it," Soloviev imagined Jews saying to Christians, "truth cannot be abstract, it cannot be separated from practice. We are a people of law, and truth itself for us is not so much an intellectual idea as it is *a law of life*. . . . Your religious ideal expresses absolute holiness, but the law of your life remains the law of sin and injustice."[18]

Soloviev recognized that Christianity and Judaism have different historical vocations, but he did not regard this as justifying Christian hostility toward the Jews. Judaism and Christianity are still in process, and both are destined for consummation in the same kingdom of God. Penultimately, there is much that the two communities can do together. In "The Jews and the Christian Question," Soloviev envisioned a three-way collaboration between the Russian Orthodox, Polish Catholic, and Jewish communities of the Russian Empire as a way of realizing the theocratic ideal in Russia and showing the rest of Europe what the right relationship between prophet, priest, and king in a modern state might look like. The significance of the scheme stands out when one compares it with the Slavophile vision: Soloviev's theocracy had become a project for all Europe, all Christendom, all communities of biblical faith.

THE UNION OF OPPOSITES

The synthesis of Christian-theocratic and liberal-universalist values that Soloviev achieved in the 1880s set him apart from most of his contemporaries. The remaking of a Romantic Christian as a liberal universalist was not unknown in nineteenth-century spiritual culture, but the conversion usually involved the abandonment of dogmatic and theocratic beliefs for a more secularized faith. Soloviev, by contrast, was able to hold the entire spectrum of values together in a highly original synthesis, the union of opposites forcing him to push at the limits of ordinary language to name his vision. It was theo-philosophical, free-theocratic, mystical-historical. The term preferred by Soloviev was *bogochelovecheskii*, "divine-human," from *bogochelovechestvo*, Godmanhood, divine humanity, humanity of God. For all its difficulties in translation, this term is the most appropriate because it refers to the source of Soloviev's intellectual confidence—the incarnation. Soloviev preached a transcendent both/and. As he saw it, people do not have to choose between Orthodoxy and modernity, religion and science, tradition and change, Christian faith and religious universalism, gospel and law, not even between God and the world. Why are these false choices? How is such wholeness of life available to us? Because "the Word became flesh and lived among us, full of grace and truth, and we have seen his glory" (John 1:14). In Christ the humanity of God, all things in heaven and on earth are reconciled and destined for incorporation in the kingdom of God. Inspired by this faith, Soloviev pursued his vocation: to advance the work of reconciliation on earth and, if need be, to storm the heavens, to wrest saints, seers, mystics, even gnostics from their ethereal mansions and enlist them in the sacred cause.[19]

In the 1890s Soloviev pulled back from the activism of the previous decade to allow more time for writing projects in academic philosophy. His shift is often interpreted as evidence of disillusion with theocracy, but a positive factor was involved as well. In 1889 Nikolai Grot, professor of philosophy at Moscow University and president of the Moscow Psychological Society, founded Russia's first professional philosophical journal, *Questions of Philosophy and Psychology*. Soloviev was one of the original collaborators in this enterprise, which called him back to his primary vocation. During the 1890s he produced brilliant philosophical essays and monographs including *The Justification of the Good* (1897). This large work, which among other things contains Soloviev's mature philosophy of law, remains the most magisterial work of moral philosophy in the Russian tradition.

In 1899–1900 Soloviev composed his final work, *Three Dialogues on War, Progress and the End of World History, with a Brief Tale of the Anti-Christ.* The last section is a literary apocalypse featuring a fight to the finish between the armies of an urbane, humanitarian Antichrist and a faithful remnant of ecumenical Christians and unassimilated Jews. The subject matter and proximity of the work to Soloviev's death—he died on July 31, 1900—have led many interpreters to suppose that Soloviev rejected activist-humanist Christianity at the end of his life and embraced radical apocalypticism. Recently, however, Judith Deutsch Kornblatt and others have shown that this view is open to serious question. It will not be adopted here.[20]

LAW AND THE THEOCRACY OF LOVE

Soloviev's first essay in the philosophy of law is embedded in the masterpiece of his early career, *The Critique of Abstract Principles* (chaps. 15–20). The social ideal advanced in *The Critique* is a symphonic wholeness in which "all constitute the end of each, and each the end of all."[21] As soon as the project of realizing this kingdom of ends begins, however, the partiality of human beings undermines the task. Even when they embrace the ideal of all for each and each for all, human beings find it difficult to do justice to both sides at once. Those who lean to "each" generate individualism; those who favor "all" generate some form of collectivism; and so the common project of building the good society is undermined. Instead of addressing living human beings in the actual world, ethicists deal with "the individual" and "society." But these are abstractions. In actuality no absolute individual exists; if he did, he would be a case of "empty personhood."[22] Conversely, no society exists except as composed of living individuals.

Soloviev's critique of abstractions was connected with his understanding of moral evil, or sin. As he saw it, the root of moral evil in humanity is the tendency to "exclusivity," that is to say, the temptation to substitute the part for the whole, to affirm oneself or one's dependents in isolation from the all-encompassing whole of things. "This abnormal attitude toward everything else—this exclusive self-assertion, or egoism, all-powerful in our practical life even though we deny it in theory, this opposition of the self to all other selves and the practical negation of other selves—constitutes the radical *evil* of our nature."[23]

The evil of exclusivity is overcome through renunciation. Renunciation does not mean self-annihilation, which is actually another sort of exclusivity, but the overcoming of partiality. The paradigm is given in Jesus, the incarnate Word who accomplishes "the double exploit of divine and human self-renunciation." Though very God, the Word lays aside his divine glory to become a human being; and as a human being Jesus does his father's will, not his own. The moral grandeur of the accomplishment is seen at the very beginning of Jesus' ministry in the temptation in the wilderness. Three times the prince of darkness invites the Messiah to self-assertion, but "Christ subordinates His human will to, and harmonizes it with, the divine will, deifying His humanity after the humanization of His Divinity."[24] Dostoevsky, too, was enchanted by the temptation story, making it the crux of Ivan Karamazov's parable of the Grand Inquisitor.

NEEDS, RIGHTS, AND LOVE OF THE WHOLE

Soloviev's critique of abstract principles began with the collectivist option, represented in his time by socialism. Soloviev was reasonably well acquainted with socialism. In his youth he had been deeply impressed by reading Saint-Simon and other early socialists, and he always evinced more sympathy for socialism than for capitalism.[25] In his estimation, socialists are right to reject plutocracy and demand an economic order embodying ethical norms. The error of socialism lies in supposing that a material or economic order by itself generates ethical norms, "that an unexampled economic set-up (some kind of fusion of capital and labor, the organization of industry by unions, etc.) is obligatory in and for itself, unconditionally normative and moral, that is, that this economic set-up as such already contains a moral principle and is the sole condition of social morality." This is a classic example of partiality: "the moral principle, the principle of the obligatory and the normative, is determined exclusively by one of the elements of the totality of human life—the economic element."[26]

Other elements, besides the material-economic, need to be accommodated in a social ethic. One of them is betrayed by the rhetoric of socialism itself. Socialists typically cloak the economic arrangements they preach in a moral discourse that reveals the transeconomic status of their ideal. Socialists call for a "just" economy and the "rights" of workers. But the concepts of justice and right cannot be derived from the material-economic process. Interests can be derived from it, but not rights. Rights derive from the freedom and rationality of human beings, features of human nature that are by definition spiritual. That such values should be realized in and through the economic order, that the latter should not be abandoned to anarchy while so-called spiritual people seek happiness in another world— these demands of socialism are quite valid. But that matter in motion and the interests generated by it are the source of freedom and rationality is a proposition Soloviev rejected. Far from being a derivative of the economic order, our consciousness of freedom and rationality points to something else: the juridical order.

A powerful personalism underlay Soloviev's appreciation for the reality of the juridical order:

> The concept of right first lends to a human being the status of *person*. Indeed, as long as I strive for material prosperity and pursue my personal interests, other people have no independent significance for me, they are merely things which I can use well or poorly [in pursuit of my interests]. But if I acknowledge that other people are not only useful to me but have rights in and for themselves, rights by virtue of which they determine my activity just as much as they are determined by it; if, when I encounter the right of another, I must say to myself, this far and no further—by this very fact I acknowledge in the other something unalterable and unconditional, something that cannot serve as the means of my material interest, and consequently something higher than this interest; the other becomes something sacred to me, that is, ceases to be a thing, becomes a person.[27]

The discovery of the juridical order represents a step forward on the path to realizing an ethical society, a kingdom of ends in which all respect the rightful claims of each, and each the rightful claims of all. But again, the task is more difficult in practice than in theory. The juridical order is no more immune than the economic order to the spell of abstract principles. In the case of law, the warring abstractions are an organic or genetic understanding of law—what Soloviev called the "abstract-historical concept of law"—and the idea of law as an external or mechanical social contract, the "abstract-utilitarian concept of law." He was referring to the split between historicist and rationalist philosophies of law, the former usually linked with Romantic conservatism, the latter with liberalism or revolution.

As always, the partisans of each abstraction tend to be right in what they affirm but wrong in what they suppress or deny. The historicists are right to insist that law does not spring full-grown and armed from the heads of political theorists but is historically embedded. Soloviev, whose debt to Slavophilism has been noted, accepted this point without difficulty. Aboriginally, all law is customary law in which "the principle of justice functions not as a principle that is theoretically grasped but as an immediate moral instinct or practical reason expressing itself in the form of symbols."[28] But historicists err when they suppose that the essence of law is satisfactorily accounted for by its historical origins. This is tantamount to replacing theory of law with history of law, which is to commit the logical error of "taking the origin or genesis of a thing in empirical reality to be the essence of that thing, confusing the historical order with the logical order, and losing the content of a thing in the process through which it is manifested."[29] Although historically conditioned, law possesses formal properties without which it would not be law, properties that are gradually clarified in the historical process itself by the emergence of concepts of personhood and freedom. Here is where the essence of law must be sought.

Still, there is a right way and a wrong way to seek this essence. The wrong way is to seize upon the formal personhood implicit in the concept of law and, isolating it from the historical process, to absolutize it. The sovereign individual who supposedly precedes history and enters into a contract with his fellows as a means of pursuing his ends is an abstraction. Historicists are right to reject it as purely hypothetical, a formula for utopianism. Soloviev sought a middle way between utopianism and Romantic conservatism in a formula acknowledging both the free-personal and the social aspects of law: "*Law is freedom conditioned by equality*," or "*the synthesis of freedom and equality*."[30]

The crafting of a definition of law provided Soloviev with an occasion to clarify his concept of natural law. Soloviev rejected the concept in the sense of an actual ordering of life preceding the rise of political associations in a supposed state of nature. To think of natural law in this way is "to take an intellectual abstraction for reality." But the concept is useful as an expression of the necessary formal properties which positive law must reflect, "to the extent that it is really law and not something else":

> The concepts of personhood, freedom, and equality constitute the essence of so-called natural law. The rational essence of law is distinguished from its historical manifestation, namely positive law. In this sense, natural law is that general algebraic formula into which history inserts the various real quantities of positive law; it exists in reality only as the general form of all positive legal relations, in them and through them.[31]

One of the prominent themes of *The Critique of Abstract Principles* is the essentially negative character of law. The idea is that law sets boundaries and establishes rules but does not prescribe moral content or ends. "For

[law] there is no *normative* end, no normative will or intention. Heroic self-sacrifice and selfish calculation make no difference to law; it does not demand the former and does not forbid the latter. A lawful government, in its ordinances, does not and cannot demand that all *should assist* each, and each all; it demands only that no one *should do harm* to anyone else."[32] In *The Justification of the Good* (1897), written much later in his career, Soloviev changed his mind on this point, having come to see that law and morality, while by no means identical, are organically linked in ways that the unsubtle distinctions of *The Critique* failed to accommodate. The rather artificial disjunction of "negative" law from "positive" morality in *The Critique* is probably to be explained by Soloviev's youthful enthusiasm for Schopenhauer, who made much of the distinction between the supposedly negative ethic of justice and the positive ethic of compassion.[33]

The motivation of Soloviev's negative theory of law seems to be moral and metaphysical rather than juridical, a pretext for an observation about the grandeur and misery of human beings as such. Law is grounded in metaphysical personhood (freedom and reason), the inalienable glory of the human being. But human beings have the capacity to misuse their personhood, "quite fully justifying Mephistopheles' observation in Goethe's *Faust*":

Ein wenig besser würd' er leben
Hätt'st Du ihm nicht den Schein des Himmelslichts gegeben;
Er nennt's Vernunft und braucht's allein,
Nur tierischer als jedes Tier zu sein.[34]

Thus personhood threatens to collapse into the abyss; the hoped-for kingdom of ends, into a barely domesticated anarchy of interests. This is surely a miserable outcome, unless of course one has overlooked the place where the truly worthy end of human life is to be found. "Unconditional form demands unconditional content. Beyond the legal order, the order of negative means, must stand a positive order defined by an absolute end."[35]

Soloviev was confident about the availability of an absolute end because he had already posited it. The absolute end is the whole of things, the symphonic unity that transcends abstractions, the Living One that gives life to all else.

Soloviev argued the case for the absolute end anthropologically, proceeding from the observable nature of human beings. The paradox of human beings is that they do not seem to be content with being themselves, that is to say, free, rational agents. They are drawn in two other directions as well: to the material world, which they love with a passion, and to the world of divine and demonic forces. "It is impossible to eliminate the fact that the human being appears to himself to be not just a human being but also and equally an animal and a god." The passions of the flesh and "the mystical attractions making [the human being] a divine or demonic being" profoundly complicate human life.[36] To deny these forces is to exchange actual human nature for the abstract model constructed by rationalism.

Mystical attractions are the various ways in which human beings are grasped by the desire to unite with all things, the yearning "to be *all*." In practical terms this can only mean attaching oneself somehow to the whole of things, since it is obvious that "the infinitely small unit" that is a human being cannot in fact be all. The desire to unite with the whole is the essence of what Soloviev calls the "religious principle." The contrast with the juridical order is clear: law demarcates, delimits, distinguishes, divides; religion connects, embraces, unites. Put another way, religion is about love—the loving union realized in "a mystical or religious community, that is to say, *the church*."[37] Loving union with the whole of things is the absolute end.

FREE THEOCRACY

The clarification of the religious principle of love, while revealing the end of life, complicates the actual business of living because of the tension between love and law. The tension would not be a problem if these values could be confined to separate spheres. But this is not possible. The religious and juridical principles are both moral principles; they pertain to "one and the same sphere, namely the sphere of practical, moral or social life." Soloviev regarded attempts to reconcile the two principles through compartmentalization as flawed. For example, he denied "that I could *actually* show Christian love to a neighbor whom, in my capacity as a judge, I send to the gallows." Love and law demand acknowledgment from the same person at the same time in the same society. An "inner, harmonious relation or synthesis" of the two must be established. But how? Soloviev's answer was, through a "free theocracy."[38]

To avoid misunderstanding Soloviev's proposal, it is crucial to underscore the attributive "free." Admittedly, readers who are put off by the term "theocracy" in the first place will regard "free theocracy" as an oxymoron. But Soloviev was quite serious about the idea, taking pains to distinguish it from what he called "false theocracy" or "abstract clericalism." False theocracy results from the absolutization of the religious principle, that is to say, from developing the religious element in human life in isolation from the others and so making it into an abstract principle. This is what happens in traditional theocracies where religious forces dominate all others and dictate to society. The antidote to this pathology is freedom: freedom of conscience first of all, and more generally the freedom to exercise rationality in all sectors of life. Soloviev's conceptuality here parallels his view of the right relationship between the juridical order and economic interest: economic initiative should not be abolished or suppressed by the law, even though law is the higher good. Similarly, the religious principle transcends the juridical, both metaphysically (it expresses the whole of things) and practically (love transcends law). But it must not abolish the juridical order. The juridical order is to be affirmed and incorporated into the free-theocratic synthesis. As Soloviev saw it, a theocracy that violates the free-rational rule of law vitiates not only law but also religion itself and the God it claims to serve. In false theocracy God is reduced to "thunder and lightning which extinguish completely the still small voice of reason and conscience."[39] But reason and conscience, and the material world itself, are God-given. A free theocracy must embrace them fully.

In his criticism of traditional theocracy, Soloviev clearly sought to distance himself from the religious and political conservatives of his day. Yet he also distanced himself from the doctrinaire liberals. Nineteenth-century European liberals, if they did not wish to expel religion from society altogether, usually embraced the formula of "a free church in a free state" to express the proper relationship between the juridical and religious principles. Soloviev rejected this formula. He accepted the need to distinguish between church and state, but not the isolation of the church from the state, which he believed the formula implied. He agreed that in a clericalist theocracy there is not enough space between church and state. But in a secularist liberal state there is not enough interaction. Soloviev believed that a sharp separation between the juridical and religious spheres is unrealistic, for in actual life, religion and law interact in all sorts of concrete ways. They *should* interact, for without a dynamic relationship, no synthesis of elements can be achieved. Of course, the synthesis must be realized in such a way as to affirm the ultimacy of the religious principle in the hierarchy of values. Otherwise the more inclusive principle is subordinated to the less. Soloviev preached theocracy, not nomocracy.

Soloviev knew that many modern legal and political thinkers rejected a value hierarchy grounded in religion, viewing "the state as the highest and final form of human society and the universal kingdom of law as the apogee of human history."[40] This statist ultimate would be valid only if human beings were free-rational creatures and nothing more. But they are more. A human being is *"a being comprising in himself* (in the absolute order) *a divine idea*, that is to say, *the whole of things* or unconditional fullness of being, *and realizing* this idea (in the natural order) *by means of rational freedom in material nature."*[41] Creatures with such an all-embracing nature need more than the state to order their affairs and give them peace; they need a church that embraces the whole of life from its material surface to its divine ground. Beyond a just society, they need a loving community; beyond their fellow human beings, fellowship with God; beyond the kingdom of ends, the kingdom of God.

Historical imagination is required to appreciate what Soloviev's theocracy meant in his time and how it might be relevant to the twenty-first century world. Soloviev actually lived in a kind of theocracy, for in the nineteenth-century, Russia was still an Orthodox Christian empire. Only secularized elites and the religious minorities questioned the arrangement. Most Russians along with their rulers regarded themselves as trustees of Orthodoxy (to them, true Christianity). Placing Soloviev's free theocracy against this background, one can see that his project was to a considerable extent a critical enterprise. Soloviev challenged his compatriots to measure the existing theocracy against the ideal concept. So, for example, Soloviev argued that freedom of conscience was an essential requirement in a true theocracy; yet there was no freedom of conscience in the Russian Empire in his lifetime. He argued that the free exercise of reason and the healthy pursuit of material interests without ascetical interference were consistent with a true theocracy, but these prescriptions hardly described the conditions of intellectual and social life in tsarist Russia. An essentially prophetic idea, Soloviev's *free* theocracy challenged the status quo.

At the same time, by preaching free *theocracy*, Soloviev made it clear that he did not finally agree with the secularist critics of Russia. The need for an establishment of religious values at the heart of society seemed clear to him; and that this establishment should be sealed by a Christian monarchy was agreeable to him as well. His celebrated appeal to Alexander III to spare the regicides of 1881 assumed the existence of a Christian monarch. Soloviev did not wish to abolish the office but to reinvigorate it. Although he became more critical of the tsarist state later in his career, Soloviev never embraced republicanism or "post-Constantinian" Christianity, nor for that matter did many of his heirs in the next generation. In the essay on Leo XIII in the Catholic companion to this volume, Russell Hittinger traces the elimination of national churches and "political Christendom" in nineteenth-century Catholicism leading to the view that the church is not in the state, nor the state in the church.[42] No such process was at work in nineteenth-century Orthodoxy, and even the catastrophes of the twentieth century have not completely dislodged the idea of a national church. Soloviev presents a good example of the ideal of national or Constantinian Christianity in action.

Besides his Constantinianism, Soloviev's theocratism was a response to the idea of the kingdom of God in the gospel. By recognizing the centrality of the kingdom in the Christian message, Soloviev was ahead of

his time. The majority of Christian theologians and ethicists in the nineteenth century were tone-deaf to the theocratic theme in the gospel. For
them, Jesus preached an inner, spiritual kingdom that was to be sharply
distinguished from the supposedly crude, nationalist theocracy of the
Jews. Soloviev rejected this one-sided spiritualizing of the gospel along
with its anti-Semitic implications. In this he anticipated Albert Sch-
weitzer and others who rediscovered the Jewish apocalyptic roots of
Christianity at the turn of the century. He also anticipated twentieth-
century theologians such as Reinhold Niebuhr, Martin Luther King, and
John Howard Yoder, who demonstrated the political seriousness of the
gospel.[43]

Soloviev's theocratism also expressed his vision of a universal love
ethic as the practical essence of Christianity. Soloviev did not believe
that a love ethic could be grounded in either the natural-economic or
the rational-juridical order of things. In the natural order, love occurs as
an instinct or passion, but there is no way to build an ethic of *universal*
love ("the inner, essential solidarity of all things") on this foundation. Love
as an instinct is too random; its range of application is too narrow. One
naturally loves family, friends, close neighbors—but "all and each?" A love
ethic cannot be grounded in the rational-juridical order of things, either.
Here human beings are recognized as free rational agents; but there is no
love, not even in the form of instinct or passion. The rational order of
things is just that: rational, intellectual. Human beings are not appreciated as "living people but only as abstract juridical persons" by virtue of
the characteristics they share with all other human beings. It cannot be
otherwise. The grandeur of the rational-juridical order lies precisely in its
generality and impersonality, its applicability to all human beings regardless of their preferences, passions, loves, or hates. Proclaiming love as the
constitutive principle of the rational order of things would be the philosophical equivalent of a judge or jury deciding cases on the basis of their
personal feelings for the individuals involved.[44]

The true ground of love lies in the mystical or divine order of things. To
function as a moral principle as distinguished from an accidental passion,
love must be "at one and the same time *a living personal force and a universal
law.*" But this is nothing less than a description of God, the absolute ground
of being. Love in the natural world is a force but not a universal law, and its
personal status is moot. In the rational order of things there is universal law
but no love, indeed no actual living beings. God is both love and law. This is
a unity transcending reason, which is why Soloviev describes it as "mystical,"
or, in the social-political context, "theocratic." An ethic of universal love is an
ethic of absolute relatedness or connectedness. One loves and serves one's
fellow human beings as ends in themselves when one recognizes them as

ends in God, acknowledging them as beings with the "power to become children of God" (John 1:12), beings whose destiny is theosis.[45]

The concept of theonomy, a terminological cousin of theocracy, might shed light on what Soloviev has in mind. The term came into currency in English-speaking theology thanks to Paul Tillich, whose thought resembles Soloviev's in a number of ways. Tillich's project in ethics and social philosophy was to transcend the antagonism between heteronomy (Soloviev's false theocracy) and autonomy (Soloviev's rational-juridical order) in an ethic of theonomy (Soloviev's theocracy of love). A theonomous ethic retains the virtues of heteronomy and autonomy (reverence and freedom) while shedding the defects (authoritarianism and selfishness) and leading us through love to the divine ground of being. Theonomy may be a better name for Soloviev's ideal than theocracy, which suggests a vicariate of some kind.[46]

JUSTICE AS THE FRAMEWORK OF LOVE

What is the impact of an ethic of universal love on law? In the history of religion and ethics, preachers of universal love have often been suspicious of law, even contemptuous of it. In Russia, Leo Tolstoy preached a Christian ethic that rejected the legal system and the state as such. Soloviev saw the matter differently. True, love stands above law in Soloviev's hierarchy of values. But unlike thinkers for whom hierarchy is a pretext for forgetting about everything below the apex, Soloviev recognized that the point of a hierarchy is to do justice to all its components. The ideal of universal love springs from the ecstatic connectedness of human beings to the divine ground of being, but this love cannot be actualized by human beings as it is in the divine ground. That would be possible only if human beings had already achieved theosis; but in fact they are unfinished creatures. Therefore universal love, although inspired from above ("mystically"), must be sought in and through engagement with the economic and juridical spheres.

Soloviev's point can be seen in his interpretation of the biblical account of the creation of human beings. In Genesis 1–2 human beings are said to be created "from the dust of the earth," "in [God's] image," and "according to [God's] likeness." Soloviev insisted that all three points are essential to a proper understanding of human nature. As dust of the earth, human beings are weak and imperfect, separated from God. As bearers of the image of God, they are endowed with the idea of perfection, a vision of the goodness and beauty which they lack. As shaped by the "likeness" of God, human beings are filled with the desire to conform themselves to the divine image, to be assimilated to the divine beauty. Three moments of moral experience follow from these determinations: confession of imperfection, contemplation of perfection, and the process of actually becoming perfect.[47] All three moments are important. A corresponding relatedness exists between the economic, juridical, and religious spheres.

In the case of love and law, Soloviev formulated the right relationship as: "*justice is the necessary framework of love*."[48] That is to say, love without respect for law will be defective, cut loose from its moorings in the ontological hierarchy and doomed to distortion through sentimentalization, self-deception, demonic obsession, or other pathologies. For example, one's love is defective if one loves a person without respecting that person's rights. That is how slave owners and serf owners "loved" their servants. A human being is a free, rational creature; and a free, rational creature, as juridical theory makes plain, is a creature endowed with inalienable rights. To violate these rights, or not to perceive them in the first place, amounts to treating a human being as something other than a human being. No appeal to "love" can rectify this original wrong. Justice is the indispensable framework of human relations.

LAW AND THE GOOD

Soloviev's most developed philosophy of law is found in his magnum opus, *The Justification of the Good* (1897), and in *Law and Morality*, a collection of essays that came out the same year.[49] In both works Soloviev treated philosophy of law as a branch of moral philosophy. The task of moral philosophy is "the justification of the Good." But what is the Good? And what does it mean to justify it?

By the Good, Soloviev meant the source of all value, that which lends meaning to the whole of life, the Good as distinguished from goods. All human beings recognize certain goods; but a list of goods does not address the issue of goodness as such. Goods, viewed analytically, are partial; they do not embrace the whole of life. The moral philosopher is looking for that which ties the partial goods together. To put it in Tillichian language, the moral philosopher seeks the ultimate concern of human beings as moral agents.

Many moral philosophers would reject this line of inquiry because it assumes that only an overarching Good can satisfy the human moral quest. What warrants this assumption? Soloviev believed it is warranted by the nature and destiny of human beings:

> "Know ye not that we shall judge angels?" [1 Cor. 6:3] St. Paul writes to the faithful. And if even the heavenly things are subject to our judgment, this is still more true of all earthly things. Man is in principle or in his destination

an *unconditional* inner form of the good as an unconditional content; all else is conditioned and relative.[50]

Here Soloviev stepped forward in the mantle of theocratic prophecy and Orthodox mysticism to relate the justification of the Good not just to the partial, unfinished world of the present, but also to the consummated kingdom of God. Human beings are conditioned by nature and history but open to eternity, destined for theosis. They bear the unconditional form of the unconditional Good.

The unconditional Good as Soloviev envisioned it bears three characteristics, all of which have ethical relevance:

The good as such is not conditioned by anything, but itself conditions all things, and is realized through all things. In so far as the good is not conditioned by anything, it is *pure*; in so far as it conditions all things, it is *all-embracing*; and in so far as it is realized through all things, it is *all-powerful*.[51]

Without a standard of purity, human beings cannot make the clear distinction between good and evil that is the essence of moral choice. Without the all-inclusiveness of the Good, morality breaks up into mutually contradictory demands. "Finally, if the good had no power, if it could not in the end triumph over everything, including 'the last enemy death' [1 Cor. 15:26]—life would be in vain."[52] Such is the Good, which the moral philosopher seeks to know. Most people call it God.

If the Good is God, what did Soloviev mean by justification? Did he presume to justify God? His preface to the second edition of *The Justification of the Good* sheds light on the question:

The object of this book is *to show the good as truth and righteousness*, that is, as the only right and consistent way of life in all things and to the end, for all who decide to follow it. I mean the Good *as such*; it alone justifies itself and justifies our confidence in it. And it is not for nothing that before the open grave, when all else has obviously failed, we call to this essential Good and say, "Blessed art Thou, O Lord, for Thou has taught [me] Thy justification" [Ps. 119:12].[53]

Soloviev was not proposing to justify the ways of God to man. The Good justifies *itself*. Human beings are justified by standing in a relationship to the Good, for which Soloviev finds the paradigm at the utter limit of human life where human weakness cannot be denied, but where the deceased nevertheless "speaks" from the dust through the mouth of the priest to bless God in the words of the great Psalm of the Law. The Slavonic version

of Psalms 119:12 pertains to the title of Soloviev's book: "teach me thy justification" (*nauchi mia opravdaniem Tvoim*; Hebr. "thy statutes"), that is,
teach me to see and acknowledge you rather than miss you, to see you as
the Good. This is the Orthodox contemplative version of what Protestants
call justification by faith. Human beings do not justify the Good by doing
it. If that were true, the Good would depend on human beings, whereas the
opposite is the case.

A word of clarification is required here, however. One should not suppose that appreciating the Good *in itself* means regarding the Good *by itself*, that is to say, construing it in isolation from the world. It is possible to
think about the Good in this way, but the consequence of such thinking is
to reduce the Good to an abstract principle. Because human life is embodied and historical, seeing the Good means seeing it in and through the
world, seeing the Good in all things and all things in the Good. This is not
easy to do precisely because of the embodied character of human life with
its pressures and distractions. But prayer, religious instruction, and moral
philosophy can help.

The connectedness of the Good to the world, that is, the fullness and
wholeness (*vseedinstvo*) of the Good, is the primary focus of *The Justification of the Good*. The themes of purity and power receive less attention.
Soloviev believed that the purity of the Good received unsurpassed treatment in Kant's moral philosophy. Soloviev did not try to better the German master on this point. But Kant did not investigate how the Good
enters into the immense process of life. His moral vision, while beautiful
in formal terms, lacked actuality and suffered from formalism. Soloviev
proposed to focus on the actualization of the Good through the "complete
and exhaustive moral norms for all the fundamental practical relations of
individual and collective life."[54]

The Justification of the Good, in its very title, shows how far Soloviev stood
from anything resembling a divine command theory of ethics. The idea that
morality means doing what God commands raises the question that Socrates
and Euthyphro debated more than two millennia ago: is something good
because God commands it, or does God command it because it is good? For
Soloviev, the very form of the question is wrong because it dissociates in
principle what is never dissociated in actuality, namely, God and the Good.
God and the Good are the same ultimate reality and are differentiated only
perspectivally depending on the aspect of the whole of things under consideration in a given context. In a work of moral philosophy, the Good is the appropriate term. Hence Socrates was right to argue against Euthyphro that
God commands only the good and, in the *Republic*, to argue that God is
good. However, this must not be taken to mean that the Good is something

other than God, since the Good as Plato and Soloviev described it—the unconditionally pure, full, ever-living source of all value—is obviously divine. To posit God apart from the Good or the Good apart form God is to create abstract principles, to generate the anticosmic ideologies of godless humanism (autonomy) and goodless religion (heteronomy). Both fail to do justice to the presence of God/Good in the actual grace-filled world.

The Russian word for grace, *blagodat'*, is helpful on this point. The term is a compound of *blago* ("good") and *dat'* ("give"); hence, the good that is given, or good gift. Western and especially Protestant theories of grace emphasize the act of giving as opposed to the gift. The Russian term suggests a more balanced view: grace is the free act of giving but also that which is given, namely the Good.[55] In adopting this view, Soloviev affirmed the traditional understanding of grace in the Orthodox tradition. The anticosmic dualism of nature and grace so common in Western theology is foreign to Orthodoxy, ancient and modern.

An oblique illustration of the difference between East and West on this point is found in Leslie Griffin's essay on Pope John XXIII included in the Catholic companion to this volume. Griffin cites Cardinal Suenens's attempt to express what was special about Angelo Roncalli:

> If one had to express it all in one word, it seems to me that one could say that John XXIII was a man surprisingly natural and at the same time supernatural. Nature and grace produced in him a living unity filled with charm and surprises. Everything about him sprang from a single source. In a completely natural way he was supernatural. He was natural with such a supernatural spirit that no one detected a distinction between the two.[56]

From an Orthodox point of view the only problem here is that the cardinal treats as an exception what should be seen as the rule, that is, as the norm of creation and sanctification alike. "A living unity [of nature and grace] filled with charm and surprises" is a good description of what the whole cosmos looked like in the beginning, still looks like in the lives of the saints and will look like in a more wonderful way in the realized kingdom of God.

THE PRIMARY DATA OF MORALITY

The Justification of the Good is a massive work, but its design is economical. Soloviev divided his subject into three parts: the Good in human nature, the Good from God, and the Good in the course of history. That is to say, one may see the Good in humanity, in divinity and in the divine-human process.

In this book Soloviev approached the discussion of human nature in a rather unexpected way. Rather than capturing his subject in a formal definition as he did in *The Critique of Abstract Principles*, or through a metaphysical doctrine of freedom, or a theological affirmation of the image of God, Soloviev undertook a quasi-empirical investigation of what he called "the primary data of morality."[57] By these he meant universally observable facts of human behavior that betoken moral consciousness and serve as the foundation for the higher moral principles. The three primary data are shame, compassion, and reverence. Shame, which expresses itself first of all in sexual modesty, is the evidence that human beings regard themselves as beings transcending material nature. The moral principle that arises from shame is asceticism (discipline, self-control). Compassion for suffering companions shows that human beings are other-regarding creatures cognizant of the neighbor's right to exist. The moral principle here is justice. Reverence, appearing first in the awe that children feel toward their parents, shows that human beings seek an object of worship. From reverence comes piety, or the religious principle. Taken together, the three principles define the right relationship to the whole of life: to nature through asceticism; to human beings through justice; to God through worship.

Soloviev used this scheme once before, in *The Spiritual Foundations of Life* (1882–84), where he described spirituality as consisting of prayer, sacrifice or almsgiving, and fasting.[58] The order is reversed, but the terms are the same: reverence, compassion, and shame.

In *The Spiritual Foundations of Life* Soloviev's purpose was edification, not systematic philosophy. In *The Justification of the Good*, however, Soloviev took as his task to show that the "primary data" are universal and logically bound to the principles he derived from them. This was not easy to do, as critics were quick to point out. In a long and extremely negative review of *The Justification of the Good*, the distinguished political and legal philosopher Boris Chicherin argued that Soloviev's treatment of the supposedly primary data of morality was arbitrary.[59] Take the case of shame. Soloviev believed that the modesty human beings feel about sexuality betokens an awareness of their transcendence over material nature, hence the beginnings of asceticism. Even if we grant that feelings of modesty toward sex are universal—a proposition that field anthropologists would have to evaluate—Chicherin pointed out that other reasons besides asceticism could be adduced to explain it. Far from implying transcendence *over* material nature, sexual restraint might be a biological adaptation to protect health and further the enjoyment *of* material nature. Chicherin also rejected the notion that shame as a moral phenomenon implies asceticism.

Human beings often feel shame because of a deficit of passions or possessions: shame over weakness, poverty, sexual inadequacy, and so on.
Chicherin accused Soloviev of making an unwarranted leap from behav-
ioral fact (if it *is* a fact) to moral principle. The same problem attended Soloviev's move from natural compassion to justice and right, and his attempt to
ground belief in God in a feeling of awe rather than in reason. Chicherin believed that Soloviev had been seduced by "the empiricist school now holding
sway" in European intellectual culture. For Chicherin, what is needed in
moral philosophy is not just facts—a "shaky foundation" for systematic
thought—but first principles, or metaphysics.[60]

It is not difficult to appreciate Chicherin's criticism of Soloviev's account of primordial human nature. That Soloviev discovered three "primary data" of morality—not two, or four, or more—is obviously related
to his abstract outline: morality in relation to that which is below human beings (material nature), on a par (fellow humans), and above them
(God). The outline is elegant but can scarcely be said to emerge from an
investigation of facts. The facts have been selected to fit the outline. Still,
it is worth asking why Soloviev began his most comprehensive work of
moral philosophy in this way.[61] Chicherin's explanation—that Soloviev
was seduced by empiricism—is implausible. The thinker who inspired
the passionate interest in God, freedom, and immortality in the Russian
religious-philosophical renaissance of the next generation was not blind
to the metaphysics of morals.

One way of accounting for Soloviev's treatment of human nature in *The
Justification of the Good* is to see it as an experiment in embodied or applied metaphysics, a rudimentary phenomenology. One must remember
that Soloviev's aim in *The Justification of the Good* was not to make the
theoretical case for God, freedom, and immortality but to show how God,
freedom, and immortality enter into actual human experience. It is appropriate, then, that the author began his book not with first principles
but with first phenomena; and in point of fact *The Justification of the Good*
is one of the most concrete works in the Solovievian corpus. A wide range
of social issues, including nationalism, crime and punishment, war, and
economic justice, is discussed.

LAW AND COLLECTIVE EVIL

Given that the issues treated in *The Justification of the Good* have to do
mainly with public order, it is not surprising that Soloviev also devoted a
good deal of attention to law. Soloviev's interest in "collective evil"
(*sobiratel'noe zlo*) reinforced his attention to the subject: if collective

evil demands attention, so presumably does the collective norm-setting designed to combat it.[62] The fact that Soloviev recognized collective evil as a matter demanding attention in its own right is significant in itself. Many nineteenth-century Christian moralists regarded social morality as an extension of individual morality. Soloviev rejected such "abstract subjectivism."[63]

Soloviev identified three quintessential manifestations of collective evil in society: the immoral relations between nations, between society and the criminal, and between social classes. The first evil manifested itself in nationalism; the second, in vengeful and punitive judicial practices such as capital punishment; the third, in economic injustice, the coexistence of luxury and squalor. A separate chapter of *The Justification of the Good* was devoted to each of these problems.[64]

On the national question Soloviev tried to steer a middle course between nationalism and cosmopolitanism (the latter based on "the abstract *man in general* of the philosophers and jurists"). The evangelical commandment to love one's neighbor as oneself transcends national boundaries and rules out national egoism. However, the actual neighbor is never an abstract being but is always embedded in a specific tribe, people, or nation. Therefore the evangelical commandment must also be taken to mean: "Love all other nations as your own." While the Christian is not called to be a "human being in general" (*obshchechelovek*), he is called to be a "pan-human" or "universal man" (*vsechelovek*). Soloviev preached a pluralist, historically concrete internationalism.[65]

A full discussion of internationalism and international law is not found in *The Justification of the Good*, although Soloviev dealt with these subjects by implication in his late essays on war. A chapter on war forms part of *The Justification of the Good*,[66] and his last book, *Three Dialogues on War, Progress and the End of World History, with a Brief Tale of the Anti-Christ* (1899–1900), offered a fuller discussion of the same theme.[67] In both essays, Soloviev aimed to challenge Tolstoyan pacifism, then at the height of its popularity in Russia. Soloviev's argument was simple and sobering: that Christian love requires us to protect the defenseless when it is in our power to do so, by force if necessary. Or more colorfully: after the murder of Abel by Cain, "justly fearing lest the same thing should happen to Seth and other peaceful men, the guardian angels of humanity mixed clay with copper and iron and created the soldier and the policeman."[68] In *Three Dialogues* Soloviev used a recent historical example: the ethnic cleansing of Armenia by Turkish and Kurdish irregulars during the Russo-Turkish War of 1877–78, a wound reopened by the Armenian Massacres of 1895. As a nineteenth-century progressivist, Soloviev believed strongly in "the approaching end of

[all] wars," but he also believed that "it would be irrational . . . to think and to act as though that approaching end had already come."[69]

Soloviev's views on war were not always well received by the liberal Christian circles that were his natural audience. The reservations expressed by the reviewer of *The Justification of the Good* in the official journal of the Moscow Theological Academy, *The Theological Herald*, are a case in point. The reviewer recognized that in *Justification of the Good* Soloviev was attempting to make the case for the "relative good" against absolutists of various types, but he felt that the clarity of the evangelical love ethic was sometimes obscured rather than illuminated by Soloviev's moderation. The critic was prepared to acknowledge that war had brought certain benefits to civilization; however,

> this does not prevent us from feeling greater sympathy for those moralists who actively summon us to cast off this inhuman means of civilization than for those who try to sooth our conscience by pointing out that the individual soldier does not harbor evil intentions toward any particular human being, "especially with the present method of fighting by means of guns and cannons against an enemy who is too far off to be *seen*." We agree with Mr. Soloviev that one cannot survive without the "relative good." But a moralist should be as careful as possible with his "justification" because, having set foot on this slippery slope, it is easy to go too far.[70]

In his treatment of criminal justice Soloviev again attempted to steer a middle course between Tolstoyan Christianity, which rejected criminal law, and its opposite, the traditional view of justice as vengeance or retribution. Both extremes fail to see the essential hallmark of justice, which is not force or retribution but "right." In a system of criminal justice there are three rights to be reckoned with: the right of the injured party to defense and compensation; the right of society to security; and the right of the criminal "to correction and reformation."[71] The first two rights are universally accepted. The third is controversial, for it entails rejecting judicial practices that assail the humanity of the criminal. These include not just bloody and cruel acts of vengeance but also any type of punishment that treats the offender simply as a means to an end. This is why Soloviev rejected capital punishment. The traditional justification of the practice in terms of vengeance or retribution clearly violates the principle of right, which is the basis of justice. The modern argument for the death penalty as a deterrent is equally bad in his opinion because it reduces a human being to the status of a means only and so undermines the common good:

The common good is *common* only because it contains in itself the good of all individual persons without exception—otherwise it would be only the good of the majority.... But from the concept of the *common* good [it] follows with logical necessity that, while limiting particular interests and aspirations precisely as common (by common boundaries), it in no way can abolish even one bearer of personal freedom, or subject of rights, taking from him life and the very possibility of free action. The common good, according to its very idea, should be the good *of this man too*.[72]

The penal system should instruct and correct the offender, not destroy him. Since correction implies the possibility of repentance and amendment of life, Soloviev also rejected mandatory life imprisonment.

In *Law and Morality*, Soloviev offered a biblical argument against capital punishment that is worth pausing over as a good example of his hermeneutics as well as of his position on the judicial issue. Soloviev regarded the Bible as the book that brought humanity out of the realm of "savage religion and religious savagery" to a kingdom of mercy and universal reconciliation. As far as capital punishment is concerned, Soloviev identified three crucial moments in biblical history: the punishment of Cain, which is reserved to God alone (Gen. 4:15); the institution of retributive justice after the Flood, an accommodation continued in the Mosaic Law; and a "return to the norm" in the prophets of Israel and in the gospel, both of which proclaim that God, and God alone, will repay sinners, and will repay them according to the principle, "I desire mercy, and not sacrifice" (Matt. 9:13 and 12:7; cf. Hosea 6:6). Soloviev was convinced that a person who considers the biblical evidence as a whole rather than seizing on bits and pieces of text will conclude that capital punishment violates the divine norm:

The Bible is a complex spiritual organism which developed over a thousand years. It is completely free of external monotony and unilinearity but amazing in its internal unity and in the harmony of the whole. To snatch out arbitrarily from this whole only intermediate parts without a beginning and an end is an insincere and frivolous business; and to rely on the *Bible in general* in favor of the death penalty—attests either to a hopeless incomprehension or a boundless insolence. Those who, like Joseph de Maistre, draw together the concept of the death penalty with the concept of a sin offering, forget that a sin offering has already been brought for all by Christ, that it has abolished all other blood sacrifices, and itself continues only in the bloodless Eucharist—an amazing lapse in consciousness on the part of persons who confess the Christian faith. Indeed, to permit any kind of sin offerings still—means to deny that which was accomplished by Christ, which means—to betray Christianity.[73]

ECONOMIC JUSTICE

Soloviev dealt with the issue of economic justice as he dealt with criminal justice: by seeking a middle way transcending one-sided approaches, in this case a way between capitalism and socialism. Once again Soloviev evinced no sympathy for unregulated market capitalism. The dislocations of early capitalism were everywhere to be seen in the big cities of Russia in the 1890s. A justification of the Good that validated plutocracy, pauperism, and other economic pathologies by invoking the "laws" of economics would be as great a travesty as pietistic theodicies that present cosmic and historical catastrophes as evidence of God's plan for the world. Even if capitalists could demonstrate beyond a reasonable doubt that the prosperity of the many was the certain outcome of the suffering of the few, their system would still be wrong for the same reason that capital punishment is wrong: it reduces some human beings to the status of a means only. The common good is "the good of all and each and not of the majority only."[74]

Applying this criterion to economic relations generally, Soloviev formulated the most celebrated concept in *The Justification of the Good*: the right of human beings to a "dignified" or "worthy" existence.[75] Human beings should live decently. An economy that makes degradation a condition of survival is immoral, and collective action should be taken to change it. "The duty of society is to recognize and to secure to each of its members the *right* to enjoy unmolested *worthy* human existence both for himself and his family."[76] "To recognize and to *secure*": Soloviev's emphasis on securing decent economic circumstances for all clearly implied the need for social and economic legislation, law being the arrangement that guarantees a certain outcome as opposed to merely recommending it.

Because of his interest in economic legislation, Soloviev has been called a "new liberal" to distinguish him from classical liberals like Chicherin.[77] The term also distinguishes Soloviev from the socialists of his day. While there is much in his criticism of capitalism that approximates socialism, Soloviev never accepted the economic determinism of socialism. He rejected its radical egalitarianism as well. "It is one thing to strive for an impossible and unnecessary equalization of property, and another, while preserving the advantages of larger property to those who have it, to recognize the right of everyone to the necessary means of worthy human existence."[78] Not equality but dignity should be the aim of economic legislation. Soloviev was an early advocate of what came to be called the democratic welfare state.[79]

Soloviev's concept of the right to a dignified existence resulted from the synthesis of his idea of law with the patristic concept of human nature as capable of theosis. Soloviev invoked the concept in the chapter on economic justice in *The Justification of the Good*:

> The absolute value of man is based, as we know, upon the *possibility* inherent in his reason and his will of infinitely approaching perfection or, according to the patristic expression, the possibility of becoming divine (*theosis*). This possibility does not pass into actuality completely and immediately, for if it did man would be already equal to God—which is not the case. The inner potentiality *becomes* more and more actual, and can only do so under definite real conditions.[80]

To appreciate the appeal to theosis here, one must keep two things in mind. First, before the revival of contemplative monasticism in nineteenth-century Russia and the labors of twentieth-century patristics scholars, the concept of theosis was in deep eclipse, even in Orthodox theology. Soloviev was one of the first modern thinkers to recognize the distinctiveness and vast implications of the idea. Second, it is highly unusual to come across the patristic concept of theosis, or any other patristic concept for that matter, in a discussion of economic justice. The paragraph quoted above comes from a passage where Soloviev discussed social statistics that show a correlation between income level and life expectancy in modern society. By interjecting the concept of theosis into this discussion, Soloviev drew on patristic piety to protest dehumanizing social conditions and so managed to connect the *summum bonum* of contemplative monks with the travails of the working class in Paris and Petersburg. Soloviev had the natural-born philosopher's ability to make connections between things that seem to most people to lie worlds apart. One can begin to appreciate why it was Soloviev and not someone else who inspired the Russian religio-philosophical renaissance of the early twentieth century. Soloviev showed that it was possible to overcome extremes, to reconcile opposites: Gospel and law, church and world, contemplation and social action, Orthodoxy and humanism, God and human beings. Soloviev loved the Good—*all* of it.[81]

Another unusual feature of Soloviev's discussion of economic issues is a fledgling environmentalist ethic. The right to a dignified existence involves the right of human beings to use nature for human ends. However, Soloviev did not regard this right as validating the unlimited exploitation of nature, nor did he regard the relationship between human beings and nature as unilateral. The right relationship between human beings and nature is neither submission nor exploitation but "looking after [nature] for one's own and its [own] sake."[82] The phraseology (*ukhazhivanie za [prirodoi] dlia sebia i dlia nee*) suggests a relationship of mutuality and intimacy. Soloviev even extended the concept of "right" to the material world, as when he wrote that "matter has a right to be spiritualized by man," suggesting a prophetic vision of nature as destined for more than it has yet become. This vision underlies Soloviev's assertion that "without loving nature for its own sake one cannot organize material life in a moral way."[83] This was an unusual claim to make in a discussion of economic justice in late-nineteenth-century Europe. Not just capitalists but even most socialists at the time assumed that nature existed solely to be exploited by human beings. Soloviev anticipated environmentalism, and more. As a recent Russian commentator observed, Soloviev's vision of the spiritualization of nature is "a cause in comparison with which the objectives of contemporary ecology seem rather modest."[84] Soloviev's environmentalism was inspired by the Pauline vision of the whole creation being destined to share in "the glorious liberty of the children of God" (Rom. 8:21).

LAW, MORALITY, AND THE CHURCH

Soloviev's view of the relation between law and morality in *The Justification of the Good* advanced beyond his position in *The Critique of Abstract Principles*. In the *Critique* Soloviev emphasized the gap between law and morality by contrasting the formal character of law with the substantive values of morality. He had little to say about how law and morality should interact concretely, even though his theocratic ideal demanded such interaction. In *The Justification of the Good* he saw a substantive relationship between law and morality, defining law as the "compulsory demand for the realization of a definite minimum of good, or for a social order which excludes certain manifestations of evil."[85] This definition rules out the view of law as a framework that can accommodate any end; law is now seen as comprising normative ends, albeit minimally conceived.[86] As we have seen, *The Justification of the Good* presented a remarkably concrete exposition of some of the moral ends that a legal order can promote in various spheres of life.

A tension between law and morality endures in the notions of a "minimum" of good and "[only] certain manifestations" of evil, restrictions which morality in its purest form would reject. Moral demands are unlimited, never finished, and effected voluntarily. "Be perfect, therefore, as your heavenly Father is perfect" (Matt. 5:48) is the standard.[87] Legal demands, by contrast, are limited, realizable, and compulsory.[88] Laws must be precise and doable; and they must actually effect, by force if necessary, the minimal good that is their raison d'être. If these characteristics are lacking, one is dealing with something other than law, or with defective laws.

The tension between law and morality need not lead to a divorce, however. Soloviev construed the evangelical call to perfection in such a way as to allow relative ethical goods including law to be affirmed:

> The *absolute* moral principle, the *demand*, namely, or the *commandment* to be perfect as our Father in heaven is perfect, or to realize in ourselves the image and likeness of God, already contains in its very nature the recognition of the *relative* element in morality. For it is clear that the demand for perfection can only be addressed to a being who is imperfect; urging him to *become* like the higher being, the commandment presupposes the lower stages and the relative degrees of advance.[89]

As a relative good, law pertains to imperfect beings. Yet as his words show, Soloviev viewed imperfection optimistically: the imperfect beings are *advancing*, heeding an upward call, participating in a process of transformation extending from here to eternity. This faith helped Soloviev to achieve his nuanced appreciation of law in *The Justification of the Good*, vindicating law as an ethical "minimum" without severing its connection to the moral and spiritual maximum.

The church has an indispensable role to play in the "moral organization of humanity as a whole," as the last chapter of *The Justification of the Good* is entitled. The church "indicates the general direction of the goodwill of mankind and the final purpose of its historical activity." Without the church and the kingdom to which it bears witness, the end of life would be opaque; history would lack a moral compass. For this reason "the state recognizes the supreme spiritual authority of the universal Church" in the moral ordering of life as Soloviev imagined it. However, this does not mean that the church may use state power to advance its mission. "The Church must have no power of compulsion, and the power of compulsion exercised by the state must have nothing to do with the domain of religion."[90] The reason for these restrictions is that piety resembles morality rather than law: it is unlimited, unfinished, and voluntarily effected. And of course the object of piety must never be construed as a "minimum." God is unlimited, unfathomable, and free, and so are the demands of piety. Soloviev's longstanding advocacy of freedom of religion in the Russian Empire also underlay his position here.

Whether Soloviev ever envisioned the formal separation of church and state is debatable. Most interpreters have emphasized the contrast between his earlier works and *The Justification of the Good*, construing the former as vehicles of theocratic utopianism, the latter as evidence of the "dissolution of theocratic views."[91] Yet the status of theocracy in Soloviev's later works has not been adequately clarified. The issue is what Soloviev meant in practical terms when he wrote that "the state recognizes the supreme spiritual authority of the universal Church." Walicki claims that, for the later Soloviev, "free theocracy was, so to speak, stripped of its millenarian features and reduced to something like a Kantian 'regulative idea' in ethics."[92] But this seems to understate the case in order to make Soloviev more acceptable to a secularist audience. In the closing pages of *The Justification of the Good* Soloviev still wrote of a "Christian state" whose "progressive task" is "to prepare humanity and the whole earth for the Kingdom of God."[93] He still entrusted the moral organization of humanity to the "harmonious cooperation" of prophet, priest, and king.[94] Is this language merely ornamentation for a proto-secular ideal? In a perverse way Boris Chicherin may have been closer to the truth when he criticized the author of *The Justification of the Good* for taking positions "which Torquemada could adopt."[95] It was an unfair comparison, of course, and would have been unfair even if Chicherin were discussing Soloviev's earlier works. Soloviev never preached clericalism, far less the Inquisition, but always a "free" theocracy. Still, Chicherin saw something that Soloviev's cultured admirers tend to minimize or to miss: for all its modernism and moderation, *The Justification of the Good* remains the work of a mystic, a prophet, and a Christian theocrat.[96]

An arresting example of the impact of Soloviev's strong Christian faith on his view of the legal order is found in his observations on Plato's *Laws* in a late essay.[97] The case is all the more poignant because of the similarity between Plato's *Laws* and Soloviev's *Justification of the Good*. Both are essays of applied ethics in which an aging philosopher attempts "to reconcile [his] ideal with practicality, combining minimalism in the former sphere with maximalism in the latter."[98] Soloviev gave a sobering account of the path that led the Plato of the *Laws*, like so many thinkers after him, to absolutize the legal and political order. Smitten as a young man by the goodness, truth, and beauty revealed in Socrates, Plato became increasingly frustrated by his inability to realize these values in the world of flesh and blood, leading him first, in the *Republic*, to accommodate such dubious means of social order as slavery, war, and tyranny, and finally, in the *Laws*, to advocate the death penalty for "any man who rejects or upsets the authority of the ancestral laws, both relative to the gods and relative to the public order. . . . Thus the greatest disciple of Socrates, who had been called to independent philosophical creativity by his indignation at the *legal* murder of his teacher, toward the end totally rests on the point of view of Anytos and Melitos, who had obtained the death sentence for Socrates precisely because of his liberal attitude to the established religious-civil order." Why did this happen? It happened, Soloviev believed, because Plato attempted "the *reform* of societal relations" without believing in "the *regeneration* of human nature"; and he did not believe in the regeneration of human nature because he did not know "the One who has the power of resurrection to eternal life." Plato knew Socrates, but not Christ, the "authentic, substantive *God-Man*." The Russian Plato would not make the same mistake. As an Orthodox Christian, he knew the Resurrected One.[99]

SOLOVIEV'S LEGACY

In the conclusion to his monograph on Soloviev's philosophy of law, Hans Helmut Gäntzel offers a generalization that few would dispute: that "the defining characteristic of the whole of Soloviev's philosophy is the unity of faith, science and life." What this means for jurisprudence is "the ultimate grounding of law in morality and, through morality, in the Christian idea of salvation."[100] Soloviev did not construe these connections in such a way as to deny the important analytical and methodological distinctions separating law, morality, and Christian faith; but he rejected all viewpoints, secular or religious, that would absolutize those distinctions. Reality for Soloviev was an ever-flowing stream issuing in the eschatological kingdom of God.

The impact of Soloviev's theo-philosophical vision on Russian intellectual culture in the next generation, usually called the Silver Age (1900–17), was enormous. Within two years of his death, Russian neoidealism issued its manifesto.[101] The young ex-Marxists Sergei Bulgakov and Nicholas Berdyaev began recreating themselves as religious philosophers, soon to be joined by others. The most important work of collective self-criticism in the history of the Russian intelligentsia, *Vekhi* (1909), struck Solovievian chords in essay after essay.[102] Even anti-Solovievian thinkers, such as Lev Shestov, could not escape his influence. Nor was Soloviev's impact limited to philosophers. The Vladimir Soloviev Religious-Philosophical Society that existed in Moscow from 1905 to 1918 numbered prominent cultural figures from many fields among its members or participants, including the poets Aleksandr Blok and Andrei Belyi, the literary critic Viacheslav Ivanov, the painter Mikhail Nesterov, and the composer Aleksandr Scriabin.[103] No Russian philosopher had ever attracted such wide attention.

Of course it was possible to take an interest in Soloviev without paying attention to his philosophy of law. It was easier to appreciate Soloviev's lit-

erary criticism, political commentary, and Sophia poems than to plough
through the 550 pages of *The Justification of the Good*. Writing in a commemorative volume six months after Soloviev's death, Pavel Novgorodtsev made an observation that applies to Soloviev's readership at all times
including our own: "The person who knows Soloviev mainly in terms of
his mystical speculations and yearnings will surely be surprised to learn
that he was a brilliant and outstanding spokesman for the philosophy of
law. It is difficult to see at first just how something as concrete and practical as the idea of law found a place among his reveries and prophecies."[104]

There were important exceptions, however, including Novgorodtsev
himself, who was already emerging as one of Russia's leading philosophers
of law. Moreover, apart from Soloviev, a new legal consciousness was
emerging in Russia at the beginning of the twentieth century. The inaugu-
ration of a quasi-constitutional order in 1905–6 strengthened this development, as did the formation of the Constitutional Democratic Party
("Kadets"), which directly or indirectly enjoyed the allegiance of many of
Russia's neoidealists and religious philosophers. A little-known fact about
Russia's early twentieth-century religious thinkers is that many of them
had received academic training in law. Sergei Bulgakov, Evgeny Trubetskoi,
Lev Shestov, Ivan Ilyin, and Boris Vysheslavtsev were all graduates of law
faculties, while others had studied law at some point in their education.
Several of the religious philosophers worked professionally in law and contributed monographs in the field. Even when they chose other paths, however, evidence of a well-formed legal consciousness can usually be found in
their work. Most early twentieth-century Russian religious philosophers
were comfortable with the view of Orthodoxy as part of a modern legal-
constitutional order, a view pioneered by Soloviev.

Among professional church theologians the attitude toward Soloviev ran
the gamut from traditionalist censure to deep admiration. Interestingly, the
first monograph on Soloviev's philosophy came not from the pen of one of
his heirs in the intelligentsia but from a teacher in a provincial Orthodox
theological seminary, Aleksandr Nikolsky (1866–1915). Nikolsky, whose
graduate degree was from the Moscow Theological Academy, exemplified
the high level of philosophical and theological culture that had been
achieved in the Russian Orthodox Church by the beginning of the twentieth century. The title of his book, *The Russian Origen of the Nineteenth Century, Vl. S. Soloviev*, presents Soloviev as a mixed blessing for the church,
much like the Alexandrian genius of the third century. Soloviev in this account was admirable in his sincere Christian faith and determination to
grapple with the eternal questions of human existence in the light of the
gospel, but deserved criticism for "approaching the examination and

investigation of the Divine mysteries with less humility and less faith in Scripture than one might have expected from a believing Christian, and with greater confidence in the power of abstract reason than one should allow on the basis of the strictly logical demands of philosophy."[105]

Unfortunately, this balanced view of Soloviev is not as widely held in the Orthodox world today as it was in Nikolsky's time. Following a brief renaissance of Solovievian theology during the 1920s and 1930s, thanks to the influence of Sergei Bulgakov, church theologians began to lose interest in him. The neopatristic school of Georges Florovsky and Vladimir Lossky, which has dominated Orthodox theology since the 1940s, judges Soloviev harshly, as do contemporary neotraditionalist theologians. One of the byproducts of the marginalization of the Solovievian legacy is the absence of work on philosophy of law by Orthodox theologians.

In Russian intellectual culture generally, on the other hand, interest in Soloviev remains significant. During the Soviet period, of course, Soloviev was a nonperson, neither published nor publicly discussed. Of course, philosophy of law as an independent discipline was not practiced, either. With the recovery of the Solovievian corpus during the *glasnost* reforms of the 1980s, Soloviev assumed a place of distinction in what is sometimes called the "Russian religio-moral philosophy of law."[106] The claim implicit in this phrase was advanced long ago by Pavel Novgorodtsev in an essay in which he argued that modern Russian philosophy of law inclines to "the establishment of a [close] bond between law and morality" and "the subordination of culture and the state to religion and Church."[107] The fact that Novgorodtsev's characterization continues to have some currency in Russian legal philosophy today is evidence of the continuing influence of Soloviev, from whom he derived it. The prominent place assigned to an article on Soloviev's philosophy of law at the head of a distinguished new collection of essays on Soloviev by Russian and non-Russian scholars is further evidence of the growing respect accorded to an aspect of the "Russian Origen's" thought which has too often been neglected.[108] As the Russian and worldwide Orthodox community seeks to contribute to the building of a stable constitutional order in the postcommunist East, Soloviev's legacy on law and human nature in the light of Christian faith can only grow in importance.

NOTES

1. The most comprehensive studies of Soloviev's life and work are K. Mochul'skii, *Vladimir Soloviev: Zhizn' i uchenie*, 2d ed. (Paris: YMCA-Press, 1951); S.M. Solov'ev, *Zhizn' i tvorcheskaia evoliutsiia Vladimira Solov'eva* (Brussels:

Foyer Oriental Chrétien, 1977), republished as *Vladimir Solov'ev: Zhizn' i tvorcheskaia evoliutsiia* (Moscow: Respublika, 1997); and A. F. Losev, *Vladimir Solov'ev i ego vremia* (Moscow: Molodaia gvardiia, 2000). For surveys in English see D. Strémooukhoff, *Vladimir Soloviev and His Messianic Work*, ed. Philip Guilbeau and Heather Elise MacGregor, trans. Elizabeth Meyendorff (Belmont, Mass.: Nordland, 1980); Jonathan Sutton, *The Religious Philosophy of Vladimir Solovyov: Towards a Reassessment* (New York: St. Martin's Press, 1988); and Paul Valliere, *Modern Russian Theology: Bukharev, Soloviev, Bulgakov* (Grand Rapids, Mich.: Eerdmans, 2000), 109–223.

2. S.M. Soloviev, *Istoriia Rossii s drevneishikh vremen*, 29 vols. (Moscow, 1854–79).

3. On Yurkevich, see P.D. Iurkevich, *Filosofskie proizvedeniia* (Moscow: Izdatel'stvo Pravda, 1990), and V.V. Zenkovsky, *A History of Russian Philosophy*, trans. George L. Kline, 2 vols. (New York: Columbia University Press, 1953), 1:313–315.

4. *The Crisis of Western Philosophy* and *Lectures on Divine Humanity* are available in English; *The Philosophical Principles of Integral Knowledge* and *The Critique of Abstract Principles* are not.

5. Schelling's extensive influence on modern Russian philosophy has been well documented. See V.F. Pustarnakov, *Filosofiia Shellinga v Rossii* (St. Petersburg: Izdatel'stvo Russkogo Khristianskogo gumanitarnogo instituta, 1998).

6. Quoted by Zenkovsky, *A History of Russian Philosophy*, 1:211–212.

7. The phrases "godless human individual" and "inhuman God" are taken from Soloviev's lecture "Three Forces" (1877); but the same conceptual scheme, with less attention to Islam, informs *Lectures on Divine Humanity*. The negative view of Islam in "Three Forces" had to do with the patriotic, not to say jingoistic, context of the lecture. Soloviev delivered it in April 1877, as Russia went to war with Turkey over the Eastern Question. The "three forces" are the humanistic but godless West, the religious but despotic Islamic East, and the synthesis of humanism and religion in Orthodoxy/Slavdom. For the text see "Tri sily," *Sobranie sochinenii Vladimira Sergeevicha Solov'eva*, ed. S.M. Solov'ev and E.L. Radlov, 2d ed., 10 vols. (St. Petersburg, 1911–14; reprint, Brussels: Foyer Oriental Chrétien, 1966), 1:227–239.

8. For a detailed discussion of the friendship between Dostoevsky and Soloviev, see Marina Kostalevsky, *Dostoevsky and Soloviev: The Art of Integral Vision* (New Haven, Conn.: Yale University Press, 1997), 49–80.

9. *The Brothers Karamazov*, part 1, book 2, chap. 5.

10. See Lecture 11–12 in Vladimir Solovyov, *Lectures on Divine Humanity*, trans. Boris Jakim (Hudson, N.Y.: Lindisfarne Press, 1995), 155–156.

11. On Soloviev's view of nationalism, see Greg Gaut, "Can a Christian be a Nationalist? Vladimir Solov'ev's Critique of Nationalism," *Slavic Review* 57 (1998): 77–94.

12. Vladimir Soloviev, *La Russie et l'Eglise universelle*, 4th ed. (Paris: Librairie Stock, 1922), lxi.

13. Mochul'skii, *Vladimir Solov'ev*, 185.

14. S. M. Solov'ev and E. L. Radlov, eds., *Sobranie sochinenii V. S. Solov'eva*, 6:18.
15. The first volume was the only one Soloviev completed as planned. For the text, see *Sobranie sochinenii V. S. Solov'eva*, 4:241–639. He composed the work in 1885–87 but could not publish it in Russia because of censorship. *La Russie et l'Eglise universelle*, which Soloviev wrote in French and published in Paris in 1889, is a version of what was to have been the third volume.
16. Vladimir Solov'ev, "Evreistvo i khristianskii vopros," in *Sobranie sochinenii V. S. Solov'eva*, 4:135–185; "Talmud i noveishaia polemicheskaia literatura o nem v Avstrii i Germanii," in *Sobranie sochinenii V. S. Solov'eva*, 6:3–32.
17. S. L. Frank, ed., *A Solovyov Anthology*, trans. Natalie Duddington (New York: Charles Scribner's Sons, 1950), 105.
18. S. M. Solov'ev and E. L. Radlov, eds., *Sobranie sochinenii V. S. Solov'eva*, 6:31.
19. Stanislav Rotsinskii underscores the centrality of the theme of reconciliation in Soloviev's thought in a recent study, *Primirenie idei i ideia primireniia v filosofii vseedinstva Vl. Solov'eva* (Moscow: Izdatel'stvo RAGS, 1999).
20. See Judith Deutsch Kornblatt, "Solov'ev on Salvation: The Story of the 'Short Story of the Antichrist,'" in *Russian Religious Thought*, ed. Judith Deutsch Kornblatt and Richard F. Gustafson (Madison: University of Wisconsin Press, 1996), 68–87.
21. V. S. Solov'ev, *Polnoe sobranie sochinenii i pisem v dvadtsati tomakh*, 20 vols. (Moscow: Nauka, 2000–), 3:117.
22. Solov'ev, *Polnoe sobranie sochinenii*, 3:120.
23. Solovyov, *Lectures on Divine Humanity*, 122–123.
24. Ibid., 160–163.
25. Soloviev equated capitalism with plutocracy and never considered the case for classical economics in positive terms. He was criticized for this not just by detractors such as Chicherin but also by some of his passionate supporters in the next generation. Sergei Bulgakov wrote that "political economy is for the most part the Achilles' heel of [this] philosopher." S. N. Bulgakov, *Ot marksizma k idealizmu: Sbornik statei (1896–1903)* (St. Petersburg: Obshchestvennaia Pol'za, 1903), 249.
26. Solov'ev, *Polnoe sobranie sochinenii*, 3:128.
27. Ibid., 133–134.
28. Ibid., 137–138.
29. Ibid., 143.
30. Ibid., 145.
31. Ibid. "Twenty years later a very similar conception was developed by the neo-Kantian legal philosopher, Rudolf Stammler, who coined the famous formula 'natural law with changing content' and is supposed to have inaugurated the revival of natural law in Germany." Andrzej Walicki, *Legal Philosophies of Russian Liberalism* (Oxford: Clarendon Press, 1987), 211.
32. Ibid., 147.
33. Walicki, *Legal Philosophies of Russian Liberalism*, 169, 181, 184–185.

34. Solov'ev, *Polnoe sobranie sochinenii*, 3:148. *Faust*, part 1:283–286 ("Prolog im Himmel"). Mephistopheles tells the Lord, "He would live a little better if You had not given him the gleam of Heaven's light; he calls it reason but uses it only to be more beastly than any beast."
35. Solov'ev, *Polnoe sobranie sochinenii*, 3:148–149.
36. Ibid., 149.
37. Ibid., 150–151.
38. Ibid., 152–155.
39. Ibid., 152.
40. Ibid., 149.
41. Ibid., 162.
42. See chapter 2, Russell Hittinger, "Introduction to Modern Catholicism," in *The Teachings of Modern Christianity on Law, Politics, and Human Nature*, ed. John Witte Jr. and Frank Alexander (New York: Columbia University Press, 2006), 39–74.
43. See Davison M. Douglas, "Reinhold Niebuhr," in *The Teachings of Modern Christianity*, 412–438; Timothy P. Jackson, "Martin Luther King Jr.," in *The Teachings of Modern Christianity*, 439–464; and Duncan B. Forrester, "John Howard Yoder," in *The Teachings of Modern Christianity*, 481–502. Soloviev was eloquent on this point: "The precept, 'Render to Caesar the things that are Caesar's, and to God the things that are God's' is constantly quoted to sanction an order of things which gives Caesar all and God nothing. The saying 'My Kingdom is not of this world' is always being used to justify and confirm the paganism of our social and political life, as though Christian society were destined to belong to this world and not to the Kingdom of Christ. On the other hand the saying 'All power is given Me in heaven and earth' is never quoted." Vladimir Solovyev, *Russia and the Universal Church*, trans. Herbert Rees (London: Centenary Press, 1948), 8.
44. Solov'ev, *Polnoe sobranie sochinenii*, 3:157–159.
45. Ibid., 158–159.
46. In fairness to Soloviev it should be noted that he never viewed the vicariate as unitary but always as a collaboration of political, ecclesiastical, and free-prophetic agents, e.g., Russian tsar, Roman pontiff, and the Jews. For discussions of Soloviev's theocratic projects, see Strémooukhoff, *Vladimir Soloviev and His Messianic Work* and the essays by Marin Terpstra, Michael Klimenko, Machiel Karskens, and Andrzej Walicki in *Vladimir Solov'ëv: Reconciler and Polemicist*, ed. Wil van den Bercken, Manon de Courten and Evert van der Zweerde (Leuven, Belgium: Peeters, 2000).
47. *Opravdanie dobra* is available in a dated but generally reliable English translation: Vladimir Solovyof, *The Justification of the Good: An Essay on Moral Philosophy*, trans. Nathalie A. Duddington (New York: Macmillan, 1918). The Duddington translation has been used for citations in this paper; the corresponding passages in *Sobranie sochinenii V.S. Solov'eva* are noted. *Law and Morality* is composed of material taken from *The Justification of the Good* and earlier writings including *The Critique of Abstract Principles*. A complete

English translation appears in Vladimir Wozniuk, ed. and trans., *Politics, Law, Morality: Essays by V. S. Solov'ev* (New Haven, Conn.: Yale University Press, 2000), 131–212.

48. Solov'ev, *Polnoe sobranie sochinenii*, 3:167. Soloviev's words are, "*Spravedlivost' est' neobkhodimaia forma liubvi.*" *Forma* here does not mean "form" in the sense of type or species, but formal structure, framework.

49. Solovyof, *The Justification of the Good* (trans. Duddington), 165–166; *Sobranie sochinenii V. S. Solov'eva*, 8:194–196.

50. Solovyof, *The Justification of the Good*, xxxi; *Sobranie sochinenii V. S. Solov'eva*, 8:22.

51. Solovyof, *The Justification of the Good*, xxxi–xxxii; *Sobranie sochinenii V. S. Solov'eva*, 8:22.

52. Solovyof, *The Justification of the Good*, xxxii; *Sobranie sochinenii V. S. Solov'eva*, 8:23.

53. Solovyof, *The Justification of the Good*, ix; *Sobranie sochinenii V. S. Solov'eva*, 8:3.

54. Solovyof, *The Justification of the Good*, xxxiii; *Sobranie sochinenii V. S. Solov'eva*, 8:23.

55. In the title of *The Justification of the Good* Soloviev used the Russian word *dobro* rather than *blago* for "good," but this does not invalidate the point about grace. Soloviev used the two terms interchangeably: "Divine grace is a *good* [*blago*], or good [*dobro*], which is given to man and not simply thought by him." *Sobranie sochinenii V. S. Solov'eva*, 3:312.

56. See Leslie Griffin, "Pope John XXIII," in *The Teachings of Modern Christianity*, 145–172.

57. Solovyof, *The Justification of the Good*, 25; *Sobranie sochinenii V. S. Solov'eva*, 8:49.

58. The English translation of this work bears a different title: Vladimir Solovyev, *God, Man and the Church: The Spiritual Foundations of Life*, trans. Donald Attwater (London: J. Clarke, 1930).

59. B. N. Chicherin, "O nachalakh etiki," *Voprosy filosofii i psikhologii* 39 (September–October 1897): 586–701. On Chicherin see G. M. Hamburg, *Boris Chicherin and Early Russian Liberalism, 1828–1866* (Stanford, Calif.: Stanford University Press, 1992) and G. M. Hamburg, ed. and trans., *Liberty, Equality and the Market: Essays by B. N. Chicherin* (New Haven, Conn.: Yale University Press, 1998).

60. Chicherin, "O nachalakh etiki," 590–591.

61. In his reply to Chicherin, Soloviev did not offer an explanation of his procedure. He sparred with Chicherin on points of logic and on practical issues that divided them. The latter were significant. Soloviev was a consistent opponent of capital punishment and mandatory life sentences; Chicherin defended them. Soloviev was a harbinger of the welfare state; Chicherin, a free market liberal. See Vladimir Solov'ev, "Mnimaia kritika. (Otvet B. N. Chicherinu)," *Voprosy filosofii i psikhologii* 39 (September–October 1897): 645–694.

62. Solovyof, *The Justification of the Good*, liv; *Sobranie sochinenii V. S. Solov'eva*, 8:xxviii.

63. Ibid., chap. 12 (part 3, chap. 3 in Duddington translation).

64. Ibid., chaps. 14, 15, and 16 (part 3, chaps. 5, 6, and 7 in Duddington translation).

65. Solovyof, *The Justification of the Good*, 284, 295–298; *Sobranie sochinenii V. S. Solov'eva*, 8:316, 328–331.

66. Ibid., chap. 18 (part 3, chap. 9 in Duddington translation).

67. *Three Dialogues* is available in English: *War, Progress and the End of History: Three Conversations Including a Short Story of the Anti-Christ*, trans. Alexander Bakshy, trans. Thomas R. Beyer Jr. (Hudson, N.Y.: Lindisfarne Press, 1990).

68. Solovyof, *The Justification of the Good*, 406; *Sobranie sochinenii V. S. Solov'eva*, 8:444.

69. Solovyof, *The Justification of the Good*, 399; *Sobranie sochinenii V. S. Solov'eva*, 8:437.

70. N. Gorodenskii, "Nravstvennaia filosofiia Vl. S. Solov'eva," *Bogoslovskii vestnik* (February 1899): 321. The words quoted by Gorodenskii appear in Solovyof, *The Justification of the Good*, 403; *Sobranie sochinenii V. S. Solov'eva*, 8:441.

71. Solovyof, *The Justification of the Good*, 323; *Sobranie sochinenii V. S. Solov'eva*, 8:357.

72. Wozniuk, *Politics, Law, Morality*, 183–184; cf. *Sobranie sochinenii V. S. Solov'eva*, 8:417, and Solovyof, *The Justification of the Good*, 379–380.

73. Wozniuk, *Politics, Law, Morality*, 176. Soloviev reiterated his opposition to the theological justification of capital punishment in his reply to Chicherin's review of *The Justification of the Good*. A good Hegelian, Chicherin defended capital punishment and appealed to gospel texts concerning eternal punishment to justify the concept of retributive justice. Cautioning Chicherin against "crude literalism" in the use of scripture, Soloviev cited a work by Archimandrite Sergy (Stragorodsky), *Pravoslavnoe uchenie o spasenii* [The Orthodox Doctrine of Salvation] (Sergiev Posad, 1895), in which the author maintains that the juridical theory of retribution "'is of accidental provenance in the Christian worldview; and so, if one is speaking about the essence of Christianity, the concept of retribution in the literal and strict sense cannot be admitted.'" Solov'ev, "Mnimaia kritika," 690. Sergy became a leading hierarch in the twentieth century, the author of the divisive declaration of loyalty to the Soviet government in 1927 and the first incumbent of the revived Patriarchate of Moscow in 1943–45.

74. Solovyof, *The Justification of the Good*, 340; *Sobranie sochinenii V. S. Solov'eva*, 8:377.

75. "Dignified" is Walicki's translation in *Legal Philosophies of Russian Liberalism*. Duddington, rendering the Russian *dostoinyi* more literally, translates "worthy."

76. Solovyof, *The Justification of the Good*, 341; *Sobranie sochinenii V. S. Solov'eva*, 8:377.

77. See Walicki, *Legal Philosophies of Russian Liberalism*, chap. 2, "Boris Chicherin: the 'Old Liberal' Philosophy of Law," and chap. 3, "Vladimir Soloviev: Religious Philosophy and the Emergence of the 'New Liberalism.'"

78. Solovyof, *The Justification of the Good*, 345; *Sobranie sochinenii V. S. Solov'eva*, 8:381.
79. The welfare state is also adumbrated in Soloviev's view of the state in *The Justification of the Good* as "collectively organized compassion" (Duddington trans. "pity"). Solovyof, *The Justification of the Good*, 448; *Sobranie sochinenii V. S. Solov'eva*, 8:488. See also Walicki, *Legal Philosophies of Russian Liberalism*, 204–245.
80. Solovyof, *The Justification of the Good*, 343; *Sobranie sochinenii V. S. Solov'eva*, 8:379.
81. Soloviev's genius in this respect can be compared with Martin Luther King's as described in Jackson, "Martin Luther King Jr.," in *The Teachings of Modern Christianity*, 439–464: "Two of King's favorite biblical passages were 'Be not conformed to this world, but be transformed by the renewing of your minds' (Rom. 12:2) and 'Let justice roll down like waters and righteousness like a mighty stream' (Amos 5:24). The ability to hold these two quotations together in a lived unity, faithful to both heaven and earth, defined King's genius."
82. Solovyof, *The Justification of the Good*, lvii; *Sobranie sochinenii V. S. Solov'eva*, 8:xxxi.
83. Solovyof, *The Justification of the Good*, lvi–lvii; *Sobranie sochinenii V. S. Solov'eva*, 8:xxxi.
84. V. V. Lazarev, *Eticheskaia mysl' v Germanii i Rossii: Shelling i Vl. Solov'ev* (Moscow: IFRAN, 2000), 154.
85. Solovyof, *The Justification of the Good*, 371; *Sobranie sochinenii V. S. Solov'eva*, 8:409.
86. Soloviev's new definition seems to have been inspired in part by the theory of Georg Jellinek. See Walicki, *Legal Philosophies of Russian Liberalism*, 200–201.
87. Solovyof, *The Justification of the Good*, 167–168; *Sobranie sochinenii V. S. Solov'eva*, 8:197–198.
88. Solovyof, *The Justification of the Good*, 369–371; *Sobranie sochinenii V. S. Solov'eva*, 8:407–409.
89. Solovyof, *The Justification of the Good*, 362; *Sobranie sochinenii V. S. Solov'eva*, 8:399.
90. Solovyof, *The Justification of the Good*, 459; *Sobranie sochinenii V. S. Solov'eva*, 8:499.
91. Evgenii Trubetskoi, *Mirosozertsanie Vl. S. Solov'eva*, 2 vols. (Moscow: Izdanie avtora, 1913), 2:190–194.
92. Walicki, *Legal Philosophies of Russian Liberalism*, 191.
93. Solovyof, *The Justification of the Good*, 455–457; *Sobranie sochinenii V. S. Solov'eva*, 8:496–497.
94. Solovyof, *The Justification of the Good*, 467–469; *Sobranie sochinenii V. S. Solov'eva*, 8:508–510.
95. Chicherin, "O nachalakh etiki," 644.
96. Pavel Novgorodtsev, one of Soloviev's admirers, acknowledged the theocratic ideal in *The Justification of the Good* but doubted that it would generate much

enthusiasm in the Russia of his time: "The idea of a model society being reflected in the collaboration of prophet, priest and king will captivate hardly anyone in our day." P. N. Novgorodtsev, "Ideia prava v filosofii Vl. S. Solov'eva," *Voprosy filosofii i psikhologii* 56 (January–February 1901): 128.

97. "Plato's Life-Drama," in Wozniuk, *Politics, Law, Morality*, 213–254. Russian text in *Sobranie sochinenii V. S. Solov'eva*, 9:194–241.

98. The analogy and cited words are Viacheslav Ivanov's in "O znachenii Vl. Solov'eva v sud'bakh nashego religioznogo soznaniia," *O Vladimire Solov'eve* (Tomsk: Izdatel'stvo Vodolei, 1997), 35. The essay was first published in 1911.

99. Wozniuk, *Politics, Law, Morality*, 249–254. Again in this essay Soloviev used the term *theosis* (248) to describe the ultimate state of regeneration.

100. Hans Helmut Gäntzel, *Wladimir Solowjows Rechtsphilosophie auf der Grundlage der Sittlichkeit* (Frankfurt am Main: Vittorio Klostermann, 1968), 289, 293.

101. For an English translation of *Problemy idealizma* (1902), see Randall A. Poole, ed. and trans., *Problems of Idealism: Essays in Russian Social Philosophy* (New Haven, Conn.: Yale University Press, 2003).

102. See Marshall S. Shatz and Judith E. Zimmerman, ed. and trans., *Vekhi/Landmarks: A Collection of Articles About the Russian Intelligentsia* (Armonk, N.Y.: M. E. Sharpe, 1994).

103. See Kristiane Burchardi, *Die Moskauer "Religiös-Philosophische Vladimir-Solov'ev-Gesellschaft" (1905–1918)*, Forschungen zur osteuropäischen Geschichte: Historische Veröffentlichungen 53 (Wiesbaden: Harrassowitz Verlag, 1998).

104. P. I. Novgorodtsev, "Ideia prava v filosofii Vl. S. Solov'eva," 112.

105. A. A. Nikol'skii, *Russkii Origen XIX veka Vl. S. Solov'ev* (St. Petersburg: Nauka, 2000), 332. The book first appeared serially in the journal *Vera i razum* (Faith and Reason) in 1902.

106. "The Russian Religio-Moral Philosophy of Law" is the title of the section on Russian thinkers in a recent textbook on the history of the philosophy of law for use in Russian law faculties: *Istoriia filosofii prava* (St. Petersburg: Izdatel'stvo Iuridicheskii institut, 1998). Another recent textbook promoting this theme is *Russkaia filosofiia prava: Filosofiia very i nravstvennosti, Antologiia* (Russian Philosophy of Law: A Philosophy of Faith and Morality—An Anthology) (St. Petersburg: Izdatel'stvo Aleteiia, 1997).

107. Novgorodtsev's "Über die eigentümlichen Elemente der russischen Rechtsphilosophie" was published in Germany in 1932 and is discussed in Gäntzel, *Wladimir Solovyows Rechtsphilosophie*, 293–294. The article appears in Russian translation in *Russkaia filosofiia prava*, 211–226 and in P. I. Novgorodtsev, *Sochineniia* (Moscow: Raritet, 1995), 367–387.

108. E. Iu. Solov'ev, "Gumanitarno-pravovaia problematika v filosofskoi publitsistike V. S. Solov'eva," in I. V. Borisova and A. P. Kozyrev, eds., *Solov'evskii sbornik*, Materialy mezhdunarodnoi konferentsii "V. S. Solov'ev i ego filosofskoe nasledie," 28–30 avgusta 2000 g. (Moscow: Fenomenologiia-Germenevtika, 2001), 29–51.

ORIGINAL SOURCE MATERIALS

AUTHOR'S PREFACE TO *THE SPIRITUAL*
FOUNDATIONS OF LIFE (1882–84)

The wickedness and futility of the way our mortal life is lived is recognized by human reason and conscience, which clamour for its improvement; but man, immersed in this life, has to find some foothold outside of it before he can begin any process of correction. The believer finds this foothold in religion, whose function it is to renew and sanctify our life and make it one with the life of God. This is in the first place a work of God himself, but it cannot be carried through without our co-operation, our life cannot be regenerated without personal action on our own part: religion is a *theandric*, that is to say a divine-human, activity.

With religion, as with everything else, it is first of all necessary to master certain fundamental methods and activities without whose practical background no progress can be made, and these things must not be chosen haphazard and arbitrarily but must be determined by the essence and object of religion itself.

Generally speaking, we live unworthily, inhumanly, enslaved by temporal things; we are in rebellion against God, we quarrel amongst ourselves, we are self-indulgent—the very opposites of the essentials of what life ought to be, a free submission to God, a unity with our neighbours, a control of our natural inclinations. The task then with which we are faced is the correction of our perverted life.

It is quite within our ability to begin to live justly. The beginning of a free submission to God, of harmony with him, is prayer; the beginning of human concord is kindness and charity; the beginning of the conquest of unsupernaturalized nature is an effort towards control of our bodily appetites: personal religion may be said to consist in prayer, alms-deeds, and fasting.[1]

But man lives a social as well as a personal or private life. He lives in an inhabited world, and he has got to live *in peace* with his fellows.[2] But how can we live in peace amid so much discord, when "the whole world lieth in wickedness" [1 John 5:19]? It is imperative not to regard this wickedness as something *unchangeable*, for wickedness is deceptive and constantly changing, and the essential purpose of the world is not evil but peace, concord, unanimity. The common good, the supreme good and truth of the world, resides in the union of all into one will directed towards the same objects; there is no truth in disagreement and separation, and it is only by co-operation, conscious or unconscious, that the universe is kept in being and carried on. No being can subsist in a state of complete isolation, for such isolation is a falsity, in no degree conformed to the truth of universal unity and peace. This unity is acknowledged, in one way or another, willingly or not, by all who seek for truth. Ask a scientist, and he will tell you that the truth of the world is the unity of its universal mechanism; the philosopher, concerned with abstractions, will say that it is manifested in the unity of logical relations that hold it all together. Fully to understand what the world is, it must be seen as a living unity, a body that is endowed with a soul and that is a vehicle of the Godhead: there is the truth of the world, and there too its beauty; when the different forms of sensible phenomena are properly related to one another the resulting harmony is seen as "the beautiful" (*kosmos*, universe, harmony, beauty).

The governing idea of the world as the expression of peace contains everything that we seek, goodness and truth and beauty. But it is impossible that the world's essential purpose should be found only in the mind; the unity that sustains, carries on, and co-ordinates everything in the universe must be more than an abstract idea. It is, in fact, a living personal power of God, and the unifying essence of this power is manifested in the divine-human person of Christ, "for in him dwelleth all the fulness of the Godhead bodily" (*Col.* ii, 9). Were it not for Christ, God would hardly be a living reality to us; all personal religion tends towards Jesus as towards its centre, and it is on him that universal religion is based.

But even Christ, the God-man, cannot be real to us if we see him as nothing more than a figure of history. He must be revealed in the present as well as in the past, and this contemporary revelation is not, cannot be, dependent on us mediocre individuals: Jesus Christ is shown to us as a living reality, independent of our limited personality, by the Church. Those who think they can dispense with any intermediary and obtain personally a full and definite revelation of Christ are certainly *not yet ripe* for that revelation; what they take to be Christ are the fantasies of their own imagination. We have to look for the fullness of Christ, not within our own limited life, but in his universal sphere, the Church.

The Church as such and in her essence holds out to us here on earth the *divine* reality of Christ. Now in this person of Christ the Godhead has united with his substance the created principle of nature and a human nature properly so called,[3] and this union of natures accomplished in the "spiritual man" Jesus Christ as an *individual personality* ought equally to be represented *collectively* in the mankind whom he has spiritualized: the state, the purely human element in social life, and the individual people, the natural element in that life, ought to be in close union and harmony with the divine element, that is, with the Church. It is the office of the Church to sanctify and, with the help of the Christian state, to transfigure the earthly life of man and of society.

It is in this work of social religion that personal religion reaches its fullness: private prayer is shaped and completed by the Holy Mysteries; private philanthropy finds a support in the institutions of a Christian state and through them joins hands with social justice; and it is only where there is a Christian system of economic life that individuals can have a fundamentally right relation with the things of this world and exercise a perfecting influence over that whole creation which "groaneth and travaileth in pain together" [Rom. 8:22] through our fault. Just as by the deflection of our own will we are made partners in the sin that surrounds us, so our amendment lessens that sin; the proper activity of man's will is to carry out, with God's help, those things which conscience presents to him as right in inward and outward, private and public affairs.

Personal religion and social religion are in complete agreement in calling on every man *to pray to God, to do good to his fellows, to restrain his impulses.* They urge him *to unite himself inwardly with Christ, the living God-man; to recognize Christ's active presence in the Church; to make it his aim to bring Christ's spirit to bear upon every aspect and detail of natural human life, that so mankind may forward the Creator's theandric aim, that earth may be oned with Heaven.*[4]

LAW AND MORALITY: ESSAYS IN APPLIED ETHICS (1897)

On the Death Penalty

1. The institution of the death penalty[5] is the last important position which *barbaric* criminal law (the direct transformation of *uncivilized* custom) still tries to vindicate in contemporary life. The matter can be considered closed. The densely numbered crowd of its defenders is gradually thinning more and more; the ancient half-rotten idol has gathered around itself what is left of them. But the idol is barely supported by two makeshift clay legs: on the theory of retribution and on the theory of deterrence.

2. . . . . In the realm of biblical ideas, a mystical bond shines through between the two grounds for "sanctification": primogeniture and crime, insofar as the firstborn of the human species, Adam, and his firstborn, Cain, were both also the first criminals—one directly against God, the second—against man.[6] Without regard to the theological aspect of the question, we note, however, that precisely the Bible, examined in its entirety, raises human consciousness high above the dark and bloody soil of savage religion

and religious savagery, which pagan nations broke loose from only partially in their higher classes, thanks to the development of Greek philosophy and Roman jurisprudence.

Three major moments relative to our question are marked in the Bible:

(1) *The proclamation of a norm* after the first murder: a criminal, even a fratricide, is not subject to human execution: "And the Lord put a mark on Cain, so that no one would kill him."

(2) *Adaptation of the norm* to the "hard-heartedness of people" after the Flood, which was called forth by extreme displays of evil in human nature: "He who spills the blood of a man—a man will spill his blood." This accommodating statute is developed at great length and made more complex in the Mosaic law.

(3) *A return to the norm* in the prophets and in the Gospels: "Vengeance is mine, says the Lord; I will repay." With what will he repay? "Mercy I desire, and not sacrifice." "I came to recover and save the lost."[7]

The Bible is a complex spiritual organism which developed over a thousand years. It is completely free of external monotony and unilinearity but amazing in its internal unity and in the harmony of the whole. To snatch out arbitrarily from this whole only intermediate parts without a beginning and an end is an insincere and frivolous business; and to rely on the *Bible in general* in favor of the death penalty—attests either to a hopeless incomprehension or a boundless insolence. Those who, like Joseph de Maistre, draw together the concept of the death penalty with the concept of a sin offering, forget that a sin offering has already been brought for all by Christ, that it has abolished all other blood sacrifices, and itself continues only in the bloodless Eucharist—an amazing lapse in consciousness on the part of persons who confess the Christian faith.[8] Indeed, to permit any kind of sin offerings still—means to deny that which was accomplished by Christ, which means—to betray Christianity. . . .

4. "No one," says a noted scholar who is an expert on this question, "even among the most fiery advocates of the death penalty, could in the defense of its necessity muster even the smallest fact, which would demonstrate that its repeal in the aforementioned States (in Tuscany and others) involved an increase in crime; that it made the social order, life and property of citizens less secure. The aforementioned repeal naturally brought the study of the death penalty down from the clouds of theory to the soil of healthy and honest experience" (Kistiakovsky, p. 11). Thanks to this experience, the personal opinion of individual leading minds *about*

the uselessness of the death penalty for the defense of society has now become a positive, experimentally demonstrated truth, and only either ignorance, unscrupulousness, or prejudice can argue against this truth.

But while the death penalty is materially useless for society, it is also spiritually harmful as an immoral action of society itself.

It is a profane, inhumane, and shameful act.

First, the death penalty is profane because in its absoluteness and finality it is an adaptation by human justice of an absolute character, which can belong only to the judgment of God as an expression of divine *omniscience*. After the deliberately and carefully considered expunging of this man from the ranks of the living, society announces: *I know* that this man is absolutely guilty in what took place, that he is absolutely worthless at present, and that he is absolutely irreformable in the future. In fact, nothing fully trustworthy is known to society and its adjudicating organs not only about the future irreformability of this man but also of his past guilt, even regarding the fact itself. Since this has been sufficiently demonstrated by the many judicial errors which have come to light, isn't this a glaringly profane infringement on eternal boundaries and a blind folly of human pride, which puts its relative knowledge and conditional justice in place of omniscient Divine truth? Either the death penalty makes absolutely no sense, or it makes profane sense.

Second, the death penalty is *inhumane*—not from the aspect of sensitivity, but from the aspect of moral principle. The question is completely one of principle: *should* there be any boundary recognized in the human individual regarding external action upon it, something inviolable and not subject to annulment from without? The horror which murder instills sufficiently demonstrates that *there is* such a boundary and that it is connected with the life of man. . . .

The special evil and horror of murder consist, of course, not in the actual taking of life but in the intrinsic renunciation of a basic moral norm, to sever decisively by one's own resolution and action the connection of common human solidarity regarding the actual fellow creature standing before me, who is the same as I am, a bearer of the image and likeness of God. But this *resolution to put an end* to a man more clearly and completely than in simple murder is expressed in the death penalty, where there is absolutely nothing apart from this resolution and carrying it out. Society only has left an *animus interficiendi* in absolutely pure form with respect to the executed criminal, completely free from all those physiological and psychological conditions and motives which darkened and obscured the essence of the matter in the eyes of the criminal himself, whether he committed the murder from calculation of gain or under the influence of a less shameful passion.[9] There can be no such complexities of motivation in the death penalty; the entire business is exposed here: its single goal—to put an end to this man in order that he not be in the world at all. The death penalty is murder, as such, absolute murder that is in principle the denial of a fundamental moral attitude toward man. . . .

While the death penalty is profane and inhumane, it also has a *shameful* nature, which was long ago secured for it by societal sensibility, as is seen in universal contempt for the *executioner*. . . . Here, a man who is unarmed and bound is in advance and wittingly killed by an armed man, risking absolutely nothing and acting exclusively out of lower self-interest. Hence the specifically shameful character of the death penalty and the limitless universal scorn for the executioner.

The direct moral consciousness and feeling so brilliantly expressed in Khomiakov's superb poem *Ritterspruch-Richterspruch* speaks here better than any abstract arguments:

> You fly—a whirlwind, on a warhorse,
> With your daring princely retinue,—
> And the defeated enemy has fallen under horse,
> And as a prisoner lies before you.
> Will you dismount, will you raise your sword?
> Will you tear off the powerless head from its shoulders?
> So, he fought with savage fury of battle.
> And laid waste cities and villages with fire—
> Now he will raise prayerful hands:
> Will you kill? O, shame and disgrace!
> And if there are many of you, will you kill
> The one who is caught in chains,
> Who is trampled in the dust, and head bowed in prayer,
> Not daring to raise it before you?
> So, his soul is black, like the gloom of the grave,
> So, the heart in him is ignoble, like a maggot in pus,
> So, he is all covered in blood and brigandage,
> Now he is powerless, the fire in his gaze is gone,
> He is tied by authority, constrained by fear . . .
> Will you kill? O shame and disgrace![10]

. . . Being contrary to the first principles of morality, the death penalty is at the same time a negation of law at its very essence. We know (see chapter 2) that this essence consists in the balance of two moral interests:

of personal freedom and the common good, from which the direct conclusion is that the latter interest (the common good) can only *restrict* the
former (personal freedom of each), but in no case can have the intention
of its complete abolition, for then obviously any balance would be violated. Therefore, measures against any person whatsoever, inspired by the
interest of the common good, in no way can reach as far as the elimination
of this person, as such, through the deprivation of his life or through the
taking away of his freedom for life. Thus, laws which allow the death penalty, life in exile with hard labor, or life imprisonment cannot be justified
from the juridical point of view, as annulling finally a given lawful relationship through the abolition of one of its subjects. And besides, the assertion that the common good in certain cases requires the ultimate
abolition of a given person also represents an internal logical contradiction. The common good is *common* only because it contains in itself the
good of all individual persons without exception—otherwise it would be
only the good of the majority. From this, it does not follow that the common good consist in the simple arithmetic sum of all particular interests
separately taken, or include in itself the sphere of freedom of each person
in all its infiniteness—this would be another contradiction since these
spheres of personal freedom in themselves can negate one another and really do so. But from the concept of the *common* good follows with logical
necessity that, while limiting particular interests and aspirations precisely
as common (by common boundaries), it in no way can abolish even one
bearer of personal freedom, or subject of rights, taking from him life and
the very possibility of free action. The common good, according to its very
idea, should be the good *of this man too*; but when it deprives him of existence and the possibility of free actions and hence the possibility of any
good whatsoever—by the same token this supposed-common good ceases
being a good for him too and thus loses its common character, itself becomes only a particular interest and therefore also loses its right to restrict personal freedom.

And in this point we see that the moral ideal fully conforms with the
true essence of law. In general, law in its particular character of coercion
toward a minimal good, although it does differ from morality in a narrow
sense, in no case can contradict it, but even in its coercive character serves
the real interest of that same morality. Therefore, if any positive law is
found in contradiction of principle with a moral consciousness of the
Good, then we can be certain in advance that it does not answer the essential requirements of rights either, and the interest of the law relative to
such statutes can in no way consist in their preservation, but only in their
lawful repeal.[11]

RUSSIA AND THE UNIVERSAL CHURCH (1889)

Introduction

A hundred years ago France, the vanguard of humanity, set out to inaugurate a new era with the proclamation of the Rights of Man. Christianity had indeed many centuries earlier conferred upon men not only the right but the power to become the sons of God (*edōken autois exousian tekna Theou genesthai*) (John i.12). But the new proclamation made by France was far from superfluous, for this supreme power of mankind was almost entirely ignored in the social life of Christendom. I am not referring so much to particular acts of injustice as to the principles which were recognised by the public conscience, expressed in the laws of the time, and embodied in its social institutions. It was by legal statute that Christian America robbed the Christian Negroes of all their human rights and ruthlessly abandoned them to the tyranny of their masters who themselves professed the Christian religion. In God-fearing England it was the law which condemned to the gallows the man who stole food from his rich neighbour to save himself from starvation. Lastly, it was the laws and institutions of Poland and of "Holy" Russia which allowed the feudal lord to sell his serfs like cattle.[12] I do not presume to pass judgment on the special circumstances of France, nor to decide whether, as distinguished writers more competent than myself declare,[13] the Revolution did this country more harm than good. But let us not forget that if each nation in history works more or less for the whole world, France has the distinction of having taken a step of universal significance in the political and social sphere.

Though the revolutionary movement destroyed many things that needed to be destroyed, though it swept away many an injustice and swept it away for ever, it nevertheless failed lamentably in the attempt to create a social order founded upon justice. Justice is simply the practical expression and application of truth; and the starting-point of the revolutionary movement was false. The declaration of the Rights of Man could only provide a positive principle for social reconstruction if it was based upon a true conception of Man himself. That of the revolutionaries is well-known: they perceived in Man nothing but abstract individuality, a rational being destitute of all positive content.

I do not propose to unmask the internal contradictions of this revolutionary individualism nor to show how this abstract "Man" was suddenly transformed into the no less abstract "Citizen", how the free sovereign individual found himself doomed to be the defenseless slave and victim of the absolute State or "Nation", that is to say, of a group of obscure persons borne to the surface of public life by the eddies of revolution and rendered the more ferocious by the consciousness of their own intrinsic nonentity. No doubt it would be highly interesting and instructive to follow the thread of logic which connects the doctrines of 1789 with the events of 1793. But I believe it to be still more important to recognise that the *prōton pseudos*, the basic falsehood, of the Revolution—the conception of the individual man as a being complete in and for himself—that this false notion of individualism was not the invention of the revolutionaries or of their spiritual forbears, the Encyclopaedists, but was the logical, though unforeseen, issue of an earlier pseudo-Christian or semi-Christian doctrine which has been the root cause of all the anomalies in the past history and present state of Christendom.

Men have imagined that the acknowledgment of the divinity of Christ relieves them of the obligation of taking His words seriously. They have twisted certain texts of the Gospel so as to get out of them the meaning they want, while they have conspired to pass over in silence other texts which do not lend themselves to such treatment. The precept "Render to Caesar the things that are Caesar's, and to God the things that are God's" [Matt. 22:21, Mark 12:17, Luke 20:25] is constantly quoted to sanction an order of things which gives Caesar all and God nothing. The saying "My Kingdom is not of this world" [John 18:36] is always being used to justify and confirm the paganism of our social and political life, as though Christian society were destined to belong to this world and not to the Kingdom of Christ. On the other hand the saying "All power is given Me in heaven and earth" [Matt. 28:18] is never quoted. Men are ready to accept Christ as sacrificing Priest and atoning Victim; but they do not want Christ the King. His royal dignity has been ousted by every kind of pagan despotism, and Christian peoples have taken up the cry of the Jewish rabble: "We have no king but Caesar!" [John 19:15]. Thus history has witnessed, and we are still witnessing, the curious phenomenon of a society which professes Christianity as its religion but remains pagan not merely in its life but in the very basis of that life.

This dichotomy is not so much a logical *non sequitur* as a moral failure. That is obvious from the hypocrisy and sophism which are characteristic of the arguments commonly used to justify this state of affairs. "Slavery and severe hardship," said a bishop renowned in Russia thirty years ago, "are not contrary to the spirit of Christianity; for physical suffering is not a hindrance to the salvation of the soul, which is the one and only end of our religion." As though the infliction of physical suffering by a man on his fellow-men did not imply in him a moral depravity and an act of injustice and cruelty which were certainly imperilling the salvation of *his* soul!

Granted even—though the supposition is absurd—that a Christian society can be insensible to the sufferings of the oppressed, the question remains whether it can be indifferent to the sin of the oppressors.

Economic slavery, even more than slavery properly so called, has found its champions in the Christian world. Society and the State, they maintain, are in no way bound to take general and regular measures against pauperism; voluntary almsgiving is enough; did not Christ say that there would always be the poor on earth? Yes, there will always be the poor; there will also always be the sick, but does that prove the uselessness of health services? Poverty in itself is no more an evil than sickness; the evil consists in remaining indifferent to the sufferings of one's neighbour. And it is not a question only of the poor; the rich also have a claim on our compassion. These poor rich! We do everything to develop their bump of acquisitiveness, and then we expect them to enter the Kingdom of God through the imperceptible opening of individual charity. Besides, it is well known that authoritative scholars see in the phrase "the eye of a needle" simply a literal translation of the Hebrew name given to one of the gates of Jerusalem (*negeb-ha-khammath* or *khur-ha-khammath*) which it was difficult for camels to pass through. Surely then it is not the infinitesimal contribution of personal philanthropy which the Gospel enjoins upon the rich, but rather the narrow and difficult, but nevertheless practicable, way of social reform.

This desire to limit the social action of Christianity to individual charity, this attempt to deprive the Christian moral code of its binding character and its positive legal sanction is a modern version of that ancient Gnostic antithesis (the system of Marcion in particular) so often anathematised by the Church. That all human relationships should be governed by charity and brotherly love is undoubtedly the express will of God and the end of His creation; but in historic reality, as in the Lord's Prayer, the fulfillment of the divine will on earth is only realised after the hallowing of God's Name and the coming of His Kingdom. The Name of God is Truth; His Kingdom is Justice. It follows that the knowledge of the truth and the practice of justice are necessary conditions for the triumph of evangelical charity in human society.

In truth all are one; and God, the absolute Unity, is all in all. But this divine Unity is hidden from our view by the world of evil and illusion, the result of universal human sin. The basic condition of this world is the division and isolation of the parts of the Great Whole; and even Man, who should have been the unifying rationale of the material universe, finds himself split up and scattered over the earth, and has been unable by his own efforts to achieve more than a partial and unstable unity, the universal monarchy of paganism. This monarchy, first represented by Tiberius and Nero, received its true unifying principle when "grace and truth" were manifested in Jesus Christ [John 1:17]. Once united to God, the human race recovered its own unity. But this unity had to be three-fold to be complete; it had to realise its ideal perfection on the basis of a divine fact and in the midst of the life of mankind. Since mankind is objectively separated from the divine unity, this unity must in the first place be given to us as an objective reality independent of ourselves—the Kingdom of God coming amongst us, the external, objective Church. But once reunited to this external unity, men must translate it into action, they must assimilate it by their own efforts—the Kingdom of God is to be taken by force, and the men of violence possess it [Matt. 11:12]. At first manifested *for* us and then *by* us, the Kingdom of God must finally be revealed *in* us in all its intrinsic, absolute perfection as love, peace and joy in the Holy Spirit.

Thus the Church Universal (in the broad sense of the word) develops as a threefold union of the divine and the human: there is the priestly union, in which the divine element, absolute and unchangeable, predominates and forms the Church properly so called (the Temple of God); there is the kingly union, in which the human element predominates and which forms the Christian State (the Church as the living Body of God); and there is lastly the prophetic union, in which the divine and the human must penetrate one another in free mutual interaction and so form the perfect Christian society (the Church as the Spouse of God).

The moral basis of the priestly union, or of the Church in the strict sense of the word, is faith and religious devotion; the kingly union of the Christian State is based on law and justice; while the element proper to the prophetic union or the perfect society is freedom and love.

The Church, in the narrower sense, represented by the hierarchy, reunites mankind to God by the profession of the true faith and the grace of the sacraments. But if the faith communicated by the Church to Christian humanity is a living faith, and if the grace of the sacraments is an effectual grace, the resultant union of the divine and the human cannot be limited to the special domain of religion, but must extend to all Man's common relationships and must regenerate and transform his social and political life. Here opens up a field of action which is man's own proper sphere. The divine-human action is no longer an accomplished fact as in the priestly Church, but a task awaiting fulfilment, the task of making the divine Truth a reality in human society, of putting Truth into practice; and Truth, expressed in practice, is called Justice.

Truth is the absolute existence of all in unity; it is the universal solidarity which exists eternally in God, but which has been lost by the natural man and recovered in principle by Christ, the spiritual Man. It remains for human activity to continue the unifying work of the God-Man by contesting the world with the contrary principle of egoism and division. Each single being, whether nation, class, or individual, in so far as it asserts its own individuality in isolation from the divine-human sum of things, is acting against Truth; and Truth, if it is alive in us, must react and manifest itself as Justice. Thus having recognised the universal solidarity, the All-in-One, as Truth, and having put it into practice as Justice, regenerate Man will be able to perceive it as his inmost essence and to enjoy it fully in the spirit of freedom and love.[14]

THE JUSTIFICATION OF THE GOOD (1897)

The Economic Question from the Moral Point of View

V In opposition to the alleged economic harmony, facts compel us to admit that starting with private material interest as the purpose of labour we arrive at universal discord and destruction instead of universal happiness. If, however, the principle and the purpose of labour is found in the idea of the common good, understood in the true moral sense—*i.e.* as the good of all and each and not of the majority only—that idea will also contain the satisfaction of every private interest within proper limits.

From the moral point of view every man, whether he be an agricultural labourer, a writer, or a banker, ought to work with a feeling that his work is useful to all, and with a desire for it to be so; he ought to regard it as a duty, as a fulfilment of the law of God and a service to the universal welfare of his fellow-men. But just because this duty is universal, it presupposes that every one else must regard the person in question in the same way, *i.e.* to treat him not as a means only but as an end or purpose of the activity of all. The duty of society is to recognise and to secure to each of its members the *right* to enjoy unmolested *worthy* human existence both for himself and his family. Worthy existence is compatible with voluntary poverty, such as St. Francis preached and as is practised by our wandering pilgrims; but it is incompatible with work which reduces all the significance of man to being simply a means for producing or transferring material wealth. Here are some instances.

"We watch the *kriuchniks* [stevedores] at work: the poor half-naked Tatars strain every nerve. It is painful to see the bent back flatten out all of a sudden under a weight of eight to eighteen puds (the last figure is not exaggerated). This terrible work is paid at the rate of five roubles per thousand puds.[15] The most a *kriuchnik* can earn in the twenty-four hours is one rouble, and that if he works like an ox and overstrains himself. Few can endure more than ten years of such labour, and the two-legged beasts of burden become deformed or paralytic" (*Novoe Vremya*, N. 7356). Those who have not seen the Volga *kriuchniks* are sure to have seen the porters in big hotels who, breathless and exhausted, drag to the fourth or fifth floor boxes weighing several hundredweight. And this in our age of machines and all sorts of contrivances! No one seems to be struck by the obvious absurdity. A visitor arrives at an hotel with luggage. To walk up the stairs would be a useful exercise for him, but instead he gets into a lift, while his things, for which, one would have thought, the lift was expressly meant, are loaded on the back of the porter, who thus proves to be not even an instrument of another man but an instrument of his things—the means of a means!

Labour which is exclusively and crudely mechanical and involves too great a strain of the muscular force is incompatible with human dignity. But equally incompatible with it and equally immoral is work which, though in itself not heavy or degrading, lasts all day long and takes up *all* the time and *all* the forces of the person, so that the few hours of leisure are necessarily devoted to physical rest, and neither time nor energy is left for thoughts and interests of the ideal or spiritual order.[16] In addition to hours of leisure, there are, of course, entire days of rest—Sundays and other holidays. But the exhausting and stupefying physical work of the week produces in holiday time a natural reaction—a craving to plunge into dissipation and to forget oneself, and the days of rest are devoted to the satisfaction of that craving.

"Let us not, however, dwell on the impression which individual facts susceptible of observation produce upon us, even though such facts be numerous. Let us turn to statistics and inquire as to how far wages satisfy the necessary wants of the workers. Leaving aside the rate of wages in the different industries, the quality of food, the size of the dwelling, etc., we will only ask of statistics the question as to the relation between the length of human life and the occupation pursued. The answer is as follows: Shoemakers live on the average to the age of 49; printers, 48.3; tailors, 46.6; joiners, 44.7; blacksmiths, 41.8; turners, 41.6; masons, 33. And the average length of life of civil servants, capitalists, clergymen, wholesale merchants, is 60–69 years.[17] Now take the figures referring to the death-rate in relation to the size of the dwellings and the amount of rent in the different parts of town. It will be seen that in parts of the town with a poor population, belonging chiefly to the working class and paying low rents, mortality is far higher than in the neighbourhood with a relatively larger number of rich people. For Paris this relation was established by Villarmé as early as the 'twenties of the present century. He calculated that during the five years from 1822 to 1826, in the II. arrondissement of Paris, where the average rent per flat was 605 francs, there was one death per 71 inhabitants, while in the arrondissement XII., where the average rent was 148 francs, there was one death per 44 inhabitants. Similar data are at hand for many other towns, Petersburg among them."[18] Hence the following true conclusion is deduced: "If a workman is not regarded as a means of production, but is recognised, like every other human being, to be a free agent and an end in himself, the average forty years of life cannot be regarded as normal, while men belonging to richer classes live on the average till sixty or seventy years. This life, the longest possible under the social conditions of the present day, must be regarded as normal. All deviation below this average, unless it can be ascribed to the peculiarities of the particular work in question, must be entirely put down to excessive labour and insufficient income which does not allow to satisfy the most essential needs and the minimum demands of hygiene with regard to food, clothing, and housing."[19]

The absolute value of man is based, as we know, upon the *possibility* inherent in his reason and his will of infinitely approaching perfection or, according to the patristic expression, the possibility of becoming divine (*theōsis*). This possibility does not pass into actuality completely and immediately, for if it did man would be already equal to God—which is not the case. The inner potentiality *becomes* more and more actual, and can only do so under definite real conditions. If an ordinary man is left for many years on an uninhabited island or in strict solitary confinement he cannot improve morally or intellectually, and indeed, exhibits rapid and obvious regress towards the brutal stage. Strictly speaking, the same is true of a man wholly absorbed in physical labour. Even if he does not deteriorate he is certainly unable to think of actively realising his highest significance as man. The moral point of view demands, then, that everyone should have the means of existence (*e.g.* clothes and a warm and airy dwelling) and sufficient physical *rest* secured to him, and that he should also be able to enjoy *leisure* for the sake of his spiritual development. This and *this alone* is *absolutely* essential for every peasant and workman; *anything above this is from the evil one.*[20]

Morality and Legal Justice

I The *absolute* moral principle, the *demand*, namely, or the *commandment* to be perfect as our Father in heaven is perfect, or to realise in ourselves the image and likeness of God, already contains in its very nature the recognition of the *relative* element in morality. For it is clear that the demand for perfection can only be addressed to a being who is imperfect; urging him to *become* like the higher being, the commandment presupposes the lower stages and the relative degrees of advance. Thus, the absolute moral principle or the perfect good is for us, to use Hegel's language, a unity of itself and its other, a synthesis of the absolute and the relative. The existence of the relative or the imperfect, as distinct from the absolute good, is a fact not to be got over, and to deny it, to *confuse* the two terms, or, with the help of dialectical tricks and on the strength of mystical emotions, to affirm them as identical, would be false. Equally false, however, is the opposite course—the *separation*, namely, of the relative from the absolute, as of two wholly distinct spheres which have nothing in common. From this dualistic point of view man himself, whose striving towards the absolute is inseparably connected with relative conditions, proves to be the incarnation of absurdity. The only rational point of view, which both reason and conscience compel us to adopt, consists in recognising that the actual duality between the relative and the absolute resolves itself for us into a free and complete unity (but not by any means into an empty identity of indifference) through the real and moral process of approaching perfection—a process ranging from the rigid stone to the glory and freedom of the sons of God.

At each stage the relative is connected with the absolute as a means for *concretely* bringing about the perfection of all; and this connection justifies the lesser good as a condition of the greater. At the same time it justifies the absolute good itself, which would not be absolute if it could not connect with itself or include in one way or another all concrete relations. And indeed, nowhere in the world accessible to us do we find the two terms in separation or in their bare form. Everywhere the absolute principle is clothed with relative forms, and the relative is inwardly connected with the absolute and held together by it. The difference lies simply in the comparative predominance of one or the other aspect. . . .

V The fact that we speak of *moral right* and moral duty, on the one hand proves the absence of any fundamental opposition or incompatibility of the moral and the juridical principles, and, on the other, indicates an essential difference between them. In designating a given right (*e.g.* the right of my enemy to my love) as *moral* only, we imply that in addition to the moral there exists other rights, *i.e.* rights in a more restricted sense, or that there exists *right as such*, which is not directly and immediately characterised as moral. Take, on the one hand, the duty of loving our enemies and their corresponding right to our love, and on the other, take the duty to pay one's debts, or the duty not to rob and murder one's neighbours and their corresponding right not to be robbed, murdered, or deceived by us. It is obvious that there is an essential difference between the two kinds of relation, and that only the second of them falls within the scope of justice in the narrow sense of the term.

The difference can be reduced to three main points:

(1) A purely moral demand, such, *e.g.*, as the love for one's enemies, is unlimited or all-embracing in nature; it presupposes moral perfection, or, at any rate, an unlimited striving towards perfection. Every limitation admitted as a matter of *principle* is opposed to the nature of the moral commandment and undermines its dignity and significance. If a person gives up the absolute moral ideal as a principle, he gives up morality itself and leaves the moral ground. Juridical law, on the contrary, is essentially limited, as is clearly seen in all cases of its application. In the pace of perfection it demands the lowest, the minimum degree of morality, that is, simply, actual restraint of certain manifestations of the immoral will. This distinction, however, is not an opposition leading to real conflict. From the moral point of view it cannot be denied that the demand conscientiously to fulfil monetary obligations, to abstain from murder, robbery, etc., is a demand for what is good—though extremely elementary—and not for what is evil. It is clear that if we ought to love our enemies, it goes without saying that we ought to respect the life and property of all fellow-men. The higher commandments cannot be fulfilled without observing the lower. As to the juridical side of the matter, though the civil or the penal law does not demand the supreme moral perfection, it is not opposed to it. Forbidding every one to murder or be fraudulent, it cannot, and indeed has no need to, prevent any one from loving his enemies. Thus with regard to this point (which in certain moral theories is erroneously taken to be the only important one), the relation between the principles of the practical life may be only expressed by saying that *legal justice is the lowest limit or the minimum degree of morality.*

(2) The unlimited character of the purely moral demands leads to another point of difference. The way in which such demands are to be fulfilled is not definitely prescribed, nor is it limited to any concrete external manifestations or material actions. The commandment to love one's enemies does not indicate, except as an example, what precisely we ought to do in virtue of that love, *i.e.* which particular actions we ought to perform and from which to abstain. At the same time, if love is expressed by means of definite actions, the moral commandment cannot be regarded as already fulfilled by these actions and as demanding nothing further. The task

of fulfilling the commandment, which is an expression of the absolute perfection, remains infinite. Juridical laws, on the contrary, prescribe or prohibit perfectly definite external actions, with the performance or non-performance of which the law is satisfied and demands nothing further. If I produce in due time the money I am owing, and pass it to my creditor, if I do not murder or rob any one, etc., the law is satisfied and wants nothing more from me. This difference between the moral and the juridical law once more involves no contradiction. The demand for the moral inner disposition, so far from excluding actions, directly presupposes them as its own proof or justification. No one would believe in the inward goodness of a man if it never showed itself in any works of mercy. On the other hand, the request to perform definite actions is in no way opposed to the inner states corresponding to them, though it does not demand them. Both the moral and the juridical laws are concerned with the inner being of man, with his will; but while the first takes this will in its universality and en-tirety, the second has only to do with particular expressions of it in respect of certain external facts, which fall within the province of justice in the narrow sense,—such as the inviolability of the life and property of each person, etc. What is of importance from the juridical point of view is pre-cisely the objective expression of our will in committing or in refraining from certain actions. This is another essential characteristic of legal justice, and, in addition to the original definition of it as a certain minimum of mo-rality, we may now say that legal justice is the demand for the *realisation* of this minimum, *i.e.* for *carrying out a certain minimum of the good*, or, what is the same thing, for doing away with a certain amount of evil. Morality in the strict sense is immediately concerned, not with the external realisation of the good, but with its inner existence in the heart of man.

(3) This second distinction involves a third one. The demand for moral perfection as an inner state presupposes free or voluntary fulfilment. Not only physical but even psychological compulsion is here, from the nature of the case, both undesirable and impossible. External realisation of a certain uniform order, on the contrary, admits of direct or indirect *com-pulsion.* And in so far as the direct and immediate purpose of legal jus-tice is precisely the realisation or the external embodiment of a certain good—*e.g.* of public safety—in so far the compelling character of the law is a necessity; for no genuine person could seriously maintain that by means of verbal persuasion alone all murders, frauds, etc., could be im-mediately stopped.

VI Combining the three characteristics indicated we obtain the follow-ing definition of legal justice in its relation to morality: *legal justice is a*

*compulsory demand for the realisation of a definite minimum of the good,
or for a social order which excludes certain manifestations of evil.*

The question has now to be asked, what is the ground for such a demand,
and in what way is this compulsory order compatible with the purely moral
order, which apparently by its very nature excludes all compulsion. . . .

The moral law has been given to man "that he might live thereby"; and if
human society did not exist, morality would remain merely an abstract
idea. The existence of society, however, depends not on the perfection of
some, but on the security of all. This security is not guaranteed by the
moral law, which is non-existent for persons in whom anti-social instincts
predominate, but it is safeguarded by the compulsory law which has actual power over every one. To appeal to the gracious power of Providence
to restrain and exhort lunatics and criminals is sheer blasphemy. It is impious to lay upon the Deity that which can be successfully performed by a
good legal system.

The moral principle demands, then, that men should freely seek perfection. To this end the existence of society is necessary. Society cannot exist
if each person wishing to do so may, without let or hindrance, rob and
murder his neighbours. Hence the compulsory law, which actually prevents these extreme expressions of the evil will, is a *necessary condition of
moral perfection*; as such it is demanded by the moral principle itself,
though it is not a direct expression of it.[21]

The Moral Organisation of Humanity as a Whole

XIII . . . *Just as the Church is collectively organised piety, so the state is collectively organised pity.* To affirm, therefore, that from its very nature the
Christian religion is opposed to the state is to affirm that the Christian religion is opposed to pity. In truth, however, the Gospel not merely insists
upon the morally binding character of pity or altruism, but decidedly confirms the view, expressed already in the Old Testament, that there can be
no true piety apart from pity: "I will have mercy and not sacrifice" [Matt.
9:13, 12:7; cf. Hos. 6:6].

If, however, pity be admitted in principle, it is logically inevitable to admit also the historical organisation of social forces and activities, which
raises pity from the stage of a powerless and limited feeling and gives it actuality, wide application, and means of development. From the point of
view of pity it is impossible to reject the institution owing to which one
can *practically pity*, i.e. *give help and protection* to tens and hundreds of
millions of men instead of dozens or at most hundreds of people.

The definition of the state (so far as its moral significance is concerned)
as organised pity can only be rejected through misconception. Some of

these misconceptions must be considered before we go on to deal with the conception of the Christian state.

XIV It is urged that the stern and often cruel character of the state obviously contradicts the definition of it as organised pity. But this objection is based on a confusion between the necessary and sensible severity and useless and arbitrary cruelty. The first is not opposed to pity, and the second, being an abuse, *is opposed to the very meaning of the state*, and therefore does not contradict the definition of the state—of the normal state, of course—as organised pity. The supposed contradiction is based upon grounds as superficial as the argument that the senseless cruelty of an unsuccessful surgical operation and the sufferings of the patient in the case even of a successful operation are in obvious contradiction to the idea of surgery as a beneficent art helpful to man in certain bodily sufferings. It is obvious that such representatives of state authority as Ivan the Terrible are as little evidence against the altruistic basis of the state, as bad surgeons are against the usefulness of surgery. I am aware that an educated reader may well feel insulted at being reminded of such elementary truths, but if he is acquainted with the recent movement of thought in Russia he will not hold me responsible for the insult.[22]

But, it will be maintained, even the most normal state is inevitably pitiless. In pitying peaceful people whom it defends against men of violence, it is bound to treat the latter without pity. Such *one-sided* pity is out of keeping with the moral ideal. This is indisputable, but again it says nothing against our definition of the state, for, in the first place, even one-sided pity is pity and not anything else; and secondly, even the normal state is not by any means an expression of the moral ideal already attained, but only one of the *chief means* necessary for its attainment. The ideal condition of mankind, or the Kingdom of God, when *attained*, is obviously incompatible with the state, but it is also incompatible with pity. When everything will once more be good there will be no one to pity. And so long as there are men to be pitied, there are men to be defended; and the moral demand for organising such protection efficiently and on a wide scale—*i.e.* the moral significance of the state—remains in force. As for the pitilessness of the state to those from whom or against whom it has to defend the peaceful society, it is not anything fatal or inevitable; and although it undoubtedly is a fact, it is not an unchangeable fact. In point of history there is no doubt that the relation of the state towards its enemies is becoming less cruel, and consequently more merciful. In old days they used to be put to painful death together with their family and relatives (as is still the case in China). Later, everyone had to answer for himself, and subsequently the very character of the responsibility has changed. Criminals have ceased to be tormented solely for the sake of inflicting pain; and at the present time the positive task of helping them morally is recognised. What can be the ultimate reason of such a change? When the state limits or abolishes the penalty of death, abolishes torture and corporal punishment, is concerned with improving prisons and places of exile, it is obvious that in pitying and protecting peaceful citizens who suffer from crimes, it begins to extend its pity to the opposite side also—to the criminals themselves. The reference, therefore, to the one-sided pity is beginning to lose force as a fact. And it is through the state alone that the organisation of pity ceases to be one-sided, since the human crowd is still for the most part guided in its relation to the enemies of society by the old pitiless maxims, "to the dog, a dog's death"; "the thief deserves all he gets"; "as a warning to others," etc. Such maxims are losing their practical force precisely owing to the state, which is in this case more free from partiality either to the one side or the other. Restraining with an authoritative hand the vindictive instincts of the crowd, ready to tear the criminal to pieces, the state at the same time never renounces the humane duty to oppose crimes,—as the strange moralists, who in truth pity only the aggressive, violent, and rapacious, and are utterly indifferent to their victims, would have it do. This indeed is a case of one-sided pity!

XV Our definition of state may lead to a less crude misconception on the part of the jurists, who regard the state as the embodiment of legality as an absolutely independent principle, distinct from morality in general and from motives of pity in particular. The true distinction between legal justice and morality has already been indicated. It does not destroy the connection between them; on the contrary, it is due to that connection. If this distinction is to be replaced by separation and opposition, an unconditional principle must be found which shall ultimately determine every legal relation as such and be altogether outside of, and as far as possible removed from, the moral sphere.

Such an a-moral and even anti-moral principle is to be found in the first place in *might* or force: *Macht geht vor Recht*. That in the order of history relations based upon right follow those based upon force is as unquestionable as the fact that in the history of our planet the organic life appeared after the inorganic and on the basis of it—which does not prove, of course, that inorganic matter is the specific principle of the organic forms as such. The play of natural forces in humanity is simply the *material* for relations determined by the conception of right and not the principle of such relations, since otherwise there could be no distinction between right and rightlessness. Right means the *limitation* of might, and the whole point is the *nature* of the limitation. Similarly, morality might be defined as *the overcoming of evil*, which does not imply that evil is the principle of morality.

We shall not advance any further in the definition of right if we replace the conception of might, derived from the physical sphere, by the more human conception of freedom. That individual freedom lies at the basis of all relations determined by law there can be no doubt, but is it really the unconditional principle of legality? There are two reasons why this cannot be the case. In the first place, because in reality it is *not unconditional*, and, secondly, because it is not the determining principle of *legality*. With regard to the first point, I mean not that human freedom is never unconditional, but that it is not unconditional in that sphere of concrete relations in which and for the sake of which law exists. Suppose that some man living in the flesh on earth actually possessed absolute freedom, that is, that he could by the act of his will alone, independently of any external circumstances and necessary intermediate processes, accomplish everything he wished. It is obvious that such a man would stand outside the sphere of relations determined by legality. If his unconditionally free will determined itself on the side of evil, no external action could limit it; it would be inaccessible to law and authority. And if it were determined on the side of the good it would make all law and all authority superfluous.

It is then irrelevant to speak of unconditional freedom in this connection, since it belongs to quite a different sphere of relations. Legality is concerned only with limited and conditional freedom, and the question is precisely as to what limitations or conditions are lawful. The liberty of one person is limited by the liberty of another, but not every such limitation is consistent with the principle of legality. If the freedom of one man is limited by the freedom of his neighbour who is free to wring his neck or chain him up at his pleasure, there can be no question of legality at all, and in any case such a limitation of freedom shows no specific characteristics of the principle of legality as such. These characteristics must be sought not in the mere fact of the limitation of freedom, but in the equal and universal character of the limitation. If the freedom of one is limited to the same extent as the freedom of the other, or if the free activity of each meets with a restriction that is common to all, then only is the limitation of freedom determined by the conception of law.

The principle of legality is then freedom within the limits of equality, or freedom conditioned by equality—consequently a conditional freedom. But

the equality which determines it is not an absolutely independent principle
either. The essential characteristic of the legal norms is that, in addition to
equality, they should necessarily answer, too, the demand for *justice*. Although these two ideas are akin, they are far from being identical. When
the Pharaoh issued a law commanding to put to death all the Jewish new-
born babes, this law was certainly not unjust on account of the unequal
treatment of the Jewish and the Egyptian babes. And if the Pharaoh subsequently gave orders to put to death all new-born infants and not only the
Jewish ones, no one would venture to call this new law just, although it would
satisfy the demand for equality. Justice is not mere equality, but *equality in
fulfilling that which is right*. A just debtor is not one who equally refuses to
pay all his creditors but who equally pays them all. A just father is not one
who is equally indifferent to all his children but who shows equal love for all
of them.

Equality, then, can be just or unjust, and it is the just equality or, in the
last resort, justice that determines the legal norms. The conception of justice at once introduces us into the moral sphere. And in that sphere we
know that each virtue is not in a cage by itself, but all of them, justice
among them, are different modifications of one or, rather, of the threefold
principle which determines our rightful relation to everything. And since
justice is concerned with man's moral interaction with his fellow-beings,
it is merely a species of the moral motive which lies at the basis of inter-
human relations, namely of pity: *justice is pity equally applied*.

In so far then as legality is determined by justice it is essentially related
to the moral sphere. All definitions of law which try to separate it from
morality leave its real nature untouched. Thus, in addition to the definition already mentioned, Jhering's famous definition declares that "law is a
protected or safeguarded interest."[23] There can be no doubt that law does
defend interest, but not every interest. It obviously defends only the just
interests or, in other words, it defends every interest in so far as it is just.
What, however, is meant by justice in this connection? To say that a just
interest is an interest safe-guarded by law is to be guilty of the crudest
possible logical circle which can only be avoided if justice be once more
taken in its essential, *i.e.* in its moral, sense. This does not prevent us from
recognising that the moral principle itself, so far as the inevitable conditions of its existence are concerned, is realised in different ways, and to a
greater or lesser degree. For instance there is the distinction between the
external, formal, or strictly-legal justice and the inner, essential, or purely-
moral justice, the supreme and ultimate standard of right and wrong being one and the same—namely, the moral principle. Possible conflict
between "outer" and "inner" justice in particular cases is in itself no

argument against their being essentially one, since similar conflict may arise in the carrying out of the simplest and most fundamental moral demands. Thus, for instance, pity may demand that I should save two men who are drowning, but being unable to save both, I have to choose between the two. The cases of difficult choice between complex applications of legal justice and morality in the strict sense are no proof of there being any essential and irreducible opposition between the two. The argument that the conceptions of justice and morality alter in the course of history is equally unconvincing. It might carry some weight if the rights and laws remained meanwhile unchanged. In truth, however, they change even more according to place and time. What conclusion, then, are we to adopt? There is change in the particular conceptions of justice, there is change in the rights and laws, but one thing remains unchangeable: the demand that the rights and laws should be just. The inner dependence of legal forms upon morality—independently of all external conditions—remains a fact. To avoid this conclusion one would have to go very far—to the country, seen by the pilgrim women in Ostrovsky's play, where lawful requests to Mahmut of Persia and Mahmut of Turkey were to begin by the phrase "Judge me, O thou *unjust* judge." [24]

XVI The connection of right with morality makes it possible to speak of the Christian state. It would be unjust to maintain that in pre-Christian times the state had no moral foundation. In the kingdoms of Judaea and of Israel, the prophets directly put moral demands to the state, and reproached it for not fulfilling these demands. In the pagan world it is sufficient to mention Theseus, for instance, who at the risk of his life freed his subjects from the cannibalistic tribute to Crete, in order to recognise that here too the fundamental moral motive of the state was pity, demanding active help to the injured and the suffering. The difference between the Christian and the pagan state is not then in their natural basis but in something else. From the Christian point of view the state is only a part in the organisation of the collective man—a part conditioned by another higher part, the Church, which consecrates the state in its work of serving indirectly in its own worldly sphere and by its own means the unconditional purpose which the Church directly puts before it—to prepare humanity and the whole earth for the Kingdom of God. From this follow the two chief tasks of the state—the conservative and the progressive: to *preserve the foundations of social life apart from which humanity could not exist*, and *to improve the conditions of its existence* by furthering the free development of all human powers which are to be the instrument of the future perfection, and apart from which the Kingdom of God could not be realised in humanity. It is clear that just as without the conservative activity of the state humanity would fall apart and there would be *no one left* to enter the fulness of life, so without its progressive activity mankind would always remain at the same stage of the historical process, would never attain the power finally to receive or to reject the Kingdom of God, and therefore there would be *nothing to live for.*

In paganism it was the conservative task of the state that was exclusively predominant. Although the state furthered historical progress, it did so involuntarily and unconsciously. The supreme purpose of action was not put by the agents themselves, it was not *their* purpose since they had not yet heard "the gospel of the kingdom." The progress itself, therefore, although it formally differed from the gradual perfecting of the kingdoms of the physical nature did not really have a purely-human character: it is unworthy of man to move in spite of himself to a purpose he does not know. God's word gives a beautiful image of the great heathen kingdoms as powerful and wonderful *beasts* which rapidly appear and disappear. The natural, earthly men have no final significance, and cannot have it; and the state, created by such men, is their collective embodiment. But the pagan state, conditional and transitory in nature, affirmed itself as unconditional. Pagans began by deifying individual *bodies* (astral, vegetable, animal, and especially human) in the multitude of their various gods, and they ended by deifying the collective body—the state (cult of the kings in the Eastern kingdoms, the apotheosis of the Roman emperors).

The pagans erred not in ascribing positive significance to the state, but only in thinking that it possessed that significance *on its own account.* This was obviously untrue. Neither the individual nor the collective body of man has life on its own account but receives it from the spirit that inhabits it. This is clearly proved by the fact of the decomposition both of the individual and of the collective bodies. The perfect body is that in which dwells the spirit of God. Christianity, therefore, demands not that we should reject or limit the power of the state, but that we should fully recognise the principle which alone may render the significance of the state actually complete—namely, its moral solidarity with the cause of the Kingdom of God on earth, all worldly purposes being inwardly subordinated to the one spirit of Christ.

XVII The question as to the relation of the Church to the state, which has arisen in Christian times, can be solved in principle from the point of view here indicated. The Church is, as we know, a divinely-human organisation, morally determined by piety. From the nature of the case the Divine principle decidedly predominates in the Church over the human. In the relation between them the first is pre-eminently active and the second preeminently passive. This obviously must be the case when the human will is in direct correlation with the Divine. The active manifestation of the human will, demanded by the Deity itself, is only possible in the worldly sphere collectively represented by the state, which had reality previously to the revelation of the Divine principle, and is in no direct dependence upon it. The *Christian* state is related to the Deity, as the Church is; it too is in a certain sense an organisation of the God-in-man, but in it the human element predominates. This is only possible because the Divine principle is realised not *in* the state, but *for* it in the Church. So that in the state the Divine principle gives *full play* to the human and allows it *independently* to serve the supreme end. From the moral point of view both the independent activity of man and his absolute submission to the Deity as such are equally necessary. This antinomy can only be solved and the two positions united by distinguishing the two spheres of life (the religious and the political), and their two immediate motives (piety and pity), corresponding to the difference in the immediate object of action, the final purpose being one and the same. Pious attitude towards a perfect God demands pity for men. The Christian church demands a Christian state. Here as elsewhere *separation* instead of *distinction* leads to *confusion*, and confusion to dissension and perdition. Complete separation of the Church from the state compels the Church to do one of two things. It either has to renounce all active service of the good and to give itself up to quietism and indifference—which is contrary to the spirit of Christ; or, zealous actively to prepare the world for the coming of God's kingdom, but, in its separation and alienation from the state, having no means at its command for carrying out its spiritual activity, the Church, in the person of its authoritative representatives has itself to seize the concrete instruments of worldly activity, to interfere in all earthly affairs and, absorbed in the question of means, forget its original purpose—an unquestionably pure and high one—more and more. Were such confusion allowed to become permanent, the Church would lose the very ground of its existence. The separation proves to be no less harmful to the other side. The state separated from the Church either gives up spiritual interests altogether, loses its supreme consecration and dignity, as well as the moral respect and the material submission of its subjects, or, conscious of the importance of the spiritual interests for the life of man, but, in its separation from the Church, having no competent and independent institution to which it could entrust the supreme care of the spiritual good of its subjects,—the task of preparing the nations for the Kingdom of God,—it decides to take that task upon itself. To do so consistently the state would have to assume *ex officio* the supreme spiritual authority—which would be a mad and dangerous usurpation recalling the "man of lawlessness" [2 Thess. 2:3] of the last days. It is clear that in forgetting its filial attitude towards the Church, the state would be acting in its own name, and not in the name of the Father.

The normal relation, then, between the state and the Church is this. *The state recognises the supreme spiritual authority of the universal Church, which indicates the general direction of the goodwill of mankind and the final purpose of its historical activity. The Church leaves to the state full power to bring lawful worldly interests into conformity with this supreme will and to harmonise political relations and actions with the requirements of this supreme purpose. The Church must have no power of compulsion, and the power of compulsion exercised by the state must have nothing to do with the domain of religion.*

The state is the intermediary social sphere between the Church on the one hand and the material society on the other. The absolute aims of religious and moral order which the Church puts before humanity and which it represents, cannot be realised in the given human material without the formal mediation of the lawful authority of the state (in the worldly aspect of its activity), which restrains the forces of evil within certain relative bounds until the time comes when all human wills are ready to make the decisive choice between the absolute good and the unconditional evil. The direct and fundamental motive of such restraint is pity, which determines the whole progress of legal justice and of the state. The progress is not in the principle, but in its application. Compulsion exercised by the state draws back before individual freedom and comes forward to help in the case of public distress. *The rule of true progress is this, that the state should interfere as little as possible with the inner moral life of man, and at the same time should as securely and as widely as possible ensure the external conditions of his worthy existence and moral development.* The state which chose on its own authority to teach its subjects true theology and sound philosophy, and at the same time allowed them to remain illiterate, to be murdered on the high-roads, or to die of famine and of infection, would lose its *raison d'être*. The voice of the true Church might well say to such a state: "It is I that am entrusted with the spiritual salvation of these men. All that thou are required to do is to have pity on their worldly difficulties and frailties. It is written that man does not live by bread *alone*, but it is not written that he lives without bread. Pity is binding upon all, and upon me also. If, therefore, thou wilt not be the collective organ of my pity, and wilt not, by rightly dividing our labour, make it morally possible for me to devote myself to the work of piety, I will once more have to set myself to do the work of pity, as I have done in the old days when thou, the state, was not yet called Christian. I will myself have to see that there should be no famine and excessive labour, no sick uncared for, that the injured should receive reparation, and injurers be corrected. But will not then all men say: What need have we of the state, which has no pity for us, since we have a Church which took pity on our bodies as well as on our souls?" The Christian state, worthy of this name, is one which, without interfering in ecclesiastical affairs, acts within its own domain in the *kingly* spirit of Christ, who pitied the sick and the hungry, taught the ignorant, forcibly restrained abuses (driving out the money-changers), was kind to the Samaritans and the Gentiles, and forbade his disciples to use violence against unbelievers.[25]

NOTES

1. It was natural to Soloviev, as an Eastern Christian, to equate bodily asceticism particularly with fasting. All three things must be understood in a representative sense: prayer as all worship, alms-deeds as neighbourly love, fasting as all "self-denial." But *cf.*, Tobit xii, 8; Matt. xvii, 21; Mark ix, 28. [Donald Attwater, the translator of Vladimir Soloviev, *God, Man and the Church* (London: James Clarke & Co., n.d. [1938]).]

2. [The sentence in Russian is simply: *Zhivia v miru, on dolzhen zhit' v mire;* "Living *in the world,* [a human being] should live *in peace*" (emphasis Soloviev's). *Mir* means both "world" and "peace" in Russian, a concept not unlike *kosmos,* which means both "world" and "thing of beauty" in Greek.]

3. The traditional theology both of East and West teaches that by the hypostatic union two natures, divine and human, were united in the person of the Word. Soloviev here subdivides the human nature, as stated. [Attwater.]

4. [Soloviev, *God, Man and the Church,* xi–xvi. Although the English title obscures it, this book is a translation of *The Spiritual Foundations of Life.* The Russian text of this selection may be found in *Sobranie sochinenii Vladimira Sergeevicha Solov'eva,* ed. S.M. Solov'ev and E.L. Radlov, 2d ed., 10 vols. (St. Petersburg, 1911–14), 3:301–304. *The Spiritual Foundations of Life (Dukhovnye osnovy zhizni)* is a good primer of Soloviev's religious thought. A work of edification rather than systematic philosophy, the book lacks the complexity of Soloviev's masterworks but nicely epitomizes his basic values, especially his ecclesiastical and social understanding of the gospel. Like all Orthodox Christians, Soloviev believed that the fullness of Christ is found not in the spirituality of isolated individuals but in the church. Unlike some of his Orthodox compatriots, he also emphasized the church's prophetic social ministry and the responsibility to collaborate with other social agencies in making the world a better place. In the translation, theandric renders the Russian *bogo-*

chelovecheskii (divine-human), from *Bogochelovek*, God-man, that is, the incarnate Christ.]

5. [Soloviev was a lifelong opponent of the death penalty. His debut as an activist on the issue came after the assassination of Tsar Alexander II by populist revolutionaries in 1881, when Soloviev called on the new tsar, Alexander III, to manifest a Christian spirit by refusing to impose capital punishment on his father's murderers. The philosopher's unsolicited appeal led to dismissal from his teaching position at St. Petersburg University. Soloviev's opposition to capital punishment reflected both the influence of modern humanitarianism and longstanding unease about judicial killing in Russia itself. One of the first policies that Grand Prince Vladimir of Kiev instituted after his conversion to Orthodox Christianity in 988 was abolition of the death penalty (subsequently rescinded). Capital punishment was less frequently applied in Russia than in Europe. The greatest writers of nineteenth-century Russia, Dostoevsky and Tolstoy, were united in their revulsion at capital punishment despite vast differences of opinion on other issues of social and political ethics. Abolished by the Provisional Government in 1917, the death penalty was restored by the new Soviet state and is still allowed in Russian law. An episcopal council of the Russian Orthodox Church addressed the issue inconclusively in 2000.]

6. The descendants of Cain, who were destroyed by the Flood, represented a third type of crime—that against nature, which was repeated afterward on a small scale in Sodom and Gomorrah. ["Sanctification" in this passage means retributive justice, as in the Latin phrase *Sacer esto*, "let it be sacred," i.e., forfeit, demanded by the gods as the penalty for an offense.]

7. Genesis 4:15; Leviticus 24:17; Romans 12:19; Deuteronomy 32:35; Hosea 6:6; Luke 19:10. [Wozniuk.]

8. Joseph Marie Maistre, Comte de (1753–1821) was a French diplomat and, at one time, the Sardinian envoy to Russia; he wrote prolifically on constitutions (*Essai sur le principe générateur des constitutions politiques et des autres institutions humaines*), social contract theory (*De la souveraineté du peuple: un anti-contrat social*), and punishment as sacrifice (*Eclaircissements sur les sacrifices*). Soloviev claimed that de Maistre was the intellectual source of Russian nationalists' cynical egoism and the degeneration of positive Russian national aspirations. See, for example, "Slavianofil'stvo i ego vyrozhdenie," *Vestnik Evropy* 11 and 12 (1889), also reprinted as a chapter in *Natsional'nyi vopros v Rossii* II, as found in *Sobranie sochinenii* 5:181–244. [Wozniuk.]

9. *Animus interficiendi*: "intent to kill." [Wozniuk.]

10. Because *Ritterspruch* is roughly "a knight's decree," and *Richterspruch*, "a judge's decree" [or "judgment"], the sense is that of the usurpation of *de jure* authority. Aleksei S. Khomiakov (1804–60) was a leading Slavophile who, along with others (e.g., Konstantin Aksakov), while being absolutely opposed to the ideas of Western liberalism for Russia, supported political and social reforms, including the emancipation of the serfs and freedom of speech.

[Wozniuk.] [The transliterated Russian text of Khomiakov's lines has been omitted.]

11. [Vladimir Soloviev, *Politics, Law, and Morality: Essays by V. S. Soloviev*, ed. and trans. Vladimir Wozniuk (New Haven, Conn.: Yale University Press, 2000), 171, 175–176, 179–184. The Russian text of this selection from *Pravo i nravstvennost'* may be found in *Sobranie sochinenii V. S. Solov'eva*, 8: 572, 577-578, 582-588.]

12. I am not forgetting that in 1861 Russia made amends by freeing the serfs.

13. See, among recent publications, the remarkable work of G. de Pascal, *Révolution ou Evolution: Centenaire de 1789* (Paris, Saudax).

14. [Vladimir Soloviev, *Russia and the Universal Church*, trans. Herbert Rees (London: Geoffrey Bles, 1948), 7–11. Soloviev composed this work in French. For the original text of this selection see Vladimir Soloviev, *La Russie et l'Eglise universelle*, 4th ed. (Paris: Librairie Stock, 1922), ix–xviii. *Russia and the Universal Church* is an exposition of Soloviev's ideal of theocracy. By theocracy Soloviev meant the reformation of social and political reality after the image of the Kingdom of God, to be realized through the collaboration of priestly (ecclesiastical), royal (political), and prophetic forces in society. Soloviev always distinguished between "false theocracy" and "free theocracy." By the former he meant traditional clericalism, the domination of society by religious institutions. By free theocracy he meant the remaking of a nominally Christian but essentially pagan social order into a just and caritative society. In *Russia and the Universal Church* Soloviev argues against religious and national isolationism to promote the twin ideals of European union and ecclesiastical reunion. An early prophet of ecumenism, Soloviev did not think that a just and caritative society was realizable without the reunion of the churches.]

15. [A *pud* is approximately 36.11 pounds.]

16. Tram conductors in Petersburg work more than eighteen hours a day for twenty-five or thirty roubles a month (see *Novoe Vremya*, N. 7357).

17. The author quoted refers here to Hanshofer's book, *Lehrbuch der Statistik*. All the figures quoted are apparently for the countries of Western Europe.

18. A. A. Isaev, *Natchala politicheskoi ekonomii* (*Principles of Political Economy*), 2nd ed., pp. 254–55.

19. Ibid., p. 226.

20. [Chapter 16 in the original Russian text; Part III, Chapter 7 in Duddington trans.]

21. [Chapter 17 in the original Russian text; Part III, Chapter 8 in Duddington trans.]

22. [Soloviev is referring to Tolstoyan anarchism.]

23. [Rudolf von Jhering (1818–1892), German historian and philosopher of law.]

24. [A. N. Ostrovsky, *The Storm*, Act 2, Scene 1.]

25. [Chapter 19 in the original Russian text; Part III, Chapter 10 in Duddington trans.] [Vladimir Soloviev, *The Justification of the Good: An Essay on Moral Philosophy*, trans. Nathalie A. Duddington (New York: Macmillan, 1918), 340–343,

362–363, 369–373, 448–460. For the Russian text see *Sobranie sochinenii V. S. Solov'eva*, 8: 376-380, 399, 406-411, 488-494, 496-500. *The Justification of the Good* (*Opravdanie dobra*) is arguably the most masterful work of moral philosophy in the Russian Orthodox tradition. Soloviev's conception of moral philosophy was very broad. It included not just the basic principles of ethics but philosophical anthropology, social and political philosophy, and the theological dimension of all of these disciplines. The wide range of subject matter treated in *The Justification of the Good* makes the book a summa of Solovievian practical reason.

While the systematic power of *The Justification of the Good* lends it the status of an enduring masterwork, the book also served a specific purpose in its historical context. Intellectual culture in nineteenth-century Russia was polarized in matters of ethics, politics, and religion. Slavophiles battled Westernizers, custodians of tsarism battled revolutionaries, Orthodox traditionalists battled Tolstoyan anarchists and other purveyors of novel religious doctrines. In *The Justification of the Good* Soloviev approached these divisions in a manner which, for the Russian tradition, was exceptional: he summoned all sides to consider the advantages of a middle way based on faith in the wholeness of the divine-human Good.

Soloviev's opposition to revolutionism did not betoken apathy about social and economic injustice. Criticism of unregulated capitalism and an economic ethic resembling that of the democratic welfare state of later times are conspicuous features of *The Justification of the Good*. It is interesting to note that Soloviev deploys the Orthodox Christian concept of theosis in this context. Theosis means the eschatological deification of human beings through the full actualization of the image of God in them. Soloviev utilizes the concept to criticize contemporary economic and social conditions, arguing that creatures called to theosis should not live in squalor but in an environment that reflects their divine nature and destiny.]

[CHAPTER 2]

Nicholas Berdyaev (1874–1948)

COMMENTARY

VIGEN GUROIAN

Nicholas (Nicholai Aleksandrovich) Berdyaev was born in 1874 in the province of Kiev to a wealthy and highly privileged family. Like so many young men of aristocratic upbringing in nineteenth-century Russia, he was sent to military academy, which he intensely disliked. He found his way to the University of Kiev, where he took up philosophy, despite the fact that he was supposed to study the natural sciences. In his posthumously published autobiographical essay *Dream and Reality* (1949),[1] Berdyaev writes, "My revolutionary and socialist sympathies and convictions had crystallized before I entered the University."[2] It was at the university, however, that Berdyaev began to associate with socialists and Marxists. He embraced radicalism from profound "ethical considerations"[3] regarding the plight of the poor and the working class under a political and economic order that he thought to be oppressive and corrupted. Because of these views and activities, Berdyaev was expelled from the university, arrested, and in 1898 sent into exile to the Volgoda region of northern Russia. Through the influence and interventions of his family, however, he spent just two and a half years there. Nevertheless, this experience left a strong and lasting impression on his thinking, as Berdyaev drew ever more resolutely toward radical socialism.

Kant and other German idealists, together with Berdyaev's Christian upbringing, tempered his attraction to Marxism from the start. In his introduction to *Slavery and Freedom* (1939), he explains, "I have never been an orthodox Marxist. I have never been a materialist and even in my Marxist period I was an idealist in philosophy. I tried to combine my idealism in philosophy with Marxism in social questions. I based my socialism upon an idealist foundation."[4] Berdyaev also detected very early the totalitarian proclivities and potentialities of Marxism. In radical circles he doggedly defended the reality and priority of freedom, goodness, and truth against every form of determinism and relativism. "I. . . . maintained the existence of truth and goodness as idealist values [embedded in the transcendental consciousness] which are independent of class struggle, of social conditions and the rest," Berdyaev wrote. "I believed in the existence of truth and justice as determining my revolutionary attitude to social reality, and not determined by it."[5]

During the late 1890s and early 1900s, Berdyaev pursued this goal of wedding Marxist social and economic analysis with Kantianism and Christianity. Nevertheless, his discontent with Marxism intensified as he edged steadily toward a personalist religious philosophy. The radicals, whose company Berdyaev kept, viewed the human individual as an instrument of the material dialectic and part of a social mass moved by historical forces. Berdyaev embraced Nietzsche's admonitions about the rise of "herd mentality" but rejected his positivism. Instead, he defended the eternal value of the human being, personal freedom, and the transcendence of spirit. In *The Meaning of the Creative Act* (1916), his favorite among his many books, Berdyaev made his case that the "creative act" is the highest and the most definitive achievement of human and divine freedom. Humankind is created in the image and likeness of God, and by virtue of this, God calls humankind to creativity, which is the consummate expression of human freedom and redemption.

On his return from exile in 1901, Berdyaev traveled to Germany, where he entered the University of Heidelberg to study with the acclaimed neo-Kantian Wilhelm Windelband. Berdyaev was already becoming disenchanted with Kant, though, and with the neo-Kantians in particular. In later years, he explained the source of his discontent, which boiled down to Kant's rationalism and legalism. Kant laid down the rule that the person should never be made the mere means to an end. Yet Kant (and even more especially the neo-Kantians) undercut the personalist bias of that rule with an ethical formalism that rendered the individual an abstraction and distilled the concreteness out of moral judgments. Kant's principle of the categorical imperative stipulates that a judgment qualifies as being morally correct when, and only when, it is universalizable, that is, equally applicable to any relevantly similar case. Berdyaev countered that this principle of universalizability makes the individual a function of the law, in service to the law, and not the other way around. The principle is potentially and often really dehumanizing. "The Gospel morality of grace and redemption," Berdyaev writes, "is the direct opposite of Kant's formula: you must not act so that the principle of your action could become a universal law; you must always act individually. . . . The universal law is that every moral action should be unique and individual, i.e., that it should have in view the concrete person and not the abstract good."[6] Thus, over and against Kantian formalism and universalism, Berdyaev embraced an existentialist contextualism and personalism.

As Berdyaev distanced himself from Kantianism and Marxism, he drew nearer to Orthodox Christianity, albeit through diverse and sometimes idiosyncratic sources. The period between his move to St. Petersburg in 1905 and the outbreak of the Bolshevik Revolution in 1917 is crucial for an understanding of Berdyaev's mature thought. In St. Petersburg (and later in Moscow), Berdyaev was associated with a rich variety of Christian intellectuals, including Dimitri Merezhkovsky, Vassil Rozanov, Vyacheslav Ivanov, Pavel Florensky, and Lev Shestov, many of whom were either imprisoned or sent into exile by the Communists. During this time Berdyaev began to write as a Christian philosopher. Indeed, soon after arriving in St. Petersburg with his new wife, Berdyaev joined Sergei Bulgakov in a joint editorship of the journal *The New Way* and, after its demise, another such enterprise entitled *Questions of Life*. Through these publications, Berdyaev and Bulgakov espoused their special blend of social and economic radicalism and Christian spirituality. Berdyaev sums up his shift from Marxism and idealism toward a distinctly Christian form of mystical religious faith and social radicalism in an article written during this period and later included in his book *Sub Specie Aeternitatis*: "Idealism was well enough for the initial criticism of Marxism and positivism. . . . but it possessed nothing creative. It is impossible to stop with it. That would be neither realistic nor religious. . . . I arrive in my articles at God-manhood, the incarnation of the Spirit in society, at the mystical union of love and freedom. From the Marxist pseudo ecumenicity, from the decadent romantic individualism, I arrive at the true ecumenicity of mystical neo-Christianity."[7]

In 1907, the Berdyaev family moved to Moscow, where Nicholas became active in the Religious-Philosophical Society, founded in memory of Vladimir Soloviev. This association of Christian intellectuals provided a refreshing and stimulating camaraderie. Berdyaev openly credited the group with expanding his religious and theological horizons. In the meantime, Berdyaev was reading deeply into the great nineteenth-century Russian Christian writers—Aleksei Khomyakov and Nicholas Fedorov, Dostoevsky and Tolstoy. Berdyaev was disappointed, however, with the Russian secular intelligentsia of both the right and left, and with the Orthodox Church. In *Dream and Reality*, Berdyaev explains how he saw things at that time: "The Russian renascence suffered from a lack of moral decisiveness and

readiness to choose and act. It was lost in a vague aestheticism and romanticism."[8] He continues, "The renascence shed hardly any light into the
wider regions of social life. The attitude of the left intelligentsia. . . . not
only of the social revolutionaries but also of the liberal-radicals, was one
of drab, moral respectability and political stringency, and they failed to
reflect profound cultural changes."[9] Although he initially supported the
revolution of 1917, Berdyaev did not favor its leaders or even its immediate
outcome:

> [The revolutionaries] were nurtured in and lived by the outworn ideas of
> Russian nihilism and positivism. . . . They were not interested in Dostoevsky,
> Tolstoy, Vladimir Solovyev, Nicolai Fyodorov and the thinkers of the turn
> of the century: they were satisfied with their Herwegh, and their Holbach,
> with their Chernishevsky and Pisarev, their standard of culture rose no
> higher than that of Plekhanov. Lenin himself was a reactionary so far as
> philosophy and culture were concerned; he was not even fully abreast of
> Marxist dialectic; for, unlike Marx he had not passed through the whole
> school of German Idealism, even though he had read Hegel.
>
> This fact had a fatal effect on the character which the great revolution in
> Russia assumed; it began by perpetuating a real pogrom against what was
> best in Russian culture.[10]

The Russian Church offered little hope, either. It was corrupt and servile
to an oppressive state, and did nothing to diffuse the situation or address
the true grievances of the Russian people in either 1905 or 1917. In an
"Open Letter" first published in the *Moscow Weekly* on August 15, 1909,
Berdyaev passionately expresses his love for and disappointment with the
Church:

> By devious and winding paths I have come to the faith of Christ and to the
> Church of Christ, which I now count as my spiritual mother. Nevertheless, I
> have not forgotten those obstacles that stood in my way. I cannot forget them
> because of the fate of those who are unable to overcome those obstacles. The
> activity of the Church, the abomination of desolation in the holy place, throt-
> tles as a heavy incubus those who seek God and his truth. . . . Is it not a stum-
> bling block that the official Christian camp, confessing the true faith and
> accordingly possessing privileges almost incomparably greater than the oth-
> ers, commits deeds of hate and evil, rather than performing acts of love? Men
> are weak and their religious will is ruined by offenses and temptations; it is
> difficult for them to withstand the most terrible offense which turns men
> from faith—the spiritual downfall and ethical decomposition of the Church

in her human, historical empirical aspects (for in her divine mystical aspects the Church is unshakable and guards eternal truth). But woe to them through whom such offense comes into the world![11]

In 1921, after a brief arrest, Berdyaev was sent out of Russia. He and his wife first settled in Berlin but in 1924 moved permanently to Paris. Berdyaev joined the rich ferment of philosophical and religious thought that stirred in Paris at that time. He established ties with Russian figures such as Sergei Bulgakov, George Fedotov, and Mother Maria Skobtsova, as well as lasting friendships with the Roman Catholic religious philosophers Jacques Maritain and Gabriel Marcel. But it is also true that Berdyaev remained an independent and often lonely voice. As he wrote many years later in *Dream and Reality*, "I never fully merged with any one movement with which I was associated. And the precariousness of my relation to them, my loneliness and misgivings sharpened my perceptions."[12]

In *Slavery and Freedom*, Berdyaev states that upon his arrival in the West, he quickly recognized that, as wrong as the Bolsheviks and Communists were, the truculent anti-Soviet mentality and easy embrace of bourgeois capitalism by so many of the Russian émigrés were barely more tolerable:

I went through a stormy inward reaction. . . . against the second, the great, Russian revolution. I considered the revolution inevitable and just; but its spiritual aspect was uncongenial to me from the very beginning. Its ignoble aspect, its encroachment upon freedom of the spirit was a contradiction of my aristocratic interpretation of personality and my cult of spiritual freedom. My refusal to accept the Bolshevik revolution was not so much on social grounds as on spiritual. I expressed this too passionately and often unfairly. I saw all the while the same triumph of the *Grand Inquisitor*. At the same time I did not believe in the possibility of any sort of restoration and I certainly did not want it. I was banished from Soviet Russia simply and solely because of my reaction in defense of freedom of the spirit.

But in Western Europe I again passed through a psychological reaction and that a two-fold one—reaction against the Russian *émigrés* and reaction against the bourgeois capitalist society of Europe. Among the Russian *émigrés* I saw the same revulsion from freedom, the same denial of it as in communist Russia. This was inexplicable, but very much less justifiable than in the communist revolution.[13]

What especially disturbed Berdyaev about life in the West was the bourgeois mentality among both religious and nonreligious people. He judged that this bourgeois mentality was hardly less materialistic than Marxism and Communism and that it was almost as destructive of freedom and personality. With clear allusions to his great spiritual mentor, Fyodor Dostoevsky, Berdyaev writes in *The Bourgeois Mind*,

> The bourgeois may be an extreme conservative or an extreme revolutionary, but in both cases he is chained to the visible world and knows no spiritual freedom. There is no grace in moralism [characteristic of the bourgeois], it proceeds from an outward source and is deaf to the music of Heaven. . . . The very idea of the rationalization of life, of an absolute social harmony, is a middle class idea which has to be opposed by the "man of the underworld," the "gentleman with a mocking reactionary face." The tower of Babel was built by the middle class, [even] the spirit of Socialism is middle-class.[14]

The atheism of Communism was self-confessed. The atheism of the bourgeois was not, and yet a denial of Christianity was entailed in all its behavior. Berdyaev continues,

> Everything the bourgeois touches, the family, the state, morality, religion, science, all is deadened. . . . The paradox of his life consists in his repudiation of tragedy. . . . Because the consciousness of guilt and sin has become so weak he is a slave of "the world," his ideal is that of worldly wealth and power; the mystery of Golgotha is unacceptable to him.[15]

Over the remaining years of his life, Berdyaev continued to oppose antihuman and anti-Christian forces on both the left and the right, in Soviet-style socialism and Western capitalism. At the same time, he produced a massive corpus in which he elaborated a philosophy of history, a theosophical spirituality, an aesthetics, and an ethics. It is to Berdyaev's ethics, however, that one must turn especially for his theological anthropology and interpretation of the origin and meaning of law. In *The Destiny of Man* Berdyaev introduces his famous threefold typology of ethics: the ethics of law, the ethics of redemption, and the ethics of creativity. Other writings that especially come into play are *The Meaning of the Creative Act* (1916), *Freedom and the Spirit* (1926), *Slavery and Freedom* (1939), and *The Beginning and the End* (1946).

Fielding Clarke, one of Berdyaev's earliest and best interpreters, was right when he observed that "the doctrines and practice of the Russian Orthodox Church are in the background . . . of all that he wrote. . . . Berdyaev was [always] a son of Orthodoxy."[16] Berdyaev himself commented: "I cannot, in all conscience, call myself a typical 'orthodox' of any kind; but

Orthodoxy was nearer to me (and I hope I am nearer to Orthodoxy) than either Catholicism or Protestantism. I never severed my link with the Orthodox Church, although confessional self-satisfaction and exclusiveness are alien to me."[17] When people in the West began referring to Berdyaev as a representative Orthodox figure, he took pains to say that he did not speak for the Church either in an official or unofficial capacity. He carefully explained that he was a philosopher, not a theologian, and certainly not a dogmatic theologian. In *Freedom and the Spirit* (1927), Berdyaev pauses to issue this strong disclaimer:

> My book is not a theological work, nor is it written according to any theological method. It belongs to no school of philosophy; rather it forms a part of "prophetic" as distinct from "scientific" philosophy, if one may employ the terminology which [Karl] Jaspers has suggested. . . . All the forces of my spirit and my mental and moral consciousness are bent towards the complete understanding of the problems which press so hard upon me. . . . I may be much mistaken, but my purpose is not to introduce heresy of any kind nor to promote fresh schism. I am moving in the sphere of Christian problematics which demands creative efforts of thought and where the most divergent opinions are naturally allowable.[18]

Berdyaev did not fit a standard mold. He was a creative, eclectic, and even eccentric thinker. Although he drew from such Eastern Patristic writers as Gregory of Nyssa and Pseudo-Dionysius, he was also steeped in the German mystics Jacob Boehme and Meister Eckhart. Berdyaev saw himself as following in the footsteps of the great nineteenth-century Russian religious philosophers Aleksei Khomyakov, Nicholas Fedorov, and Vladimir Soloviev, but Friedrich W. J. Schelling, Arthur Schopenhauer, and especially Immanuel Kant were formative influences. The care that Berdyaev took to describe himself as a philosopher and explain what he meant merits further attention. For he revealed much about his purposes and goals as well as his relationship to the extraordinary ferment of religious thought in Russia up to the Revolution of 1917. From this we begin to understand how his thought fits into the larger context of religious philosophy in the West from the Enlightenment through the first half of the twentieth century.

In *The Destiny of Man* (1931), Berdyaev distinguishes between doing philosophy and doing theology. The philosopher, he says, seeks to find meaning for existence through rational reflection on human experience, whereas the Christian theologian explores the meaning of redemption in the knowledge of God's triune being gained by faith in the God-Man,

Jesus Christ. Berdyaev, of course, allowed for the possibility that a philosopher might, like himself, be a believer in "religious revelation." In this case, the philosopher's "thought is bound to be nurtured by" that revelation. Indeed, "he may acquire the mind of Christ and this will make his philosophy different from that of non-Christian thinkers."[19] The philosopher's thought will no longer be simply anthropological, but his or her anthropology will be theological and the God-Man the norm of philosophical reflection.

Nonetheless, Berdyaev insists that under no circumstance must revelation "force upon philosophy any theories or ideal constructions.... Philosophy is led to its conclusions by the cognitive process itself; unlike theology it cannot have the results of knowledge forced upon it from without." For philosophy "to be at all possible," he continues, "it must be free; it brooks no constraint."[20] In this claim for the independence of philosophy—although he does not say it is autonomous—one detects the influence of Immanuel Kant and, in the definition of religious philosophy, the impact of Vladimir Soloviev.

Not all of Berdyaev's contemporaries agreed with his claim for the independence of philosophy or accepted his disclaimers about dogmatic theology. And insofar as Berdyaev wrote with the voice of a Christian believer, especially an Orthodox believer, some critics accused him of misspeaking concerning the faith. Thus, to read Berdyaev is to engage a brilliant intellect and sensitive spirit constantly in tension and controversy with prevailing orthodoxies, including, one might add, orthodoxies about the origin, meaning, and purposes of ethics and law.

THE ORIGIN OF ETHICS

In *The Destiny of Man*, Berdyaev holds that the origin of ethics is commensurate (or simultaneous) with the origin of the distinction between good and evil, and that both are consequent to what the Christian faith refers to as the Fall into sin. He writes, "It might be said that the world proceeds from an original absence of discrimination between good and evil to a sharp distinction between them and then, enriched by that experience, ends by not distinguishing them any more."[21] In other words, "Paradise is the state of being in which there is no valuation or distinction"[22] between good and evil: likewise, the kingdom of God is "beyond" good and evil. In between this beginning and this end is the only world that we know in the ordinary sense of knowing, and in that world the distinction between good and evil tries and tests us at every turn. One can say,

Berdyaev continues, that "it is bad that the distinction between good and evil has arisen, but it is good to make the distinction once it has arisen; it is bad to have gone through the experience of evil, but it is good to know good and evil as a result of this experience."[23]

Berdyaev argues that in order to get to the heart of the meaning of ethics, an epistemology of original sin is needed. The knowledge of good and evil indicates commission of the original sin and loss of original innocence. Original sin is an act of imagination and will that distances human beings from God. It triggers a fundamental shift in human consciousness. The whole of human history is the legacy of this original sin and the fallen consciousness of humankind; as a result, humankind is plunged into "a godless experience of life."[24] Yet the very knowledge of good and evil, which is gained at the awful cost of alienation from God and mortality, paradoxically also gives rise to conditions wherein and whereby human beings may be reawakened to the presence and existence of God and inherit eternal life. "Awareness of original sin both humbles and exalts man. Man fell from a height, and he can rise to it again,"[25] but not, says Berdyaev, by mere moralism or the law. The character of the kingdom of God is not merely ethical, as moralists imagine; nor is it achieved by even the strictest adherence to the law. "The triumph of a 'good' based in valuation and distinctions is . . . not paradise or the Kingdom of God. The Kingdom of God . . . is on the other side of the distinction."[26] It is beyond good and evil.

THE FAILURE OF LEGALISM AND MORALISM

"It is the Fall [also] that made moralists of us,"[27] Berdyaev argues. Moralism and legalism go together. Both are incapable of reaching the kingdom of God. Both are premised on the mistaken belief that the solution to human suffering is the triumph of good over evil achieved by adherence to law. Leo Tolstoy is an example of someone who put all his hope for the kingdom of God in obedience to moral law. Tolstoy interpreted good and evil, which are the symptoms of a much deeper disorientation of human existence and disturbance of consciousness, as objective forces pitted against one another, the victory of good over evil ensuring perfection and peace. Tolstoy's moralism is an extreme example of the ethics of law with all of its limitations, and this ethics of law is the first of the three kinds of ethics Berdyaev discusses in *The Destiny of Man*.

Berdyaev held that law is impotent "to change human nature" or redeem humankind from a seemingly interminable struggle of good and evil. In the depths of their souls, human beings know this is so and yearn for something more. "Man thirsts for redemption, for deliverance not only from evil but from the legalism and the distinction between good and evil."[28] Genuine redemption "destroys the roots of sin and evil" and erases the distinction between good and evil. The ethics of redemption bridges "the gulf" between God and humanity that was objectified by sin and the law. It announces the entrance of the transcendent good, of divine life itself, of grace, "into the very depths of" human existence, into the very heart of the world.[29] It promises liberation from sin and death and the restoration of humankind to communion with the living God. The sum of this redemptive action is what the Gospel of John calls eternal life.

REDEMPTION

In setting forth his theology of redemption, Berdyaev rejected the theory of atonement of St. Anselm of Canterbury (ca. 1033–1190) that had come to dominate various forms of Roman Catholicism and Protestantism. This doctrine described the atonement as an act of sacrifice rendered on our behalf by Christ for the violation, due to original sin, of God's righteousness and honor. It defined Christ's death as a satisfaction or substitution that propitiates the wrath or righteous indignation of God. Some Protestant versions of this doctrine are purely forensic, insofar as they understand atonement as a purely vicarious act of Christ on behalf of human beings, since the debt owed to God is far greater than any one human being except Christ could possibly pay. Other typically Roman Catholic teachings interpreted this act in strongly reconciliatory terms as making right of our relationship with God.

Berdyaev, like many other Eastern Orthodox Christians, regarded this kind of atonement theory as overly legalistic and juridical. Furthermore, he argued that it is alien to the spirit of the New Testament and classical Christianity: "The Redemption achieved by the Son of God is not a judicial verdict, but a means of salvation; it is not a judgment, but a transformation and illumination of nature—in a word, its sanctification."[30] The juridical concept, whether understood in forensic terms or reconciliatory terms, represented "the relations between God and man . . . [as] of a purely external character."[31] Such an atonement does not remedy the mortal sickness and weakness of post-Edenic humanity that prevents human beings from entering into genuine communion with God. Berdyaev argues, "Redemption is not justification, but the acquiring of perfection."[32] It is not God who is unable or unwilling to forgive, "but man who cannot pardon himself, any more than he can absolve himself from his apostasy from God"[33] or make reunion with divine life possible. Salvation is God acting from "within" the human being through the incarnation of the Son who by his perfect life and sacrifice cures humankind of sin and death so that they may participate in the divine life.

THE ETHICS OF REDEMPTION AND THE KINGDOM OF GOD

Berdyaev embraced an "ontological" or "physicalist" interpretation of redemption highly characteristic of Eastern Church Fathers reaching back to Ireneaus and Athanasius. Berdyaev writes, "The spiritual nature of man does not merely demand pardon for sin, but rather its final defeat and extermination, that is to say, the transfiguration of human nature. The meaning of Redemption lies in the coming of the Second Adam, the new spiritual man, in the coming of the love of which the Old Adam was ignorant, in the transformation of the lower nature into the higher."[34] On this ground, Berdyaev argued that the ethics of redemption overcomes the ethical dualism of good and evil that is the mainstay of unredeemed naturalistic ethics and law. On the foundation of this cure of sin and perfection of our human nature accomplished by the God-Man Jesus Christ, a new spiritual ethics is made possible. According to this ethic, grace is the opposite of necessity and not, as is often argued, the opposite of freedom. The grace of God is a divine love healing human nature as well as a divine freedom creatively engaging human freedom toward the end of the sanctification of life.

The ethics of redemption paves the path to the kingdom of God; however, it does not encompass the whole of salvation. For the ethics of redemption still bears the terrible mark of the Fall into sin. Its paving "stone" is suffering love, divine and human, whereas the kingdom of God is not only beyond good and evil but also transcends every kind of human suffering.

THE ETHICS OF CREATIVENESS AND FREEDOM OF THE SPIRIT

The ethics of creativeness, Berdyaev's unique contribution to Christian ethics, is the fruit that grows from the seed sown by grace in our wounded humanity. Or another way of putting it: the ethics of creativity is the service to God's kingdom that Christians are empowered to do by virtue of the fact that the Son of God has rehabilitated human nature in God's own person and restored humankind to freedom in the Spirit. Humanity's creative powers are weakened by the Fall. Through Christ, human nature is redeemed and restored; humanity is saved from sin. The old human being is reborn into a new creature. "Christ [the Creator Word] became immanent in human nature, and this makes man a creator like the Creator God."[35] There is nothing explicit in the gospel about humanity's creative vocation; it would have been a mistake had such a thing been included in the New Testament, since a person must pass through redemption before he or she can understand fully the meaning of God's calling to creativity. When a person is reborn into the freedom of the Spirit, that vocation is clarified and he or she may act upon it with a complete sense of purpose. "Creativeness is a work of man's God-like freedom, the revelation of the image of the Creator within him. Creativeness is not in the Father, neither is it in the Son but in the Spirit,"[36] and reaches beyond the Old and New Testaments.[37] As St. Paul puts it, "Where the Spirit of the Lord is, there is freedom" (2 Cor. 3:17 RSV). Indeed, Berdyaev insists that "the whole of St. Paul's teaching about various gifts is concerned with man's creative vocation. The gifts are from God, and they indicate that man is intended to do creative work."[38] The creative capacity of the human person, especially when liberated by Christ in the Spirit, anticipates, is a proleptic sign of, the transfiguration of the world. Indeed, "man is called to extraordinary activity, to creative upbuilding of profit for the Kingdom of God, which is known as God-humanity."[39]

ETHICS AND SIN

In sum, for Berdyaev, human beings have invented ethics in response to "the criterion of good and evil . . . the genesis of morality and the origin of moral distinctions and valuations."[40] Ethics, however, is not just a theoretical discipline; nor is it, as the common person often thinks, simply the judicious application of law to regulate a social world. The ethics of law and the ethics of redemption take into account at various levels what biblical religion calls sin. They are means by which human beings can cope with and overcome the dissension, division, and conflict that sin and the bitter knowledge of good and evil introduce into life. The ethics of law envisions a social good and seeks to effect it principally through prohibitions and punishments. This form of ethics is "both very human and well adapted to human needs and standards"; however, it can be "pitiless" toward the individual in his or her concrete circumstances and severely constrict freedom.[41] And it is powerless to solve the riddle of the dualism of good and evil that shadows human existence everywhere.

The ethics of redemption overcomes fallen nature and reaches beyond good and evil. Wherever it is present, Christ is known and the Spirit is acting. The ethics of redemption is illumined by the knowledge of the humanity of God in Jesus Christ and the perfection of God's own image and likewise in the Incarnate Son's humanity. It is about love and not law, about freedom and not sanction. The ethics of redemption posits in the light of Christ that the conflict between good and evil, which is alien and obstructive to the personal, free, and loving communion of divine life may be transcended. Nevertheless, Berdyaev adds,

> Man's chief end is not to be saved but to mount up, creatively. For this creative upsurge salvation from sin and evil is necessary. From the religious point of view, the epoch of redemption is subordinated to the epoch of creativeness. A religion of thirst for salvation and terror of perdition is only a temporary passage through a dualistic division [of good and evil and nature and spirit]. . . . Creativeness is the final revelation of the Holy Trinity—its anthropological revelation. . . . God himself, who gave His Only Son to be broken on a tree, atones for the sin of man and he expects that man, having partaken of the mystery of redemption, will accomplish the great deed of creativeness, will realize his positive destiny."[42]

The ethics of creativeness, therefore, completes the spiritual work of redemption. "Human nature, redeemed and saved from evil, has a positive content and purpose. This content and purpose can only be creativeness. . . . That the image and likeness of God the Creator cannot fail to be himself a creator is an anthropological truth" which Judaism and Christianity bring into the world.[43] The ethics of creativeness is humanity's response to God's call to enact and embody, through imagination and will, the values of love and freedom that belong to the kingdom of God.

HUMAN AND DIVINE NATURES

At this stage, a review of Berdyaev's philosophical and religious reflection on human and divine natures is needed. It is the basis for an understanding of his position on the relationship of law and Christianity. Christianity insists that the human person is an indivisible compound of nature and spirit, said Berdyaev. He cautioned, however, that Christianity is not about a body-soul or mind-body dualism. The human person is spirit insofar as God is Spirit and God has created humanity in God's own image and likeness. It makes no difference that human beings do not possess an "objective spiritual nature or substance comparable to their psychic or corporeal substance." That which is spiritual in human beings is even more integral to their nature. That which is spiritual "is, as it were, a Divine breath, penetrating human existence and endowing it with the highest dignity, with the highest quality of existence, with an inner independence and unity."[44] According to Berdyaev, it is for this reason that if one intends to speak of human nature and destiny with any depth of seriousness or understanding, one must also speak of God. Human existence and Divine Existence, anthropology and theology, are inextricably intertwined for two reasons: "(1) man is the image and likeness of God the Creator and, (2) God became man, the Son of God manifested Himself to us as the God-Man."[45]

THE IMAGE OF GOD AND THE IMAGE OF HUMANITY

Berdyaev held that personality is the image of God in humankind: "The image of human personality is not only a human image, it is also the image of God."[46] Personality is the lynchpin of Berdyaev's existentialist ethics; for him, it was "an axiological category. . . . Personality is *the* moral principle, and our relations to all other values [are] determined by reference to it." The ethical is itself grounded in the even deeper metaphysical and theological nature of personality. Personality "rises above the natural life. . . . It is not the product of the biological process or of social organization. Personality is spiritual and presupposes a spiritual world. . . . In other words, the existence of personality presupposes the existence of God,"[47] as well as the Spirit of God in human beings.

Personality, however, must not be confused with mere individuality or autonomy. Personhood is relational and depends upon being in community with others. Human beings are fully human to the extent that they are in community and that their social existence reflects the perfect communion of the three divine persons through participation in the divine life that God has made possible in Jesus Christ. Human existence is fundamentally "theanthropic" (or God-directed), said Berdyaev. God calls (or invites) humankind into a communion with divine life, leading to the *theosis* (or divinization) of humankind. Genuine human togetherness, or what Russian theology calls *sobornost*, is possible because God, in whose image human beings are created, is perfect *sobornost*, perfect communion. Theosis of the isolated individual is not possible. In God there is *perichoresis*, a perfect interpenetration of love of the three divine persons in and through love. Likewise, "the absolute Heavenly Man is both the unique man and the whole *soborny* humanity" drawn together by love and in communion with the divine Trinity.[48]

Through this, it can be seen that the Christian belief in the God-Human Jesus Christ profoundly deepens our understanding of personhood. Christ reveals, once and for all, that the human being "bears within himself [or herself] the image which is both the image of man and the image of God, and is the image of man in so far as the image of God is actualized."[49] Christ actualized (perfected) this image of God in his Person. That is what St. Paul means when he speaks of Jesus as the "first born of all creation" (Col. 1:15 NKJV) and also the first of the heavenly humanity (I Cor. 15:48–49). Christ, who perfects our humanity, fulfills in his Person this vocation of God-manhood that sin has hindered and obstructed ever since the Fall. By becoming a human being and living a life without sin, the Son of God has made it possible for humankind to obtain this goal of God-manhood that sin had prevented. And Christ has sent the Spirit into the world so that every human being might effectively use his or her freedom to embrace divinity, as God has embraced humanity.

ON THE HUMANITY OF GOD

It is hard to name another Christian theologian of Berdyaev's era who insisted more strongly that theology is as much about humanity as it is about God and that anthropology is as much about God as it is about humanity. No one, except perhaps Sergei Bulgakov, made this case in quite the same fashion. For example, Karl Barth in his later years spoke with great force about the humanity of God. "In Jesus Christ," Barth wrote in his famous address entitled "The Humanity of God," "there is no isolation of man from God or God from man."[50] In Jesus Christ, God affirms humanity and fully enacts human freedom so that the communion between God and human beings is complete. "God is *human*" through God's complete identification with humanity in Jesus Christ.[51] By the incarnation, God "*encloses* humanity" in God's divinity. In Christ "the fact is once and for all established that God does not exist without man."[52]

Both Berdyaev and Barth offered fundamentally christological arguments about the nature of God and humanity. They parted company, however, in their respective interpretations of how the incarnation narrows the gap between God and humanity. Barth employed Reformed covenantal theology: "In Him [Christ] we encounter the history, the dialogue, in which God and man meet together and are together, the reality of the covenant *mutually* contracted, preserved, and fulfilled by them."[53] Berdyaev invoked the Orthodox vision of the union of the human and the divine expressed in the doctrine of theosis. He began with the radical premise that whatever is truly human is original in God and is fulfilled by participation in the life of God. "The birth of man in God is a theogenic process." Berdyaev writes. "In the eternal idea of him, man is rooted in God-manhood and linked with the God-man," the Lamb who is slain from the foundation of the world. On these grounds, "it may [even] be said that a pre-eternal manhood exists in God."[54] Therefore, "true human-ness," Berdyaev continues, "is likeness to God; it is the divine in man," the *imago dei*. "The divine in man is not the 'super-natural' and it is not a special act of grace; it is a spiritual principle which is in man as a particular reality." The human being at present "is to but a small extent human; he is even in-human. It is not man who is [fully] human but God,"[55] and the fullness of our humanity is contingent upon complete participation in the divine life (2 Pet. 1:3–4). Berdyaev affirms this as a mystagogical and eschatological truth. For him, the divinity of humanity and the humanity of God are a dual mystery symbolized in the Christian myths of creation and redemption. The entire anthropological significance of the christological dogma, Berdyaev concludes, is not yet understood because humankind still is simply humankind and not yet eschatological divine humanity.

MYTH AND SYMBOL

Berdyaev offered these bold assertions about the nature of humanity with an important qualifier—namely, that the knowledge revealed about human nature and human destiny by the incarnation is not reducible to rational conceptualization. It is not knowledge in the ordinary, scientific, or historical sense. It is knowledge that is wrapped in divine mystery. And it is expressed principally through myth and symbol. "Behind the myth are concealed the greatest realities, the original phenomena of the spiritual life. . . . Myth is the concrete recital of events and original phenomena of the spiritual life symbolized in the natural world, which has engraved itself on the language, memory, and creative energy of the people. . . . Myth presents to us the super-natural in the natural, the supra-sensible in the sensible, the spiritual life in the life of flesh; it brings two worlds symbolically together."[56] Contrary to the claims and expectations of the modern schools of demythologization, divine knowledge is lost rather than gained by demythologizing. Both "pure philosophy" and rational theology unburdened of myth and religious experience "cannot know God"[57] in God's personhood. When God is turned into a concept and object of study, little can be understood about God that affects human salvation.

Human beings make myths, but God reveals the truth in myths. All religious language is inherently mythological and symbolic. Myths employ symbolic speech because it is the only kind of language that bridges nature and spirit. "Symbols presuppose the existence of two worlds and two orders of being, and they would not exist were there only one order. A symbol shows us that the meaning of one world is to be found in another, and the meaning itself is revealed in the latter." Likewise, "God can only be perceived symbolically, for it is only by means of symbols that it is possible to penetrate the mystery of His Being. Divinity cannot be rationally determined and remains outside the scope of logical concepts."[58] Biblical myth does not attempt to lift the veil from the face of God, and yet it draws human beings nearer to God than rational conceptualization. It does not externalize God or render God a mere object of cognition, an idea or a thing. The language of myth ably represents God as a person and agent, and pictures the world as filled with God's Spirit. "Academic 'rational' theology [has] transgressed the limits of its competence in one direction by regarding the mysteries of divine life as entirely accessible to itself, and, in the other, by supporting agnosticism, assigned fixed limits to spiritual experience, and the knowledge of the divine."[59]

Similarly, argued Berdyaev, neither scientific nor historical knowledge is capable of comprehending or explaining the whole measure and meaning of our humanity. If Christian theology needs to stay near to symbolic speech and myth, so, too, must theological anthropology. A theological anthropology that embraces myth and symbol as legitimate ways of knowing is needed, for the human person is the intersection of two worlds—nature and spirit—and myth alone can capture their relation and interpenetration. "The very fact of the existence of man," Berdyaev writes in *The Destiny of Man*, "is a break in the natural world and proves that nature cannot be self-sufficient but rests upon a supernatural reality."[60]

Berdyaev believed that this understanding of the doctrine of the God-Man ought to settle once and for all that myth is needed in theology and anthropology. Mystery cannot be "unpacked" and translated into pure conceptual knowledge about God and human beings, although some may try. In the doctrine of the incarnation, Christian theology and anthropology are convincingly joined not by rational concepts but by myth and symbol. If human reason cannot solve the paradox of the dual nature of humankind, neither can we expect it to unravel the riddle of the two natures of Christ: "It is impossible to form a [pure] conception of the dual nature of Christ. . . . Two natures in one single personality" cannot be grasped "by reason."[61] New Testament writers employed symbolic speech in order to communicate the intersection and interaction of nature and spirit and God and humanity. The incarnation (that is, the birth, death on the cross, resurrection and ascension of the God-Man) is the great Christian myth. From this constellation of images, the New Testament writers constructed a myth, albeit a historicized myth that uniquely recorded historical events that within this mythic framework are shown to hold transhistorical significance.

SUFFERING OF GOD

There is one final feature of Berdyaev's doctrine of God and the relation of the divine and the human that calls for some attention. Berdyaev rejected the traditional notion that God is a perfect act and being and, therefore, that God does not change, is not moved, and does not experience emotion or loss. He opined that this doctrine of the unchanging and immovable character of divine life reflects an unfortunate adaptation of the myth of the biblical God to the Aristotelian idea of the Unmoved Mover. But the living God of the Bible, Berdyaev argued, is assuredly not this static and lifeless God of rational theology. Once again the incarnation is illustrative. If the New Testament writers are trustworthy, then there is drama even in the "inner" (or immanent) life of God, the "drama of love"[62] shared and communicated among the Three Divine Persons. And if God is love, then God is open to suffering. The myth of the incarnation suggests the same inasmuch as the Father loves the Son who is crucified and dies. Love is not love if it is not open to suffering, even, no especially, divine love, since it is the model of all love. What the myth of the incarnation certainly affirms is that "the Son of God suffers not only as Man but also as God."[63] Therefore, to deny tragedy in the divine life, Berdyaev remarks, "is only possible at the cost of denying Christ, His cross and crucifixion, the sacrifice of the Son of God."[64] That drama and tragedy are played out in this world and in the spiritual realm, in human life and in the life of God the Father, the Son, and the Holy Spirit.

Berdyaev concluded, therefore, that rational theology creates "a profound gulf between the idea of perfection in humanity and in God. Self-satisfaction, self-sufficiency, stony immobility, pride, the demand for continual submission, are qualities" that this theology attributes to God's perfection and yet "considers vicious and sinful" when speaking of human beings. If one follows this line of reasoning, what possible sense can be made of the gospel injunction: "Be ye perfect as your Father in Heaven is perfect"?[65] Is holiness in Jesus' own life not accompanied by suffering? Would not God the Father's yearning for the Son entail agony when the Son dies on the cross and even descends among the dead? Does not St. Paul state that "the Spirit Himself makes intercession for us with groanings which cannot be uttered" (Rom. 8:26 NKJV)? In Berdyaev's view, the paradoxical double truth that God is absolutely "other" and also our most immediate Friend is held together by the mystical truth that God's perfection is not an Aristotelian completeness of act and being. It is rather a holiness forged in the love borne by the Father, the Son, and the Holy Spirit for one another.

"It is more worthy of God to ascribe to Him longing for the loved one, a need for sacrificial self-surrender"[66] than to say that God is self-sufficient, passionless, and perfect immobility, Berdyaev concluded. The mythological anthropomorphizing of the Old and New Testaments is infinitely preferable and certainly more accurate about the character of God and God's relation to humanity than the backhanded anthropomorphizing of rational theology. Rational theology exchanges the symbol for analogy, and ultimately exchanges analogy for concepts that break as they try to express this tragic, redemptive, and creative divine-human drama at the meeting of nature and spirit.

DIVINE AND HUMAN FREEDOM: THE *UNGRUND*

The idea that divine and human personality and freedom emerge from the *Ungrund*, the primal, uncreated freedom and pure potentiality (the meonic "nonbeing") "outside" of God is perhaps the most controversial theme in Berdyaev's religious philosophy. This idea of *Ungrund* may not be essential to understanding Berdyaev's theological anthropology, ethics, and views on law and politics. It is integral to his thought, however, and so needs to be discussed. At the start, we should listen carefully to Berdyaev when he says that the *Ungrund* is not a concept but an intuition, a mythological picture of what is rationally unknowable but utterly important for a proper understanding of personality and freedom. The *Ungrund* is a symbol that transcends human conceptualization.

Berdyaev borrowed this idea of the *Ungrund* from the German mystic Jacob Boehme (1575–1642), but said that he used the term differently from Boehme. Boehme claimed that the *Ungrund* is within the godhead; Berdyaev, however, maintained that the *Ungrund* is "outside" of God and is the pure primal meonic potentiality from which God brings everything into existence. God did not create the *Ungrund*. In fact, the godhead issues from the *Ungrund* in an eternal theogenic process. Nevertheless, argued Berdyaev, the *Ungrund* is not some "thing" that exists over and against God. It is not a "thing" or a "nothing" but is pure potentiality. For that matter, neither is God a being in the same way that the human individual is a being. The trinitarian godhead is the personal creator who freely brings the world into existence out of this "nothingness" of pure potentiality or primal freedom.

How does God accomplish this? Berdyaev's answer was a form of theological voluntarism, which drew on Boehme as well as medieval philosophers John Duns Scotus and William of Ockham. God *wills* Creation into existence by imagining it. "The faculty of imagination is the source of all creativeness," he said. "God created the world through imagination. In Him imagination is an absolute ontological power."[67] Thus, on one hand, God did not create *freedom* and, on the other hand, God brought everything that is *freely* into existence through an imaginative act of will. But Berdyaev rejected the traditional way of framing this issue of God's willing and freedom. "It is equally wrong," he argued, "to say that God is bound to will the good and that the good is that which God wills." In other words, God's will is neither arbitrary nor bound by external law or norm. "We cannot judge God from our side of the distinction[s] between good and evil" and freedom and necessity. Quite simply, "God is above good. And there cannot be in Him any evil that is on this side of the distinction. . . . [And] when we ask whether God is free to will evil we apply to Him the categories of a fallen world."[68]

Let me summarize what I have said about Berdyaev's views on God, freedom, and human morality with five postulates. First, God did not create freedom; rather freedom is uncreated. Second, God brought everything that is into existence out of this uncreated freedom. Third, humanity is both "child" of God and "child" of this uncreated freedom—of nonbeing, of *ton me on*. Fourth, human moral valuation originates from a distinction between good and evil that is generated by human sin and applies solely to a fallen world. Moral good and evil are products of creaturely imagination and will, and do not come from God. Fifth, human moral valuation does not touch upon the character of God. God is beyond good and evil.

THE MEANING OF THE FALL AND ITS RELATION TO LAW

God's creative act constitutes a call to humankind from the depths of freedom to join God as a co-creator of beauty and truth. God, however, risks rebellion in issuing this call, since a person, as we just reviewed, is both a "child" of freedom and a "child" of God. Human beings in their rebellion make a "hell" out of their lives by choosing to live in falsehood and ugliness, apart from God, and descend back toward nonexistence. The Fall is a corruption of human will and imagination; corrupted will and imagination spawn enslaving powers, processes, and authorities that together with fallen angelic agents stand over and against personality and freedom. A hitherto nonexistent dualism of good and evil enters into human life, and this moral dualism gives rise to law and ethics, which represent humanity's struggle to ward off the chaos and dissolution caused by sin.

The Fall is a myth, however, and not a proper subject of scientific history, in Berdyaev's view. It "did not occur in the phenomenal world or in time." Rather, "the phenomenal world and its time are a product of the Fall."[69] The Fall symbolizes the coming to be of the phenomenal world, that is, the determinate and lawbound nature. Before the Fall, the relationship between God and humankind was wholly intersubjective, and humankind's relationship to nature was harmonious. After the Fall, history, marked by objectification and conflict, comes into being. Henceforth, humankind experiences the world as externality, largely incommunicable and unmovable; even God is objectified in human consciousness. Despite their weakened state, human beings intuitively recognize the tragic and deadly force of this objectification of God and the world as a consequence of sin. There remains a universal yearning in the human heart for the peace and harmony of paradise.

The Fall not only affects human beings, but its tragic consequences also permeate the whole of creation. Original sin sullies and depersonalizes all of life, as well as alienating humankind from God. God experiences this loss and is pained by the agony of God's creature, who heads into nonexistence. "God longs for His 'other,' His friend," Berdyaev writes.[70] Yet because God loves perfectly, he cannot and will not abbreviate or contradict human freedom. God cannot and will not unilaterally impose paradisiacal communion upon rebellious human beings and angels, even though he suffers for their separation from him. Nor can the knowledge of good and evil that humankind has gained be reversed.

According to one traditional interpretation of the Fall, the knowledge of good and evil is the Fall itself. When I know good and evil, when I make distinctions and valuations, I lose my innocence and wholeness, fall away from God, and am exiled from paradise. But another interpretation is possible, one that stands in a somewhat paradoxical relationship to the first. "Knowledge in itself is not a sin and does not mean falling away from God."[71] Rather, knowledge "is good and means discovery of meaning."[72]

The evil of original sin, the Fall in its essence, is the act of plucking the fruit of the tree of knowledge against God's wishes. This rebellion, prompted by vain imaginings of autonomy, self-sufficiency, and power over the world, transposes humankind from paradise into "an evil and godless experience of life."[73]

According to this alternative interpretation of the Fall, there is no reason to expect or hope that human beings will return to the state of original naiveté. Human beings mature with knowledge, even though they may also use knowledge in self-defeating and self-destructive ways. In other words, knowledge can be used for good or evil. Meanwhile, God acts to heal the rupture between God and humanity and to stop and reverse the process of corruption unto death that sin starts in the human being like yeast in batter. God sends God's "Only Begotten Son" who "suffers and is crucified, an innocent suffer."[74] "The Lamb is slain from the foundation of the world' (Rev. 13:8 NKJV), says the seer of the book of Revelation." "The Divine sacrifice forms part of the plan of creation from the first," Berdyaev writes.[75] By an act of immense sacrificial love, God renews God's call to communion through the blood of the Lamb. "Man is not free if God stands to him in the relation of a Creator, but he is free if God's relation to him is that of giving him grace."[76]

Too often in Christian theology, said Berdyaev, God's grace is represented as an external power that compels or forces conformity to God's will, whereas grace is not alien to human nature. For that reason grace rehabilitates and transforms human nature from "within." It restores the image of God in the human person. The truth is that God's grace is eternal love freely given, resonant with personality and rehabilitative of human nature. Grace restores human nature from the "inside" so that God's call to communion reverberates throughout the person's whole being, as if he or she were in paradise. And the person is enabled to respond effectively to God's call. This redemptive and sanctifying effect of Christ's sacrifice and restoration of human nature puts in place the conditions under which law, which is born of sin, is no longer needed. But before we take that penultimate step along Berdyaev's theological path, it is necessary to explore more fully how an objectified world has come into being and how and why human sin brings law into existence.

OBJECTIFICATION AND THE ORIGIN OF LAW

As I have intimated already, Berdyaev maintained that the Fall brings about a shift in human consciousness from existential, intersubjective knowing and encounter, wherein the I-Thou relationship prevails, to a way of imagining and relating to God, the human other, and nature that is depersonalizing and objectifying. In a fallen state, human beings experience the world as external, fragmented, and ruled by causal necessity. The primal *sobornost* of existence is broken. The I and the Thou have become competing egos, self-centered selves that view each other as objects, things, means to an end. This process of "objectification" introduces into human society all the instrumentalities of depersonalization, coercion, and force that characterize a fallen world. The whole of the creation is affected. The broken harmony of paradise devolves into exploitation and commodification of every living and nonliving thing.

At root, objectification is the "ejection of man into the external, it is an exteriorization of him. . . . [It] is the uprising of an exteriorized 'not-I' in place of the 'Thou' of the primordial communion of being. The exteriorized I, the egoistic, self-alienated self, experiences" the world as external, an obstacle to happiness or an object for possession, use, or self-gratification. From the Fall onward, human thought, will, and imagination have taken this unholy experience of the created order to be what reality really is. Since at least the time of Immanuel Kant, argued Berdyaev, most of modern philosophy has been blind to the paradox "that what is called 'objective' is precisely what is 'subjective' and what is called 'subjective' is 'objective'. . . . Objectivity was accepted as identical with general validity." In truth, however, "the subject is the creation of God in personal relation with God while the object" is the sinful subject's projection of a world governed and connected by causal law rather than love.[77] Thus human beings conceive even God as an object related to them as external supreme cause or law or objective good and not as a subject of personal communion; they no longer view this relationship as an existential encounter.

Berdyaev insisted that this process of objectification is not merely a figment of the mind or imagination. The objectified world is "real" insofar as fallen existence is an actual condition, an environment, in which "exteriorization and alienation are [always and continually] taking place."[78] Human beings are an inseparable part of that milieu. Just as "'uncreated freedom' is a limiting notion that symbolically does not lend itself to logical definition," so, too, "objectification" is "a symbolical description of the fallen state of the world in which man finds himself subservient to necessity and disunion."[79] Berdyaev summarizes:

> [The] Fall is a matter of importance in the theory of knowledge. Objectification and the unauthentic character of the phenomenal world are by no

means to be taken as meaning that the world of men and women, animals and plants, minerals, stars, seas, forests and so on is unreal and that behind it is something entirely unlike it—the things-in-themselves. It means rather that this world is in a spiritual and moral condition in which it ought not to be, it is a state of servitude and loss of freedom, of enmity and alienation, of ejection into the external, of subjection to necessity.[80]

The difference between the life of the spirit and objectification is the difference between personal communion and historical social existence, or the difference between love and justice. Social existence and the laws that govern it imprison personality in an environment of externalized power and coercion designed to control the disintegrative effects of sin; whereas, communion and love preserve and deepen the integrity of personality in an environment of free existential communion.

THE ORIGIN, NATURE, AND PURPOSE OF LAW

On the basis of this foundational inquiry, Berdyaev's outlook on the origin, purpose, and meaning of law can be explained. Law, said Berdyaev, is the expression of "a vision of the Divine Will distorted by sinful nature." Law is not "an original expression of God's feelings toward man";[81] rather, objectification, social existence, and law go hand in glove. Traditional Christian theology embraces St. Paul's judgment that the law came into the world because of sin and death, and that law makes sin manifest. Law "denounces sin, limits it, but cannot conquer it."[82] The primary evil is not the law, of course, but sin, which necessitates law. In order, however, for the human person to attain the fullness of life of which Paul also speaks, he or she must not only be delivered from sin and death but from law as well.

Berdyaev maintained that law and the ethics of law are refined and partially transformed expressions of the universally human desire for revenge. All human "valuation, judgment and condemnation contain an element of primitive vengeance in sublimated form," Berdyaev argued. But while law and justice may be rooted in the primal human desire for revenge, that desire when expressed through law and justice never has been merely an expression "of cruelty or ferocity." Among the ancients "it was preeminently a moral feeling and a religious duty . . . [as] can be seen from the Greek tragedy."[83] This moral feeling or impulse is originally grounded in fear and awe, and later in the higher forms of ethics in religious law and conscience.

THE NATURE OF LAW

Berdyaev's analysis of the origin, nature, and purposes of law belongs to his "epistemology of original sin." "The realm of objectification, which is a consequence of sin, is a social realm, . . . made for the average person, for mankind in the mass, for the ordinary and the hum-drum, for *das man*."[84] Where genuine communion no longer exists, historical social existence comes into being, and this social world depends upon law in order to continue. Through law, society regulates disruptive, disintegrative, and dissimulating effects of sin. By the use of law, society protects the endangered individual from destructive forces and makes room for a measure of personal freedom. Ironically, however this freedom and security is bought at the price of continued devaluation and diminution of personality and communion. But law sees only the outer human being whose personal visage blends into the mass and common herd. While protecting the individual, law tends to move from the particular to the general. In this respect, Christian theology errs profoundly whenever it describes God as law or as the enforcer of law. God is a Person and the Lover of persons in their uniqueness and particularity. Love, and not law, is the appropriate symbol of personality.

Wherever there is the fear that the stability and peace of society are under threat, law trumps love and personality. Law by its very nature—whether it is positive, natural, moral, or divine law—deals in abstraction and generality and is allied with external force. But personality can never be subsumed under an objective norm, nor is force in a sinful world finally amicable to love, freedom, and personality. For this reason the ethics of the gospel reverses the method of the ethics of law. Under the ethics of redemption "it is impossible," Berdyaev argues, "that in the same circumstances one ought always and everywhere to act the same way," by the same rule or norm. "It is impossible if only because circumstances never are quite the same."[85] It is impossible also because the goal of grace is the salvation of the unique person and not of the objectified and externalized social order. Personality, freedom, and love are concerned with the inner human being in all of his or her discreteness as an icon of God, personal agent, and potential God-man or God-woman.

LAW AND FREEDOM OF THE WILL

Based upon Berdyaev's strong strain of Christian personalism, one might expect, as happens often in Western theology, that he embraced the doctrine of freedom of the will. In fact, he rejected the concept. Berdyaev's view was that the doctrine of freedom of the will is a mistake representing a wrong turn in Christian philosophy. "The doctrine of free will was modeled to suit a normative, legalistic morality," Berdyaev remarked.[86] It is, in a sense, the counterpart in Christian ethics of the juridical doctrine of redemption. It satisfies society's need to attribute moral responsibility to the person. According to "legalistic normative ethics," freedom of the will is "the condition of fulfilling the moral law," and by this exercise a person is "justified if he chooses the good and fulfills the law, and condemned if he chooses evil and fails to fulfill the law."[87] But freedom, according to Berdyaev, "must not be understood . . . merely as the possibility given to man of fulfilling the law and justifying himself by good works."[88] Recall that Berdyaev argued strenuously that freedom is the primal reality and that its integrity and creative potential do not dependent upon the existence of law. Freedom is ontologically precedent to law and is therefore in no sense a function or correlative of law. Also, freedom eschatologically surpasses the law, since law does not exist in the kingdom of God. So it certainly makes no sense to say that the freedom of the will belongs to the essence of humanity. In the beatific life of communion with God there is no such freedom of will. As for the present, said Berdyaev, "man is enslaved by the necessity to choose between that which is forced upon him and carrying out the law under fear of penalties. He proves to be least free in that which is connected with his 'free will.'"[89]

Berdyaev felt that in this respect, Luther had it at least partly correct when he rebelled "against justification by works connected with free will."[90] The ethics of redemption embraces this vision with its promise of eternal life free of sin, suffering, and death. It proclaims that, through Jesus Christ and the Spirit, the kingdom of God enters the lives of all believers. True liberation comes through grace and not from free will; human beings are free when they no longer need to fear failing to do the right or the good prescribed by law, when they need not choose between good and evil because good and evil, together with sin itself, no longer exist having been consumed by the love of God and the sanctifying fire of Pentecostal grace.

Like the idea of a legalistically described moral order, the doctrine of the free will is rooted in fear and driven by fear. And it can be an enslaving doctrine, said Berdyaev, since the ethical apparatus that human beings devise to judge the will manifest all of the objectifying and depersonalizing characteristics of law and the juridical understanding of redemption. Thus, concluded Berdyaev, it was a mistake for Catholic moral theology and Protestant ethics to adopt a doctrine of free will in order to secure human dignity. Yes, free will may serve, as in the case of law, to control the destructive effects of sin. But the doctrine of free will must not be mistaken for true freedom of personality, which is not contingent upon or correlative to the distinction between good and evil or a doctrine of free will. True freedom of personality is creative energy that envisions and brings into existence new values and realities.

In summary of Berdyaev's view, the ethics of law and the doctrine of freedom of will are both premised on the concept of a binding moral order external to personal existence. This concept of a single universally binding moral order, however, is itself a product of objectification. Objectification causes us to experience *autexousion*, the deep and transcendent capacity within every human being for self-determination, as an external norm. This objectification contradicts personality and obscures the image of God in humankind. It even invites us to imagine a will that stands over and against this moral order and is "free" to obey or defy it. But at the source of their existence, human beings are not creatures of law. Humankind is personality brought into existence by a divine act of love. God intends for communion that is without fear or coercion. For love is the opposite of fear, and love transcends law. Human love is movement toward God, which we may call will, but not free will. It is simply contradictory to speak of a free will that stands poised between willing God and willing against God. How can love will against itself? "There is no fear in love; but perfect love casts out fear, because fear involves torment. . . . He who fears has not been made perfect in love. We love Him because he first loved us (1 John 4:18–19 NKJV)."

THE POSITIVE PURPOSE OF LAW

Just as "the realm of objectification is a social realm," so too is law. "The ethics of law is essentially social. . . . The Fall subordinated human conscience to society. Society became the bearer and guardian of the moral law."[91] Yet even though law has this "negative" origin, it does have a positive purpose. For in a sinful world, Berdyaev maintained, personal well-being cannot depend solely upon the spiritual or moral character of others: "It is a paradox, but the exclusive predominance of an ethics of grace in a sinful world would endanger the freedom and the existence of personality."[92] And a "society that chose to be based solely upon grace and declined to have any law would be a despotic society. Thus Communist society may be said in a sense to be based upon grace and not upon law, of course, it is not grace in the Christian sense of the term. The result is a tyranny, a theocracy reversed."[93] Law serves a positive good in so much as it clears space for the exercise of personal freedom and human creativity.

But this is not all that needs to be told. In a fallen and sinful world, "justice is righteousness refracted in the common life of every day."[94] We are faced with this profound paradox that reason and human effort alone cannot wholly clarify or resolve: "The law does not know the concrete and unique, living personality or penetrate into its inner life, but it preserves that personality from interference and violence on the part of others, whatever their spiritual condition."[95] So unredeemed, "man requires law and is therefore naturally inclined to see law at work everywhere."[96] Yet, in the last analysis, although it may be true that "Christ did not indeed reject law," Christ did reveal "a spiritual world where love and freedom enlightened by grace effectively triumph over law."[97] Grace and love, not law, are the "radiating energy"[98] of life, and life could not go on without that energy.

FREEDOM, IMAGINATION, AND CREATIVENESS

"By the side of the self-contained moral world of laws and rules to which nothing can be added," writes Berdyaev in *The Destiny of Man*, "man builds up in imagination a higher, free and beautiful world lying beyond ordinary good and evil. . . . The Kingdom of God is the image of a full, perfect, beautiful, free and divine life. . . . But the most perfect fulfillment of the law," he added, "is not the same as the perfect life."[99] The ethics of redemption promises life free of sin, suffering, and death. It proclaims that the kingdom of God enters the lives of all who believe in the crucified and resurrected Lord.

The ethics of redemption also indicates the eclipse of the ethics of law and points to the ethics of creativeness without explicitly setting it forth. This is appropriate, says Berdyaev, for "if the ways of creativeness were [explicitly] indicated and justified in the Holy Scriptures, then creativeness would be obedience [to a command], which is to say that there would be no creativeness. . . . The compulsory revelation of creativeness as a law, as an indication of the way to go, would contradict God's idea of man, God's desire to see in man the creator, [freely] reflecting His own divine image."[100] Nonetheless, Jesus' parables of the kingdom of God are about "the fruit which the seed must bring forth if it falls on good soil and of talents given to man which must be returned for profit. Under cover of parable Christ refers in these words to man's creative activity, to his creative vocation."[101]

As with God, so also with human beings, creativity is an imaginative exercise. The human imagination, however, has been warped and distorted by sin just as much as reason and the will. Therefore, it should not be surprising that law, which combats the effects of sin, also polices and inhibits imagination. Berdyaev writes, "The ethics of law forbids man to imagine a better world and a better life; it fetters him to the world as given and to the socially organized herd life, laying down taboos and prohibitions everywhere. But the ethics of creativeness breaks with the herd-existence and refuses to recognize legalistic prohibitions. "To the 'law' of the present life it opposes 'the image' of a higher one."[102] Redemption is liberation from this fallen age. The mind of Christ is a mind that is freed to imagine and envision a new creation. Indeed, "God expects from man the highest freedom, the freedom of the eighth day of creation."[103]

Berdyaev argued that the whole fabric of human life depends upon creativeness for vision and vitality. Short of the kingdom of God, however, "there is always a tragic discrepancy between the burning heat of the creative fire in which the artistic image is conceived and the cold of its formal realization. Every book, picture, statue, good work, social institution is an instance of this cooling down of the original flame."[104] Yet Pentecost is a sign, emblem, and foretaste of the new creation wherein this paradox of flame and dying ember is transcended. Berdyaev's ethics of creativeness is an ethics of this age of the Holy Spirit where freedom comes into its own as the power to imitate divine creativity. Freedom, according to the ethics of law, means "acceptance or rejection of the law of the good and responsibility for doing one or the other."[105] By contrast, genuine freedom, according to the ethics of creativeness, is the liberty of the children of God to participate in the realization of the kingdom of God, wherein the old morality of right and wrong and good and evil exists no more.

The ethics of the old creation is always either teleological or deontological. According to teleology, the good is defined as the ultimate goal or purpose in life toward which the ethical person strives. According to deontology, the good is an overarching norm under which the ethical person performs his or her duty. Both teleology and deontology are bound up with law and inhibit the growth of the moral imagination. Law "is limited to imagining compliance with, or violation of, its behests." But "the most perfect fulfillment of the law" is not even a shadow of the new creation in Christ.[106] Law, no matter how it is conceived or lived out, governs the Old Adam and not the New Adam. The Christian faith redefines the moral life. Obedience to law for the sake of the good is replaced by creative activity inspired by a vision of the beauty of God and God's kingdom. "From the ontological and cosmological point of view," Berdyaev writes, "the final end of being must be thought of as beauty and not as goodness,"[107] not fulfillment of law but the synergy of divine and human creative freedom for the sake of the eternal kingdom of Love. Indeed, good that is defined as the opposite of evil contradicts beauty in the same way that the sinful and enslaving structures of objectification contradict the kingdom of God.

The ethics of creativeness resembles no other ethics; indeed, it confounds our habitual association of law with ethics and the formal distinction between ethics and aesthetics. One may ask, "How can beauty be the final goal of life rather than the good?" Is not beauty an aesthetic appraisement? That might be true in a world of sin and objectification, but Berdyaev's eschatological imagination pressed beyond such distinctions and categories. In Christian ethics, God is frequently described in terms of the final Good, but in Berdyaev's view, even this concept of the final Good has not been purged of ethical dualism. Good that functions as the opposite of evil is only a means, a path at best, to the kingdom of God, whereas "beauty lies beyond the knowledge of good and evil" and all of the division and disharmony of sin. The perfect perichoresis of the Father, the Son, and the Holy Spirit is Beauty. The communion of saints in the kingdom of Heaven is Beauty. God is the Good only if "evil is already forgotten," but in that case *good is beauty.*"[108]

BERDYAEV'S CHRISTIAN REALISM

Berdyaev was not starry-eyed about beauty; he knew that the diabolical may even—and often does—mimic beauty. But he said that this is not true beauty. "There can be no moral deformity in beauty, [for] that is a property of evil. The beauty of evil is an illusion and a fraud."[109] This fraudulent beauty does not hold truth and is in a process of decay, and ultimately the fraud will be exposed. The veneer will wash off and expose an essence that is ugly or grotesque. The ethics of creativeness discovers the kingdom of God "as the reign of beauty."[110] This is an active process, for "beauty is never objectivity in itself, which asks for nothing but mere passivity in relation to itself, it is always transfiguration."[111] The beauty of the kingdom of God is not an object but the quality of transfigured relationships reached through and by the synergy of human and divine energies. It is a transfigured relation, harmony, and mutuality, transcending not just law and coercive force but the very distinction between good and evil. The beauty of the kingdom of God is holiness. Holiness is a communion of love and not merely a possession of the independent ego.

For all of this talk of synergy and perfection, however, there is not a trace of liberal progressivism or secular utopianism in Berdyaev. He was a Christian realist, albeit not a typical one. "The Christian faith tells us to seek first the kingdom of God and divine perfection," he writes. But, he quickly adds, Christianity "will have nothing to do with the day-dreaming, utopias, or false imagination; it is realist, and the Fathers of the Church are always appealing for spiritual sobriety. Christian consciousness has a clear perception of all the difficulties that beset the way to perfection, but it knows that 'the kingdom of Heaven suffereth violence and the violent take it by force.'"[112]

Berdyaev powerfully invoked the Christian doctrine of original sin, although with a different sort of emphasis and theological outcome than what we have learned to expect from Reinhold Niebuhr or Karl Barth. Berdyaev described the human being as a "sick being, with a strong unconscious life"[113] and an imagination that readily turns idolatrous and diabolical. He constantly pointed out these idolatries and how human beings are enslaved to them. His realism was truly dialectical in that he held forth the utterly transcendent holiness of God as the standard of perfection over and against which we measure human sinfulness and evil. While he may have been pessimistic about the degree of holiness possible in history, he was optimistic about the possibility of human redemption and salvation. In his remarkable essay "The Worth of Christianity and the Unworthiness of Christians," Berdyaev writes:

> The negation of Christianity due to the shortcomings of Christians is essentially the ignoring or misunderstanding of original sin. Those who are conscious of original sin see in the unworthiness of the Christian not a flat contradiction of the worth of Christianity, but a confirmation of it. It is the religion of redemption and salvation, and is not forgetful that the world finds pleasure in sin. There are many teachers who claim that the good life can be compassed without any real overcoming of evil, but Christianity does not think so; it insists on this victory, a rebirth; it is radical and more exacting.[114]

Berdyaev's realism was personalist and christological, communalist and trinitarian. He had the highest expectations for human perfection, while keeping his eyes wide open to the corrupting and divisive force of sin in the world. Only the *metanoia*, the conversion of the person, and not "any program imposed externally" upon the individual or society, enables human beings to reach the heights of goodness and holiness. "Compulsion will never make good Christians or a Christian social order," Berdyaev remarks. "There must be an effective and real change in the hearts of persons and of peoples, and the realization of this perfect life is a task of infinite difficulty and endless duration."[115] The kingdom of God is not a program; nor is it the inevitable outcome of an evolutionary or ameliorative process. Berdyaev criticized Vladimir Soloviev's political theology on this score. Solovyev presented his theory of Godmanhood as if it were "a necessary determined process of evolution."[116] In him there were "no tragic conflicts and yawning gulfs, such as are disclosed in Dostoyevsky."[117] Berdyaev thought that Soloviev's theory was not sufficiently serious about either the reality of human freedom or the persistence of human sin that prevents the coming of the fullness of the kingdom of God. In *The Russian Idea*, Berdyaev commends an active rather than passive eschatology: "The end of this world, and the end of history, depend . . . upon the creative act of man."[118] And yet, even as he made this commendation, Berdyaev adds that no amount of human creativeness guarantees that the kingdom will come: "I have shown the tragedy of human creativeness, which consists in the fact that there is a lack of correspondence between creative purpose and created product. Man is not creating a new life or a new form of existence, but cultural products" all of which are affected and distorted by "objectivization which is based upon alienation, the loss of freedom and personality, and subjection to the general and necessary."[119]

Berdyaev opposed the humanistic ideas of progress. He insisted that the Christian must vigilantly guard at all times against the lure of the multifarious cultural artifacts, ideologies, and institutions that would lay claim to the whole of humankind and promise worldly redemption. In *Slavery and Freedom* (1939), he included among these family, sex, money, and property, collectivism and capitalism, the state and revolution. It seems that nothing in this world is "safe," or the source of human salvation. Even Christ prayed for the kingdom of God as gift of the Father and, just as important, made his prayer the model for every Christian.

Fielding Clarke stated that we should not expect from Berdyaev a program of social, economic, or political reform. Berdyaev made no claim to having "produced a new theology or a new sociology. He speaks of 'personalistic socialism,' for example, as his aim, but it is with principles not details that he is concerned. *It is not programmes but perspectives which he gives us.*"[120] For Berdyaev, human personality cannot exist without community. Thus community is itself part of human nature. Nevertheless, no particular historical structure of society is perfectly suited to human beings. Berdyaev was true to the spirit of the Hebrew prophets. Like them, he warned against every possible form of human pride and idolatry of self or society. Like them, he envisioned salvation as a communion of being and saw justice as a sign of the birth of the kingdom of God. He strongly insisted that Christians must move beyond a concern with their own individual salvation and act in ways that affirm that in Christ the kingdom has already been made present. In other words, Berdyaev's ethic of creativeness was an integral element of his realism. It brought the eschatological hope of Christian faith up front and center, and from this standpoint radically relativized every human achievement. Yet Christ's parables and the Spirit-filled events of Pentecost also open up a positive vision of divine and human community that should outweigh a negative fixation upon personal struggle with sin and evil and inspire creative acts that help bring about social, economic, and political justice.

THE LEGACY

More than fifty years after his death in 1949, and despite his sometimes heterodox views, Nicholas Berdyaev quite deservedly ranks as one of the most brilliant and creative twentieth-century exponents of Eastern Christian mystical theology and spirituality. My teacher, the late Will Herberg, justifiably included Nicholas Berdyaev with Jacques Maritain, Martin Buber, and Paul Tillich in his influential *Four Existentialist Theologians*, published in 1960.[121] If that book were compiled today, no doubt Berdyaev would retain his position among the great existentialist and personalist theologians of the twentieth century.

Sadly, however, little of Berdyaev's work is now in print in English. His enormous notoriety during the mid-twentieth century diminished as time wore on, and he fell out of the corpus of theologians routinely read in seminaries and graduate schools. Whereas Protestants, Roman Catholics, and Jews kept alive the legacies of Berdyaev's companions in Herberg's anthology, the Orthodox in the English-speaking world neglected Berdyaev.

For important reasons, those Russian theologians of Berdyaev's generation and the generation following who founded a neopatristic school of Orthodox thought took center stage. The likes of Vladimir Lossky, Georges Florovsky, and John Meyendorff sought, in T. S. Eliot's words, to "purify the dialect of the tribe"[122] as they clarified the historical, dogmatic, and liturgical riches of Orthodoxy. They actively participated in the burgeoning modern ecumenical movement and made a tremendous gift of Orthodoxy to Western Christian thought and the churches. They founded and populated Orthodox seminaries, thus giving new life to the tradition. They defined the mainstream of Orthodox historical, systematic, and liturgical theology for our time.

Nonetheless, the neglect of Berdyaev (and Sergei Bulgakov to a somewhat lesser extent) has cost Orthodoxy in originality and energy. Berdyaev seriously reflected on the nature of religious experience and was deeply engaged with modern philosophical and religious thought. His work breathed new life into a church theology that had grown formalistic and stale. Today, his thought may be in a unique position to address the post-modernist controversy and reinvigorate Orthodox theology as the neopatristic school shows signs of growing tired and becoming disconnected from the everyday life of Orthodox Christians.

Ironically, during the very same years that Berdyaev's reputation suffered in the Western diaspora, Russian dissidents and religious intelligentsia rediscovered and wholeheartedly embraced him. From the 1960s through the collapse of the Soviet Union, Berdyaev was ascendant as the Russian brand of a liberation theologian. His strong emphasis on Christianity and freedom inspired hope and resistance against Soviet tyranny. His critique of Marxism and Bolshevism and his historical interpretation of Russian religion and culture helped to explain what was happening and what needed to be done in order finally to shed Communism. His influence may be found in such dissidents and religious leaders of the era as Alexander Solzhenitsyn and Father Alexander Men. During visits I made to Russia in 1990 and 1991, Berdyaev came up in conversations more frequently than any other modern Russian religious thinker. Those with whom I spoke drew heavily from his prophetic analysis in such works as *The Origin of Russian Communism* (1937) and *The Russian Idea* (1946). Since then, Berdyaev's influence has receded, mainly because of the pressing need to stabilize the church and recover the theological and dogmatic tradition. Yet his legacy is secure in Russia. His writings are back in print, and Berdyaev will continue to be read and studied as one of the towering figures of modern Russian religious philosophy.

NOTES

1. In this and following instances, the date in parentheses after a title is the original publication date in the language in which the book was first published, whether Russian, French, or English.
2. Nicholas Berdyaev, *Dream and Reality* (New York: Macmillan, 1951), 115.
3. Ibid., 115.
4. Nicholas Berdyaev, *Slavery and Freedom* (New York: Charles Scribner's Sons, 1944), 13.
5. Ibid.
6. Nicolas Berdyaev, *The Destiny of Man* (New York: Charles Scribner's Sons, 1960), 137.
7. Quoted by Matthew Spinka in *Nicolas Berdyaev: Captive of Freedom* (Philadelphia: Westminster Press, 1950), 20.
8. Berdyaev, *Dream and Reality*, 154.
9. Ibid., 153.

10. Ibid., 154–155.
11. Translated by Matthew Spinka and quoted in *Nicholas Berdyaev*, 35–36. The letter is also included in Nicholas Berdyaev's *The Spiritual Crisis of the Intelligentsia* (St. Petersburg, 1910), 299.
12. Berdyaev, *Dream and Reality*, 155.
13. Berdyaev, *Slavery and Freedom*, 16–17.
14. Nicolas Berdyaev, *The Bourgeois Mind and Other Essays* (London: Sheed & Ward, 1934), 24.
15. Ibid., 24–25.
16. Fielding Clarke, *Introduction to Berdyaev* (London: Geoffrey Bles, 1950), 18.
17. Berdyaev, *Dream and Reality*, 177.
18. Nicholas Berdyaev, *Freedom and the Spirit* (London: Geoffrey Bles, 1935), xix.
19. Berdyaev, *Destiny of Man*, 7
20. Ibid.
21. Ibid., 47.
22. Ibid.
23. Ibid., 49–50.
24. Ibid., 49.
25. Ibid., 53.
26. Ibid., 47.
27. Ibid.
28. Ibid., 133.
29. Ibid., 135.
30. Berdyaev, *Freedom and Spirit*, 173–174.
31. Ibid., 175.
32. Ibid., 174.
33. Ibid., 175.
34. Ibid., 175–176.
35. Nicolas Berdyaev, *The Meaning of the Creative Act* (New York: Harper & Brothers, 1954), 101.
36. Ibid., 98.
37. Berdyaev, *Destiny of Man*, 162.
38. Nicolas Berdyaev, *The Beginning and the End* (New York: Harper & Brothers, 1957), 174.
39. Berdyaev, *Meaning of the Creative Act*, 99.
40. Berdyaev, *Destiny of Man*, 23.
41. Ibid., 112.
42. Berdyaev, *Meaning of the Creative Act*, 105–106, 110.
43. Ibid., 110–111.
44. Nicholas Berdyaev, *Spirit and Reality* (New York: Charles Scribner's Sons, 1939), 6.
45. Berdyaev, *Destiny of Man*, 69.
46. Berdyaev, *Slavery and Freedom*, 44.
47. Berdyaev, *Destiny of Man*, 72.

48. Berdyaev, *Freedom and Spirit*, 138.

49. Berdyaev, *Slavery and Freedom*, 45.

50. Karl Barth, *The Humanity of God* (Atlanta: John Knox Press, 1960), 46.

51. Ibid., 51.

52. Ibid., 50.

53. Ibid., 46.

54. Nicholas Berdyaev, *The Divine and the Human* (London: Geoffrey Bles, 1949), 111.

55. Ibid., 110.

56. Berdyaev, *Freedom and Spirit*, 72.

57. Ibid., 64.

58. Ibid.

59. Ibid., 66–67.

60. Berdyaev, *Destiny of Man*, 60.

61. Berdyaev, *Freedom and Spirit*, 73.

62. Ibid., 210.

63. Berdyaev, *Slavery and Freedom*, 51.

64. Berdyaev, *Destiny of Man*, 38.

65. Ibid., 37.

66. Ibid., 38.

67. Ibid., 97.

68. Ibid., 56.

69. Berdyaev, *Beginning and End*, 241.

70. Berdyaev, *Destiny of Man*, 25.

71. Ibid., 49.

72. Ibid.

73. Ibid.

74. Ibid., 41.

75. Ibid., 44

76. Ibid., 45.

77. Berdyaev, *Beginning and End*, 17.

78. Ibid., 60.

79. Berdyaev, *Dream and Reality*, 288.

80. Berdyaev, *Beginning and End*, 59–60.

81. Berdyaev, *Freedom and Spirit*, 75.

82. Berdyaev, *Destiny of Man*, 110.

83. Ibid., 114.

84. Berdyaev, *Beginning and End*, 70.

85. Berdyaev, *Destiny of Man*, 170.

86. Ibid., 25.

87. Ibid.

88. Ibid., 26.

89. Ibid., 25–26.

90. Ibid., 25.

91. Ibid., 112.
92. Ibid., 119–120.
93. Ibid., 130
94. Ibid., 120.
95. Ibid., 130.
96. Berdyaev, *Freedom and Spirit*, 175.
97. Ibid.
98. Berdyaev, *Destiny of Man*, 178.
99. Ibid., 183.
100. Berdyaev, *Meaning of the Creative Act*, 97, 99.
101. Berdyaev, *Destiny of Man*, 162.
102. Ibid., 184.
103. Berdyaev, *Meaning of the Creative Act*, 158.
104. Berdyaev, *Destiny of Man*, 166.
105. Ibid., 170.
106. Ibid., 184.
107. Ibid., 185.
108. Berdyaev, *Divine and Human*, 139 (emphasis added).
109. Ibid.
110. Ibid.
111. Ibid., 143.
112. Berdyaev, *Bourgeois Mind*, 126.
113. Berdyaev, *Destiny of Man*, 68.
114. Berdyaev, *Bourgeois Mind*, 126–127.
115. Ibid, 126.
116. Nikolai Berdyaev, *The Russian Idea* (Hudson, N.Y.: Lindisfarne Press, 1992), 188.
117. Ibid., 109.
118. Ibid., 257.
119. Ibid.
120. Clark, *Introduction to Berdyaev*, 183.
121. Will Herberg, ed., *Four Existentialist Theologians* (Garden City, N.Y.: Doubleday, 1958).
122. T. S. Eliot, "Little Gidding," in *Collected Poems 1909–1962* (New York: Harcourt Brace, 1963), 204.

ORIGINAL SOURCE MATERIALS

ON THE NATURE AND VALUE OF PERSONALITY

Our conception of man must be founded upon the conception of personality. True anthropology is bound to be personalistic. Consequently it is essential to understand the relation between personality and individuality. Individuality is a naturalistic and biological category, while personality is a religious and spiritual one. . . . Personality is spiritual and presupposes the existence of a spiritual world. The value of personality is the highest hierarchical value in the world, a value of the spiritual order. . . .

The value and unity of personality does not exist apart from the spiritual principle. The spirit forms personality, enlightens and transfigures the biological individual and makes him independent of the natural order. Personality is certainly not an abstract norm or idea suppressing and enslaving the concrete, individual living being. The idea or ideal value of personality is the concrete fullness of life. . . . Conflict between good and evil or between any values can only exist for a person. Tragedy is always connected with the personality—with its awakening and its struggles. A personality is created by the Divine idea and human freedom. The life of personality is not self-preservation as that of the individual but self-development and self-determination. The very existence of personality presupposes sacrifice, and sacrifice cannot be impersonal. . . .

. . . Personality from its very nature presupposes another—not the "not-self" which is a negative limit, but another person. Personality is impossible without love and sacrifice, without passing over to the other, to the friend, to the loved one. A self-contained personality becomes disintegrated. Personality is not the absolute, and God as the Absolute is not a Person. God as a Person presupposes His other, another Person, and is love and sacrifice. The Person of the Father presupposes the Persons of the Son and of the Holy Spirit. The Holy Trinity is a Trinity of Persons just because they presuppose one another and imply mutual love and inter-communion.

On another plane the personality of God and of man presuppose each other. Personality exists in the relation of love and sacrifice. It is impossible to conceive of a personal God in an abstract monotheistic way. A person cannot exist as a self-contained and self-sufficient Absolute. Personalistic metaphysics and ethics are based upon the Christian doctrine of the Holy Trinity. The moral life of every individual person must be interpreted after the image of the Divine Tri-unity, reversed and reflected in the world. A person presupposes the existence of other persons and communion between them. Personality is the highest hierarchical value and never is merely a means. But it does not exist as a value apart from its relation to God, to other persons and to human society. Personality must come out of itself, must transcend itself—this is the task set to it by God. Narrow self-centeredness ruins personality.

. . . The complexity of man lies in the fact that he is both an individual, a part of the genus, and a person, a spiritual being. The individual in his biological self-assertion and self-centredness may sever himself from the life of the genus, but this alone never leads to the affirmation of personality, its growth and expansion. Hence Christian ethics is personalistic, but not individualistic. The narrow isolation of personality in modern individualism is the destruction and not the triumph of personality. Hardened selfhood—the result of original sin—is not personality. It is only when the hardened selfhood melts away and is transcended that personality manifests itself.[1]

PERSONALISM V. EGOISM

Personalism transfers the centre of gravity of personality from the value of objective communities—society, nation, state, to the value of personality, but it understands personality in a sense which is profoundly antithetic to egoism. Egoism destroys personality. Egocentric self-containment and concentration upon the self, and the inability to issue forth from the self is original sin, which prevents the realization of the full life of personality and hinders its strength from becoming effective. . . . Personality presupposes a going out from self to an other and to others, it lacks air and is suffocated when left shut up in itself. Personalism cannot but have some sort of community in view.

At the same time this going out of the personality from itself to an other does not by any means denote exteriorization and objectivization. Personality is I and Thou, another I. But the Thou to whom the I goes out and with whom it enters into communion is not an object, it is another I, it is personality. With an object, indeed, no communion is possible, no state of community can be shared with it, there can be only mutual obligation. The personal needs an other, but that other is not external and alien: the relation of the personal to it is by no means exteriorization. Personality is to be found in a series of external relations with other people and in acts of communion with them. External relations mean objectivization, whereas communion is existential. External relations, being in the world of objectivization, are to be classed as determination and therefore do not liberate man from slavery. Communion on the other hand, being in the existential world, and having no cognizance of objects, belongs to the realm of freedom, and means liberation from slavery. Egoism denotes a double slavery of man—slavery to himself, his own hardened selfhood, and slavery to the world, which is transformed exclusively into an object which exercises constraint from without. The egocentric man is a slave, his attitude to everything which is non-I is a servile attitude. He is aware of non-I only, he has no knowledge of another I, he does not know a Thou, he knows nothing of the freedom of going out from the I. The egocentric man usually defines his relation to the world and to people in a way that is not personalistic, he very readily adopts the point of view of the objective scale of values. There is something lacking in the humanity of the egocentric man. He loves abstractions which nourish his egoism. He does not love living concrete people.[2]

PERSONALITY AND THE ANDRIC EXISTENCE

... Human personality is the andric existence. Theologians will reply in alarm that Jesus Christ alone was God-man, and that man is a created being and cannot be God-Man. But this way of arguing remains within the confines of theological rationalism. Granted man is not God-man in the sense in which Christ is God-man, the Unique One; yet there is a divine element in man. There are, so to speak, two natures in him. There is within him the intersection of two worlds. He bears within himself the image which is both the image of man and the image of God and is the image of man in so far as the image of God is actualized.

This truth about man lies beyond the dogmatic formulas and is not completely covered by them. It is a truth of existential spiritual experience which can be expressed only in symbols, not in intellectual concepts. That man bears within himself the image of God and in virtue of that becomes man, is a symbol. One cannot work out an intellectual concept about it. Divine-humanity is a contradiction for the line of thought which inclines towards monism or dualism. Humanistic philosophy never rose to such a height as to understand the paradoxical truth about divine-humanity. Theological philosophy, however, has endeavoured to rationalize this truth. All theological doctrines of grace have been but the formulations of the truth about the divine-humanity of man, and about the inward action of the divine upon the human. But it is absolutely impossible to understand this mystery of divine-humanity in the light of the philosophy of identity, monism, immanentism. The expression of this mystery presupposes a dualistic moment, an experience of the process of transcendence, of falling into an abyss and of escaping from that abyss. The divine is that which transcends man, and the divine is mysteriously united with the human in the divine-human image. It is for this reason only that the appearance in the world of personality which is not a slave to the world is possible. Personality is humane and it surpasses the human, which is dependent upon the world. Man is a manifold being; he bears within him the image of the world, but he is not only the image of the world, he is also the image of God. Within him conflict between the world and God takes place. He is a being both dependent and free. The image of God is a symbolic expression and if it is turned into a concept it meets with insuperable difficulties. Man is a symbol, for in him is a sign of something different, and he is a sign of something different. With this alone the possibility of liberating man from slavery is connected. This is the religious foundation of the doctrine of personality—not the theological foundation but the religious, that is to say, the spiritually empirical, the existential. The truth about God-humanity is not a dogmatic formula, not a theological doctrine, but an empirical truth, the expression of spiritual experience.[3]

PERSONALITY AND COMMUNION

This same truth of the twofold nature of man, twofold and at the same time integral, has its reflection in the relation of human personality to society and to history. But here it is turned upside down, as it were. Personality is independent of the determination of society, it has its own world, it is an exception, it is unique and unrepeatable. And at the same time personality is social, in it there are traces of the collective unconscious. It is man's way out from isolation. It belongs to history, it realizes itself in society and in history. Personality is communal; it presupposes communion with others, and community with others. The profound contradiction and difficulty of human life is due to this communality. Slavery is on the watch to waylay man on the path of his self realization and man must constantly return to his divine image.

Man is subjected to forcible socialization during the very time that his human personality must be in free communion, in free community, in communality which is based upon freedom and love. And the greatest danger to which a man is exposed on the paths of objectivization is the danger of mechanization, the danger of automatism. Everything mechan-

ical, everything automatic in man is not personal, it is impersonal, it is antithetic to the image of personality. The image of God, and the image of
mechanism and the automaton clash against each other, the choice is either God-man or automatic humanity, machine-humanity. Man's difficulty is rooted in the fact that there is no correlation and identity between
the inward and the outward, no direct and adequate expression of the one
in the other. This is indeed the problem of objectivization. When he ob-
jectivizes himself in the external man enslaves himself to the world of objects; and at the same time, man cannot but express himself in the external,
cannot dispense with his body, cannot but enter actively into society and
history.

Even the religious life of humanity is subject to this objectivization. In
a certain sense it may be said that religion in general is social; that it is a
social link. But this social character of religion distorts the spirit, subordinates the infinite to the finite, makes the relative absolute, and leads away
from the sources of revelation, from living spiritual experience. In the in-
terior world, personality discovers its image through the image of God,
through the penetration of the human by the divine. In the exterior world
the actualization of truth denotes the subordination of the world, of society, and of history to the image of personality, it signifies permeation by
personality. And that is personalism.[4]

CHRISTIANITY AND REDEMPTION

Christianity is the religion of Redemption and therefore presupposes the
existence of evil and suffering. It is therefore idle to invoke them as evidence against the Christian faith. The very reason why Christ came into
the world is because of its sin, and Christianity teaches us that the world
and man must bear the Cross. If suffering is the result of evil it is also the
path by which we are to be freed from it. For Christian thought suffering
is not necessarily an evil, for God Himself, that is God the Son, suffers.
The whole creation groaneth and travaileth together waiting for its deliverance. But the opponents of Christianity constantly base their attacks
upon the fact that the coming of the Saviour has not delivered the world
from suffering and evil. Almost two thousand years have passed since the
coming of the Redeemer and the world is still full of bloodshed, while humanity is racked with pain and the amount of evil and suffering has actually increased. The old Jewish argument seems to have won the day. The
true Messiah will be he who will finally deliver humanity from evil and
suffering here below.

But we forget that Christianity recognizes the positive value of the sufferings which mankind endures on earth, and that it has never promised us happiness or blessedness here. Besides which Christian prophecy as to the fate of humanity has been fairly pessimistic in character. Christianity has never upheld the view that universal peace and the Kingdom of God upon earth would be achieved by the intervention of some overwhelming power. On the contrary, it recognizes the freedom of the human spirit in a very high degree, and it regards the realization of the Kingdom of God without its participation as an impossibility. If the justice of Christ is not realized in the world, that is due rather to human injustice. The religion of love is not responsible for the fact that hate predominates in our natural world. . . .

It is impossible for us to conceive the mystery of Redemption rationally any more than any other mystery of the divine life. The juridical theory of redemption, which from the days of St. Anselm of Canterbury has played such a big part in Catholic theology and from which Orthodox theology is not entirely free, is a rationalization of this mystery, which is thus interpreted according to a scheme of relationships existing in the natural world. This juridical conception was simply an attempt to adapt celestial truth to the level of the natural man. It is not a spiritual conception at all. To regard the universal tragedy as a judicial process initiated by an angry Deity against offending man is quite unworthy. To think in this fashion is to adapt the divine life which is always mysterious and unfathomable to pagan conceptions and the spirit of tribal vengeance. God, according to pagan-Jewish thought, is regarded as a fearful tyrant Who punishes and takes vengeance for every act of disobedience, Who demands a ransom, a propitiatory victim, and the shedding of blood. . . . Upon the juridical theory of redemption the stamp of Roman and feudal conceptions regarding the rehabilitation of man was irrevocably set. The transgression of the Divine Will leads to a judicial process and God demands repayment; He must receive compensation in order to pacify His wrath. No human sacrifice will satisfy Him or make Him yield. Only the sacrifice of the Son is proportionate to the crime committed and the offence it has caused. . . .

The Redemption achieved by the Son of God is not a judicial verdict, but a means of salvation; it is not a judgment, but a transfiguration and illumination of nature—in a word, its sanctification. Salvation is not justification, but the acquiring of perfection. The conception of God as judge is that of the natural man and not the spiritual, to whom a quite different aspect of the divine nature is revealed. It is impossible to attribute to God the kind of sentiments which even men themselves regard as blameworthy, as, for instance, pride, egoism, rancour, vengeance, and cruelty. The natural man has given to the world a monstrous idea of God. According to the juridical conception of Redemption the religion of Christ is still a legal religion in which grace is not conceived ontologically.

In Christianity Redemption is the work of love and not that of justice, the sacrifice of a divine and infinite love, not a propitiatory sacrifice, nor the settlement of accounts. "For God so loved the world that He gave His only-begotten Son that whosoever believeth in Him should not perish, but have everlasting life." Bukharev, on the theory that the Lamb was slain from the foundation of the world, puts forward the remarkable idea that the voluntary sacrifice of the Son of God was part of the initial plan of creation. God Himself longs to suffer with the world. The juridical interpretation of the evolution of the universe transforms Redemption into a judicial process. . . .

The meaning of Redemption lies in the coming of the Second Adam, the new spiritual man, in the coming of that love of which the Old Adam was ignorant, in the transformation of the lower nature into the higher. It certainly does not lie in the mere regulation of the external relationships between the Old Adam and God, nor in the pardon and satisfaction granted to one party by the other. The meaning of the coming of Christ into the world lies in a real transfiguration of human nature, in the formation of a new type of spiritual man, and not in the institution of laws, by the carrying out of which the spiritual life may be acquired. . . . Man hungers for a new and higher kind of life which is in accordance with his dignity and is eternal. It is this which really constitutes the revelation of the New Covenant. In Christianity the central idea is that of transfiguration, not justification. The latter has occupied too prominent a place in Western Christianity. In Eastern Christianity and in the Greek Fathers, on the other hand, the idea is modified in human nature. But the idea of transfiguration and of divinization was fundamental.

The coming of Christ and Redemption can be spiritually understood only as a continuation of the creation of the world, as the eighth day of this creation, that is to say, as a cosmogonic and anthropogonic process, as a manifestation of divine love in creation, as a new stage in the freedom of man. The advent of the new spiritual man cannot merely be the result of the evolution of human nature. On the contrary it presupposes an entry of the eternal and spiritual into this natural time-world of ours. The natural evolution of humanity leaves us shut up within the restraints and limits of natural reality. Original sin, the evil which lies at the root of this world, continues to isolate the terrestrial world and hold it in bondage. Deliverance can only come from above. The power of the spiritual and divine world has to come into our fallen natural reality, and by transfiguring our nature, break down the barriers dividing the two worlds. Thus the history of Heaven becomes that of earth. The human race which is that of the Old Adam had to be prepared historically to receive the new spiritual man who comes from another world; a preparatory spiritual development had to take place first. Within the sphere of humanity and in the natural world there had to be a pure and spotless being capable of receiving the divine element, a feminine principle enlightened by grace. The Virgin Mary, the Mother of God, was simply the manifestation of this principle, through which the human race was to receive the Son of God and the Son of Man. In Christ, the God-Man, the infinite divine love met the answering love of man. The mystery of Redemption is that of love and liberty. If Christ is not only God but also man (which is what the dogma of the Two Natures teaches us) then in Redemption not only the divine Nature played its part but also human nature, that is, the heavenly spiritual nature of mankind. Christ as God-Man reveals the fact not only that we belong to an earthly race but that the spiritual man, thanks to Him, abides in the very depths of divine reality.

In Christ, as Man in the absolute sense, summing up in Himself the whole of spiritual humanity, man makes a heroic effort to overcome by sacrifice and suffering both sin and death, which is the consequence of sin. And this he does in order to respond to the love of God. In Christ human nature co-operates with the work of Redemption. Sacrifice is the law of spiritual ascent and with the birth of Christ a new era in the life of creation begins. Adam underwent the trial of his freedom and failed to respond to the divine call by an expression of free and creative love. Christ, the New Adam, makes this response to the love of God and thereby points out the way to this response to all who are spiritually His.

Redemption is a dual process in which both God and man share; yet it is but one process, not two. Without human nature and the exercise of human freedom it would be impossible. Here, as everywhere else in Christianity, the mystery of the theandric humanity of Christ is the key to any true understanding. There is no final solution to this mystery except in the Trinity, for it is in the Spirit that the relations between the Father and the Son are resolved. Evil cannot be overcome except by the participation of human freedom in the process. But evil undermines and alters the character of this freedom which alone permits of its defeat.

Here we have the fundamental antinomy which finds its solution in the dual mystery of Christ's nature. The Son of God, the Second Hypostasis of the Divine Trinity, overcomes the opposition between human freedom and divine necessity by the suffering of the Cross. In the passion of the Son of God and the Son of Man on Calvary freedom becomes the power of divine love, which enlightens and transfigures human freedom in the saving of the world. Truth in the guise of suffering and love makes us free without constraint; in fact it creates a new and higher kind of freedom. The freedom which the truth of Christ gives us is not the result of necessity. Redemption cannot be understood as a return of human nature to its primitive state before the fall of Adam. Such a conception would indeed make nonsense of the whole process of the universe. But the new spiritual man is superior not only to fallen Adam, but to Adam before the Fall, and his advent marks a new stage in the creation of the world. The Old Adam gives us no clue to the mystery of infinite love and the new type of freedom, for that mystery is only revealed in Christ. . . .

The appearance of Christ marks a new era in the destiny of the world, a new moment in the creation both of the world and of man. Not only human nature but the whole universe and the whole of cosmic life was transformed after the coming of Christ. When the Blood of Christ shed upon Calvary touched the earth, earth became a new thing, and it is only the limitations of our receptive faculties which prevent us from seeing it with our very eyes.[5]

THE FALL: THE ORIGIN OF GOOD AND EVIL

Christianity has adopted the myth of the Fall and of the Garden of Eden; thinkers who have given up Christianity and do not want a religious basis for ethics reject it. But the problem of ethics cannot even be formulated unless it be admitted that the distinction between good and evil had an origin in time and had been preceded by a state of being "beyond" or "prior to" good and evil. "Good" and "evil" are correlative and in a sense it may be said that good comes into being at the same time as evil and disappears together with it. This is the fundamental paradox of ethics. Paradise is the state of being in which there is no valuation or distinction. It might be said that the world proceeds from an original absence of discrimination between good and evil to a sharp distinction between them and then, enriched by that experience, ends by not distinguishing them any more. . . .

The origin of the knowledge of good and evil has two essentially different aspects, and this leads to a paradox. It is possible to interpret the knowledge of good and evil as the Fall. When I know good and evil, when I make distinctions and valuations, I lose my innocence and wholeness, fall away from God and am exiled from paradise. Knowledge is the loss of paradise. Sin is the attempt to know good and evil. But another interpretation is possible. Knowledge in itself is not a sin and does not mean falling away from God. Knowledge is good and means discovery of meaning. But plucking the fruit of the tree of knowledge indicates an evil and godless experience of life, an attempt on the part of man to return to the darkness of non-being, a refusal to give a creative answer to God's call and resistance to the act of creation. Yet knowledge connected with this act is a manifestation of the principle of wisdom in man, a transition to a higher consciousness and a higher state of existence. It is equally wrong and contradictory to say that the knowledge of good and evil is good and to say that it is evil. Our terms and categories are inapplicable to that which lies beyond the state of being which has given rise to those terms and categories.

Is it a good thing that the distinction between good and evil has arisen? Is good-good, and evil-evil? We are bound to give a paradoxical answer to this question: it is bad that the distinction between good and evil has arisen, but it is good to make the distinction, once it has arisen; it is bad to have gone through the experience of evil, but it is good to know good and evil as a result of that experience. When Nietzsche substituted for the distinction between good and evil the distinction between the fine and the low, he thought he was replacing moral and cognitive categories by natural and elemental; i.e., by paradisiacal categories. But it was an Eden after the Fall. Nietzsche cannot find his way to paradise. "Beyond good and evil," i.e. in paradise, there ought to be neither good nor evil in our sense of these terms, but with Nietzsche evil remains. Man has chosen the knowledge of good and evil through experience, and he must follow that painful path to the end; he cannot expect to find Paradise half-way. The myth of the lost paradise symbolizes the genesis of consciousness in the development of the spirit. . . .

The origin of good and evil is expressed by a myth, and ethics is bound to have a mythological basis. Both at the beginning and the end ethics comes upon a realm which lies beyond good and evil: the life of paradise and the life of the Kingdom of God, the preconscious and the superconscious state. It is only the "unhappy" consciousness with its dividedness, reflection, pain and suffering that is on "this side" of good and evil. And the most difficult question of all is what is the nature of the "good" before the distinction between good and evil has arisen and after it has ceased to be? Is there "good" in paradise and in the Kingdom of God? This is the essential metaphysical problem of ethics which is seldom considered.[6]

GOD IS BEYOND GOOD AND EVIL

It is obvious that God is "beyond good and evil," for on "this side" of it is our fallen world and certainly not God. God is above good. And there cannot be in Him any evil that is on this side of the distinction. When we ask whether God is free to will evil we apply to Him the categories of our fallen world. One can only think of the subject in terms of negative theology. God certainly is not bound by the moral good and is not dependent upon it. He *is* the Good as an absolute force. But we have at once to add that He is above good, for the category of goodness is not applicable to Him. It is impossible to pass judgment on God, for He is the source of all the values by reference to which we judge. God reveals Himself to us as the source of values, as infinite love. Theodicy can judge God only in the light of what God has revealed to us about Himself. It defends God against human conceptions of Him, against human slander.[7]

FREEDOM, FREE WILL, AND VALUES

The problem of the relation between freedom and values is even more troublesome. It may be said that man in his freedom is confronted with ideal norms or values which he has to realize; his failure to do so is an evil. This is the usual point of view. Man is free to realize the good or the values which stand above him as for ever laid down by God, forming an ideal normative world, but he is not free to create the good, to produce values. The scholastic conception of free will comes precisely to this, that man can and must fulfil the law of goodness, and if he fails to do so, it is his own fault and he is punished. This choice between good and evil is forced upon him from without. Freedom of will is not a source of creativeness, but of responsibility and possible punishment. This purely normative conception has been specially worked out for legal purposes. True freedom, however, consists not in fulfilling the law, but in creating new realities and values. As a free being man is not merely a servant of the moral law, but a creator of new values. Man is called upon to create the good and not only to fulfil it. Creative freedom gives rise to values. As a free being, a free spirit, man is called to be the creator of new values. The world of values is not a changeless ideal realm rising above man and freedom; it is constantly undergoing change and being created afresh. Man is free in relation to moral values, not merely in the sense that he is free to realize or not to realize them. Similarly, in relation to God man is free not merely in the sense that he can turn towards God or away from Him, can fulfil or not fulfil His will. Man is free in the sense of being able to co-operate with God, to create the good and produce new values.[8]

THREE TYPES OF ETHICS

There exist three types of ethics—the ethics of law, of redemption and of creativeness. Ethics in the profound sense of the term must teach of the awakening of the human spirit and not of consciousness, of creative spiritual power and not of laws and norms. The ethics of law, the ethics of consciousness which represses subconsciousness and knows nothing of superconsciousness, is the result of the primitive emotion of fear, and we, Christians, see in it the result of original sin. Fear warns man of danger, and therein lies its ontological significance.

The awakening of spirit in man is very painful. At the early stages the spirit divides and fetters man's vital energy, and only later does it manifest itself as creative energy. The spiritual superconscious principle separates man out of nature, and, as it were, dementalizes nature, depriving it of its daemonic power. In man too there is a struggle between spirit and nature. Consciousness becomes the arena of that struggle. The awakening of the spirit may be inspired by the idea of redemption or by creativeness. The idea of redemption subjects the soul to new dangers. The thought of perdition and salvation may become a morbid obsession. In that case salvation of the soul from being possessed by the idea of salvation comes from creative spiritual energy, from the shock of creative inspiration. Redemption is only completed through creativeness. This is the fundamental conception of the new ethics.[9]

THE ETHICS OF LAW

The ethics of law is the pre-Christian morality; it is to be found not only in the Old Testament but in paganism, in primitive communities, in Aristotle and the Stoics, and within Christianity in Pelagius and to a considerable extent in St. Thomas Aquinas. At the same time the ethics of law contains an eternal principle which must be recognized by the Christian world as well, for sin and evil are not conquered in it. The ethics of law cannot be interpreted chronologically only, for it co-exists with the ethics of redemption and of creativeness. Its history in the Christian world is extremely complicated. Christianity is the revelation of grace, and Christian ethics is the ethics of redemption and not of law. But Christianity was weighed down by extraneous elements and underwent changes in the course of time. It has often been interpreted in a legalistic sense. Thus, the official Roman Catholic theology is to a considerable extent legalistic. The Gospel itself has been constantly distorted by legalistic interpretations. Legalism, rationalism and formalism have actually introduced an element of law into the truth of the Christian revelation. Even grace received a legalistic interpretation. Theologians were alarmed by St. Paul's doctrine and did their best to limit and modify it. An element of rationalistic, almost Pelagian legalism penetrated into the very consciousness of the church. Luther protested ardently against the law in Christianity, against legalistic ethics, and attempted to take his stand beyond good and evil. But Luther's own followers were alarmed by him; they tried to render harmless his passionate protests and modify and rationalize his irrationalism. Only the school of K. Barth, following Kierkegaard, has returned to Luther's paradoxality. Throughout the history of Christianity there has always been a struggle between the principles of grace and spiritual regeneration and the formal, juridical and rationalistic principles.

Legalistic morality is deeply rooted in human society and goes back to the primitive clans with their totems and taboos. The ethics of law is essentially social as distinct from the personal ethics of redemption and creativeness. The Fall subordinated human conscience to society. Society became the bearer and the guardian of the moral law. Sociologists who maintain that morality has a social origin have unquestionably got hold of a certain truth. But they do not see the origin of this truth or the depth of its meaning. The ethics of law means, first and foremost, that the subject of moral valuation is society and not the individual, that society lays down moral prohibitions, taboos, laws and norms to which the individual must submit under penalty of moral excommunication and retribution. The ethics of law can never be personal and individual, it never penetrates into the intimate depths of personal moral life, experience and struggle. It exaggerates evil in personal life, punishing and prohibiting it, but does not attach sufficient importance to evil in the life of the world and society. It takes an optimistic view of the power of the moral law, of the freedom of will and of the punishment of the wicked, which is supposed to prove that the world is ruled by justice. The ethics of law is both very human and well adapted to human needs and standards, and extremely inhuman and pitiless towards the human personality, its individual destiny and intimate life. . . .

The primitive moral consciousness is communal and social. Its moral subject is the group united by kinship and not the individual. Vengeance as a moral act is also communal: it is carried out by one group of kinsmen against another, and not by one individual against another. Blood vengeance is the most characteristic moral phenomenon of antiquity and persists in the Christian world in so far as human nature in it is not transfigured and enlightened. . . .

In antiquity vengeance was not at all connected with personal guilt. Vengeance and punishment were not primarily directed against the person who was personally guilty and responsible. The conception of personal guilt and responsibility was formed much later. Blood vengeance was impersonal. When the state took upon itself the duty of avenging and punishing crime, the idea of personal guilt and responsibility began to develop. The law, which always has a social character, demands that the primeval chaos of instincts should be suppressed; but it merely drives that chaos inwards and does not conquer it or regenerate it. Chaotic primeval instincts have been preserved in the civilized man of the twentieth century. The world-war and the communistic revolution have shown this.

After the Christian revelation vengeance, which was at first a moral and religious duty, became an immoral unruly instinct that man had to overcome through the new law. The ancient awe-inspiring tyranny of the clan and kin with its endless taboos and prohibitions ceased to be a moral law as it was in antiquity, and became a part of atavistic instincts against which a higher moral consciousness must struggle. This is one of the important truths of social ethics. To begin with, society subdues and disciplines man's instincts, but afterwards, at the higher stages of moral development, ideas and emotions which had been instilled into man for the sake of disciplining him become, in their turn, unruly instincts. This happened in the first instance with vengeance. Society deprived the individual of freedom because he was possessed by sinful passions; but social restraint of freedom became an instinct of tyranny and love of power. Superstitions, tyranny and caste privileges had once served the purpose of bringing order into chaos and establishing a social cosmos; but they degenerated into instincts which stand in the way of a free social organization. Law plays a double part in the moral life of humanity: it restrains unruly instincts and creates order, but it also calls forth instincts which prevent the creation of a new order. This shows the impotence of the law. . . .

The fatal consequence of the legalistic discrimination between good and evil is tyranny of the law which means tyranny of society over the person and of the universally binding idea over the personal, the particular, unique and individual. The hard-set crystallized forms of herd life in which the creative fire is almost extinct oppress like a nightmare the creative life of personality. The law thwarts life and does violence to it. And the real tragedy of ethics lies in the fact that the law has its own positive mission in the world. It cannot be simply rejected and denied. If this were possible there would be no conflict of principles. The ethics of law must be transcended, the creative life of personality must be vindicated. But the law has a positive value of its own. It warps the individual life, but it also preserves it. It is a paradox, but the exclusive predominance of the ethics of grace in a sinful world would endanger the freedom and, indeed, the very existence of personality. A person's fate cannot be made to rest solely upon other people's spiritual condition. This is where the significance of law comes in. No one can be made to depend upon his neighbours' moral qualities and inward perfection. In our sinful world personality is doomed to share to some extent the herd life which both thwarts it and preserves it by means of law and justice. Justice is righteousness refracted in the common life of every day. The realm of the herd-man, *das Man*, is the result of the Fall; indeed, it *is* the fallen world. The life of personality is inevitably warped in it, and even Christian revelation becomes distorted. The primary evil is not in the law as such which makes sin manifest, but in the sin which gives rise to the law. But the law which denounces sin and puts a limit to the manifestations of it has a way of degenerating into evil. . . .

From its very nature law inevitably inspires fear. It does not regenerate human nature, does not destroy sin, but by means of fear, both external and inward, holds sin within certain bounds. Moral order in the world is maintained in the first place through religious fear, which later on assumes the forms of the moral law. Such are the direct consequences of the Fall. In the life of the state and the community we find at this stage cruel punishments and executions to which moral significance is attached. The characteristic feature of the ethics of law is that it is concerned with the abstract norm of the good but does not care about man, the unique and individual human personality and its intimate inner life. This is its limitation. It is interested not in man as a living being with his joys and sufferings, but in the abstract norm of the good which is set for man. This is the case even when it becomes philosophic and idealistic and proclaims the principle of the intrinsic value of human personality. Thus in Kant the conception of personality is purely abstract and normative, and has no relation to the concrete and irreplaceable human individuality in which Kant never took any interest. . . .

The law neither cares about the individual's life nor gives him strength to fulfil the good which it requires of him. This is the essential contradiction of the ethics of law, which inevitably leads to the ethics of grace or redemption. Dried up formal virtue deprived of beneficent, gracious and life-giving energy is frequently met with in Christian asceticism, which may prove to be an instance of legalistic morality within Christianity. A monastically ascetic attitude to life, a kind of resentment towards it, is the expression of the ethics of law within the religion of grace and redemption;

it is powerless to raise life to a higher level. Only when asceticism is combined with mysticism it acquires a different character. The moral law, the law of the state, of the church, of the family, of civilization, of technics and economics, organizes life, preserves it and passes judgment upon it; sometimes it warps life but never sustains it with a gracious power, never illuminates or transfigures it. The law is necessary for the sinful world and cannot be simply cancelled. But it must be overcome by a higher force; the world and man must be freed from the impersonal power of the law. . . .

The ethics of law is not only religious and social; it is also philosophical and claims to be based upon freedom and autonomy. But even then its Old Testament character makes itself manifest. Philosophical ethics of law is normative and idealistic; it is not based upon any external authority but is autonomous. This is pre-eminently true of the Kantian system, which is the most remarkable attempt of constructing a philosophical ethics of law. Though Kant's ethics is autonomous, it is based on the conception of law, as the very term autonomy indicates. It is legalistic because it is concerned with the universally binding moral law, with man's moral and rational nature which is the same in all; it is not in the least interested in the concrete living man as such, in his destiny, in his moral experience and spiritual conflicts. The moral law, which man must freely discover for himself, automatically gives directions to all, and is the same for all men and in all cases of life. Kant's moral maxim that every man must be regarded not only as a means but also as an end in himself is undermined by the legalistic character of his ethics, because every man proves to be a means and an instrument for the realization of an abstract, impersonal, universally binding law. Morality is free in so far as it is autonomous; man, however, is not free or autonomous at all, but is entirely subject to law. Consequently Kant completely denied the emotional side of the moral life, provoking Schiller's famous epigram. Human personality has really no value for Kant and is merely a formal and universally binding principle. Individuality does not exist for Kantian ethics, any more than do unique and individual moral problems which demand unique and individual, i.e. creative, moral solutions. . . .

The moral philosophy of Tolstoy is as legalistic as that of Kant. It is not based on any external authority. Tolstoy regards the Gospel as an expression of the moral law and norm, and the realization of the Kingdom of God is for him on a par with abstention from tobacco and alcohol. Christ's teaching consists for him of a number of moral precepts which man can easily carry out, once he recognizes their rationality. Tolstoy was a severe critic of Christian falsity and hypocrisy, but he wanted to subordinate life to the tyrannical power of legalistic morality. There is something almost daemonic in Tolstoy's moralism which would destroy all the richness and fullness of life. Both Kant and Tolstoy had grown up against a Christian background, but in spite of their love of freedom their teaching is a legalistic distortion of Christianity. They preach righteousness achieved through fulfilling the law, i.e. they return to a philosophically refined form of pharisaism and Pelagianism, which also upheld moralism and had no need of grace.

It was against Pelagian moralism and rationalism, i.e. against legalism in the Catholic church, that Luther rebelled; but in its further development Lutheranism, too, became legalistic. The legalistic element was strong in Christianity at all times, and even the doctrine of grace was interpreted in that sense. Pharisaism was by no means overcome. Moralism in all its forms was essentially pharisaical. Asceticism assumed a legalistic character. A moralist as a type is a stickler for the law who does not want to know anything about the concrete, living individual. Amoralism is a legitimate reaction against this. The imperatives of legalistic ethics are applicable only to very crude, elementary instances—one must not indulge in vice, steal, commit murder, tell lies—but they are of no help in the more subtle and complex cases which demand an individual, creative solution. The law has been made for the Old Adam, vindictive, tyrannical, greedy, lustful and envious. But the real problem of ethics lies deeper; it is bound up with the individual complexity of life, which is due to conflicts between the higher values and to the presence of the tragic element in life. And yet it is generally supposed that the business of ethics is to teach that one ought not to be a pick-pocket! . . .

The complexity and paradoxality of the Christian attitude to the law is due to the fact that although Christ denounced pharisaism, He said that He came to fulfil the law and not to destroy it. The Gospel transcends and cancels the ethics of law, replacing it by a different and higher ethics of love and freedom. But at the same time it does not allow us simply to reject the law. Christianity opens the way to the Kingdom of God where there is no more law, but meanwhile the law denounces sin and must be fulfilled by the world which remains in sin. Sinners need salvation, and salvation comes not from the law but from the Saviour; salvation is attained through redemption and not through law. But the lower sphere of the law exists all the time, and law remains in force in its own domain. The social life of Christendom is still under the power of the law almost to the same extent as the life of the primitive clans and totems. The law is improved and perfected while remaining the same in principle. There is an eternal element in it. . . .

We are thus faced with the following paradox: the law does not know the concrete, unique, living personality or penetrate into its inner life, but it preserves that personality from interference and violence on the part of others, whatever their spiritual condition may be. Therein lies the great and eternal value of law and justice. Christianity is bound to recognize it. It is impossible to wait for a gracious regeneration of society to make human life intolerable. Such is the correlation of law and grace. I must love my neighbour in Christ, this is the way to the Kingdom of Heaven. But if I have no love for my neighbour I must in any case fulfil the law in relation to him and treat him justly and honourably. It is impossible to cancel the law and wait for the realization of love. That, too, would be sheer hypocrisy. Even if I have no love I must not steal, must not commit murder, must not be a bully. That which comes from grace is never lower but always higher than that which comes from the law. The higher does not cancel the lower, but includes it in a sublimated form. A legalistic misinterpretation of love and grace is an evil and leads to violence, denial of freedom and complete rejection of the law. This then is the relation between the ethics of law and the ethics of redemption. The latter cannot take the place of the former: if it does, it becomes despotic and denies freedom. The two orders co-exist, and the order of grace stands for regeneration and enlightenment, and not for tyranny. The highest achievement of the ethics of law is justice.[10]

THE ETHICS OF REDEMPTION

To every sensitive mind it is clear that it is impossible to be content with the law and that legalistic good does not solve the problem of life. Once the distinction between good and evil has arisen, it is beyond the power of man to annul it, i.e. to conquer evil. And man thirsts for redemption, for deliverance not only from evil but from the legalistic distinction between good and evil. The longing for redemption was present in the pre-Christian world. We find it in the ancient mysteries of the suffering gods. In an embryonic form it is present in totemism and the totemic eucharist. The thirst for redemption means an earnest hope that God and the gods will take part in solving the painful problem of good and evil and in human suffering. God will come down to earth like fire, and sin and evil will be burnt up, the distinction between good and evil will disappear, and so will the impotent legalistic good which does nothing but torture man. The thirst for redemption is the longing to be reconciled to God, and it is the only way to conquer atheism inspired by the presence of pain and evil in the world. Redemption is the meeting with the suffering and sacrificial God, with a God, i.e., who shares the bitter destiny of the world and of man. Man is a free being and there is in him an element of primeval, uncreated, pre-cosmic freedom. But he is powerless to master his own irrational freedom and its abysmal darkness. This is his perennial tragedy. It is necessary that God Himself should descend into the depths of that freedom and take upon Himself the consequences of pain and evil to which it gives rise. . . .

Everyone knows that the Gospel morality is totally different from the morality of law. But the Christian world has managed to live and to formulate its doctrine as though there had never been any conflict between them. No one can deny that there is an opposition between the Christian and the legalistic ethics. The Gospel morality is based upon the power of grace, unknown to the law, so that it is no longer morality in the old sense. Christianity means the acquisition of power in and through Christ, of power that truly regenerates man and does not fear life or death, darkness or pain. The real opposition is between power and law, between something ontologically real and something purely ideal and normative. This is why abstract moralism, so natural to all legalistic and normative theories, is not at all typical of Christianity. We touch here upon the central point of Christian ethics and of ethics in general. The fundamental question of ethics may be formulated as follows: can the idea of the good be the aim of human life and the source of all practical valuations? Moralists are only too ready to base their systems upon the idea of the supreme good and think it, indeed, indispensable to ethics. But as soon as the idea of the supreme good is put at the basis of ethics, ethics becomes normative and legalistic. . . .

The ethics of the Gospel is based upon existence and not upon norm, it prefers life to law. A concrete existent, a living being, is higher than any abstract idea, even if it be the idea of the good. The good of the Gospel consists in regarding not the good but man as the supreme principle of life. The Gospel shows that men, out of love for the good, may be vile and hypocritical, that out of love for the good they may torture their fellows or forget about them. The Sabbath is for man and not man for the Sabbath—this is the essence of the great moral revolution made by Christianity, in which man for the first time recovered from the fatal consequences of distinguishing between good and evil and from the power of the law. "The Sabbath" stands for the abstract good, for the idea, the norm, the law, the fear of defilement. But "the Son of man is the lord of the Sabbath." Christianity knows no abstract moral norms, binding upon all men and at all times. Therefore for a Christian every moral problem demands its own individual solution, and is not to be solved mechanically by applying a norm set once for all. It must be so, if man is higher than "the Sabbath," the abstract idea of the good. Every moral act must be based upon the greatest possible consideration for the man from whom it proceeds and for the man upon whom it is directed. The Gospel morality of grace and redemption is the direct opposite of Kant's formula: you must not act so that the principle of your action could become a universal law; you must always act individually, and everyone must act differently. The universal law is that every moral action should be unique and individual, i.e. that it should have in view a concrete living person and not the abstract good.

Such is the ethics of love. Love can only be directed upon a person, a living being and not upon the abstract good. To be guided in one's moral actions by the love for the good and not for men means to be a Scribe and a Pharisee and to practise the reverse of the Christian moral teaching. The only thing higher than the love for man is the love for God, Who is also a concrete Being, a Person and not an abstract idea. The love of God and the love of man sum up the Gospel morality; all the rest is not characteristically Christian and merely confirms the law. Christianity preaches love for one's neighbour and not for "those far off." This is a very important distinction. Love for "the far off," for man and humanity in general, is love for an abstract idea, for the abstract good, and not love for man. And for the sake of this abstract love men are ready to sacrifice concrete, living beings. We find this love for "the far off" in humanistic revolutionary morality. But there is a great difference between humanistic and Christian love. Christian love is concrete and personal, while humanistic love is abstract and impersonal; Christian love cares above all for the individual, and humanistic for "the idea," even though it be the idea of humanity and its happiness. There is, of course, a strong Christian element in humanism, for humanism is of Christian origin. Christianity affirmed the supreme value of man through the words of Christ that man is higher than Sabbath and His commandment of love for one's neighbour. But just as in Christianity the Scribes and Pharisees began to gain the upper hand, and "the Sabbath," the abstract idea of the good, was set above man, so in humanism its Scribes and Pharisees put the idea of human welfare or progress above man as a concrete living being. . . .

We have already seen that the Gospel morality is opposed to the legalistic morality of salvation by one's own efforts through carrying out the moral law. Since it is based not upon the abstract good but upon the relation to man as a concrete living person, it is highly dynamic in character. Christianity does not recognize the fixed types of "the wicked" and of "the righteous." An evil-doer may turn into a righteous man, and *vice versa*. St. John of the Ladder says: "You will be careful not to condemn sinners if you remember that Judas was one of the Apostles and the thief was one of a band of murderers; but in one moment the miracle of regeneration took place in him." This is why Christ teaches us "judge not, that ye be not judged." Up to the hour of death no one knows what may happen to a man and what a complete change he may undergo, nor does anyone know what happens to him at the hour of death, on a plane inaccessible to us. This is why Christianity regards "the wicked" differently than this world does; it does not allow a sharp division of mankind into two halves; "the good" and "the wicked"—a division by which moral theories set much store. . . .

The Gospel makes a complete change in our moral valuations, but we are not conscious of its full significance because we have grown used to it and adapted it too well to our everyday needs. "I am come to send fire on the earth." In this fire are burnt up all the old, habitual moral valuations, and new ones are formed. The first shall be last, and the last first. This means a revolution more radical than any other. Christianity was born in this revolution, it has sprung from it. But Christian humanity was unable to introduce it into life, for that would have meant rising "beyond good and evil" by which the world lives. When the mysterious words of the Gospel were made into a norm, "the last" became the new "first". It was just as it is in social revolutions when the oppressed class comes into power and begins to oppress others. This is the fate of all the Gospel words in so far as they are turned into a norm. The paradox is that the oppressed never can be masters, for as soon as they obtain mastery they become the oppressors. The poor never can be masters, for as soon as they obtain mastery they become rich. Therefore no external revolutions can correspond to the radical change proclaimed in the Gospel. The Gospel does not preach laws and norms, and cannot be interpreted in that sense.

The gospel is the good news of the coming of the Kingdom of God. Christ's call to us is the call to His Kingdom and can only be interpreted in that sense. The morality of the Kingdom of God proves to be unlike the morality of the fallen world, which is on this side of good and evil. The Gospel morality lies beyond the familiar distinction between good and evil according to which the first are first and the last are last. The ethics of redemption is in every way opposed to the ideas of this world. Most of what Christ says takes the form of "it hath been said, but I say unto you." Tareyev is right when he insists that the Gospel is absolute in character and incommensurable with the relative naturally historical life. "But I say unto you that ye resist not evil." The ordinary moral life is based upon resisting evil. "Love your enemies, bless them that curse you, do good to them that hate you, and pray for them which despitefully use you, and persecute you." If this call of the Gospel be understood as a law, it is impracticable; it is senseless from the point of view of the ethics of law, it presupposes a different and a gracious order of being. "Seek ye first the Kingdom of God and His righteousness, and all these things shall be added unto you." Herein lies the essence of the Gospel and of Christianity. . . .

It is impossible to understand the Gospel as a norm or law. If it is understood in that sense it becomes hostile to life and incompatible with it. The absolute character of the Gospel teaching about life then becomes unintelligible and impracticable. The chief argument that the world has always brought against the gospel is that it is impracticable and opposed to the very laws of life. And indeed the morality of the Gospel is paradoxical and contrary to the morality of our world even at its highest. The Gospel is opposed not only to evil but to what men consider good. Usually people have tried to make the Gospel fit the requirements of this world and so make it acceptable. But this has always meant a distortion of Christianity. How then are we to understand the absolute, transcendental and uncompromising character of the truth proclaimed in the Gospel? The Gospel is the good news of the coming of the Kingdom of God. This is the essence both of the Gospel and of Christianity as a whole. "Seek ye first the Kingdom of God and all these things will be added unto you." The Gospel reveals the absolute life of the Kingdom, and everything in it proves to be unlike the relative life of the world. The Gospel morality is not a norm or a law because it is the morality of paradise and is beyond our good and evil, beyond our legalistic distinctions between good and evil. . . .

Christ came to bring down fire on earth, and everything that men regard as valuable, all the kingdoms built up by them, are consumed in that fire. Be perfect as your Father in heaven is perfect. Is that a norm and a rule of life? Of course not. The perfection of the Heavenly Father cannot be the norm for a sinful world; it is absolute, while a law or rule is always relative to sin. It is a revelation of an absolute, divine life, different from the sinful life of the world. Thou shalt do no murder, thou shalt not steal, thou shalt not commit adultery—all this can be a norm or a rule for the sinful life of the world and is relative to it. But the perfection of the Heavenly Father and the Kingdom of God are not relative to anything and cannot be made into a rule. The Gospel appeals to the inner, spiritual man and not to the outer man, a member of society. It calls not for external works in the social world but for the awakening and regeneration of the spiritual life, for a new birth that is to bring us into the Kingdom of God. The Gospel is addressed to the eternal principle in the human soul independent of historical epochs and social changes, and in a certain sense it is not social. Everything in the Gospel is connected with the person of Christ and is incomprehensible apart from that connection. The injunctions of the Gospel are utterly unrealizable and impossible as rules of action. But what is impossible for man, is possible for God. Only in and through Christ is the perfection similar to the perfection of the Heavenly Father realized, and the Kingdom of God actually comes. The Gospel is based not upon law, even if it be a new law, but upon Christ Himself, upon His personality. Such is the new ethics of grace and redemption.[11]

THE ETHICS OF CREATIVENESS

The Gospel constantly speaks of the fruit which the seed must bring forth if it falls on good soil and of talents given to man which must be returned with profit. Under cover of parable Christ refers in these words to man's creative activity, to his creative vocation. Burying one's talents in the ground, i.e. absence of creativeness, is condemned by Christ. The whole of St. Paul's teaching about various gifts is concerned with man's creative vocation. The gifts are from God and they indicate that man is intended to do creative work. These gifts are various, and everyone is called to creative service in accordance with the special gift bestowed upon him. It is therefore a mistake to assert, as people often do, that the Holy Writ contains no reference to creativeness. It does—but we must be able to read it, we must guess what it is God wants and expects of man.

Creativeness is always a growth, an addition, the making of something new that had not existed in the world before. The problem of creativeness is the problem as to whether something completely new is really possible. Creativeness from its very meaning is bringing forth out of nothing. Nothing becomes something, non-being becomes being. Creativeness presupposes non-being, just as Hegel's "becoming" does. Like Plato's Eros, creativeness is the child of poverty and plenty, of want and abundance of power. Creativeness is connected with sin and at the same time it is sacrificial. True creativeness always involves catharsis, purification, liberation of the spirit from psycho-physical elements and victory over them. Creation is different in principle from generation and emanation. In emanation particles of matter radiate from a centre and are separated off. Nor is creation a redistribution of force and energy, as evolution is. So far from being identical with evolution, creation is the very opposite of it. In evolution nothing new is made, but the old is redistributed. Evolution is necessity, creation is freedom. Creation is the greatest mystery of life, the mystery of the appearance of something new that had never existed before and is not deduced from, or generated by, anything. Creativeness presupposes non-being μή όν (and not ούκ όν) which is the source of the primeval, pre-cosmic, pre-existent freedom in man. The mystery of creativeness is the mystery of freedom. Creativeness can only spring from fathomless freedom, for such freedom alone can give rise to the new, to what had never existed before. Out of being, out of something that exists, it is impossible to create that which is completely new; there can only be emanation, generation, redistribution. But creativeness means breaking through from non-being, from freedom, to the world of being. The mystery of creativeness is revealed in the biblical myth of the creation. God created the world out of nothing, i.e., freely and out of freedom. The world was not an emanation from God, it was not evolved or born from Him, but created, i.e. it was absolutely new, it was something that had never been before. Creativeness is only possible because the world is created, because there is a Creator. Man, made by God in His own image and likeness, is also a creator and is called to creative work. . . .

Man cannot produce the material for creation out of himself, out of nothing, out of the depths of his own being. The creative act is of the nature of marriage, it always implies a meeting between different elements. The material for human creativeness is borrowed from the world created by God. We find this in all art and in all inventions and discoveries. We find this in the creativeness of knowledge and in philosophy which presupposes the existence of the world created by God—objective realities without which thought would be left in a void. God has granted man the creative gift, the talent, the genius and also the world in and through which the creative activity is to be carried out. God calls man to perform the creative act and realize his vocation, and He is expecting an answer to His call. Man's answer to God's call cannot entirely consist of elements that are given by and proceed from God. Something must come from man also, and that something is the very essence of creativeness, which brings forth new realities. It is, indeed, not "something" but "nothing"—in other words it is freedom, without which there can be no creative activity. Freedom not determined by anything answers God's call to creative work, but in doing so it makes use of the gift or genius received from God and of materials present in the created world. When man is said to create out of nothing it means that he creates out of freedom. In every creative conception there is an element of primeval freedom, fathomless, undetermined by anything, not proceeding from God but ascending towards God. God's call is address to that abyss of freedom, and the answer must come from it. Fathomless freedom is present in all creativeness, but the creative process is so complex that it is not easy to detect this primary element in it. It is a process of interaction between grace and freedom, between forces going from God to man and from man to God. . . .

Man's creative activity alone bears witness to his vocation and show what he has been destined for in the world. The law says nothing about vocation, nor does the ethics of redemption as such. The Gospel and St. Paul's Epistles speak of man's gifts and vocation only because they go beyond the mystery of redemption. True creativeness is always in the Holy Spirit, for only in the Spirit can there be that union of grace and freedom which we find in creativeness. Its meaning for ethics is twofold. To begin with, ethics must inquire into the moral significance of all creative work, even if it has no direct relation to the moral life. Art and knowledge have a moral significance, like all activities which create higher values. Secondly, ethics must inquire into the creative significance of moral activity. Moral life itself, moral actions and valuations have a creative character. The ethics of law and norm does not as yet recognize this, and it is therefore inevitable that we should pass to the ethics of creativeness, which deals with man's true vocation and destiny.

Creativeness and a creative attitude to life as a whole is not man's right, it is his duty. It is a moral imperative that applies in every department of life. Creative effort in artistic and cognitive activity has a moral value. Realization of truth and goodness is a moral good. There may, however, be a conflict between the creation of perfect cultural values and the creation of a perfect human personality. The path of creativeness is also a path to moral and religious perfection, a way of realizing the fullness of life. The frequently quoted words of Goethe, "All theory is grey but the tree of life is eternally green," may be turned the other way round: "All life is grey but the tree of theory is eternally green." "Theory" will then mean creativeness, the thought of a Plato or a Hegel, while "life" will stand for a mere struggle for existence, dull and commonplace, family dissensions, disappointments and so on. In that sense "theory" means rising to a higher moral level. . . .

The ethics of creativeness differs from the ethics of law first of all because every moral task is for it absolutely individual and creative. The moral problems of life cannot be solved by an automatic application of universally binding rules. It is impossible to say that in the same circumstances one ought always and everywhere to act in the same way. It is impossible if only because circumstances never are quite the same. Indeed, the very opposite rule might be formulated. One ought always to act individually and solve every moral problem for oneself, showing creativeness in one's moral activity, and not for a single moment become a moral automaton. A man ought to make moral inventions with regard to the problems that life sets him. Hence, for the ethics of creativeness freedom means something very different from what it does for the ethics of law. For the latter the so-called freedom of will has no creative character and means merely acceptance or rejection of the law of the good and responsibility for doing one or the other. For the ethics of creativeness freedom means not the acceptance of the law but individual creation of values. Freedom is creative energy, the possibility of building up new realities. The ethics of law knows nothing of that freedom. It does not know that the good is being created, that in every individual and unrepeatable moral act new good that had never existed before is brought into being by the moral agent whose invention it is. There exists no fixed, static moral order subordinated to a single universally binding moral law. Man is not a passive executor of the laws of that world-order. Man is a creator and an inventor. His moral conscience must at every moment of his life be creative and inventive. The ethics of creativeness is one of dynamics and energy. Life is based upon energy and not upon law. It may be said, indeed, that energy is the source of law. The ethics of creativeness takes a very different view of the struggle against evil than does the ethics of law. According to it, that struggle consists in the creative realization of the good and the transformation of evil into good, rather than in the mere destruction of evil. The ethics of law is concerned with the finite: the world is for it a self-contained system and there is no way out of it. The ethics of creativeness is concerned with the infinite: the world is for it open and plastic, with boundless horizons and possibilities of breaking through to other worlds. It overcomes the nightmare of the finite from which there is no escape.

The ethics of creativeness is different from the ethics of redemption: it is concerned in the first place with values and not with salvation. The moral end of life is for it not the salvation of one's soul or the redemption of guilt but creative realization of righteousness and of values which need not belong to the moral order. The ethics of creativeness springs from personality but is concerned with the world, while the ethics of law springs from the world and society but is concerned with the personality. The ethics of creativeness alone overcomes the negative fixation of the spirit upon struggle with sin and evil and replaces it by the positive, i.e. by the creation of the valuable contents of life. It overcomes not only the earthly but the heavenly, transcendental selfishness with which even the ethics of redemption is infected. Fear of punishment and of eternal torments in hell can play no part in the ethics of creativeness. It opens a way to a pure, disinterested morality, since every kind of fear distorts moral experience and activity. It may indeed be said that nothing which is done out of fear, whether it be of temporal or of eternal torments, has any moral value. The truly moral motive is not fear of punishment and of hell, but selfless and disinterested love of God and of the divine in life, of truth and perfection and all positive values. This is the basis of the ethics of creativeness.[12]

CREATIVENESS AND IMAGINATION

The ethics of creativeness presupposes that the task which confronts man is infinite and the world is not completed. But the tragedy is that the realization of every infinite task is finite. Creative imagination is of fundamental importance to the ethics of creativeness. Without imagination there can be no creative activity. Creativeness means in the first instance imagining something different, better, and higher. Imagination calls up before us something better than the reality around us. Creativeness always rises above reality. Imagination plays this part not only in art and in myth making, but also in scientific discoveries, technical inventions and moral life, creating a better type of relations between human beings. There is such a thing as moral imagination which creates the image of a better life; it is absent only from legalistic ethics. No imagination is needed for automatically carrying out a law or norm. In moral life the power of creative imagination plays the part of talent. By the side of the self-contained moral world of laws and rules to which nothing can be added, man builds up in imagination a higher, free and beautiful world lying beyond ordinary good and evil. And this is what gives beauty to life. As a matter of fact life can never be determined solely by law; men always imagine for themselves a different and better life, freer and more beautiful, and they realize those images. The Kingdom of God is the image of a full, perfect, beautiful, free and divine life. Only law has nothing to do with imagination, or, rather, it is limited to imagining compliance with, or violation of, its behests. But the most perfect fulfillment of the law is not the same as the perfect life.

Imagination may also be a source of evil; there may be bad imagination and phantasms. Evil thoughts are an instance of bad imagination. Crimes are conceived in imagination. But imagination also brings about a better life. A man devoid of imagination is incapable of creative moral activity and of building up a better life. The very conception of a better life towards which we ought to strive is the result of creative imagination. Those who have no imagination think that there is no better life at all and there ought not to be. All that exists for them is the unalterable order of existence in which unalterable law ought to be realized. Jacob Boehme ascribed enormous importance to imagination. The world is created by God through imagination, through images which arise in God in eternity.[13]

CREATIVENESS AND BEAUTY

... From the ontological and cosmological point of view, the final end of being must be thought of as beauty and not as goodness. Plato defined beauty as the magnificence of the good. Complete, perfect and harmonious being is beauty. Teleological ethics is normative and legalistic. It regards the good as the purpose of life, i.e. as a norm or a law which must be fulfilled. Teleological ethics always implies absence of moral imagination, for it conceives the end as a norm and not as an image, not as a product of the creative energy of life. Moral life must be determined not by a purpose or a norm but by imagery and the exercise of creative activity. Beauty is the image of creative energy radiating over the whole world and transforming it. Teleological ethics based upon the idea of the good as an absolute purpose is hostile to freedom, but creative ethics is based upon freedom. Beauty means a transfigured creation, the good means creation fettered by the law which denounces sin. The paradox is that the law fetters the energy of the good, it does not want the good to be interpreted as a force, for in that case the world would escape from the power of the law. To transcend the morality of law means to put infinite creative energy in the place of commands, prohibitions, and taboos.[14]

CREATIVENESS AND THE KINGDOM OF HEAVEN

... All efforts to create new life, whether in historical Christianity, by social revolutions, or by the information of sects and so forth, alike end in objectivization, and adaptation to dull, everyday normality. The old rises in new forms, the old inequality, love of power, luxury, schisms and the rest. Life in our aeon is only a testing and a pathway, but the testing has a meaning and the path leads to a consummating end. It would become easier for man if he were aware of the fact that a further revelation of the unknown is at hand, a revelation not only of the Holy Spirit but of a new man and a new cosmos. . . .

The greatest religious and moral truth to which man must grow, is that we cannot be saved individually. My salvation presupposes the salvation of others also, the salvation of my neighbour, it presupposes universal salvation, the salvation of the whole world, the transfiguration of the world. The very idea of salvation arises from the oppressed condition of man; and it is associated with a forensic conception of Christianity. This ought to be replaced by the idea of creative transformation and enlightenment, by the idea of perfecting all life. 'Behold I make all things new'. It is not only God Who makes all things new, it is man too. The period of the end is not only a period of destruction, but also a period of divine-human creativeness, a new life and a new world. The Church of the New Testament was a symbolic image of the eternal Church of the Spirit. In the Church of the Spirit the eternal Gospel will be read. When we draw near to the eternal Kingdom of the Spirit the torturing contradictions of life will be overcome and sufferings which towards the end will be increased, will pass into their antithesis, into joy. And this will be the case not only for the future but also for the past, for there will be a reversal of time and all living things will share in the end.[15]

NOTES

1. [Nicholas Berdyaev, *The Destiny of Man* (New York: Charles Scribner's Sons, 1937), 71–75.]

2. [Nicholas Berdyaev, *Slavery and Freedom* (New York: Charles Scribner's Sons, 1944), 42–43]

3. [Ibid., 45–46.]

4. [Ibid., 46–47.]

5. [Nicholas Berdyaev, *Freedom and the Spirit* (London: Geoffrey Bles, 1935), 171–174, 176–179.]

6. [Berdyaev, *Destiny of Man*, 47, 49–50, 52.]

7. [Ibid., 56–57.]

8. [Ibid., 57.]

9. [Ibid., 100–101.]

10. [Ibid., 111–112, 115–116, 119–120, 122–126, 128–131.]

11. [Ibid., 133–142, 157–159.]

12. [Ibid., 162–165, 169–171.]

13. [Ibid., 182–184.]

14. [Ibid., 185.]

15. [Nicholas Berdyaev, *The Divine and the Human* (London: Geoffrey Bles, 1949), 199–202.]

[CHAPTER 3]

Vladimir Nikolaievich Lossky (1903–1958)

COMMENTARY

MIKHAIL M. KULAKOV

Vladimir Nikolaievich Lossky was born in 1903 in St. Petersburg into the family of a well-known Russian intuitionist philosopher, Nikolay Onufri-yevich Lossky. He studied briefly at the universities of Petrograd and Prague before matriculating at the University of Paris, from which he eventually graduated with a degree in medieval studies in 1927. In 1922 Vladimir was exiled from Russia with his father's family and other notable intellectuals who had refused to cooperate with the new Soviet government. After a two-year stay in Prague, the family settled in Paris, where Lossky im-mersed himself in study of Western theology and spirituality under the guidance of the influential Thomist scholar Etienne Gilson.

Lossky devoted a great deal of time to the study of Meister Eckhart's negative mysticism. He detected a certain affinity between this German Dominican friar and the Byzantine mystics. Eckhart rejected the earlier attempts of Western medieval mystics to encounter God with prayer, using one's rational abilities. He was convinced that it is easier to say what God is not than to attempt to formulate what God is. To seek a di-rect and immediate fellowship of the soul with the inexpressible and un-approachable God was, for Eckhart, a much more fruitful endeavor. Yet, Lossky did not find Eckhart (particularly Eckhart's *Gottheit*) to be suffi-ciently personalist in his negative (or apophatic, from the Greek *apo-phasis*, "denial") approach. Nor was Eckhart able to overcome the tendency of considering "common nature" before the persons of the Trinity. Lossky's brilliant study *Theologie négative et connaissance de Dieu chez Maitre Eckhart* was published in Paris posthumously in 1960. The study of the Western scholastic and mystical traditions led Lossky to a thorough investigation of the roots of spiritual and doctrinal divergence between East and West and a search for points of contact and unity.

Lossky accepted his forced exile from Russia as a call to become a living witness of Eastern Orthodoxy to Christians in the West. He distanced himself from Orthodox circles in France that promoted the utopian ideas of Holy Russia and Slavophile exclusivism. Instead, he channeled his energies toward the construction of a patristically based, comprehensive theological system. Already in 1928 Vladimir was playing a leading role in the Brotherhood of St. Photius, an émigré missionary society in Paris, which Lossky envisaged as an "order of Christian knights" engaged in Orthodox witness and creative dialogue with the West. Lossky's centrist stand among the various groups of Russian emigration in Paris was demonstrated by his staunch support of the Moscow Patriarchate, the canonical authority of which had been challenged by radical anti-Soviet factions on the right and liberal circles on the left that were in contact with the Patriarch of Constantinople and were locally associated with Metropolitan Evlogii. Among the more influential representatives of these liberal circles in Paris were philosopher Nicholas Berdyaev and theologian Sergei Bulgakov.

Lossky was deeply involved in the controversies and debates of the 1930s. His lengthy tract *The Sophia Controversy*, published in 1936, contained ferociously destructive criticism of the highly complex and vastly influential philosophical theology of Bulgakov. Following Soloviev, Bulgakov envisaged the existence of a world-soul, or a "fourth hypostasis," described as an "eternal femininity" in God that dominates the cosmic process. Lossky denounced Bulgakov's teaching for its hidden determinism, its slavish dependence on philosophy, and personification of nature, which led to a reduced and inadequate notion of divine and human persons robbed of genuine self-determination.[1] Lossky saw it as his task to liberate Russian religious thought from its enslavement to philosophy in general and to nineteenth-century German idealism and Slavophile exclusivism in particular. His theological work is thus a reaction to these tendencies in Khomyakov and Soloviev in the nineteenth century, as well as in his contemporaries Bulgakov and Berdyaev.

Unlike Bulgakov and Berdyaev, who were suspicious of the official Russian Church within the Soviet Union, Lossky pled for fidelity to it in its concrete, historical form. He was deeply saddened by the dismemberment of the Russian Church brought about by the tragic events of the Bolshevik Revolution. He felt that both conservative and liberal Russian emigrants betrayed the Orthodox Church within Russia. In contrast to his universal vision of the church, their notions of the "true ecclesia" were too dependent on certain political, cultural, or national conditions (or ideals not related directly to the historical church as a canonical institution, as in the case of Berdyaev and Bulgakov). In *Mystical Theology*, Lossky portrayed the Orthodox Church as the "center of the universe, the sphere in which its destinies are determined."[2] In "Temptations of Ecclesial Consciousness," first published in Paris in 1950, he wrote that each one is called "to the ministry of the Church at the present moment in the existing conditions." He urged his readers to discern, in the humiliated and persecuted Russian Church, the "true Church," which had a crucial task.[3] He warned that one should not wait "for a normal period (such periods do not exist)."[4]

Lossky certainly did not wait for a better period. He engaged in intense dialogue with Catholic and Protestant theologians. He labored tirelessly for the recognition of the French Orthodox community of the Western rite. He supported the embattled leaders of the Moscow Patriarchate, and held in high esteem the patriarchal *locum tenens*, Metropolitan Sergii (Stragorodskii), maintaining an intensive correspondence with him over a number of years.[5] He exemplified the same realism in his position on war and on the use of force.

Lossky made every effort to get involved in the French resistance movement during the Nazi occupation of France. His *Sept jours sur les routes de France* contains his candid reflections on French Catholic heritage and culture, divine and human justice, "holy wars," and "just wars." Lossky's commitment to active resistance to aggression was not unqualified. He denounced the spiritualist heresy of infusing a war with an artificial soul and drew a distinction between absolute reality and relative or secondary concepts and values. His reflections warned of the danger of human persons becoming victims of religious, social, and political myths. He further developed these ideas in his eschatological essay *Dominion and Kingship* (1953).[6]

Lossky not only stimulated a fruitful ecumenical exchange in France, but he also led an Anglican-Orthodox dialogue at the annual conferences of the Anglo-Russian Fellowship of St. Alban and St. Sergius in Abingdon, England. He had many followers among younger Anglican theologians, associated with the Fellowship of St. Alban. The English translation of his *Essai sur la théologie mystique*, published in 1958, was the work of these Anglican friends and disciples of Lossky.

APOPHATIC FOUNDATIONS OF LOSSKY'S TEACHING

The most characteristic elements of Lossky's theology, which shaped not only the interpretation of law and ethics but also his entire theological system, were his Chalcedonian distinction between the categories of "person"

and "nature," his apophatic (or negative) approach to theology, his challenging doctrine of the Trinity, and his wholehearted devotion to a "genuine" Orthodoxy rooted in the teachings of the fathers of the Eastern
Church.

Central to Lossky's theology was his insistence that the person and nature are distinct but not separate. Lossky rejected as inadequate all theol-
ogizing that focuses on the level of "nature" and presupposes the "primacy"
of the divine essence over the divine persons. He charged the Western
theological tradition with "depersonalization" of the Trinity and elevation
of the abstract divine essence above the living God of Abraham, Isaac, and
Jacob. He insisted that theological thought should not lower itself to
the level of abstract speculations, since truth can only be lived and experienced. Truth is a "living body," and it "should not be dissected as a corpse."[7]
Lossky was highly critical of the Western juxtaposition of the ideas of nature and grace, which forces one to accept a mechanistic concept of human nature to which grace is added as a "magical substance." His
characteristically Eastern Orthodox personalistic view of salvation explained his rejection of juridical and external morality. Obedience and
purity for Lossky were negative concepts; they imply the "exteriority of
God and the instrumental submission of man."[8] Salvation is not accomplished by God's external activity or through one's rational comprehension of propositional truths. Salvation is deification; it is a conscious
and voluntary union with God—"the synergy, the harmony of two cooperating wills."[9]

KNOWING THE UNKNOWABLE

In *Mystical Theology*, Lossky argues that this emphasis on intimate union
with the "Incomprehensible and the Unknowable" represents the "fundamental character of all theological thought within Eastern Tradition."[10] It
is a humble recognition of what God is not, rather than an insistence on
what God is. It is a move beyond speculation to actual union. This contemplative approach, as we shall see, provides a distinctively different
foundation for ethics, as well as for a social and political image of the
church.

Unlike the Eastern Orthodox, Western Christians seek to analyze and
explain God, subjecting their faith to the test of reason. As Wolfhart Pannenberg, one of the most notable Protestant proponents of critical rationality, aptly remarks, "Every theological statement must prove itself on the
field of reason and can no longer be argued on the basis of unquestioned

propositions of faith."[11] In the Catholic tradition one finds a partial recognition of the apophatic way. Augustine, as Rowan Williams points out, acknowledged the need for transfiguration of intellect, but not for its complete transcendence. For Augustine, knowledge ultimately replaces ignorance.[12] In Western Christianity, the encounter with God is still a reaching out "in thought."[13]

Lossky claimed that Thomas Aquinas, reflecting on the apophatic (negative) and the affirmative theology of the Eastern mystic Dionysius the Pseudo-Areopagite (ca. 500), reduced the two ways of Dionysius[14] to one. This, for Lossky, effectively made "negative theology just a corrective to affirmative theology" and denied Dionysius's insistence that the negative (apophatic) way ultimately surpasses the affirmative (kataphatic).[15] In the Christian East, apophaticism received a classic exposition in the writings of Gregory Palamas. In the Catholic West, certain parallels to Eastern apophaticism can be found in the works of Meister Eckhart, whom Lossky diligently studied, and in the writings of Eckhart's followers, such as Henri Suso, John Tauler, and Nicholas of Cusa.

Negative theology in Lossky is neither a "prohibition upon knowledge" nor some esoteric individualistic exercise in mysticism. The negative or apophatic way is the only adequate existential theology involving man's entire being. It is an honest and responsible recognition of the inadequacy of our discursive reason in the presence of the living God. Discursive reason has its role and place in the initial stages of one's gradual ascent to union with God. Lossky says, "Speculation gradually gives way to contemplation, knowledge to experience; for, in casting off the concepts which shackle the spirit, the apophatic disposition reveals boundless horizons of contemplation at each step of positive theology."[16] The apophatic way of union with God is the true *metanoia*, the "change of heart" from selfish isolation of individual nature to truly personal plenitude and completeness in the synergy of the divine and human spirit. Herein lies the cause of Lossky's rejection of the external juridical approach to theology and ethics and the key to the understanding of his personalism and his trinitarian vision.

TRIUNE GOD: LAW AND JUSTICE PERSONIFIED

In the chapter of *Mystical Theology* devoted to the "Two Aspects of the Church," Lossky states that from the outset the "Church, according to St. Cyril of Alexandria, is the holy city which has not been sanctified by observing the law—for the law made nothing perfect (Heb. VII, 19)—but by becoming conformed to Christ."[17] He thus put the personhood of God at the foundation of moral life of the Christian community: "The pre-eminently catholic dogma of the Trinity is the model, the *canon* for all the canons of the Church, the foundation of the whole ecclesiastical economy."[18]

The divergence of the Greek and the Latin interpretations of the Trinity represents the very heart of the dispute between the Eastern and the Western Christendom, highlighting the unique distinctions of the two traditions. Lossky charged the Western Church with the heresy of subordinating of the Spirit to the Son and claimed that this error is directly connected with the Western confusion about the real meaning of the "person" both in God and in man.[19] Lossky insisted that the "Western doctrine" of the double procession of the Holy Spirit from the Father and the Son—that is, the revision of the Nicene Creed by the Western Church to say that the Holy Spirit proceeds from the Father *and the Son*[20]—was the "primordial cause, the only dogmatic cause, of the breach between East and West."[21] The fallacy of the Western position, in Lossky's view, was its departure from the patristic understanding of the Father as the "unique source of Godhead and principle of the unity of the three."[22] The Western Church instead posited an abstract and impersonal concept of common divine nature (or essence) that was logically prior to and above the persons of the Trinity. Thus, in the Western doctrine formulated by Augustine and perfected by Thomas Aquinas, the unity of the persons of the Trinity lay not in the person of the Father but in this impersonal concept of common essence. The person of the Spirit is perceived merely as a "reciprocal bond between the Father and the Son."[23] Moreover, the Western doctrine of the procession of the Holy Spirit from the Father and the Son tended, in Lossky's view, to weaken the persons of the triune God by confusing the Father and the Son in the "natural act of spiration." This Western creedal formulation ultimately obscured the living reality of the personhood of God in the Trinity.[24]

Not all Orthodox theologians share Lossky's radical position regarding the importance of the *Filioque* ("and the Son") issue in the theological disputes between the East and the West.[25] Yet, for Lossky the *Filioque* is a "negation of personalism."[26] In this protest against the betrayal of the living God of Abraham, Isaac, and Jacob, Lossky has been compared with Pascal, Kierkegaard, and Barth in their denunciation of the "rebelliousness of the human intellect which flees from the *metanoia* and *kenosis* demanded by the revelation of the living God."[27]

Lossky contrasts the philosophical abstractions of the "God in general" of Descartes, of Leibniz, and of the "dechristianized Deists" with the living persons of the Trinity.[28] For Lossky, the doctrine of the Trinity forms the heart of negative theology. It is a "cross for human ways of thought."[29] It is a primordial revelation and, at the same time, the source of all revelation and all reality. It is the "ultimate reality, [the] first datum which cannot be deduced, explained or discovered by way of any other truth; for there is nothing which is prior to it."[30] The fullness of being, the end and the meaning of existence, can be found in the Trinity alone. "Between the Trinity and hell there lies no other choice."[31] When the concept of a "common nature" takes precedence in one's formulation of trinitarian teaching, a "certain philosophy of essence" prevails, which overshadows the living reality of the Trinity itself.[32] Lossky insisted that the reality of the personal God—the "divine hypostasis (the particular in God) cannot be reduced to an "essence" (the common in God).[33] Personhood must be deconceptualized. Neither divine nor human persons can be expressed in abstract concepts. The mutual coinherence of divine hypostases in the Trinity reveals the true meaning of personhood.[34]

Rowan Williams correctly observes that in Lossky the doctrine of the Trinity "overturns our understanding of individuality as the most basic category."[35] Yet, Lossky was often unjust and inaccurate in his criticism of the Western scholastic understanding of the nature of the Trinity, and of the distinction between "person" and "individual."[36] Some of Lossky's generalizations contain factual errors. In his discussions of the Eastern patristic understanding of the hypostasis as distinct from the individual, he ascribes greater consistency and clarity to the Eastern Fathers than one can actually find in them.[37] The same is true regarding his interpretation of the patristic teaching on the image of God in man. While undoubtedly building on certain patristic notions, Lossky clearly went beyond Augustine[38] and beyond the church fathers. These historical errors, however, do not undercut Lossky's main point about the prevalence of philosophy in much of Western theology and the need to prostrate one's intellect "before the living God, radically ungraspable, unobjectifiable and unknowable."[39]

TRANSCENDING ONE'S NATURE

Lossky called for the same radical deconceptualization of personhood in Christian anthropology that he demanded in trinitarian theology. He insisted that personhood cannot be expressed through any conceptual paradigm or captured in any definition.[40] The same distinction between "person" and "nature" that is crucial for the understanding of the Trinity applies to the understanding of the human person. In Eastern doctrines of the Trinity, the person of the Father is the source and the principle of unity, not the "common essence" as in Western rationalism. Likewise, in

Eastern anthropology personality is not a mode of nature, but rather nature is just a content of the person. Creatively developing the insights of Gregory of Nyssa and Maximus the Confessor, Lossky envisaged personhood as freedom in relation to nature—freedom granted so that nature would thus be transfigured and deified.

Lossky argued that ancient philosophy had nothing remotely comparable to the Christian understanding of personhood as revealed in the Trinity. "Greek thought did not go beyond the 'atomic' conception of the individual. Roman thought, going from mask to the role, defined *persona* through juridical relationships. Only the revelation of the Trinity, [the] unique foundation of Christian anthropology, could situate personhood in an absolute manner."[41] Lossky argued that the principal distinction between person and "common nature" in Eastern trinitarian theology provides the only sound foundation for personal uniqueness and diversity. Objects are determined and defined by their substance and their nature. Persons, by contrast, have the capacity to govern their nature, charging it with new meaning, surpassing and transcending it.[42] This capacity is God-given freedom. Lossky cited Gregory Nazianzen in support of his claim that freedom is one of the characteristic traits of the divine image in man.[43]

Lossky further clarified the distinct meaning of personhood by drawing a crucial distinction between the individual and the person (*hypostasis*, understood as a fullness of the nonconceptual reality of a self-determined human being). The notion of the individual is atomistic and deterministic. It does not imply social relationships, but conveys the idea of an element, something disunited and fragmented, and it does not contain the concept of freedom as self-determination.

THE FREEDOM OF CHOICE

As a devout antideterminist, Lossky did not share the Protestant reformers' doctrine of man's total depravity. He rejected the reformers' claim that the image of God in man was completely obliterated as a result of the Fall. This is one of the major points of divergence between the classic reformers' teaching on human nature and that of the Eastern Orthodox.[44] The Orthodox maintain that the image of God in the human person is indestructible. Lossky, too, insisted that even when someone "removes himself as far as possible from God, and becomes unlike Him in his nature, he remains a person."[45]

Lossky understood freedom in the tradition of Pseudo-Macarius and Maximus the Confessor. Human freedom, for Lossky, lay in the image-character of man's being—in the fact of human persons being created in the image of God. Human beings have the capacity for self-determination (*autexousion*) because God in whose image they are created is free and sovereign. Following Maximus the Confessor, Lossky distinguished natural will, which belongs to us as persons, from the choosing will (or gnomic will) which is a faculty of our nature. For Lossky, "nature wills and acts" while the person "chooses, accepting or rejecting that which the nature wills."[46] In Maximus's view, a perfect nature knows naturally what is good and consequently has no need of choice. Lossky, too, held that "our free choice (*gnome*) indicates the imperfection of fallen human nature, the loss of the divine likeness."[47] "Choice" for our fallen human nature becomes a necessity, and "free will" is understood as a "hesitation in our ascent toward the good."[48] True liberty for Lossky and for the Eastern ascetical tradition as a whole rests in a "free renunciation of one's own will, of the mere *simulacrum* of individual liberty, in order to recover the true liberty, that of the person, which is the image of God in each one."[49]

FREEDOM AND THE JURISPRUDENCE OF THE HEART

Lossky's personalistic, internalized, and experiential understanding of law and ethics is in perfect agreement with Orthodox distinction between the superior spiritual capacity of self-determination, which belongs to us as persons, and the will, which is strictly the faculty of our nature. In order to appreciate this distinction, we must recall that in Lossky our understanding of the "person" cannot be reduced to the notion of human nature. For Lossky, the nature is the "content of the person" and the "person is the existence of the nature."[50] The weakened and fallen human nature, with its conflicting passions and desires, constantly wills and acts within us. Yet the ultimate decision rests with the person who accepts or rejects "that which the nature wills," through engagement of the spiritual capacity of self-determination (often described by the Eastern spiritual authors as self-consciousness, or the spiritual intellect, or the heart).[51]

In a chapter of *Mystical Theology* devoted to the image and likeness, Lossky explains that when man sinned he sinned freely by exercising his faculty of self-determination. That is why all divine laws and commands are addressed not to certain features of fragmented human nature, but to the person, to his or her spiritual self-determination.[52] In this, Lossky closely follows Eastern monastic anthropology with its emphasis on the spirit and the heart. Deification through spiritual coinherence in God is the reversal of defragmentation through passions. The human spirit "must find its sustenance in God, must live from God; the soul must feed on the spirit; the body must live on the soul."[53] The spirit and the heart in the Eastern ascetical tradition represent the moral and spiritual center of the human person (as distinct from the purely emotional and discursive realms). Lossky's use of the monastic teaching of Nikiphoros the Hesychast on "uniting of the [human] spirit with the heart" and the "descent of the spirit into the heart"[54] is highly enlightening. He points out that, according to Macarius of Egypt, the heart, understood as the seat of all intellectual and spiritual activity, is the "workshop of justice and injustice."[55] Thus, according to the apophatic teaching of the Eastern Church, an authentic jurisprudence must above all be a jurisprudence of the heart.[56] It cannot but be personalist, dynamic, and internalized in contrast to the Western external and rationalist theories. As we will see, even divine Law, in its written form found in the Old Testament, is assigned a temporary place in the divine economy.[57] Likewise, positive law should never be absolutized and objectified. It cannot claim to be an accurate reflection of absolute spiritual reality and should not be turned into "an idol."[58] The dignity and freedom of the human person should not be sacrificed by those who fall prey to social and political myths.

TEACHING REGARDING THE WORLD

The same concern for safeguarding the self-determination of divine and human persons can be observed in Lossky's reflections on the origin of the world, the role of man in the cosmos, and the value of human civilization. Lossky's lectures on creation reveal that he read with interest the works of the French intuitivist philosopher Henri Bergson. There are even some affinities in Lossky's teaching with the thought of Bergson, particularly the rejection of the intellectualist conceptions of reality as inadequate, which is clearly manifest in both authors. Yet, Lossky was strongly opposed to Bergson's notion of God as a "God of creative evolution" or as a "vital impulse, an absolute in becoming."[59] For Lossky, recognition of creative evolution would mean a rejection of divine omnipotence.

Lossky constructed his cosmology, his teaching on the origin and the nature of the world and the universe, on the basis of his personalist trinitarian theology and his anthropology. He demonstrated his personalism in drawing a sharp contrast between the Hellenic and Origenistic notions of the eternal "cyclical repetition of worlds" and the Christian doctrine of "absolute creation," a creation from nothing (*ex nihilo*). Matter is not eternal, and the created world is not a quasi-necessary outcome of God's own being. The personal triune God is the creator exclusively by his sovereign will, Lossky insisted; "the name of creator is secondary to the three names of the Trinity."[60] Lossky's personalism is further exemplified by his designation of the earth as being spiritually central to all creation. The earth is spiritually central to creation because of the unique role of the human person destined to unite the material and the spiritual: "at the center of the universe beats the heart of man."[61] "The earth is spiritually central because . . . man, penetrating the indefiniteness of the visible to bind it again to the invisible, is the central being of creation."[62] "Divine freedom is accomplished through creating this supreme risk: another freedom."[63] In his lecture "The Creation," Lossky, echoing Maximus the Confessor, elaborates on the grand mission of the human person created to be the microcosm and the mediator. "Man is not a part, since a person contains everything within himself."[64]

In his collection of lectures published as *Orthodox Theology,* Lossky points out that one should not only observe the difference between the Hellenic and Christian understanding of creation (an eternal creation as opposed to creation out of nothing). One should also note the principal difference between the static and impersonalist interpretation of the manner of creation by some Latin Fathers (namely Augustine) and the more apophatic and personalist notion of the Greek Fathers (namely Gregory of Nyssa and John of Damascus). Lossky emphasized that, for the Greek Fathers, the ideas of all things were contained not in the abstract divine essence of the being of God, but rather in the will and the wisdom of the free and personal God.[65] Augustine had Christianized the Platonic notion of the world of ideas by refashioning it into the world of exemplary causes, or ideas of things to be created in the mind and the being of God. Lossky strongly rejected this notion as that which undermines the originality and value of creation and the creator Himself.[66] "For Orthodoxy," writes Lossky, "*nihil* from which the world was created" is an indication of the nondivine nature of the world, of its principal newness in relation to God. Created in this unique manner, the world will always exist.[67] The creation of the world always assumed the cosmic process of its deification.

While it is an "immense compensation for the absence of God," human civilization cannot replace paradise.[68] Human nature must be transfigured by grace, following the ascetic path of sanctification. This sanctification embraces both the spiritual and the bodily realms, thus acquiring genuinely cosmic dimensions. Eastern Orthodox cosmology is thoroughly ecclesiological: "The entire universe is called to enter within the Church, to become the Church of Christ."[69] Having in mind Soloviev, Fedorov, and his contemporary Bulgakov (and perhaps being unduly harsh), Lossky observes in *Mystical Theology*, "Even when it has strayed furthest from the line of tradition, even, indeed, in its very errors, the thought of Eastern Christians in recent centuries—and Russian religious thought in particular—reflects a tendency to envisage the Cosmos in ecclesiological terms."[70]

Lossky insisted that the living monastic ideal of radical self-denial and active virtue have a lasting significance "for the entire universe."[71] The impact on culture and politics of such great Orthodox spiritual centers as the monasteries of Mount Sinai and of Studion, the "monastic republic" of Mount Athos (which attracts spiritual aspirants from both the East and the West), and the famous Russian *lavras* in Kiev and Moscow has been great indeed. "The outward forms may change, the monasteries may disappear, as in our own day they disappeared for a time in Russia, but the spiritual life goes on with the same intensity, finding new modes of expression."[72] The world was created that it might be deified.

Lossky's cosmology was not only thoroughly ecclesiological; it also presents a powerful defense of divine omnipotence and of divine and human self-determination. In Berdyaev, the freedom of personality is uncreated and creation is conceived as a joint venture between God and man.[73] In Lossky, creation is not coeternal with God.[74] In Berdyaev, God has no ultimate power over the "uncreated freedom"—reflecting Boehme's concept of a "primitive, predeterminate *Ungrund*" which is prior to good and evil. In Lossky, creation is a free act of the Trinity.[75] Defending divine omnipotence in creation, Lossky highlighted the dignity and the value of human freedom. To be truly innovative, God creates "the other," a personal being endowed with an ability to reject his Creator. "God becomes *powerless* before human freedom: He cannot violate it since it flows from his own omnipotence."[76] That is why catholicity (free unity in diversity) of the universal Christian community in Lossky can be the sole foundation of divine "dominion and kingship."[77] Moreover, unlike Berdyaev, who was highly critical of historical Christianity and the church as an institution,[78] Lossky was convinced that genuine personal dignity and freedom can only be fully attained and discovered within the unity of the concrete historical church.[79]

THE CHURCH AS A SOCIAL IDEAL

Lossky would have been far from sympathetic with the widespread individualistic rejection of "organized religion" in Western society today. He emphasized the exclusive cosmic status of the church and its universal mission. He denounced two extreme views of the church prevalent in his day: the conservative mummification of the church as a socially irrelevant spiritual entity and the liberal confusion of the church with the world in which striving for the kingdom of God on earth and for the realization of social justice become the sole purpose of the church. He was deeply convinced in the unique and inimitable nature of the church as both divine and human organism and consequently in its unique spiritual mission.[80]

Lossky was critical of medieval Catholic ecclesiology, with its emphasis on external, administrative unity[81] and its preoccupation with "abstract universalism of a doctrine imposed by the hierarchy."[82] Such ecclesiology, in Lossky's view, is too far removed from the living union of human persons with the persons of the Trinity and is primarily concerned with submission to external principles.[83] And more specifically, the role of the Holy Spirit in the Western doctrine of the church is rather obscure.[84] While admitting important affinities between his personalist ecclesiology and the organic ecclesiologies of Catholic Tübingen theologians of the romantic period, particularly that of Moehler, Lossky still rejected them as inadequate.[85] He recognized that, in portraying the church as a christological organism, Moehler came closer to the Orthodox vision of the church. Yet in Lossky's judgment, Moehler's ecclesiology was incomplete and rather deterministic. Human persons are "absorbed in a supra-Person" of Christ who acts as a "supra-consciousness of the whole church."[86] Lossky even rejected the corrective to Moehler's organic model advanced by his notable Orthodox predecessor, Khomyakov. Lossky acknowledged that Khomyakov's emphasis on the role of the Holy Spirit in the church is a valuable improvement; yet, Khomyakov, too, failed to recognize the self-determined reality of human persons and reduced the consciousness of the church to the "function" of the third person of the Trinity.[87] The Holy Spirit becomes the "supra-Person," the "supra-consciousness" of the church.

Lossky rejected both of these models by comparing them with a personalist reading of the scriptures, namely John 15:26–27 and 14:26. In both models the individual is hopelessly lost. Lossky pointed out that the scripture clearly speaks of two kinds of witness to the truth within the church: the witness of the Holy Spirit and the human witness of Jesus' disciples of all ages ("You also are witnesses"). Thus Lossky argued that the consciousness of the church consists not only in the witness of the Holy Spirit himself, but also in the free and conscious witness of unique human persons enabled, reminded, and taught by the Holy Spirit.[88] In contrast to Moehler and Khomyakov, Lossky was not willing to sacrifice the self-determination, uniqueness, and dignity of human persons to the organic togetherness of the ecclesial supraconsciousness. For him there cannot be a forced uniformity in the catholic consciousness of the church, "for there is no measure common to all where persons are concerned."[89]

Lossky's polemic with the French Catholic theologian Yves Congar further clarified the contours of his personalist teaching on the church. Lossky rejected Congar's representation of unity and catholicity as one and the same "mark" of the church.[90] That in his view would stress only formal, external unity and would obliterate the emphasis on the "full human consciousness" of the body of Christ.

Lossky was critical of Protestant ecclesiologies (and their Orthodox varieties) on rather different counts. He saw the root of Protestant fragmentation and disaggregation of the body of Christ in the "revolutionary-anarchic" spirit of Protestant individualism, in the "distrust and even hidden disbelief in the fact that the Church (not the abstract heavenly church, but the specific historical Church) received from Christ himself the mandate to bind and to loose."[91] He strongly opposed the Protestant distinction between a visible and an invisible church, the historic church on earth and the church in heaven. Lossky described this distinction (originally believed to have been made by Luther[92]) as an "ecclesiological Nestorianism," analogous to the heretical christology of Nestorius, which divided Christ into two persons, divine and human. Lossky maintained that "ecclesial Nestorians," on one hand, deprive the body of Christ of its concrete physical dimension by turning it into an abstract "spiritual principle" and, on the other hand, indistinguishably confuse the church with the world.[93] Lossky asked: Is there not a middle ground between an "anticatholic subjectivism" and an "impersonal objectivism"?[94] He presented his notion of catholicity as a golden middle that mediates between the juridical institutionalism of Roman Catholicism and the extreme individualism of Protestantism.

Lossky's trinitarian personalism penetrated his teaching on the church as profoundly as it influenced his anthropology. In fact, he conceived the whole Christian church as an image of the Holy Trinity and as a living "theandric" organism that embraces and harmoniously unites divine and human realms.[95] Lossky took pains to show that Eastern Orthodox ecclesiology has nothing in common with artificial conceptual constructs. The intimate coinherence and mutual love of the Father, Son, and Holy Spirit must be reflected and glorified in the "very ordering of ecclesiastical life."[96] Catholicity, the central biotic principle on which the life of the Ecclesia (or the whole "divine economy") is built, is the principle of unity in diversity. This "unity-diversity" of the Christian community is the only context in which the persons of the godhead can be truly revealed and human beings can attain their personal completeness.[97] The roles of the two divine persons sent into the world are not the same.

Lossky distinguished between the unifying role of Christ and the diversifying role of the Holy Spirit, and, correspondingly, between the christological element and the pneumatological element of the church.[98] There is a seeming antinomy between the role of Christ and the role of the Holy Spirit: "the Holy Spirit diversifies what Christ unifies."[99] Thus, the christological element represents Christ uniting through the Incarnation our human "created" nature with our divine "uncreated" nature.[100] Lossky portrayed this as an objective union of potentiality. It relates not to our persons, but to our created nature "in so far as it is received into the person of Christ."[101] This unifying work of Christ thus creates a new foundation, a fertile environment, an "ecclesiastical organism"[102] for the development of a totally new "diversity of persons."[103]

To highlight the radically different nature of this diversity (as compared to the generally accepted secular notions of diversity) Lossky pointed out that outside of the church there is multiplicity. Yet this multiplicity is an isolating selfish multiplicity of corruption: "the multiplicity is that of the individuals which divide up humanity."[104] By contrast, within the church, "through the deifying flames of the Holy Spirit," human beings acquire a multiplicity of redemption of a diametrically opposite ethical nature.[105] They become capable of selfless (kenotic) love exemplified in the life of the Trinity. Thus, the pneumatological element in Lossky's system stands for the diversifying ministry of the Holy Spirit, which leads individuals to selfless authentic personhood. The all-encompassing notion describing this dynamic interaction of divine and human persons is catholicity. It is one of the four traditional "notes of the Church," yet, it is creatively expanded to convey Lossky's delicately balanced personalist ecclesiological model.

CATHOLICITY: SPIRITUAL KNOWLEDGE
AND INTERPERSONAL ETHICS

To illustrate the unique nature of catholicity in which an individual is not absorbed into a faceless supra-consciousness, Lossky recalls the argument used by Maximus the Confessor in the controversy with the Monothelites:

The Church as a whole is called ecumenical, a qualification which does not apply to any portion of her; but every smallest portion of the Church—even one single faithful—can be called catholic. When St. Maximus, to whom ecclesiastical tradition gives the title of Confessor, replied to those who desired to force him to be in communion with the Monothelites, "Even if the whole world . . . should be in communion with you, I alone should not be," he was opposing his catholicity to an ecumenicity which he regarded as heretical.[106]

Of the four traditional marks of the church (unity, holiness, catholicity, and apostolicity), Lossky singled out catholicity, presenting it as the "golden thread" and as a "mode of knowledge of the Truth proper to the Church, in virtue of which this truth becomes clear to the whole Church, as much to each of her smaller parts as to her totality."[107] The individual retains personal distinctiveness while partaking of the fullness of the catholic truth.

Lossky contrasted his personalist interpretation of catholicity as unity in diversity with the Roman Catholic interpretation of catholicity as external universality of the visible organization, universalism of the church's doctrine, its global geographic presence or ancient history.[108] He was also critical of the Protestant understanding of catholicity, which rejected episcopal authority and transplanted the secular democratic principle of the majority vote, and in certain instances replaced the authentic meaning of catholicity with the relativist notion of "ecumenism."[109] To be sure, Lossky was actively involved in ecumenical dialogue with a number of Catholic and Anglican theologians; yet, he could not accept the relativism and individualism of liberal Protestant and Orthodox ecumenists. He insisted that ecumenism can never take the place of authentic catholicity. This emphasis on diversity at the expense of unity is the disaggregation of the church: the truth that is attributed to individual inspirations becomes multiple and therefore relative; catholicity is replaced by "ecumenism."[110]

ECCLESIASTICAL AUTHORITY

The divine authority of the episcopate to apply the canons of the church to safeguard its unity was nonnegotiable for Lossky. The most representative statements of his views on intellectual freedom and ecclesiastical authority are found in his *Mystical Theology,* the tract *Spor o Sofii* (*The Sophia Controversy*), and in his open letter to Berdyaev, published by Berdyaev in his journal *Put'*.[111] While in *Mystical Theology* Lossky states flatly that the "submission to the will of the bishop is submission to the will of God,"[112] he subsequently made clear that the authority and the actions of the bishop are not totally unqualified. Lossky recognized that a personal element is inevitably involved in episcopal action. The principle of catholicity as free unity in diversity is foundational to the understanding of Lossky's notion of ecclesiastical authority. Catholicity in Lossky is not some abstract universalism of a dogma imposed by the hierarchy: "The obligation of defending the Truth is incumbent on every member of the church." "A layman is even bound to resist a bishop who betrays the Truth and is not faithful to the Christian tradition."[113]

DEMOCRACY

In his wartime journal *Sept jours sur les routes de France,* Lossky recognized the positive value of democracy in the secular political context. Yet, he stressed that the "struggle for democracy, for freedom, for human dignity" can be truly just only when it is "based on a living experience" and "springs from a deep and healthy source."[114] While he recognized the value of democracy in the secular political realm, however, Lossky strongly opposed its application to the life of the church. He regarded the principle of the majority vote as an impoverished and inadequate surrogate for the spiritual reality of catholicity.[115]

Elaborating on his distinction between the notion of personhood as distinct from the notion of the individual, Lossky contrasted catholicity with collectivity and showed the crucial difference between the principle of catholicity and the principle of democracy. Catholicity as a spiritual unity in diversity utilizes spiritual resources and dynamics and is thus distinct from the democratic election process and the majority rule (the principle that the greater number should exercise greater power). Lossky emphatically states in his essay "Concerning the Third Mark of the Church" that democracy in the sense of majority rule is "foreign to the Church, a caricature of catholicity."[116] In support of his argument he quotes Khomyakov, who said that the "Church does not consist in the greater or lesser quantity of her members but in the spiritual bond that unites them."[117] But Lossky was equally adamant that catholicity has nothing in common with totalitarian enforcement of one common vision on the multitude of human persons comprising the body of Christ. Forced uniformity is alien to persons guided by the Spirit of God: "There is no measure common to all where persons are concerned."[118] The preservation of the voluntary nature of unity and of personal distinctiveness is absolutely crucial:

> Evidence of Truth, the memory or tradition of the church, that which constitutes the content of consciousness, is one and the same for all; but that does not mean that there is one single consciousness of the Church, which is

imposed uniformly on all, as a "supra-consciousness" belonging to a "collective person."[119]

A few sketchy reflections in *Sept jours* represent Lossky's first attempts to formulate his political views. It seems that he was not quite accurate in his evaluation of the role of Gallicanism as a positive, creative initiative in the history of France.[120] Perhaps the ruthless policies of the French eighteenth-century revolutionary leaders toward the church in France and the terror that followed influenced Lossky's negative assessment of the *Declaration of the Rights of Man and of Citizen* (1789). In *Sept jours* he mused whether the *Declaration* was not just a "false reflection" of an authentic catholicity degenerated into Latinism (understood by Lossky as a rationalistic and bureaucratic alien influence on the French national mentality).[121]

Lossky abhorred political authoritarianism and the servility of the Russian Church. In this, he was much like his liberal Orthodox contemporaries Bulgakov and Berdyaev. Yet, Lossky was never willing to compromise his fidelity to the catholic truth and to the authority of the episcopate.[122] He chastised Berdyaev for his refusal to "render voluntary obedience to the Truth" by "dying to self." He argued that the "defense of one's individual freedom in the face of highest freedom in the church would be tantamount to a defense of one's limitations, that is one's slavery." The "very issue of the defense of our rights in the Church is a misconception, because these rights are unlimited,"[123] in the sense that the right to defend the catholic truth is distinct from the right to defend one's controversial opinion.

"IN THE WORLD, OF THE CHURCH"

Throughout his theological writings, Lossky consistently advocated the vision of a spiritual and independent church conceived as a social ideal. There is a striking affinity between Lossky's vision of the church and that of the Russian sixteen-century nonpossessors (*nestiazhateli*) led by Nil Sorskii, who conceived the church as "unencumbered by worldly responsibilities, serving as a spiritual and moral beacon in a dark and evil world."[124] Lossky's view also presents a contrast to the traditional Byzantine *Imperium Christianum* model of church-state relations referred to as *symphonia*. Lossky's most explicit statements on this theme came in *Soblazny*, his lecture "The Creation," and his open letter to Berdyaev in *Put'*. (The only misleading exception is found in Lossky's early reflections in *Sept jours*, where he expresses his Francophile admiration of French monarchy.)

In *Soblazny* Lossky insists, "The Church is not of this world, but it is in this world and exists for this world in the same manner as Christ."[125] Although the church as an institution should maintain political neutrality and independence, her members individually are expected to be creatively engaged in the life of society: "The Church is the center of the world . . . , her members, at one and the same time, are also members and builders of the earthly city, they do not abandon the world, but live in the world and are called to act and be creative in it." "Each of us . . . is at one and the same time a product and a creator of contemporary culture."[126] In "The Creation" Lossky is more emphatic and direct; he portrays the "children of God" as the mind and the conscience of the world and highlights the physical dimensions of deification:

> We are therefore responsible for the world. We are the word, the logos, through which it bespeaks itself, and it depends solely on us whether it blasphemes or prays. Only through us can the cosmos, like the body that it prolongs, receive grace. For not only the soul, but the body of man is created in the image of God.[127]

Except for the strong emphasis on the independence and spiritual nature of the church, all the accents in Lossky's social teaching are traditionally Eastern Orthodox: Anthropology is at the foundation of cosmology, cosmology is an element of an all-embracing, radically eschatological ecclesiology, and the world is "at the threshold of the Kingdom of God."

What are some of the characteristic differences between the social theologies in the East and the West? The perceptive comparison of Catholic, Protestant, and Orthodox social conceptions drawn by Konstantin Kostyuk in 1997 points out some of the differences and helps to see much clearer the essence of Lossky's characteristically Eastern Orthodox social vision:

> Having formulated the principles of solidarity, subsidiarity and of the common good, Catholicism has thereby limited its social message to representatives of a specific culture and concrete historical epoch (naturally, modern democratic Europe). The idea of social progress embedded in this message devalues the life of past generations and non-European cultures. Protestantism on the whole, from its very inception, developed its social teaching within the framework of the "spirit of capitalism," the spirit "of this world." Formulating social ethics Western churches are almost forced to put their ethical teaching in opposition to the individual Gospel ethics of the Sermon on the Mount and subjecting themselves to the laws of the "social world"

they distort the message of the Kingdom, "which is not of this world." Eastern Orthodoxy does not desire to limit the task of salvation to specific generations and nations and therefore it cannot place at the foundation of its social message the ethics of bourgeois relations; it refuses to sacrifice the purity of the Gospel teaching in order to please secular culture.[128]

Though he advocated a universal vision and a "meta-historical" conception of the church, Lossky was never guilty of cultural insensitivity. In *Temptations of Ecclesial Consciousness* (1950) Lossky observes, "Certain political, national, social, cultural . . . interests and tendencies are unavoidable in the Christian community." He adds, "To revolt against those would be to revolt against life itself, against its richness and diversity."[129]

Lossky's liberal opponents were campaigning for a more vocal and a more politically and socially active church. Lossky, by contrast, while admitting that the church does possess "inexhaustible resources on which could draw all those called to rule the earthly kingdoms,"[130] maintained that it is not the responsibility of the church to dictate its will in the temporal realm: "The Church does not proscribe to anyone certain political views, social doctrines or cultural specifics."[131] The church should always remember its spiritual prerogatives:

> Just as Christ, being free of the world, kept silence before the court of Pilate, the Church often standing silent before the powers of this world, preserves her transcendental freedom. Although it is at times difficult for us to recognize this freedom of hers under the external appearance of humiliation. "The scandal for the Jews" –- the cross is also insurmountable for many Christians. Many would prefer to see in the Church one of the forces of history, comparable to other worldly factors and the "inferiority complex" before the powerful administration of Roman Catholicism is a temptation from which many Orthodox are not free.[132]

Lossky was convinced that the primary task of the church is to fertilize the world spiritually. Although he expresses romantic admiration for the French monarchy in his early sketchy comments in *Sept jours*, Lossky denounced the confusion of the spiritual with the temporal that was so characteristic of the Frankish empire of Charlemagne. He regarded as inadmissible the interference of ecclesiastical authorities into the internal affairs of the state.[133] He recognized the essential nature of the state and describes it in *Sept jours* as "that indispensable convention so necessary to human societies," and, on an apophatic note, as "that great fictitious reality, anchored in our consciousness to the point of being part of ourselves."[134]

Lossky offered no definitive theological analysis of the state and of its relation to the church comparable to that of Soloviev. In *Sept jours*, Lossky warns about the deadly poison hidden in the temptation of secular power. He also recognized the extreme complexity of the task of making the right distinction between the realm of God and the realm of Caesar.[135] He critically examined the ideologies of conservative monarchism and revolutionary radicalism in France and dismissed both as bankrupt. He found comfort in the thought that "all those called to rule the earthly kingdoms" can find inexhaustible resources in the Christian church, which is full of vitality and driven by eschatological vision.[136]

THE DISEASE OF NATIONALISM

At a time when the Russian Church abroad was torn by political, ethnic, and cultural antagonism (1935–50), Lossky saw his task to free Eastern Orthodox ecclesiology from any type of national or cultural orientation.[137] In this emphasis, he was distinctively different from Bulgakov and Berdyaev, who, as Rowan Williams points out, "felt themselves to be, in some sense, the true heirs and spokesmen of Russian Orthodoxy" and represented an "implicit refusal to recognize that the Church could continue to function authentically in a dechristianized society" as well as an "implicit belief that the Church was necessarily bound to certain cultural or national structures."[138] In *Temptations of Ecclesial Consciousness*, Lossky appeals to the splintering groups, pleading for unity and a broader universal vision of the church. This appeal recurs in his *Mystical Theology* and in his essay "Catholic Consciousness," where he pronounces the expression "national church" to be heretical because it fragments and devalues the unity of the body of Christ.[139] "The view which would base the unity of a local church on a political, racial or cultural principle is considered by the Orthodox Church as a heresy, specially known by the name of *philetism*."[140]

In "Catholic Consciousness," Lossky speaks to this and other related divisive issues with greater directness and passion:

> No differences of created nature—sex, race, social class, language, or culture—can affect the unity of the Church; no divisive reality can enter into the bosom of *Catholica*. Therefore it is necessary to regard the expression "national Church"—so often used in our day—as erroneous and even heretical, according to the terms of the condemnation of phyletism pronounced by the Council of Constantinople in 1872. There is no Church of the Jews or of the Greeks, of the Barbarians or of the Scythians, just as there is no Church of

slaves or of free men, of men or of women. There is only the one and total Christ, the celestial head of the new creation which is being realized here below, the Head to which the members of the one Body are intimately linked.[141]

To Lossky the breadth of kenotic selflessness acquired through this "intimate link"—one's surrender to God's Spirit—is the only cure from any type of fragmentation of the body of Christ: "Renouncing his separate good, he endlessly expands, and is enriched by everything that belongs to all."[142] This is what Lossky actually meant by freedom from the limitations of one's fragmented nature and by the need to transcend one's nature through kenotic "renunciation of self."[143] In fact, in *Image and Likeness*, enlisting the support of Gregory of Nyssa, Lossky pronounces this kenotic "renunciation of self" as "the basis . . . of all evangelical morality."[144] The roots of this emphasis can be traced to the ascetic monastic spirituality of the Orthodox East.

Lossky used the term *phyletism* to mean an "ideology that raises the nation to an element of faith."[145] Others define it as a "belief that one's national identity is greater than one's baptism and faith in Jesus Christ." Various forms of religious nationalism continue to persist among the Orthodox both in traditionally Orthodox lands such as Russia and former Yugoslavia and in the Orthodox diaspora.[146] In Russia, these sentiments go as far back as 1453, when Constantinople was captured by the Turks and Moscow became the "third Rome." Presently the transformed manifestations of these sentiments in Russia of the twenty-first century are being described by some liberal Orthodox not as *phyletism*, but rather as a "heresy" of "Orthodox provincialism."[147] Lossky's admonitions are as relevant as ever. While he is criticized for his Francophile musings, Lossky's ideal of a nation is far removed from nationalistic conceptions. Lossky's students rightly point out that his talent and passion as a first-rate controversialist was not directed to defending Byzantine or Slavophile exclusiveness but to portraying his vision of what was truly Christian. Nation for Lossky, in the words of his son Nikolai, is "rather a unity of responsible individuals whose ideal is expressed in the lives of the saints, whereas sainthood is understood as a vocation of every human being."[148]

JUST WARS VS. "HOLY WARS"

In *Sept jours*, Lossky reflects on the possibility of a just war, on "holy wars," and on divine and human justice. Though sketchy and incomplete, these reflections burn with passion to uphold the value of the human person and the supreme reality of the Church of Christ. It is a creative and novel

approach to the issue of Christian attitude to war with distinctively Eastern Orthodox personalist concerns.

Lossky was eager to expose the danger of "mythic thinking" regarding
war, of mistaking false abstractions of ideologies of war for absolute values and absolute reality. He recognized relative, local, and national values
and emphatically denied the legitimacy of military action in defending
absolute values. Military action is justifiable only on the condition that
those involved in a conflict have a clear realization that the values they
fight for are relative. The sacrifice of one's life in such a war acquires absolute value. Lossky designated this type of action as a "human war."[149] He
distinguished between three kinds of wars: the conventional warfare
conducted by a secular state ("physical war"), "human war" (understood
as national resistance to aggression), and "holy war," conducted under the
auspices of the church.[150]

Lossky's notion of a "human war" is deeply rooted in his distinction between absolute reality and abstractions, between absolute values and relative, secondary, or derived values. He set off false abstractions of the
ideologies of "holy war" and of the fascist war for "pure race" against the
reality of the "human war." He also reminded readers that in reflections
on war one always needs to distinguish between abstract ideas of democracy, freedom, Western culture, and Christian civilization and the concrete realities of the "soil, the land, the Homeland." The injustice and the
cruelty of all so-called religious wars lies in the heresy of "infusing war
with an artificial soul" and in presenting relative values as absolutes. He
argued that "if we oppose the idol of the pure race with the more humane
idols of law, liberty and humanity they would not be any the less idols for
it, ideas rendered hypostasized and absolute: the war would still be a war
of idols and not a human war."[151]

It would be a mistake, however, to assume that Lossky believed that
all political action should be based on relative values. He portrayed the
church of Christ as the only absolute reality, and, referring to Peter's attempt to defend his Lord in Gethsemane with a sword, reminded readers
that the church "needs neither our material defense nor our childish
swords."[152] As the icon of the Holy Trinity and as the body of Christ (the
authentic "unity in diversity"), the church does not stand in need of our
swords, but rather presents a limitless resource of vision and strength
"for all those who are called to rule the earthly kingdoms."[153]

In his reflections on divine and human justice in *Sept jours*, Lossky
challenged the rationalist view of God's immutable justice presented by
the clergy of the Roman Catholic Church in France. He contrasted their
static, rationalist notion with the Orthodox apophatic and personalist

understanding of divine justice. Thus, on June 18, 1940, Lossky made the following entry in his journal:

> I had heard a great prelate at Notre Dame speak before thousands of faithful about our just cause, call upon God that He would grant us victory in the name of this just cause. If we followed his thought to its logical end God would find himself obliged to help us because He is just and we are defending justice. He could not act nor wish otherwise without contradicting Himself, without renouncing His attribute of justice, immutable (as is everything about God written in religious works and theological guides). So if we lost this war after all, after calling on God to give us victory in the name of His justice, what would there be left to say?[154]

This is another example of Lossky's unwillingness to accept the abstract, external notion of justice and a static view of the eternal law of God as an objective body of norms outside the will of God to which he conforms his will. In these reflections Lossky, once again, implicitly contrasted his dynamic personalist concept of direct divine economy with the Western rationalist view, which he described as a "fixed divine plan of immutable preordinations." In a distinctively apophatic way, Lossky emphasized the danger of equating our finite notions of justice with divine justice: "We should have prayed for victory with tears and great contrition, bearing in mind this fearsome Justice, before which we are all unjust. We should not have called on Justice, which is beyond our measure, which we could not bear, but on the infinite mercy which made the Son of God descend from Heaven."[155]

CANON LAW

Unlike the Roman Catholic Church, the Orthodox Church does not regard canon law as juridical. But the Orthodox also part company with Protestants who (except for German Protestant jurists), following Martin Luther, rejected this whole body of ecclesiastical rules and laws as binding on Christians. The history of the Orthodox Church certainly abounds with various extreme interpretations of canon law, those of the legalistic Byzantine canonists and of the liberal anarchists. Yet the guiding principle, the notion of *oikonomia*, understood as "following the spirit rather than the letter of the law," serves as an important safeguard in interpreting and applying ecclesiastical rules.

Lossky saw his task to bring to light the most valuable intuitions of his predecessors in the Eastern patristic and canonical tradition and to root and incorporate canon law into his trinitarian system. His major contribution to the interpretation of the Orthodox canonical tradition lay in restoring the connection between the dogma and the canons and in placing trinitarian personalism and catholicity (understood as personal unity in diversity) at the heart of canon law. In *Mystical Theology*, he emphatically states that the preeminently "catholic" dogma of the Trinity is the model, the canon, for all the canons of the church, the foundation of the whole ecclesiastical economy.[156] He acknowledged that in the Orthodox East the "sociology of the Church" (the practical application of the teachings of the church to the life of the Christian community) is not to be found in the dogmatic tradition per se, but rather in the canonical tradition. Yet, even in the realm of practical application of canons, the emphasis is on deification (the spiritual transfiguration of persons) rather than on external administration of discipline.

Father Michael Azkoul points out the difference between the interpretation of canon law in the West and in the East. In his tract on the differences between the Roman Catholic and Orthodox theologies, he perceptively observes that "unlike the Latins, the Orthodox Church does not think of canons as laws, that is, as regulating human relationships or securing human rights; rather, Orthodoxy views canons as the means of forging the new man or new creature through obedience. They are training in virtue. They are meant to produce holiness."[157]

Lossky would not have chosen the word "obedience." He preferred to speak of the "plurality of personal consciousnesses" coexisting in "unity and multiplicity."[158] His personalist, apophatic, and experiential understanding of the truth never allowed Lossky to view canon law as juridical statutes. He could not accept any other criterion of truth than the truth itself.[159] He believed that catholicity as free and harmonious participation of persons in the life of the Trinity is the only safeguard against dictatorial rule and coercion in the Christian community. In *Mystical Theology* he writes,

> In the light of the canons this society [the Christian Church] would appear as a "totalitarian collectivity" in which "individual rights" do not exist; but, at the same time, each person in this body is its end and cannot be regarded as a means. This is the only society in which the reconciliation of individual interests with those of the society as a whole does not present an insoluble problem, for the ultimate aspirations of each one are in accord with the supreme end of all, and the latter cannot be realized at the expense of the interest of any.[160]

PATRISTIC ROOTS OF LOSSKY'S PERSONALISM

It would perhaps be more helpful to acknowledge that the Eastern Orthodox tradition has a distinctive attitude to law rather than to speak of its
expressed "antijuridicalism." In contrast to the Western static and external notion of the eternal law of God, the Eastern Orthodox tradition embraces a more dynamic and personalist understanding of justice. The
Eastern tradition stresses the supremacy of the personal divine will and of
direct divine economy. Divine commands are rather understood as tran-
sient, symbolic representations of dynamic spiritual realities. Thus Maximus the Confessor (ca. 580–662), whose writings exerted a great influence
on Lossky, emphasized that there is a deeper spiritual knowledge, a divine
principle "hidden mystically" in the letter of the Law. What did he mean
by a "divine principle"? In his *Centuries*, Maximus elaborated on the Pauline distinction between the spirit and the letter of the Mosaic law (2 Cor.
3:6) and denounced legalistic and external observance.[161] Maximus
pointed out the disparity between the "symbols through which the law is
expressed and the divine realities which these symbols represent."[162] He
believed that, only under the guidance of the Spirit, can our spiritual intellect, as distinct from the cognitive capacity of rational reason, penetrate
into the "divine and spiritual beauty contained within the letter of the
law"[163] and acquire a spiritual (noetic) "vision of the nature of created beings and the inner principles implanted in them by their Creator.[164] He rejected literal, legalistic apprehension of the Mosaic law exclusively on
personalist grounds. Literal understanding of the law diverts the creature
away from union with the Creator to the worship of creation. "God did not
order the Sabbath," insisted Maximus, "the new moons and the feasts to
be honored because he wanted men to honor the days themselves. . . . On
the contrary, He indicated that He Himself was to be honored symbolically through the days. For He is the Sabbath. . . . He is the Passover. . . . He
is the Pentecost."[165] Maximus called for a contemplative approach to the
Law and taught that contemplation "mediates between figurative representations of the truth and the truth itself." Maximus taught that all "outward and evanescent interpretation[s] of the Law, subject to time and
change" must be rejected by the one who seeks through contemplation to
ascend to the heights of spiritual knowledge.

The notion of natural law is present in the Eastern patristic tradition,
yet it has not been developed in the East into a comprehensive theory
comparable to the natural law theory in Catholic theology. In his *Five*

Centuries of Various Texts, Maximus drew a clear distinction between "natural law," "written Law" (meaning Mosaic law), and the "law of grace." He emphasized the social function of the natural law and saw its task in bringing "into harmony all men's voluntary relationships with one another"[166] and in granting "equal rights to all men in accordance with natural justice."[167] He described the function of the "written law" as that of "preventing wrongdoing through fear" and as making one accustomed to doing what is right.[168] He regarded the law of grace as superior to the other two laws because it directly teaches the attainment of "similitude to God, in so far as it is possible for man."[169] Thus the law of grace, by contrast, describes not a rational ascent to an intellectual principle, but a transformation of human nature through deification without "altering its fundamental character."[170] It is a revelation of the archetype of human nature and union with Him.[171]

The later Orthodox tradition did little to develop these potent Maximian distinctions between natural law, written law, and the law of grace. And today, natural law teaching does not have the same status in the Eastern Orthodox theology as it does in the Western Thomistic system, where it forms the basis for the development of positive law.

Although it is certainly justifiable to speak of the Eastern Orthodox tradition as "antijuridical" and as that which propagates the censure of the law, it would be inadmissible to ignore the enormous role of the Orthodox Church and of the Eastern canonical tradition in particular in the development of legal systems in the Orthodox East. The overall impact of the Orthodox tradition on the formation of legal consciousness and positive law in the countries of the Orthodox East is a much more complex and contradictory phenomenon.

In order to identify the principal difference between the status and the role of ethics and law in Eastern and Western Christianity, it is important to distinguish from the outset between canon law (understood as the law of the church for purposes of order, ministry, and discipline) and rational legal theory of the church (understood as the teaching of the church on the civil or positive law of a society). It is also necessary to highlight yet another distinction between the actual social influence of the church as an institution and the distinctive social teaching of the church as an independent spiritual entity. Having drawn these distinctions, if we were to ask whether the Orthodox Church had an impact on the development of legal systems and positive law in Byzantium and in Russia, the answer would certainly be in the affirmative. Thus, for instance, the Byzantine *nomocanons* were used in Russia as a basis for *Kormchaya Kniga,* the most ancient collection of Russian ecclesiastical and secular codes. Yet, when the question is asked as to whether the Eastern Orthodox Church has had a distinctive legal theory or social doctrine comparable to those of the Catholic and Protestant churches, the answer would be a negative one. It is a telling anecdote that, until the year 2000, none of the Orthodox churches had a written statement of its social teaching. The first such document, "Bases of the Social Concept," was adopted in 2000 by the Jubilee Bishop's Council of the Russian Orthodox Church in Moscow.

In Byzantine society, according to John Meyendorff, a "charismatic understanding of the state" which, as he admits, "obviously lacked political realism and efficiency" implies that the state is conceived as a "universal counterpart of a universal church."[172] An assumption of unstable "dynamic polarity" between God and the world does not allow for a possibility of clear-cut formulae and legal absolutes in the realm of social ethics. The predominance of charismatic, experiential, otherworldly, and eschatological concepts in the Eastern Christendom shaped a principally different understanding of the function of the church in the world from that of the Western Christendom. This charismatic and prophetic understanding of its mission by the Byzantine church kept it from spelling out a clearly delineated legal and canonical criterion for interpreting Christian action in the world.[173]

LOSSKY'S TEACHING ON "DIVINE LAW" AND LEGAL ORDER

Lossky did not share the Western understanding of the eternal law of God, the *lex aeterna* as an objective body of norms outside the will of God to which he conforms his will. Lossky contrasted the dynamic personalist concept of direct divine economy, which entails risk on the part of God, to the Western rationalist view, which he described as a fixed "divine plan" of "immutable preordinations."[174] This personalist stance shaped Lossky's understanding of the divine Law and legal order. Citing St. Paul's qualification of the law as that "which was added because of transgressions" (Gal. 3:19), Lossky insisted that the "divine Law is proper to the catastrophic state of created being in subjection to the law of sin and death." Thus, if one is to use the terminology accepted in the West, Lossky believed God's commands to be postlapsarian in origin (that is, formulated after the Fall). Lossky speaks of the "eschatological call" and the profound meaning of God's law, which should not be understood as a static reality and the means of justification. The divine law in Lossky is an expression of divine economy and is essential to the Old Testament, where the relationship between man and God assumes the form not of a union but of alliance guaranteed by loyalty to the law. Lossky warns of the danger of attaching an absolute value to such legal situation and "projecting it onto the very nature of God."

In order to assess better the major objections of the Eastern Orthodox to the Western natural law theory, it would be helpful to recall that in the Roman Catholic system the human attribute of reason or intelligence plays an essential role. As Angela Carmella rightly points out: "The conviction that we can know natural law is based upon the premises that the person is intelligent, that nature is intelligible, and that natures intelligibilities are laws for the mind that grasps them."[175] Thus, in the Roman Catholic philosophy of law, the natural law or the intelligible moral order becomes the criteria of the ethical content of the positive law of a society. "An intelligible moral order," continues Carmella, "means that the positive law of a society can be measured against those moral principles."[176]

The Greek Fathers operated on a different understanding of the nature of human reason. They distinguished between spiritual intellect and discursive reason. Discursive reason is incapable of direct apprehension of spiritual reality. Spiritual reality is of a principally different nature from the phenomena perceived by the senses. Moreover, the Eastern Orthodox and particularly Lossky's understanding of divine order in the universe is expressly personalist, apophatic, and experiential in contrast to the Catholic rational notion of natural law. Discursive reason is incapable of direct apprehension of dynamic divine economy. Truth is also understood experientially, rather than rationally. Following Khomyakov, Lossky insists on two specific attributes of the truth. First, the "Truth can have no external criteria."[177] It stands on the basis of its own internal evidence. Second, "gnosis" [authentic knowledge] is inseparable from love." Thus, by connecting gnosis with love Lossky highlights the ethical and communitarian dimensions of the Eastern Orthodox epistemology. He follows Khomyakov, who insisted that the "Truth can only be apprehended in brotherly love." At the foundation of Catholic legal consciousness and ethics lie the rational notion of natural law and the key role of human reason in the apprehension of this natural law. Lossky's ethics, by contrast, could be described as the internalized and experiential ethics of transfiguration through participation in the divine nature. *Theosis*, or deification, is at the heart of Lossky's ethics.[178]

It must be made clear that there are very few direct references to positive law in Lossky's theological works or his wartime journal. Lossky's *Mystical Theology* and the collections of his essays such as *In the Image and Likeness of God* and the *Orthodox Theology* contain profound reflections on canon law and the place of the divine law in the Old Covenant.[179] Yet, apart from his statements in *Sept jours* about the dangers of absolutizing positive law and turning it into an idol,[180] he never addressed at length the issues of the relationship between positive law and the Christian teaching.

This question was not at the forefront of his theological and social vision. Lossky did not raise the question whether the church should assume direct responsibility for guiding the society in its constitutional reconstruction. He did not reflect on the issue whether the church should or should not develop a Christian philosophy of positive law. Yet, as we have seen, Lossky's vision was not limited to the realm of personal ethics, as is the case with many Orthodox writers. Following Maximus the Confessor, he insisted on the social and cosmic dimensions of deification. In his lecture "Christological Dogma," he speaks of the "deification of men and by them, of the whole universe."[181] In another instance, he writes that the role of the human person in the world is to "bind the visible to the invisible" and to reunite in himself the "sensible and the intelligible."[182] He concludes: "We are therefore responsible for the world. We are the word, the logos, through which it bespeaks itself, and it depends solely on us whether it blasphemes or prays."[183]

CONCLUSIONS

Vladimir Lossky is probably the best known and most widely followed modern Orthodox theologian. His classic work *The Mystical Theology of the Eastern Church* (1944) is a milestone in the ongoing dialogue between Eastern and Western Christianity. Lossky's brilliant critique of "Catholic essentialism" and "Protestant existentialism" has had a profound impact on both Western European and Eastern theology. His portrayal of Orthodoxy as that which mediates between the two Western traditions continues to attract attention in both camps. Pope John Paul II expressed his admiration of the "courageous research" of Vladimir Lossky and compared his work in its speculative value and spiritual significance to the contributions of Jacques Maritain and Étienne Gilson in the West and Vladimir Soloviev and Pavel Florensky in the East.[184] Lossky's "originality and imagination in interpreting the Eastern fathers," writes the Anglican theologian Rowan Williams, "should secure him a firm place among twentieth century theologians, and practically all Eastern Orthodox ecclesiology in the past few decades has taken his scheme as a starting-point."[185]

Emphasizing the principal "dogmatic dissimilarity between the Christian East and the Christian West,"[186] Lossky focused on the apophatic (negative) foundations of theology understood as a "personal encounter with God in silence." Building on this contemplative foundation, Lossky called for a radical deconceptualization of personhood both in trinitarian theology and in human anthropology. He incorporated into his creative synthesis the insights of the Cappadocian fathers, Symeon the New Theologian and Maximus the Confessor, the spiritual masters of the Greek *Philokalia*, and Gregory Palamas. Lossky insisted that a person cannot be reduced to his nature or expressed in concepts. Nature can only be described as the "content of the person and not as the person."[187] There is an ethical depth in Lossky's ascetic teaching on personhood. The drive for self-transcendence and kenotic "self-forgetting" is the primordial foundation and the nerve of authentic personhood.

Lossky was not a philosopher of law like Vladimir Soloviev, and in his theological writings he certainly did not address political, social, and ethical issues with the same directness and comprehensiveness that one finds in the works of Berdyaev or Soloviev. Yet, in today's Eastern Orthodox world Lossky is indisputably more influential than Soloviev and Berdyaev.

In the Soviet era, limited publications of Lossky's works within Russia provided believers with some access to the vibrant streams of creative contemporary Orthodox theology engaged in dialogue with the West. Yet, the Soviet government censors forced the Russian Orthodox publishers to remove from the *Mystical Theology* Lossky's denunciations of brutal persecution of believers within Russia and his admiration of their enduring courage.[188] Within Russia, Lossky is more appreciated by the stricter, more traditional wing of Russian theologians due to the apologetic nature of his writings. His work has been one of the major shaping factors in the prevalence of the neopatristic approach in the Russian theology in the last century. Since the time of *perestroika*, Lossky's teachings have been popularized by Deacon Andrei Kuraev, a conservative, controversial apologist of the Russian Orthodox Church. Of the younger, more recent Russian theologians who continue to expound the themes of mysticism and the vision of God in the Eastern monastic tradition, the name of patristic scholar Hilarion Alfeyev is the most notable.

In Great Britain Lossky exerted considerable influence on certain Anglican theologians associated with the Anglo-Russian Fellowship of St. Alban and St. Sergius. Derwas J. Chitty, one of the best Anglican authorities on Egyptian monasticism, was inspired by Lossky to "proclaim to the world an Orthodoxy that was not peculiar to any one country." Timothy Ware, now known as Bishop Kallistos, a former student and admirer of Chitty's, joined the Orthodox Church and became a leading promoter of Eastern Orthodoxy and of the neopatristic approach to British theologians. While Kallistos frequently cites Lossky in his own writings, he deliberately avoids the controversial style so characteristic of much of Lossky's work. Kallistos counts Lossky with the "hawks" and not the "doves" of Orthodox theology for his "stricter view of the *Filioque* issue."[189] Anglican theologian Eric L. Mascall critically engaged Lossky's insights into his ecumenical discussion of the openness of Being and the concepts of Grace and Nature in East and West. Rowan Williams, the current Archbishop of Canterbury, is a distinguished scholar of Eastern Orthodox theology and a critical interpreter of Lossky's legacy to British theological circles. Of the more ecumenically minded Catholic theologians in France on whom Lossky made a positive impact, one must mention Yves Congar and Louis Bouyer. Of the French Orthodox writers of importance, Olivier Clément, Lossky's friend and disciple, applies Lossky's personalist insights in his creative essays on political theology. Olivier Clément and the prominent Greek theologian Christos Yannaras are the only two followers of Lossky's personalism who write directly on issues of social and political ethics. In the United States, Lossky's writings have been widely circulated by St. Vladimir's Press, an Orthodox publishing house. Daniel B. Clendenin, an American Protestant scholar of Eastern Orthodoxy, insightfully communicates to American Protestant readers the bases of the Orthodox apophatic (mystical) theology using extensively Lossky's writings.

Although Vladimir Nikolaievich Lossky is primarily appreciated for his theological vision, his critique of nationalist and deterministic tendencies in Russian religious philosophy, his analysis of the pitfalls of Western conceptualism and juridicalism, and his holistic vision of human freedom contain profound implications for contemporary discussions of law, politics, and society.

NOTES

1. See Vladimir Lossky, "Spor o Sofii," II, §13, §2, §4, §13 in *Bogoslovie i Bogovidenie*, ed. Vladimir Pislyakov (Moscow: Izdatel'stvo Svyato-Vladimirskogo Bratstva, 2000), 407–408, 412–415, 445–455. See also the excellent pioneering study by Rowan D. Williams, now the archbishop of Canterbury, to which I am greatly indebted and use extensively in this chapter: "The Theology of Vladimir Nikolaievich Lossky: An Exposition and Critique" (D.Phil. thesis, Oxford University, 1976). Lossky rejected Bulgakov's interpretation of the doctrine of incarnation as heretical on the grounds that it indirectly introduces Apollinarian notions and, assuming the deterministic concept of Sophia (the divine nature) as foundational, distorts the kenotic nature of divine incarnation representing it not as a personal divine agape, the voluntary "self-giving" of God, but as an act of some objectively predetermined natural necessity.

2. Vladimir Lossky, *The Mystical Theology of the Eastern Church* (Cambridge: James Clarke, 1991), 178.

3. Lossky, "Soblazny tserkovnogo soznaniya," in *Bogoslovie i Bogovidenie*, 567.

4. Ibid.

5. See Vladimir Lossky, "Lichnost' i mysl' svyateishego Patriarkha Sergiya," in *Bogoslovie i Bogovidenie*, 503–511. This epitaph by Lossky was published for the first time in Moscow in 1947 in the collection *Patriarkh Sergii i ego dukhovnoye nasledstvo*.

6. Vladimir Lossky, *In the Image and Likeness of God*, ed. John H. Erickson and Thomas E. Bird (Crestwood, N.Y.: St. Vladimir's Seminary Press, 2001), 225–227.

7. Cited by Lossky's son Nicolas in his preface to *Sept jours sur les routes de France: Juin 1940* (Paris: Les Éditions du Cerf, 1998), 13.

8. Lossky, "Original Sin," in *Orthodox Theology: An Introduction*, trans. Ian and Ihita Kesarcodi-Watson (Crestwood, N.Y.: St. Vladimir's Seminary Press, 2001), 86.

9. Lossky, *Mystical Theology*, 207.

10. Ibid., 239.

11. Wolfhart Pannenberg, *Basic Questions in Theology*, trans. George H. Kehm, 2 vols. (Philadelphia: Westminster Press, 1983), 2:54. Cited by Daniel B. Clendenin in *Eastern Orthodox Christianity: A Western Perspective* (Grand Rapids, Mich.: Baker Books, 2002), 50.

12. See Rowan D. Williams, "The Via Negativa and the Foundations of Theology: An Introduction to the Thought of V. N. Lossky," in *New Studies in Theology*, ed. Stephen Sykes and Derek Holmes (London: Duckworth, 1980), 1:97.

13. Augustine, *Confessions* IX, 10, trans. R. S. Pine-Coffin, *Saint Augustine* (Harmondsworth, England: Penguin, 1983), 198; cited in "Via Negativa," *New Studies in Theology*, 1:97.

14. As expounded in his *De mystica theologia*, 3.

15. Lossky, *Mystical Theology*, 26.

16. Ibid., 40.

17. Ibid., 177.

18. Ibid.

19. See Lossky, *In the Image and Likeness of God*, 76–77; A. M. Allchin, "Vladimir Lossky," in *The Kingdom of Love and Knowledge: The Encounter Between Orthodoxy and the West* (New York: Seabury, 1982), 203.

20. The *Filioque* clause was first added to the Nicene Creed at the local Council of Toledo in 589.

21. Lossky, *Mystical Theology*, 56.

22. Ibid., 62.

23. Ibid.

24. Ibid., 62–65.

25. See Timothy Ware, *The Orthodox Church* (London: Penguin, 1993), 218.

26. Williams, "The Theology of Vladimir Nikolaievich Lossky," 131.

27. Ibid., 132.

28. Lossky, *In the Image and Likeness of God*, 88–89.

29. Lossky, *Mystical Theology*, 66.

30. Ibid., 64.

31. Ibid., 66.

32. Ibid., 64.

33. Lossky, *In the Image and Likeness of God*, 114–115.

34. Lossky, *Mystical Theology*, 144–145.

35. Williams, "Eastern Orthodox Theology," in *The Modern Theologians: An Introduction to Christian Theology in the Twentieth Century*, ed. David F. Ford, 2 vols. (Oxford: Basil Blackwell, 1989), 2:161.

36. See Williams, "The Theology of Vladimir Nikolaievich Lossky," 106; see also Alar Laats, "Doctrines of the Trinity in Eastern and Western Theologies: A Study with Special Reference to K. Barth and V. Lossky," in *Studies in the Intercultural History of Christianity* (Frankfurt am Main: Peter Lang, 1999), 114:77, 148.

37. See Lossky, *Mystical Theology*, 50–62, Williams, "The Theology of Vladimir Nikolaievich Lossky," 106, 122; Allchin, *Kingdom of Love and Knowledge*, 203.

38. Williams, "The Theology of Vladimir Nikolaievich Lossky," 122.

39. Lossky, *Orthodox Theology*, 24.

40. See Lossky, *In the Image and Likeness of God*, 115.

41. Lossky, *Orthodox Theology*, 42.

42. Lossky, *Mystical Theology*, 122.

43. Gregory Nazianzen, quoted in ibid., 124 n. 3.

44. See Lossky's objection to Calvin's claim that human nature no longer possesses freedom of the will in "Spor o Sofii" II, §11 in *Bogoslovie i Bogovidenie*, 446.

45. Lossky, *Mystical Theology*, 124. More recently this position has been shared by some liberal Protestant theologians in the West.

46. Ibid., 125.

47. Ibid.

48. Ibid.

49. Ibid., 122.

50. Ibid., 123.

51. Ibid., 125, 131, 201.

52. Ibid., 130.

53. Ibid., 128.

54. Ibid., 201.

55. Ibid.

56. Cf. Hebrews 8:10 (NASV): "For this is the covenant that I will make with the house of Israel after those days, says the Lord: I will put My laws into their minds, and I will write them upon their hearts."

57. Lossky, *In the Image and Likeness of God*, 216; *Orthodox Theology*, 86. Cf. Jaroslav Pelikan, *The Spirit of Eastern Christendom (600–1700)* (Chicago: University of Chicago Press, 1977), 215.

58. Lossky, *Sept jours*, 22.
59. Lossky, *Orthodox Theology*, 19.
60. Ibid., 53.
61. Ibid., 64.
62. Ibid.
63. Ibid., 54.
64. Ibid., 67.
65. Ibid., 57.
66. Ibid.
67. Ibid., 61.
68. Ibid., 86.
69. Ibid., 113.
70. Lossky, *Mystical Theology*, 112.
71. Ibid., 18.
72. Ibid., 19.
73. Nikolay Berdyaev, "Smysl tvorchestva," in *Filosofiya tvorchestva, kul'tury i iskusstva*, 2 vols. (Moscow: Izdatel'stvo Isskustvo, 1994), 2:144–145. See also Vasili V. Zen'kovsky, *Istoriya russkoi filosofii*, 2:75, and Williams, "The Theology of Vladimir Nikolaievich Lossky," 237.
74. Lossky, *Orthodox Theology*, 53.
75. Ibid., 52.
76. Ibid., 73.
77. Lossky, *In the Image and Likeness of God*, 214–215.
78. See Berdyaev's statement cited by Matthew Spinka in *Nicolas Berdyaev: Captive of Freedom* (Philadelphia: Westminster Press, 1950), 35–36. See also chapter 2, this volume.
79. Lossky, "Soblazny," 562.
80. Ibid., 561.
81. Lossky, *In the Image and Likeness of God*, 178.
82. Ibid., 176.
83. Ibid.
84. Ibid., 177.
85. Ibid., 190–191.
86. Ibid., 191.
87. Ibid., 190, 191.
88. Cf. John 14:26: "He will teach you all things, and bring to your remembrance all that I have said to you." Cited ibid., 191.
89. Ibid., 192.
90. Ibid., 176–177.
91. Lossky, "Soblazny," 565.
92. See Louis Berkhof, *Systematic Theology* (Grand Rapids, Mich.: Eerdmans, 1979), 565.
93. Lossky, "Soblazny," 560; *Mystical Theology*, 186.
94. Lossky, *In the Image and Likeness of God*, 186.

95. Ephesians 1:17–23, cited by Lossky, *Mystical Theology*, 183.

96. Ibid., 176.

97. Lossky, *In the Image and Likeness of God*, 178.

98. It is also highly significant that the same distinction between nature and person which lies at the foundation of Lossky's doctrine of the Trinity runs across his teaching on the unifying role of Christ and the diversifying role of the Holy Spirit in the church. The one nature "common to all men," "split up by sin," and "parceled out among many individuals" is reestablished by Christ and objectively united in his body—the Church. See Lossky, *Mystical Theology*, 121. Yet the church is not only one common human nature objectively "recapitulated" in the person (hypostasis) of Christ—it consists of a multitude of persons (hypostases) in need of being freely and consciously deified and united to God. This free and personal deification, the collaboration between grace and human freedom is accomplished in each member by the Holy Spirit. Lossky, *In the Image and Likeness of God*, 177–178.

99. Ibid., 178.

100. Lossky, *Mystical Theology*, 185.

101. Ibid., 183.

102. Lossky, *In the Image and Likeness of God*, 179.

103. Ibid., 178.

104. Lossky, *Mystical Theology*, 182.

105. Ibid.

106. Lossky, *In the Image and Likeness of God*, 175.

107. Ibid.

108. Ibid., 174–175.

109. Lossky, "Spor o Sofii," I.1, in *Bogoslovie i Bogovidenie*, 396–397; *In the Image and Likeness of God*, 179.

110. Ibid., 179.

111. See "Pis'mo V. Losskago N. A. Berdyaevu," *Put'* 50:27–32.

112. Lossky, *Mystical Theology*, 188.

113. Lossky, *In the Image and Likeness of God*, 175–176.

114. Lossky, *Sept jours*, 21–22. Later Lossky affectionately speaks of France, claiming that even under the old regime it kept the "spirit of the democratic state" (44).

115. Lossky, *In the Image and Likeness of God*, 181.

116. Ibid.

117. Ibid.

118. Ibid., 192.

119. Ibid.

120. Williams, "The Theology of Vladimir Nikolaievich Lossky," 18.

121. Lossky, *Sept jours*, 54.

122. See Lossky's letter to Berdyaev, *Put'* 50:28–29.

123. Ibid., 29.

124. Richard Pipes, *Russia Under the Old Regime* (London: Penguin, 1995), 230.

125. Lossky, "Soblazny," 561.

126. Ibid., 561–562.

127. Lossky, *Orthodox Theology*, 71.

128. Konstantin Kostyuk, "Stanovlenie sotsial'nogo ucheniya v pravoslavii," in *Sotsial'no-politicheskii zhurnal* (1997): 6. Page 1 of the e-text is available at http://www.civitasdei.boom.ru/person/orthlehr.htm (in Russian). Translation mine. Yet, having said this Kostyuk (referring to much more recent times, in anticipation of the "Bases of the Social Concept" adopted by the Russian Orthodox Church in 2000) acknowledges that the "absence of such social teaching is acutely sensed by the church as well as the society," that it "upsets the political balance" in society, undermines the spiritual impact of the Orthodox Church on society and "demonstrates the Church's inability to spiritually nourish the nation."

129. Lossky, "Soblazny," 562.

130. Lossky, *Sept jours*, 45.

131. Ibid.

132. Lossky, "Soblazny," 561; cited from the English translation. "The Temptations of Ecclesial Consciousness," in *St. Vladimir's Theological Quarterly* 32, no. 3 (1988): 247. Translation revised.

133. Lossky, *Sept jours*, 44–45.

134. Ibid., 16.

135. Ibid., 45.

136. Ibid.

137. Expounding his notion of catholicity as a free and harmonious union of unique persons united by Christ and empowered by the Holy Spirit, Lossky elucidates and develops the creative intuitions of such nineteenth-century Slavophiles as Ivan Kireevsky and Aleksei Khomyakov. Yet, what is noteworthy is that while doing so Lossky deliberately avoids the use of the Russian term *sobornost*, not because of its inaccessibility to the uninitiated, but primarily because of its "Russianness" and its nationalistic connotations. He replaces *sobornost* with catholicity—one of the four traditional marks of the Church. See Lossky, *In the Image and Likeness of God*, 170 n. 1.

138. Williams, "The Theology of Vladimir Nikolaievich Lossky," 10.

139. Lossky, *In the Image and Likeness of God*, 184.

140. Lossky, *Mystical Theology*, 15. Lossky refers to the 1872 Synod of Constantinople, citing Mansi, *Coll. concil.*, 45:417–546, and the article by M. Zyzykine, "L'eglise orthodoxe et la nation," *Irénikon* (1936): 265–277.

141. Lossky, *In the Image and Likeness of God*, 184.

142. Lossky, *Orthodox Theology*, 128.

143. See Lossky, *Mystical Theology*, 182, cf. 144–145, 148.

144. Lossky, *Orthodox Theology*, 128.

145. So defined by one of Lossky's most influential students, French theologian Olivier Clement, "Serbian Church must undergo examination of conscience: Orthodox Theologian Analyzes Responsibility in Kosovo Conflict," in *Zenit*

Daily Dispatch, Rome (June 22, 1999), cited from e-text available at http://www.zenit.org/english/archive/9906/ZE990622.html.

146. Ibid. See also the remark of the editor of *St. Vladimir's Theological Quarterly*, who laments that "ethno-phyletism" continues as a spiritual disease, particularly in America," in Lossky, "The Temptations of Ecclesial Consciousness," *St. Vladimir's Theological Quarterly* (1988) 32, no. 3: 250.

147. Aleksandr Kyrlezhev, "Vozmozhen li sintez politicheskoi ideologii na osnove pravoslavia?" http://religion.ng.ru/concepts/2000-10-11/5_sintes.html.

148. Nikolai Lossky, in *Sept jours*, 10.

149. Ibid., 21.

150. Ibid.

151. Ibid., 21–22.

152. Ibid., 22.

153. Ibid., 45.

154. Ibid., 23.

155. Ibid.

156. Lossky, *Mystical Theology*, 177.

157. Father Michael Azkoul, "What Are the Differences Between Orthodoxy and Roman Catholicism?" http://www.ocf.org/OrthodoxPage/reading/ortho_cath.html.

158. Lossky, *In the Image and Likeness of God*, 192.

159. Ibid., 181.

160. Lossky, *Mystical Theology*, 175–176.

161. Maximus the Confessor, "Fifth Century of Various Texts," §§33, 34, in *Philokalia*, 4 vols., trans. G. E. H. Palmer et al. (London: Faber and Faber, 1990), 2:268.

162. Maximus, "Fifth Century," §35, *Philokalia* 2:268.

163. Ibid., §21, *Philokalia* 2:265.

164. Ibid., §27, *Philokalia* 2:266.

165. Ibid., §46, *Philokalia* 2:272. Lossky echoed Maximus in his lecture on the *Original Sin* where he speaks of the spirit, "historical dynamism" and the "eschatological call" of the Law. Lossky, *Orthodox Theology*, 89.

166. Maximus, "Fifth Century," §10, *Philokalia* 2:262.

167. Maximus, "Second Century," §41, *Philokalia* 2:196.

168. Ibid., §11, *Philokalia* 2:263.

169. Maximus, "Second Century," §41, *Philokalia* 2:196.

170. Maximus, "Fifth Century," §13, *Philokalia* 2:264.

171. Ibid.

172. John Meyendorff, *Byzantine Theology: Historical Trends and Doctrinal Themes* (New York: Fordham University Press, 1979), 216.

173. Ibid.

174. Lossky, *In the Image and Likeness of God*, 218.

175. Angela C. Carmella, "A Catholic View of Law and Justice," in *Christian Perspectives on Legal Thought*, ed. Michael W. McConnell, Robert F. Cochran Jr., and Angela Carmella (New Haven, Conn.: Yale University Press, 2001), 262.

176. Ibid.

177. Lossky, *Mystical Theology*, 188.

178. Lossky, *Orthodox Theology*, 128.

179. See Lossky, *Mystical Theology*, 175–176; *In the Image and Likeness of God*, 216–217; and *Orthodox Theology*, 85–89.

180. Lossky, *Sept jours*, 22.

181. Lossky, *Orthodox Theology*, 110.

182. Ibid., 64.

183. Ibid., 71.

184. Pope John Paul II, *Fides et ratio*, VI, 74.

185. Williams, "Eastern Orthodox Theology," 163.

186. Lossky, *Mystical Theology*, 12–14, 21–22.

187. In Lossky the person is the existence of nature: "There is nothing in nature which properly pertains to the person, who is always unique and incomparable." Ibid., 121. The human person is not to be controlled by nature but is rather called to control nature and continually transcend himself in grace. Ibid., 241.

188. Compare the English version of *Mystical Theology*, 16, also 245–246, and the Russian version *Ocherk misticheskogo bogosloviya vostochnoi tserkvi* (Moscow, 1991), 16, 185.

189. See Ware, *The Orthodox Church*, 213.

ORIGINAL SOURCE MATERIALS

SEPT JOURS SUR LES ROUTES DE FRANCE

... I HAD THE IMPRESSION that the State—that indispensable convention so necessary to human societies, that great fictitious reality, anchored in our consciousness to the point of being part of ourselves—was ceasing to exist. But order, the State's function, carried on nevertheless, through a sort of inertia, an innate discipline, or—more likely—through the mute solidarity of French people suffering the same fate.

Did the Third Republic really exist anymore, with its Government, civil servants, courts, bailiffs, stamped papers, and with all its administrative symbolism? Or, going back in time ten centuries, would we find ourselves suddenly transported back to the era of the Norman invasions, the time when the kingship of the last Carolingians was disappearing; the royal feeling withdrawing into peoples' consciousness to be replaced by other instincts and other ties, more concrete and more personal—the instinct for companionship, the man-to-man ties that were the basis of feudal society, with its manly and solid virtues? ...

I was following my conscience when I made the decision to leave. Three days earlier, on Monday night, the TSF (radio) had communicated the order from the military governor of the Seine for all eligible men who had not yet been called up. Potential conscripts were to leave the Paris region within six days, starting Thursday June 13, and retreat to the provinces, to the destinations that would be assigned to them by the mobile guards at the main exit points on the south side of the capital. Above all else, my friend and I wanted to sign up to participate in the defense of Paris (we still expected the city to be defended). At the recruitment center on rue St. Dominique, our fate was resolved in an unexpected way: my friend—a Russian refugee—could not be accepted into the Foreign Legion due to his poor health. But I—French and eligible for mobilization—was told to wait until I was called up, and could not speed things up with a voluntary enlistment. "But I want to help defend Paris." The lieutenant shrugged, with a bitter smile. "Try to sign up with the territorial guards, at the police station." Same shrug and unhappy smile at the police station ... The only thing left to do was to leave, "retreat to the provinces." My friend, who wanted to follow me, not obtaining in time the permit foreigners need, finally had to resign himself to staying behind. I prepared to leave.

At the Chevrot farm we were met by a sergeant's coarse kindness. They made room for us on the straw in a very large barn, next to other "eligible recruits." The other half of the barn sheltered refugee families. We each received a pack of 'troop' cigarettes—the Army's first welcome. Tomorrow I will finally be a soldier. I will have my place—modest, but clear and well defined—among those who would resist. I will have my nameless regimental number, one "unknown soldier" among so many others. I will no longer be on the sidelines of the communal job to be done. I will no longer be an intellectual set apart from the national destiny—a fragile and sensitive instrument that constantly turned in on itself to meditate, a being for whom life stops to make room for a thought. I will finally simply do my duty: no thoughts, no anguish—just gritting my teeth and staring straight at this monstrous reality that was still impossible to take in: the Germans are in Paris. . . .

But then [during the Hundred Years War] the enemy was "driven out of the Kingdom of France." The miracle of Joan of Arc took place at the limits of all human hope, where the resources—of valiant captains with prowess at arms, of wise counselors adept in political matters—reached their end. The miracle of Joan of Arc, this act of God, took place at the limit where all the prelates' magisteria and all the philosophy doctors' theology were nothing more than useless verbiage, incapable of reanimating the faith of the Christian people—vain words, like the insane comments made by Job's rational friends. . . .

Every day since the war started, we had heard words light in judgment but heavy in consequences, because it is always words that condemn, that deliver us to our destiny. They told us, "We will win this war because we are stronger, because we are richer. We will win because we want to." As if weapons were enough in themselves to secure the victory. As if the war were just a huge industrial endeavor, a question of capital. Military *matériel* war—inhuman war—materialistic war. Yet without a doubt we lost that war. We must have the courage to say it. And there's more: France could not have won that war, as it was presented to us. Otherwise France would no longer be France, a humane place par excellence. Otherwise, having won the war of military *matériel* (as it was presented to us), the country would have lost perhaps the most precious thing it possesses: the foundation of its being. France would have lost that which is France, that which differentiates it from every other country on Earth, if it had won that war without a human face. Everywhere where we resisted the enemy, that was an act of human courage; the French courage that gave up the battle to enemy *matériel*, superior in number and strength.

Despite the laws of *"matériel* war," we defended the soil, the land. Without a doubt we lost the *matériel* war. But the human war, the French war, was not lost. The Germans are in Paris; they may already be on the Loire, on the Garonne, everywhere. But France is not yet conquered: the human war has just begun. It may last a century, like that other great time of trouble; the era that gave rise to a new France—the era we call the Hundred Years' War.

There was another heresy—spiritualist this time—that tried to superimpose itself on the *"matériel* war," to infuse that war with an artificial soul. This was the ideology of a "holy war," of a "crusade." The ideology had several nuances: the struggle for the democracies, for freedom, for human dignity, for Western culture, for Christian civilization, and finally for divine justice. I say 'heresy' because these ideas—while often just in themselves—were not based on a living experience. They did not spring from a deep and healthy source that alone could have transformed them into "idea-forces." And these words rang false, as all abstractions do. They especially rang false because they tried to present secondary, relative concepts and values as *absolutes*. Even Christian civilization, as a civilization, is no more than a product, a creation, an external manifestation of an absolute reality, which is the faith of the Christian peoples. Holy war is not waged for cathedrals, for theological works, for missals. These are merely the trappings of the Church—Christ's clothes divided up by the soldiers at the foot of the Cross. As for the Church, source of all these secondary goods, it needs neither our material defense nor our childish swords. It is pointless to repeat Peter's naive gesture of slashing the slave's ear in the garden of Gethsemane . . . War is not fought for absolute values. This was the great error of the so-called "religious" wars and the main cause of their inhuman atrocities. War is equally not waged for relative values that we attempt to render absolute, for abstract concepts we cloak in religion. If we oppose the idol of the "pure race" with the more humane idols of law, liberty and humanity, they would not be any the less idols for it, ideas rendered hypostasized and absolute; the war would still be a war of idols, and not a human war. Human war, the only just war (inasmuch as any war may be called just) is a war for relative values, for values that we know to be relative. It is a war where man—a being called for an absolute goal—dedicates himself spontaneously and without hesitation for a relative value that he knows to be relative: the soil, the land, the Homeland. And this sacrifice acquires an absolute value, imperishable and eternal for the human person. Joan of Arc's divine mission had a relative value as its goal: taking the Dauphin to Reims to return France's king to her. Joan had no animosity toward the English she would "drive out of France." This is one of the primary characteristics of the human war she waged. It is also characteristic of France's soul, of which Joan of Arc is the most perfect image. . . .

We also talked about Justice, and even the justice of God, in the name of which we should fight so that justice (which is an attribute of God) would triumph in the face of our adversaries' iniquity. "Our cause is just. This is why God will grant us victory." This is how the prelates spoke, the people's spiritual leaders. The just cause often triumphed in "God's judgment," those judicial duels waged between two parties in conflict. But those two parties abandoned their justice, abandoned their just cause, to give place to divine justice alone—without possibility of appeal—which would manifest through their feat of arms. And again, the Church was obliged to oppose this practice eight hundred years ago. . . . I had heard a great prelate at Notre Dame speak before thousands of faithful about our just cause, call upon God that He would grant us victory in the name of this just cause. If we followed his thought to its logical end, God would find Himself obliged to help us because He is just, and we are defending justice. He could not act nor wish otherwise without contradicting Himself, without renouncing His attribute of Justice, immutable (as is everything about God written in religious works and theological guides). So if we lost this war after all, after calling on God to give us victory in the name of His justice, what would there be left to say? It came down to this: either our cause was not the just cause, or God is unjust. Yes, He is unjust, if we wish to put it that way, because He is greater than justice, because His justice is not our justice, because His ways are not our ways. Because before His justice, which will one day shake the foundations of the universe, our poor justice is nothing less than injustice. . . . We should have prayed for victory with tears and great contrition, bearing in mind this fearsome Justice, before which we are all unjust. We should not have called on Justice, which is beyond our measure, which we could not bear, but on the infinite mercy which made the Son of God descend from Heaven.

"Lord, we are all unjust before You, and our justice is vain; yet come to our aid, because we are unjust and blind, and cannot find Your way. Stay Your sword of justice, and grant us the victory over our enemy, whom You have allowed to invade France. For nothing is done that is not Your will, and You are the Master of the peoples of the Earth, whom you punish for their own greater good."

But the blindness of an 'autonomous' lay morality hardened hearts, even among people of the Church. We have long since forgotten what Philippe de Commines, wise counselor to Louis XI and an historian well-versed in politics, knew: "Thus it seems that God tries to show us the way and give us many signs, and also strikes us with many rods for our bestial nature and our evil, which I think is better. Who can remedy this if God does not?"

At the crossroad, in the center of Arpajon, a sergeant—a Moroccan with a complacent smile—was acting the policeman. With a triumphant gesture he kept pointing out the same direction to all those who had the bad luck of turning toward his lights. Military convoys, troupes, refugee families were all heading toward La Ferté-Allais, instead of taking the Estampes route just a little below. I naively relied on him as well, and it cost me a detour of a few kilometers. Finally, having reached the right road by taking paths across fields, I headed once again toward Estampes, the ultimate goal of my long trip and certain refuge, where I will at last stop being an "individual" to become a member of the collective group, which carried out the huge task of national defense.

Strange failure awaited those great "trips abroad,"—the Crusades, that mysterious push toward the East. In spite of what is usually said, it was not just the cupidity of the noblemen, greedy for booty, nor the taste for war adventures peculiar of the feudal world, which made the Western Christians leave their families and worldly goods, in order to take the Cross and head out toward the unknown lands of the Middle East, overtaken by an irresistible impulse. It was above all an enormous pilgrimage, an armed pilgrimage, a movement of religious nature, to which other motives, other interests, were soon added on. At times, the legends which arise around an existing event, the poetry which it inspires, reveal to us the depth hidden in an historic act, while remaining unnoticed by historians who base themselves on "positive data." They traveled toward the East to deliver the Saint Sepulcher. They went also to find the mysterious country where the apostle St. John lived eternally, reigning over a Christian people. They went there above all pushed by a vague religious uneasiness, which will later find its expression in the mystical poem on "The Search of the Holy Grail," where the chalice of the Last Supper would symbolize the plenitude of the Gifts of the Holy Spirit, the Christian plenitude. But the Crusades became a war of pillage and destruction, relentless against the Orthodox Christian. In place of the spiritual kingdom of St. John, they founded an ephemeral kingdom, "the Latin Empire"; in place of the Holy Grail, the knights brought to the West the Manichean heresy of the Bulgarians. It is then that a new Crusade stirred the French people of the North against those of the South. The first "religious war" bloodied the French soil. The Languedoc would be bound to know others, three centuries later.[1]

THE MYSTICAL THEOLOGY OF THE EASTERN CHURCH

Image and Likeness

Men have therefore a common nature, one single nature in many human persons. This distinction of nature and person in man is no less difficult to grasp than the analogous distinction of the one nature and three persons in God. Above all, we must remember that we do not know the person, the human hypostasis in its true condition, free from alloy. We commonly use the words "persons" or "personal" to mean individuals, or individual. We are in the habit of thinking of these two terms, person and individual, almost as though they were synonyms. We employ them indifferently to express the same thing. But, in a certain sense, individual and person mean opposite things, the word individual expressing a certain mixture of the person with elements which belong to the common nature, while person, on the other hand, means that which distinguishes it from nature. In our present condition we know persons only through individuals, and as individuals. When we wish to define, "to characterize" a person, we gather together individual characteristics, "traits of character" which are to be met with elsewhere in other individuals, and which because they belong to nature are never absolutely "personal." Finally, we admit that what is most dear to us in someone, what makes him himself, remains indefinable, for there is nothing in nature which properly pertains to the person, which is always unique and incomparable. The man who is governed by his nature and acts in the strength of his natural qualities, of his "character", is the least personal. He sets himself up as an individual, proprietor of his own nature, which he pits against the natures of others and regards as his "me," thereby confusing person and nature. This confusion, proper to fallen humanity, has a special name in the ascetic writings of the Eastern Church—αὐτότης, φιλαυτία or, in Russian, *samost,* which can perhaps be best translated by the word egoism, or rather if we may create a Latin barbarism "ipseity."

A difficulty is met with in reference to the Christological dogma which would see the will as a function of the nature; for us it is easier to envisage the person as willing, asserting and imposing himself through his will. However, the idea of the person implies freedom *vis-à-vis* the nature. The person is free from its nature, is not determined by it. The human hypostasis can only realize itself by the renunciation of its own will, of all that governs us, and makes us subject to natural necessity.

Made in the image of God, man is a personal being confronted with a personal God. God speaks to him as to a person, and man responds. Man,

according to St. Basil, is a creature who has received a commandment to become God.[2] But this commandment is addressed to human freedom, and
does not overrule it. As a personal being man can accept the will of God; he
can also reject it. Even when he removes himself as far as possible from
God, and becomes unlike Him in His nature, he remains a person. The image of God in man is indestructible. In the same way, he remains a personal
being when he fulfills the will of God and in his nature realizes perfect likeness with Him. For according to St. Gregory Nazianzen, "God honoured
man in giving him freedom, in order that goodness should properly belong
to him who chooses it, no less than to Him who placed the first fruits of
goodness in his nature."[3] Thus, whether he chooses good or evil, whether he
tends to likeness or unlikeness, man possesses his nature freely, because he
is a person created in the image of God. All the same, since the person cannot be separated from the nature which exists in it, every imperfection, every "unlikeness" in the nature limits the person, and obscures "the image of
God." Indeed, if freedom belongs to us as persons, the will by which we act
is a faculty of our nature. According to St. Maximus, the will is "a natural
force which tends towards that which is conformed to nature, a power
which embraces all the essential properties of nature."[4] St. Maximus distinguishes this natural will (θέλημα φυσικόν) which is the desire for good to
which every reasonable nature tends, from the choosing will (θέλημα
γνωμικόν) which is a characteristic of the person.[5] The nature wills and acts,
the person chooses, accepting or rejecting that which the nature wills.
However, according to St. Maximus, this freedom of choice is already a sign
of imperfection, a limitation of our true freedom. A perfect nature has no
need of choice, for it knows naturally what is good. Its freedom is based on
this knowledge. Our free choice (γνωμή) indicates the imperfection of fallen
human nature, the loss of the divine likeness.[6]

THE WAY OF UNION

Source of all intellectual and spiritual activity, the heart, according to St.
Macarius of Egypt, is "a workshop of justice and injustice."[7] It is a vessel
which contains all the vices, but where at the same time, "God, the angels,
life and the Kingdom, light and the apostles, and the treasures of grace are
to be found."[8] "Where grace fills the pastures of the heart, it reigns over all
the parts and the thoughts: for there inhabit the intelligence (νοῦς) and
all the thoughts of the soul."[9] In this way grace passes by way of the heart
into the whole of man's nature. The spirit (νοῦς, πνεῦμα), the highest part
of the human creature, is that contemplative faculty by which man is able

to seek God. The most personal part of man, the principle of his conscience and of his freedom, the spirit (νοῦς) in human nature corresponds most nearly to the person; it might be said that it is the seat of the person, of the human hypostasis which contains in itself the whole of man's nature—spirit, soul and body. This is why the Greek Fathers are often ready to identify the νους with the image of God in man.[10] Man must live according to the spirit; the whole human complex must become "spiritual" (πνευματικός), must acquire the "likeness." It is in fact the spirit which becomes united with baptismal grace, and through which grace enters into the heart, the centre of that total human nature which is to be deified. "The uniting of the spirit with the heart," "the descent of the spirit into the heart," "the guarding of the heart by the spirit"—these expressions constantly recur in the ascetic writings of the Eastern Church. Without the heart, which is the centre of all activity, the spirit is powerless. Without the spirit, the heart remains blind, destitute of direction. It is therefore necessary to attain to a harmonious relationship between the spirit and the heart, in order to develop and build up the personality in the life of grace-for the way of union is not a mere unconscious process, and it presupposes an unceasing vigilance of spirit and a constant effort of the will.

Love is inseparable from knowledge—"gnosis." There is an element of personal awareness necessary, without which the way towards union would be blind, and without any certain object, "an illusory discipline" (ἄσκησις φαινομένη), according to St. Macarius of Egypt.[11] The ascetic life, "apart from gnosis" (οὐκ εν τῇ γνώσει), has no value, according to St. Dorotheos;[12] only a spiritual life that is fully aware—ἐν γνώσει—a life in constant communion with God, is able to transfigure our nature by making it like the divine nature, by making it participate in the uncreated light of grace, after the example of the humanity of Christ who appeared to the disciples on Mount Tabor clothed in uncreated glory.[13]

REDEMPTION AND DEIFICATION

. . . When the dogma of the redemption is treated in isolation from the general body of Christian teaching, there is always a risk of limiting the tradition by interpreting it exclusively in terms of the work of the Redeemer. Then theological thought develops along three lines: original sin, its reparation on the cross, and the appropriation of the saving results of the work of Christ to Christians. In these constricting perspectives of a theology dominated by the idea of redemption, the patristic sentence, "God made Himself man that man might become God," seems to be

strange and abnormal. The thought of union with God is forgotten because of our preoccupation solely with our own salvation; or, rather,
union with God is seen only negatively, in contrast with our present
wretchedness. . . .

It was Anselm of Canterbury, with his treatise *Cur Deus Homo,* who
undoubtedly made the first attempt to develop the dogma of redemption
apart from the rest of Christian teaching. In his work Christian horizons
are limited by the drama played between God, who is infinitely offended
by sin, and man, who is unable to satisfy the impossible demands of vindictive justice. The drama finds its resolution in the death of Christ, the
Son of God who has become man in order to substitute Himself for us and
to pay our debt to divine justice. What becomes of the dispensation of the
Holy Spirit here? His part is reduced to that of an auxiliary, an assistant in
redemption, causing us to receive Christ's expiating merit. The final goal
of our union with God is, if not excluded altogether, at least shut out from
our sight by the stern vault of a theological conception built on the ideas
of original guilt and its reparation. The price of our redemption having
been paid in the death of Christ, the resurrection and the ascension are
only a glorious happy end of His work, a kind of apotheosis without direct
relationship to our human destiny. This redemptionist theology, placing
all the emphasis on the passion, seems to take no interest in the triumph
of Christ over death. The very work of the Christ-Redeemer, to which this
theology is confined, seems to be truncated, impoverished, reduced to a
change of the divine attitude toward fallen men, unrelated to the nature of
humanity.

We find an entirely different conception of the redeeming work of
Christ in the thought of St. Athanasius.[14] "Christ," he says, "having delivered the temple of His body to death, offered one sacrifice for all men to
make them innocent and free from original guilt, and also to show Himself victorious over death and to create the first fruits of the General Resurrection with His own incorruptible body." Here the juridical image of
the Redemption is completed by another image, the physical—or rather
biological—image of the triumph of life over death, of incorruptibility tri-
umphing in the nature which had been corrupted by sin.

In the Fathers generally, as well as in the Scriptures, we find many images expressing the mystery of our salvation accomplished by Christ.
Thus, in the Gospel, the Good Shepherd is a "bucolic" image of the work
of Christ.[15] The strong man overcome by the "stronger than he, who ta-
keth away his arms and destroys his power," is a "military" image,[16]
which is often found again in the Fathers and in the Liturgy: Christ victorious over Satan, trampling upon the gates of hell, making the Cross

his standard of triumph.[17] There is also a "medical" image, that of a sickly nature cured by salvation as the antidote to a poison.[18] There is an image which could be termed "diplomatic," the divine stratagem which deceives the devil in his cunning.[19] And so it goes. At last we come to the image used most often, taken by St. Paul from the Old Testament, where it was borrowed from the sphere of juridical relations.[20] Taken in this sense, redemption is a juridical image of the work of Christ, found side by side with many other images.[21] When we use the word "redemption," as we do nowadays, as a generic term designating the saving work of Christ in all its fullness, we should not forget that this juridical expression has the character of an image or simile: Christ is the Redeemer in the same sense that He is the Warrior victorious over death, the perfect Sacrificer, *etc.*

Anselm's mistake was not just that he developed a juridical view of the redemption, but rather that he wanted to see an adequate expression of the mystery of our redemption accomplished by Christ in the juridical relations implied by the word "redemption." Rejecting other expressions of this mystery as inadequate images, *quasi quaedam picturae*, he believed that he had found in the juridical image—that of the redemption—the very body of the truth, its "rational solidity," *veritatis rationabilis soliditas*, the reason why it was necessary for God to die for our salvation.[22]

The impossibility of proving rationally that the work of redemption was necessary, by making use of the juridical meaning of the term "redemption," was demonstrated by St. Gregory of Nazianzus in a magisterial *reductio ad absurdum....*[23] For St. Gregory of Nazianzus, the idea of redemption, far from implying the idea of a necessity imposed by vindictive justice, is rather an expression of the dispensation, whose mystery cannot be adequately clarified in a series of rational concepts. He says, in later passage, that "it was necessary for us that God should be incarnate and die that we might live again" (c. 28). "Nothing can be compared with the miracle of my salvation: a few drops of blood re-make the whole universe" (c. 29).

After the constricted horizons of an exclusively juridical theology, we find in the Fathers an extremely rich idea of redemption which includes victory over death, the first fruits of the general resurrection, the liberation of human nature from captivity under the devil, and not only the justification, but also the restoration of creation in Christ....

... Thus each person is an absolutely original and unique aspect of the nature common to all. The mystery of a human person, which makes it absolutely unique and irreplaceable, cannot be grasped in a rational concept and defined in words.[24]

THE TEMPTATIONS OF ECCLESIAL CONSCIOUSNESS

The Church is not of the world, but She is in the world and exists for the world in the same manner as Christ is not of the world, yet He came into the world for the sake of the world. Just as Christ, being free of the world, kept silence before the court of Pilate, the Church often standing silent before the powers of this world, preserves her transcendental freedom. Although it is at times difficult for us to recognize this freedom of hers under the external appearance of humiliation. "The scandal for the Jews"—the cross is also insurmountable for many Christians. Many would prefer to see in the Church one of the forces of history, comparable to other worldly factors and the "inferiority complex" before the powerful administration of Roman Catholicism is a temptation from which many Orthodox are not free.

Each of us, being of the earth, belongs to a definite political structure, a definite social class; each is in part the product of and at the same time a creator of modern culture, and so on—but each of us, participating in the unity of the Church, can and must become more than his political interests, more than his class, more than his culture, because the Church affords us the opportunity of being *free* of our limited nature. It is inevitable that there will be among Christians a variety of opinions and of political, ethnic, social, cultural, and other interests. To protest against these opinions and interests would be as absurd (and heretical) as to wish to suppress life with all its richness and complexity. The Church has never prescribed for her members any political views, social doctrines, or cultural peculiarities. This is why She cannot tolerate the interests or arrangements of individuals or groups being passed off as "the Church's interests," because her first concern must be the observance of unity, outside of which there is no catholicity, no certitude, no distinctions between the Church and the world.[25]

TRADITION AND TRADITIONS

One can say that Tradition represents the critical spirit of the Church. But, contrary to the "critical spirit" of human science, the critical judgment of the Church is made acute by the Holy Spirit. It has then quite a different principle: that of the undiminished fullness of Revelation. Thus the Church, which will have to correct the inevitable alterations of the sacred texts (that certain "traditionalists" wish to preserve at any price, sometimes attributing a mystical meaning to stupid mistakes of copyists), will be able at the same time to recognize in some late interpolations (for example, in the *comma* of the "three that bear record in heaven" in the first epistle of St. John) an authentic expression of the revealed Truth. Naturally authenticity here has a meaning quite other than it has in the historical disciplines.[26]

DOMINION AND KINGSHIP: AN ESCHATOLOGICAL STUDY

We need first of all to examine the terms which we are using here, in speaking of God's "dominion" and of its "fulfillment." Dominion is a relative concept implying, as its counterpart, submission to some dominant thing or person. But to speak of submission means necessarily to admit a possibility of "insubmissiveness" and rebellion against the dominion which is exerted. Only that which offers or is capable of offering resistance is dominated. The God of Aristotle is not lord over his eternal world: he is only the unconditioned first condition for the necessary operation of the machine of the universe, from which all contingency is excluded. Aristotle would have been astounded indeed if anyone had sought to give his God—the first unmoved Mover, the Thought which thinks itself—the name of Κύριος, Lord.

Now, the God of the Bible is the Lord, the Lord of the celestial hosts, of all spirits and of all flesh. His dominion is "from generation to generation"; it is exerted "in every place." Although it is impossible to escape from this universal dominion (which is made all the more absolute by the fact that the God of the Jews and Christians is the *Creator* of all things), one can, nevertheless, *resist* it; and the uttered curses of a man seeking to reach God in order to contend with Him face to face are not, in the Bible, what they are in ancient tragedy: the desperate outcry of a liberty falling back on itself and recognizing its absurd and illusory quality in face of a Destiny equally inexorable for gods and mortals.

We see, indeed, that God justifies Job, who contended with him, while his wrath is kindled against Eliphaz and his friends, who have spoken in favor of the irresistible and necessary absolutism of his dominion: "You have not spoken of me what is right, as my servant Job has" (Job 42 :7). For Job's protest, his refusal to accept a dominion which allowed of no dialogue between God and man, was a negative witness to the true nature of God's dominion. Job's complaint is a praise which exalts God higher, which enters more profoundly into His mystery, by refusing to halt at the abstract idea of His dominion which others make for themselves. This is a theology which aims higher than all clumsy theodicies, of which the speeches of Job's comforters are the prototype. While it is true that the absolute dominion of God is attested by many passages of the Old Testament, yet the Book of Job compels us to see in it something more than the anthropomorphic expression of a divine determinism.

It is true that in extension the dominion of the Creator includes all that exists, and even, according to St. Paul, reaches beyond existence, as a necessity to exist because of the creative word by which everything is maintained in being and can no more return into non-existence. Nevertheless this dominion, in its intensive aspect, is never uniform and invariable, but changing and dynamic. . . .

If the God of the philosophers and the learned is only a First Necessity who ordains the chain of cause and effect and corrects automatically every chance deviation which introduces itself, taking no more notice of human freedom than of a grinding noise in the machinery, the God of the Bible reveals Himself by His very wrath as He who undertook the risk of creating a universe whose perfection is continually jeopardized by the freedom of those in whom that perfection ought to reach its highest level. This divine risk, inherent in the decision to create beings in the image and likeness of God, is the summit of almighty power, or rather a surpassing of that summit in voluntarily undertaken powerlessness. For "the weakness of God is stronger than men" (I Cor. 1:25): it surpasses to an infinite degree all the attributes of majesty and dominion which the theologians enumerate in their treatises *De deo uno*. This category of divine risk, which is proper to a personal God freely creating personal beings endowed with freedom, is foreign to all abstract conceptions of the divine dominion—to the rationalist theology which thinks it exalts the omnipotence of the living God in attributing to him the perfections of a lifeless God who is *incapable* of being subject to risk. But he who takes no risks does not love: the God of the theology manuals can love only himself, and it is his own perfection which he loves even in his creatures. He does not love any *person:* for personal love is love for another than oneself. . . .

Since the fulfillment of God's dominion coincides with the final deification of created being, and since this ultimate vocation of the creation cannot be realized automatically, without the free cooperation of the person, both in angels and men, it is necessary for each stage of the way which leads to this end to include an agreement of the two wills: the will of God and the will of creatures. From the time of the First Adam's sin, which rendered man (and through him the whole of the earthly cosmos) incapable of progress in the way of his vocation, until the moment when Christ "the last Adam" (ὁ ἔσχατος Ἀδάμ, I Cor. 15:45) "will re-capitulate" (according to St. Irenaeus) fallen humanity—the harmony of the two wills can be only external. The successive covenants of the Old Testament are precisely of this kind: that made with Noah, with Abraham, and finally with Moses, imposing God's dominion as *Law* on the people whom He had chosen for Himself to realize the redemptive work which He alone could accomplish. The Law which convicted man of sin, making sin "exceeding sinful" according to St. Paul, manifested the slavery of man to a dominion *other* than that of God. This is a "third will," to which the First Adam submitted himself freely, seduced by the promise of a false deification outside the love of God. Along with this perverse will of a spiritual power at enmity with God, the dominion of sin and death entered the world, through man's sin. The Law of Moses, given by the mediation of angels (Gal. 3:19) showed to those who received it the helplessness of man in face of the "law of sin" through which is exerted the dominion of the angels of Satan, now prince of this world. Harmony with the will of God is henceforth expressed by confession of sin, by recognition that it is impossible to be saved from the present situation except by God's own intervention, and finally by faith in the Promise which accompanies the Law, the Promise without which the Law could not be an expression of the divine economy, a "school-master to bring us unto Christ" (Gal. 3: 24). . . .

"Why then the law? It was added because of transgressions, till the offspring should come to whom the promise had been made: and it was ordained (διαταγεὶς) by angels" (Gal. 3:19). There is a close connection between the dominion of the Law and the law of sin and death, between the revealed Law and the law of sin which it makes manifest, between the legal order imposed by the agency of the angels of the Lord and the power exerted over the world since the Fall by the angels of Satan. There is no difficulty at all in recognizing that the divine Law is proper to the catastrophic state of created being in subjection to the law of sin and death. But we must also distinguish, in this miserable state imposed on the earthly creation by the sin of man, in that very law which St. Paul calls the "law of sin and death," the existence of an infallible order by means of which the dominion of God rules amid the disorders of the fallen world, preserving it from total destruction, setting bounds to the dominion of the powers of darkness. And there is more: even the dominion of the rebellious Angel over the fallen creature is not outside the scope of the will of God, who gives this captivity a certain legal character. God is sole Lord, and the spirits in revolt against him could not exercise their usurped dominion if in the last resort they did not remain subject, despite themselves, to his unique dominion. Though wishing to frustrate God's plan, the evil one finds himself finally compelled to serve it. . . .

The divine economy makes use of the rebel will to fulfill the design of the Creator, in spite of all the obstacles set up by human or angelic free will. If this is so, God's design, which is fixed as to the end in view (the deification of all created beings), must be likened, as to its execution, to a strategy of ever-changing tactics, infinitely rich in possibilities, to a multiform (πολυποίκιλος) Wisdom of God in action. But it is not so for the rationalist theologians. The devitalized theology of the Christian descendants of Job's comforters has accustomed us to think of the divine plan *sub specie aeternitatis,* lending to the eternal Will of God the only characteristic of eternity which they know: that of necessary and immutable preordinations, in the likeness of the miserable fixed eternity which is usually attributed to the truths of mathematics.

The magnitude of Satan's spiritual power, shown to Job, demonstrates the vastness of the cosmic catastrophe brought about by man's sin, the blindness and helplessness of his perverted freedom. All this is to show the beneficent character of the law of mortal existence, which rules by necessity over the new state established by God's will for His creation, enslaved by sin. The repentance of Job (whose "words without knowledge" had "darkened counsel") consists in recognizing, besides the necessary and ineluctable character of the dominion which he had refused to accept, the contingency of the divine economy, which always directs the terrestrial world towards the realization of its supreme vocation, that realization in which fallen man has become incapable of cooperating.

Job's attitude in accusing God is opposite to that of his friends, who, in assuming the hypocritical role of defenders of God, defended, without knowing it, Satan's right to an unlimited dominion. Like most defenders of the *status quo,* in wishing to justify the legitimate character of the present condition of humanity, they gave an absolute value to the legal situation, projecting it on to the very nature of God. In this wrong perspective, the different levels of human, demonic, angelic, and divine reality, bound up in the complex and shifting economy of salvation, are telescoped together, welded together and crystallized in a single vision of a God-Necessity, comparable to the inexorable and impersonal Fate ('Ανάγκη) of Greek paganism. They speak solely of the God of the Law, but not of the God of the Promise; God dominates their creation but does not become involved in it, does not run the risk of being frustrated in His love. This God is only a dictator, not a King. But Job aimed higher than his friends, for he believed the Promise, without which the Law would have been a monstrous absurdity and the God of the Old Testament could not have been the God of Christians. That is why the Book of Job is the first of the books of the Old Testament, in the traditional order, to open up the eschatological horizon, by placing the dominion of God and the condition of man in their true perspective—something which we must take into account in speaking of the fulfillment of the dominion.

St. Paul tells us that the creation awaits with impatience the revelation of the sons of God, which will set it free from the bondage of corruption, from the fixed law of birth and death, from the round of seasons, and the repeated cycles of existence. For the whole of terrestrial nature, of creation dependent on man, did not submit voluntarily to this universal necessity which Ecclesiastes and St. Paul call "vanity." The terrestrial universe, which was corrupted by man's sin, must also participate in the liberty of the glory of the sons of God (Rom. 8:19–22). When the cyclical law of repetition suddenly stops its rotating movement, creation, freed from vanity, will not be absorbed into the impersonal Absolute of a Nirvana but will see the beginning of an eternal springtime, in which all the forces of life, triumphant over death, will come to the fullness of their unfolding, since God will be the only principle of life in all things. Then the deified will shine like stars around the only Star, Christ, with whom they will reign in the same glory of the Holy Trinity, communicated to each without measure by the Holy Spirit.

. . . "We are not contending against flesh and blood" but against the "spiritual hosts of wickedness in the heavenly places" (Eph. 6:12). This struggle which began in the spiritual spheres of the angelic heavens is continued in the earthly cosmos, and in the struggle human freedom is at stake. The spiritual level where this war for the inheritance of the sons of God is waged is more profound than any of the superficial layers of reality which are accessible to analysis by the human sciences. None of the sciences—not psychology, nor sociology, nor economics, nor the political sciences—can detect the true origin of the different evils which they observe and attempt to define, in their efforts to exorcise them or at least to restrict the damage they do. Even philosophy, though it speaks of the human spirit and uses the terms "person" and "nature," cannot reach the level at which the problem of human destiny is posed. The terms which it uses are, for the most part, the result of the decadence and secularization of theological ideas. Philosophy is never eschatological: its speculation never goes to the furthest extremes, it inevitably transposes into ontology truths which are metaontological. Its field of vision remains on this side of the two abysses which theology alone can name, with fear and trembling:

the uncreated abyss of the Life of the Trinity and the abyss of hell which opens within the freedom of created persons. . . .

We know that the gates of hell shall never prevail against the Church, and that hell's power, shattered by Christ, remains unreal so long as our will does not make common cause with that of the enemy of our final vocation. The Church strives only for the realization of this final goal set before all creation. All other conflicts in which we are obliged to take part in this world are restricted to the interests of a group, a party, a country, a human ideology: they inevitably exclude and sacrifice our enemies. Here, however, no one is excluded or sacrificed: even when the Church takes action against men, it is still for the salvation of these men that she continues to strive.

This is the guiding principle of her struggle, and its field extends ever wider as our eschatological involvement becomes more intense. But what is this intense involvement if not sanctity realized?[27]

THE THEOLOGICAL NOTION OF THE HUMAN PERSON

Thus, in the light of Christological dogma, Boethius' definition, *substantia individua rationalis naturae*, appears insufficient for establishing the concept of human person. It can only be applied to the "enhypostasized nature" (to use the expression created by Leontius of Byzantium) and not to the human hypostasis or person itself. We understand why Richard of Saint-Victor rejected Boethius' definition, remarking with finesse that substance answers the question *quid,* person answers the question *quis.* Now, to the question *quis* one answers with a proper noun which alone can designate the person.[28] Hence the new definition (for the divine persons): *persona est divinae naturae incommunicabilis existentia.*

. . . "Person signifies the irreducibility of man to his nature—"irreducibility" and not "something irreducible" or "something which makes man irreducible to his nature" precisely because it cannot be a question here of "something" distinct from "another nature" but of *someone* who is distinct from his own nature, of someone who goes beyond his nature while still containing it, who makes it exist as human nature by this overstepping and yet does not exist in himself beyond the nature which he "enhypostasizes" and which he constantly exceeds. I would have said "which he ecstacizes," if I did not fear being reproached for introducing an expression too reminiscent of "the ecstatic character" of the *Dasein* of Heidegger, after having criticized others who allowed themselves to make such comparisons.[29]

CATHOLIC CONSCIOUSNESS

No differences of created nature—sex, race, social class, language, or culture—can affect the unity of the Church; no divisive reality can enter into the bosom of the *Catholica*. Therefore it is necessary to regard the expression "national Church"—so often used in our day—as erroneous and even heretical, according to the terms of the condemnation of phyletism pronounced by the Council of Constantinople in 1872. There is no Church of the Jews or of the Greeks, of the Barbarians or of the Scythians, just as there is no Church of slaves or of free men, of men or of women. There is only the one and total Christ, the celestial Head of the new creation which is being realized here below, the Head to which the members of the one Body are intimately linked. At this point any private consciousness which could link us with any ethnic or political, social or cultural group must disappear in order to make way for consciousness "as a whole" (καθ' ὅλον), a consciousness greater than the consciousness which links us to humanity at large. In fact, our unity in Christ is not only the primordial unity of the human race, which has only one origin, but the final realization of this unity of human nature, which is "recapitulated" by the last Adam— ὁ ἔσχατος Ἀδάμ. This eschatological reality is not some kind of ideal "beyond" but the very condition of the existence of the Church, without which the Church would not be a sacramental organism: her sacraments would have only a figurative sense, instead of being a real participation in the incorruptible life of the Body of Christ.

If we wish to apply the notion of consciousness to ecclesial reality, we must understand that in this reality there are many personal consciousnesses but only one subject of consciousness, only one "self-consciousness" (*Selbstbewusstsein*), which is the Church. In this sense the Fathers of the Church—and all those who, freed from their individual limitations, follow in their steps—are the fathers of the consciousness of the Church, those by whom Truth could be expressed in the councils in the form of dogmas, not as the "supra-conscious" constraint of a *deus ex machina*, but in full personal consciousness, engaging human responsibility. It is precisely this which permits us to make judgments in questions of faith and to say with catholic audacity: "It has seemed good to the Holy Spirit and to us" (Acts 15:28).[30]

ORTHODOX THEOLOGY: AN INTRODUCTION

The Creation

We are . . . responsible for the world. We are the word, the logos, through which it bespeaks itself, and it depends solely on us whether it blasphemes or prays. Only through us can the cosmos, like the body that it prolongs, receive grace. For not only the soul, but the body of man is created in the image of God.

Original Sin

Evil certainly has no place among the essences, but it is not only a lack: there is an activity in it. Evil is not a nature, but a state of nature, as the Fathers would say most profoundly. It thus appears as an illness, as a parasite existing only by virtue of the nature he lives off. More precisely, it is a state of the will of this nature; it is a fallen will with regard to God. Evil is revolt against God, that is to say, a personal attitude. The exact vision of evil is thus not essentialist but personalist.

The Old Testament did not know the intimate sanctification by grace, yet it knew saintliness, for grace, from outside, aroused it in the soul as an effect. The man who submitted to God in faith and lived in all righteousness could become the instrument of His will. As is proved by the vocation of prophets, it is not a question of agreement between two wills, but of lordly utilization of the human will by that of God: The Spirit of God swoops upon the seer, God takes possession of man by imposing Himself from outside on his person. God, invisible, speaks: His servant listens. The darkness of Sinai is opposed to the light of Tabor like a veiled mystery to an unveiled mystery. Man prepares himself to serve in the obscurity of faith, by obedience and purity. Obedience and purity are negative concepts: they imply the exteriority of God and the instrumental submission of man who, even when just, cannot free himself from his state of sin and death. Saintliness, as active sanctification of all being and the free assimilation of human nature to that of God, can only manifest itself after the work of Christ, by the conscious grasping of this work. That is why the Law is essential to the Old Testament, and the relationship of man and God is not union but alliance, guaranteed by loyalty to the Law.

Thus the history of the Old Testament is not only that of the foreshadowings of salvation but that of man's refusals and acceptances. Salvation approaches or withdraws as man prepares or not to receive it. The καιρὸς of Christ, His moment, will depend on human will. The entire meaning of the Old Testament lies in these fluctuations underlining the double aspect of Providence. The latter is not unilateral. It takes into account the human waiting and call. Divine pedagogy scrutinizes man, tests his dispositions.

This testing is sometimes a struggle, for God wishes that human liberty should not only resist Him but force Him, if not to reveal His name, at least to bless: thus Jacob becomes Israel "for you have wrestled with God and with man and you have won" (Gen. 32:29). And the patriarch *becomes* the people, and when this people is captive in Egypt, God raises up Moses to deliver it. On Sinai, God passes in His glory before Moses but prevents him seeing His Face "for man cannot see Me and live": divine nature remains hidden. But the election of Israel, the decisive stage, is affirmed in a new alliance: that of the Law. A written obligation to which the chosen people must submit, the Law is accompanied by divine promises that the Prophets will continue to make precise. Thus the Law and the Prophets complement each other; and Christ will always evoke them together to underline their completeness. The Prophets are the men whom God chose to announce the profound meaning of His Law. In contrast to the Pharisees, who gradually turned the Law into a static reality and the means of justification, the Prophets explain its spirit, its historical dynamism, the eschatological call that it contains in making man take cognizance of his sin and his helplessness before it.[31]

NOTES

1. [Vladimir Lossky, *Sept Jours sur les Routes de France*, (Paris: Les Editions du Cerf, 1998), 16–17, 19–20, 20–24 , 26–27, 64–65. Eng. trans. for chapter: Heather Jones and Elizabeth Icks, "Superior Translations." Despite the fact that Lossky's diary (which he wrote in June of 1940) was first published forty years after his death in 1998, it seemed justifiable to make an exception and to place the following excerpts from it at the beginning of our selection. All the other selections in this chapter follow a chronological order on the basis of the date of first publication.]

2. Words of St. Basil reported by St. Gregory Nazianzen in "In laudem Basilli Magni, or. XLIII, 48", *P.G.*, t. 36, 560 A.

3. "In sanctum Pascha, or. XLV, 8", *P.G.*, t. 36, 632 C.

4. "Opuscula theologica et polemica, Ad Marinum", *P.G.*, t. 19, 45 D–48 A.

5. *Ibid.*, 48 A—49 A, 192 BC. In St. John Damascene, "De fide orth, III, 14", *P.G.*, t. 94, 1036–7; 1044–5.

6. [Vladimir Lossky, "Image and Likeness," *The Mystical Theology of the Eastern Church*, 121–122, 124–125.]

7. "Hom. Spirit., XV, 32", *P.G.*, XXXIV, 597 B.

8. *Ibid.*, XLIII, 7, 776 D.

9. *Ibid.*, XV, 20, 589 B.

10. See above, the chapter "Image and Likeness." [In the 1991 English edition of *The Mystical Theology of the Eastern Church*, the chapter referred to is found on pages 114–134.]

11. "Spiritual homilies, XL, I", *P.G.*, XXXIV, 761.

12. "Doctrina, XIV, 3", *P.G.*, LXXXVIII, 1776–80.

13. ["The Way of the Union," *The Mystical Theology of the Eastern Church*, 201–202, 215.]

14. *De incarnatione verbi* 20; *P.G.* 25, col. 129D-132A.

15. Matt. 18:12–14, Luke 15:4–7, John 10:1–16.

16. Matt. 12:29, Mark 3:27, Luke 11:21–22.

17. St. Athanasius, *De incarnatione verbi* 30; *P.G.*, 25, col. 148.

18. St. John of Damascus, *De imaginibus* III, 9; *P.G.*, 94, col. 1332D. The image of Christ as the physician of human nature, wounded by sin, is often found in connection with the parable of the Good Samaritan, which was interpreted in this way for the first time by Origen, Homily 34 on St. Luke, *P.G.*, 13, cols. 1886–1888; *Commentary on St. John* 20, 28; P.G. 14, col. 656A.

19. St. Gregory of Nyssa, *Oratio catechetica magna* 22–24; *P.G.*, 45, cols. 60–65.

20. Rom. 3:24, 8:23; I Cor. 1:30; Eph. 1:7, 14:30; Col. 1:14; Hebr. 9:15, 11:35, with the sense of deliverance. I Tim. 2:6; I Cor. 6:20, 7:22; Gal. 3:13, with the sense of a ransom paid.

21. For St. Paul, the sacrificial or sacerdotal image of the work of Christ is basically identical to the juridical image—that of purchase or redemption properly so called—but it also completes and deepens it. In effect, the idea of propitiation in blood (Rom. 3:26) ties together the two images—the juridical and the sacrificial—in the notion of the expiatory death of the just man, a notion characteristic of the messianic prophecies (Isaiah 53).

22. *Cur Deus homo* I, 4; *P.L.*, 158, col. 365.

23. [*Or.* 45, 22; *P.G.* 36, col. 653.]

24. [Vladimir Lossky, "Redemption and Deification," trans. Edward Every, in *In the Image and Likeness of God*, 98–102, 107.]

25. [Vladimir Lossky, "The Temptations of Ecclesial Consciousness," trans. Thomas E. Bird, in *St. Vladimir's Theological Quarterly* 32, no. 3 (1988): 247, 248. Translation revised.]

26. [Vladimir Lossky, "Tradition and Traditions," trans. G. E. H. Palmer and E. Kadloubovsky, in *In the Image and Likeness of God*, 156.] Origen, in his homilies on the Epistle to the Hebrews, after having expressed his views on the source of this epistle, of which the teaching is Pauline but the style and composition denote an author other than St. Paul, adds this: "If, then, some church considers this epistle as written by St. Paul, let it be honored also for that. For it is not by chance that the ancients have transmitted it under the name of Paul. But who wrote the epistle? God knows the truth." Fragment quoted by Eusebius, *Historia Ecclesiastica* VI, 25; P.G. 20, col. 584C.

27. [Vladimir Lossky, "Dominion and Kingship: An Eschatological Study," trans. Thomas E. Bird, in *In the Image and Likeness of God*, 212–218, 220, 225, 226–227. It is hardly accidental that Lossky published this powerful essay on divine dominion of love and freedom in 1953—the year in which the Soviet dictator Josef Stalin died.]

28. *De Trinitate* IV, 7; P.L. 196, cols. 934–935.

29. [Vladimir Lossky, "The Theological Notion of the Human Person," in *In the Image and Likeness of God*, 118–120.]

30. [Vladimir Lossky, "Catholic Consciousness: Anthropological Implications of the Dogma of the Church," trans. Thomas E. Bird, in *In the Image and Likeness of God*, 184, 194.]

31. [*Orthodox Theology: An Introduction*, 71, 80, 85–86, 88–89.]

[CHAPTER 4]

Mother Maria Skobtsova (1891–1945)

COMMENTARY

MICHAEL PLEKON

The way to God lies through the love of people. At the Last Judgment I shall not be asked whether I was successful in my ascetic exercises, not how many bows and prostrations I made. Instead I shall be asked, Did I feed the hungry, clothe the naked, visit the sick and the prisoners. That is all I shall be asked. About every poor, hungry and imprisoned person the Savior says "I": "I was hungry and thirsty, I was sick and in prison." To think that he puts an equal sign between himself and anyone in need. . . . I always knew it, but now it has somehow penetrated to my sinews. It fills me with awe.

—MOTHER MARIA SKOBTSOVA

The nun, radical social activist, and martyr we know as Mother Maria Skobtsova (1891–1945) had many names, roles, and identities in her life.[1] The diverse sides of her personality, the many gifts with which she was endowed, and the various ways in which she exerted her spiritual, artistic, and philanthropic energies are at first overwhelming. It is as if she could not live just one life. She was an artist but also a political activist. She distanced herself from the faith into which she had been baptized, yet later, Christ, the gospel, and the direct care of suffering people defined her existence.

Born Elisaveta Iurevna Pilenko in Riga, Latvia, she grew up in her family's homes in St. Petersburg and in Anapa, by the Black Sea in the south of Russia. Her birth was difficult, requiring a Caesarian section. All her biographers cite her mother Sophie Pilenko's observation that during her life, Liza, as her family called her, became well acquainted with death. At her baptism, she almost suffocated during the triple immersion. Her father Iouri died suddenly in 1906, propelling her already weakened faith into a crisis. How could a good God permit such a good man to die when his family so needed him? She would bury two of her three children before her own death and know that the third, her son Iouri, was interned in a Nazi concentration camp, as she was. For much of her adult life, she was surrounded by the poor, emotionally distraught, and chronically ill people she sheltered, cared for, and buried. She would spend the last months of her life consoling fellow concentration camp inmates, all of them observing daily the endless plumes of smoke rising from the crematoria.

She was also known as Elisabeth Kuzmina-Karavaeva, from her first impulsive and short-lived marriage to Dimitri Kuzmin-Karavaev. Through her second marriage she became Elisabeth Skobtsova. She was the mother of two daughters, Gaiana, from her first marriage, and Nastia, as well as a son, Ioura, from her second marriage to Daniel Skobtsov. A White Army officer, he had presided as military judge over her trial. Her offense had been serving as the first woman mayor of Anapa after the Bolshevik mayor fled in the face of the White Army. Given her outspoken personality and her predecessor's politics, she was suspected of membership in the hated Bolshevik movement. However, she had earlier also escaped arrest and likely execution by the Bolsheviks by claiming friendship with Lenin's wife.

She was finally given the name of the great ascetic, St. Mary of Egypt, when she made her monastic profession, received tonsure and the habit on March 7, 1932. In receiving her into monastic life, her bishop, the remarkable Metropolitan Evlogy (Georgievsky) said that as the first Mary, of Egypt, retreated to the desert after a life of passion, so this second Mary, named for the first, should go into and speak and act in the desert of suffering human hearts. "The world," he said to Mother Maria on another occasion, "is your monastery." A pastor of amazing discernment, he encouraged many to take risks, to encounter and embrace this world just as Christ had encountered and embraced the Palestine of the first century.[2] Among those he urged and, when necessary, protected, were, among others, the great theologian and priest Father Sergei Bulgakov, scholars such as Fathers Lev Gillet, Cyprian Kern, Nicolas Afanasiev, Basil Zenkovsky, Georges Florovsky, Bishop Cassian Bezobrazov, George Fedotov, Anton Kartashev, and Constantine Mochulsky, philosophers Simeon Frank, Nicholas Berdyaev, and Paul Evdokimov, as well as Mother Maria.[3] There was hardly a group, conference, or meeting from the 1920s to the 1940s at which Evlogy was not present: meetings and summer camps of the Russian Christian Students' Association, ecumenical gatherings, and graduations at St. Sergius Theological Institute, which he was instrumental in opening in Paris.[4] And at these gatherings, the metropolitan was surrounded by exactly the individuals just named: canon law and liturgical specialists, patristics and scripture scholars, literary critics and philosophers, all of them passionate people of the Orthodox Church. What an intriguing, gifted assembly of persons of faith he supported in the hard times of forced emigration, the Depression, World War II, and the Nazi occupation of France. Only in recent years, through the work of Antoine Arjakovsky, Paul Valliere, Rowan Williams, and Anastassy Brandon Gallaher, among others, are these marvelous thinkers becoming known.[5]

Of these lights of the Russian emigration, Mother Maria is one of the greatest treasures of creativity, compassion, holiness, and sacrifice that the Eastern Orthodox Church has ever offered to the rest of the churches and the world. Trained in literature, theology, and the fine arts, a gifted poet and essayist, she was a groundbreaking figure in many respects. Among the first women allowed to study theology formally in the St. Petersburg Academy, she was a confidant of the influential procurator general of the Russian Church, C. P. Pobedonostev, a St. Petersburg neighbor. While still in her student years she became a member of the circle of the great poets Vyachyslav Ivanov and Alexander Blok. Poet and theologian, political activist, spouse, and parent, she would never have guessed that she would spend the last decades of her life as a professed nun, running hostels for the homeless, troubled, and ill in Paris and its suburbs.

Despite the demands of feeding and sheltering the residents of her hostels, she managed to keep up a productive life as a writer and scholar, participating in the Religious-Philosophical Society led by Nicholas Berdyaev, contributing essays to the famous journal he edited, *Put'* (The Way) and other publications. She embroidered vestments, altar cloths, and tapestries and painted icons for the chapels in her hostels. She continued to participate in the Russian Christian Students' Movement she helped found. After futile but instructive personal efforts to be an advocate for impoverished immigrants, she began the Orthodox Action group, yet another organization for serving those in need, and set up the hostels where the basic needs of life could be met. Once, after a lecture on Russian literature to immigrant workers, she was told that what they needed more was clean laundry and a good meal. She directly provided these things.

Despite her administration and hands-on direction of the hostels, she remained engaged in the theological debates of her era. In her published essays, one can, for example, read her radical thoughts about a renewal of monastic life for the twentieth century, not a rejection of the essentials of prayer, work, and love of neighbor, but a rethinking of how these would be lived in a time of economic depression rather than in the well-endowed monasteries of Russia and Eastern Europe. She took on a spirited defense of her radical social activism by a discerning examination of both the scriptures and the writings of saints and church leaders down through the ages. She wrote about the blessing that the Russian revolution, despite all its horror, brought to the Russian people and their church. In what has become the best known of her essays, "Types of Religious Lives," she examines several different types of religiosity, concluding with an inspired statement of what she termed the "Gospel" or "evangelical" type of Christian faith and life. She had perhaps the greatest Orthodox theologian of the twentieth century and a mystic as her spiritual father, Sergei Bulgakov. Her close friends included the lights of the Russian emigration in Paris, Father Bulgakov and Berdyaev, as well as Simeon Frank, Basil Zenkovsky, Sister Joanna Reitlinger, and Constantine Mochulsky, among others.

During the Nazi occupation of France, her efforts to assist the suffering multiplied. She applied for and received state authorization and support for her hostels as public canteens, supplying food rations to destitute citizens. Likewise, she sought out work contracts and thereby employed her hostel residents in an array of wartime industries. She fearlessly visited, fed, and consoled many of the almost seven thousand French Jews, half of them children, whom the Vichy government herded into the Paris cycling stadium, Velodrome d'Hiver, in July 1942. She was able to save several children, smuggling them out in trashcans. During the Nazi occupation, many fearing arrest were given shelter and new identities in her hostels. With her chaplain, she devised ways to hide and protect both Jews and others whom the Nazis sought to exterminate; Father Dimitri issued baptismal certificates, and eighty new parishioners were registered as members of the Orthodox parish lodged in the chapel at the hostel in rue de Lourmel.

In life as well as after her death, Mother Maria had her critics and enemies. Recently, even her "Types of Religious Lives" has been attacked by traditionalists in Russia. Her insightful descriptions of the hypocrisy and introversion of certain forms of Orthodox piety have been rejected as biased and distorted. Her critique of monastic life and her proposals for its renewal have also been characterized, along with her own existence, as a misunderstanding of the monastic tradition and modern rejection of it. In her own time, as her contemporaries have witnessed, including Metropolitan Anthony Bloom, theologian Elisabeth Behr-Sigel, and the late Sophie Koloumzine, Mother Maria was an embarrassment for many in the Russian Paris. Her avid participation in intellectual circles, her continuing to write for journals, her expeditions hunting for food for her hostels, her seeking out the homeless in Parisian bars and bistros, the state of her monastic habit with its marks of cooking, her attachment to

Gauloise cigarettes—all of this made her a nonconformist, a persona non grata.

Metropolitan Anthony Bloom has written regretfully of his disapproval of her. Father Basil Zenkovsky, in his perceptive yet acerbic memoirs, grudgingly admits her dedication to serving others, but with little compassion or approval. And this was the assessment of a priest who knew her for fifteen years, from the Russian Christian Students Association, and who sat on the board of her hostels. Her other mentor, the philosopher Nicholas Berdyaev, was ambivalent about her attempting radical social work as a monastic, and even her friend Father Lev Gillet wondered whether her seeking monastic profession really added anything to her nonetheless heroic work. He tried to dissuade her from this step, but after she was received and tonsured, he supported her, not only as her chaplain in life but also in the years after her death. Along with Metropolitan Anthony, Father Lev did not hesitate to call Mother Maria a modern saint.

It is most likely that she and Father Dimitri were betrayed to the Gestapo by fellow Russians, possibly even some who assisted in the hostels and who were either scandalized or fearful of her humanitarian activities during the occupation. In February 1943 both Mother Maria and Father Dimitri were arrested, along with her son Yuri. All were eventually sent to concentration camps, she to Ravensbrücjk and Yuri and Father Dimitri to Mittelbau-Dora, a work camp annex of Buchenwald. Mother Maria's time in the camp is well documented.[6] At first, almost energized by the hard labor, Mother Maria became a source of hope, an oasis in the death camp. But the work, meager rations, and sickness took their toll on her. She comforted fellow inmates, led prayers and Bible studies, even embroidered the invasion of Normandy in the style of the Bayeux tapestry. She survived surprising long, given the conditions and despite debilitating illness, until March 31, 1945, when, according to witnesses, she took the place of another inmate scheduled to be gassed that day. Less than two weeks later, American soldiers liberated the camp.

Many have called her a martyr, an apostle of compassion, a saint for our times. There are testimonies not only to her heroic work in the concentration camp but also to her years of service to the poor and suffering in the Paris hostels. As with her contemporary, the Lutheran pastor, theologian, and martyr Dietrich Bonhoeffer, her status has not been without controversy and disagreement. In 1985 the Supreme Soviet inscribed her posthumously into the order of national heroes of the war. Yad Vashem, the Holocaust Martyrs' and Heroes' Remembrance Authority in Jerusalem, recognized her as one of the "righteous among the Gentiles," planting a tree in her memory there on August 14, 1987. In February 2003, a commemorative plaque was affixed to the external walls of the building at 77 rue de Lourmel by the Paris city government, acknowledging Mother Maria's work for the suffering and her heroism.[7]

The petition for her formal recognition as a saint in the Orthodox Church has not been acted upon by the Patriarchate of Constantinople for more than fifteen years, and repeated inquiries about its status remain unanswered. Metropolitan Anthony Bloom's published words about her capture her personality and passion:

> Mother Maria is remembered in the context of the Russian emigration, the French Resistance or Ravensbrück concentration camp. But her achievement extends beyond the circumstances of her life and it outlives them. For above all, by way of her Christian dedication and in her own distinctive style, she demonstrated what it means to be human. . . . Infinite pity and compassion possessed her; there was no suffering to which she was a stranger; there were no difficulties which could cause her to turn aside. She could not tolerate hypocrisy, cruelty or injustice. The Spirit of Truth which dwelt in her led her to criticize sharply all that was deficient, all that was dead in Christianity and, particularly, in what she mistakenly conceived to be classical monasticism. Mistakenly, for what she was attacking was an empty shell, a petrified form. At the same time, with the perception of a seer, she saw the hidden, glorious content of the monastic life in the fulfillment of the Gospel, in the realization of divine love, a love which has room to be active and creative in and through people who have turned away from all things and—above all—from themselves in order to live God's life and be his presence among men, his compassion, his love. . . . Mother Maria is a saint of our day and for our day: a woman of flesh and blood possessed by the love of God, who stood fearlessly face to face with the problems of this century.[8]

It is with good reason that Mother Maria Skobtsova is included in this volume. Not just despite the controversial aspects of her person and life, but rather because of them, she very much embodies the times in which we live. By traditional standards, her life was far from a model. Some reject her precisely because of her outspoken and passionate character as well as the turns her life took. Yet, as her writings reveal, she was a faithful voice of the Christian tradition, a true person of the church precisely in her willingness to criticize what was in need of reform and in thinking creatively about the paths of renewal. Although the major part of her adult life was taken up with caring for the marginal and suffering, she nevertheless managed to retain a dynamic intellectual and spiritual existence.

She did not leave a systematic body of social and theological reflection; yet we have a great deal of what she was able to write: four volumes of poems, plays, reviews, studies of saints' lives, and essays, not to mention correspondence. Mother Maria's voice is an important one amid the others of persons of faith in the Eastern Orthodox tradition. Situated in the very midst of the twentieth century's most turbulent years, she offers us a radical view of the consequences of the Incarnation, of God's becoming human and of humanity's becoming godly.

Though Mother Maria has not yet been officially recognized as a saint in the Orthodox Church, she is greatly revered. Here and there one can find icons of her. In one, she holds not the martyr's cross but a burning candle, like St. Genevieve, the patron of Paris, who saved her city from destruction. The flickering flame of one candle seems weak and insignificant, especially in the yawning darkness of the years in which Mother Maria lived. Yet her life, for all its complexity and the darkness of her era, was radiant, incandescent. Her weakness, even her dying, was the power of God and resurrection for all around her.

INTELLECTUAL AND CULTURAL CONTEXT: "RUSSIAN PARIS" AND ITS LIGHTS

Mother Maria was an integral and prolific contributor to the intellectual creativity of the Russian emigration in Paris. She was formed not only by the "Russian religious renaissance," as Nicolas Zernov calls it before the revolution, but also, and even more so, by the results of Russian intellectuals' encounter with Western scholars, churches, politics, and culture in the emigration years. Antoine Arjakovsky, in his magisterial study of the Russian émigré intelligentsia in Paris, locates Mother Maria as a participant in all the important study groups and discussion circles and in the journal *Put'* in these years.[9]

The influences on Mother Maria were many and diffuse. One could think, for example, of the archconservative Pobedonostev, the head of the state ministry that controlled the Orthodox Church, this structure having been one of Peter the Great's creations. While a warm, almost parental affection existed between the two and while the young Liza Pilenko surely absorbed her mentor's piety, his suspicion of any development, growth, or freedom either in the life of the church or in other sectors of society must have fueled the almost insatiable desire on the young woman's part for freedom and creativity in spiritual and cultural life. One could take the poet Alexander Blok, another of her mentors, and find there an astonishing similar pattern of influence. Blok's pessimism and despair seemed to nurture Elisabeth Pilenko's zest for life and hunger for personal experience, her indomitable spirit, manifest at the very end of her life, in her poems' defiance of the gas chambers and crematoria of the concentration camp. Some of her most pointed essays, such as "A Justification of Pharasaism," were a response to Father Sergius Chetverikov's very conservative ideas about preserving Russian spirituality.[10]

On a more positive note, her relationship to her bishop in Paris, the already mentioned and remarkable Metropolitan Evlogy, can be seen as immensely significant in a number of ways. Not only did Evlogy clear the way for Maria's monastic tonsure, invoking an ancient canon, to accept the ecclesiastical divorce between Daniel Skobtsova and Maria, but he also gave her freedom to develop her hostels not as reproductions of Russian monasteries but as houses of both prayer and hospitality. Whenever she took over a new property, the very first unit to be set up was the chapel. She was foremost what Paul Evdokimov calls an "ecclesial being." Reading her essays, one is struck by her classic sense of the centrality of the scriptures, the Eucharist, and prayer in her life and in all her activities. But she also saw the need to pray and celebrate the liturgy, the "sacrament of the brother/sister," well beyond the daily cycle of services in the hostel chapel. To be sure, she often was absent from morning prayer, but where was she? She was scavenging the greengrocers, butchers, and other food wholesalers at Les Halles, all to feed the residents of her hostels. As she puts it in "Types of Religious Lives" and other essays, this is authentic Gospel Christianity. To feed the hungry, listen to the sad and anxious, to find jobs and lodging for the desperate—this was "the liturgy outside the church-building," what Ion Bria would call the "liturgy after the liturgy," echoing St. John Chrysostom:[11]

> Our communion with people passes mostly on the level of earthly encounters and is deprived of the authentic mysticism that turns it into communion with God. And we are given a perfectly real possibility in our communing in love with mankind, with the world, to feel ourselves in authentic communion with Christ. And this makes perfectly clear what our relations to people, to their souls, to their deeds, to human destiny, to human history as a whole should be. During a service the priest does not only cense the icons of the Savior, the Mother of God and the saints. He also censes the icon-people, the image of God in the people who are present. And as they leave the church precincts, these people remain as much the images of God, worthy of being censed and venerated. . . . We like it when the "churching" of life is

discussed but few people understand what it means. Indeed, must we attend all the church services to "church" our life? Or hang an icon in every room and burn an icon-lamp in front of it? No, the churching of life is the sense that the whole world as one church, adorned with icons that should be venerated, that should be honored and loved, because these icons are true images of God that have the holiness of the Living God upon them.... We believe that the sacrament of the Eucharist offers up the Lamb of God, the Body of Christ, as a sacrifice for the sins of the world. And being in communion with this sacrificial Body, we ourselves become offered in sacrifice... the "liturgy outside the church" is our sacrificial ministry in the church of the world, adorned with living icons of God, our common ministry, an all-human sacrificial offering of love, the great act of our spirit. In this liturgical communion with people, we partake of a communion with God, we really become one flock and one Shepherd, one body, of which the inalienable head is Christ.[12]

Despite this sense of liturgy and life interpenetrating each other, Mother Maria was criticized by some, including Father Cyprian Kern, her chaplain, and Mothers Evdokia and Blandina, for not attending all the daily services, for not observing all the fasting prohibitions in her cooking, for departing from the traditional patterns of monastic observance and churchly piety. All three sought transfer to a more orderly ecclesiastical and monastic setting. Yet the great mystic who also was her chaplain, Father Lev, supported her commitment to the suffering and her unconventional style of life, as did her last chaplain, Father Dimitri Klepinine, and her bishop, as well as a number of colleagues and friends, including Nicholas Berdyaev. Others who were constant in their support were several on the left of the spectrum in the Russian Paris: Feodor Pianov and Ilya Fondaminsky-Bunakvov, who were both imprisoned by the Gestapo, the latter also dying in the camps; scholar Constantine Mochulsky, known for his work on Dostoevsky; and the specialist in Russian spirituality George Fedotov. It should not be surprising that Mother Maria's own socialist commitment to the poor and suffering would have been supported by the more liberal members of the Paris emigration and scorned by monarchist, conservative factions.

Just as we note Mother Maria's gifts in the many roles and activities of her life, it is also possible to see her own the distinctive synthesis of radical faith and radical love for the neighbor we hear in her essays and see lived out in the hostels she directed. Thomas Merton said in the very last talk he gave, in Bangkok on December 10, 1968, that in the modern era, each monastic and every Christian is to some extent "on his/her own." His actual words were those of a Tibetan abbot to a fellow monk when asked what should be done in light of the Communist Chinese takeover of monastic buildings and the very country. "From now on, Brother," he said, "everybody stands on his own feet."[13]

So many of the individuals of the Russian emigration in Paris were and remain attractive as persons of faith in action, not only because of their great intelligence and holiness but also because they dared to do precisely what the abbot and Merton said. Metropolitan Evlogy pushed them out, gave them the blessing of freedom to find their own paths, supported and even protected them. Mother Maria certainly exemplifies what Merton quoted. As even some of her critics observed, she was seldom unsure of her position and herself. Yet, she also was constantly a student, a novice in formation, thus profoundly shaped by several of her friends and colleagues. From Nicholas Berdyaev and the teacher-become-priest Alexander Elchaninov, she absorbed and lived out the radical freedom that Christianity gives. Less concerned with details of this freedom than Berdyaev was, she recognized it being enhanced by the revolution, which liberated the Russian Church and Christian faith from both the Russian state and Russian culture. Reading Berdyaev's provocative essay, "The Worth of Christianity and the Unworthiness of Christians" and "The Bourgeois Mind," it is easy to think of Mother Maria both as an example as well as one whose conversation, in Berdyaev's circle, may have contributed to the radical ideas within.[14] Of her many essays, two that appear in the new English-language anthology are particularly relevant, statements of her vision of the positive aspects of the revolution.[15] Another very powerful meditation on freedom, "Birth and Death," is explicitly indebted to Berdyaev and is drawn from some of the personal tragedies of her own life.[16]

Chief among those who shaped her thinking was the great theologian and priest, Father Sergei Bulgakov. Called the "Russian Origen," surrounded to this day by controversy and the suspicion that he made the figure of Divine Wisdom almost a member of the Trinity, Father Bulgakov's enormous theological creativity and personal holiness are only recently becoming known outside a small circle of specialists.[17]

Father Bulgakov wrote about many subjects: the Mother of God, John the Baptist, the angels, the Eucharist, the icons, the possibilities of healing the great schism, the nature of the church. His larger trilogy is not only a look at the essential dogma of the Trinity but also, more particularly, a more positive or constructive statement of the dogma of Chalcedon, that of Christ and the Incarnation and the implications of this for the world and all of humankind. His vision of the Incarnation is cosmic, but what is

riveting is his boldness in thinking about the church in both her exten-
siveness and the limits and limitations of her institutional expression. He
also confronts the captivity of so much theology, church practice, and
even piety to an overly temporal or this worldly pattern.[18] In Christ's incarnation and resurrection, ascension and coming down of the spirit, the
kingdom of heaven, like God himself, has forever become part of the life
of creation, of human beings. Yet, creatures of time and space, the limiting
features of these are all too often imposed upon God and the kingdom
where they are not relevant.[19]

For Bulgakov, in the Incarnation, human life has become divinized and
God's life humanized. Soloviev's idea of *Bogochelovechestvo*, or "the humanity of God," also translated as "Godmanhood," is what distinguishes
the gospel, the life of the church, and the existence of every Christian.
Divinity and humanity might be said to have interpenetrated each other,
so that a new dimension of reality has been created, a new economy of
salvation. Writing on the "second Gospel commandment," Mother Maria
observes,

> The commandment of love for one's neighbor, the second and equal in value
> to the first, calls mankind in the same way today as when it was first given.
> For us Russian Orthodox people it may be easier to understand than for
> anyone else, because it was precisely this commandment that captivated
> and interested Russian religious thought. Without it, Khomiakov would
> have been unable to speak of the *sobornost'* of the Orthodox Church, which
> rests entirely on love, on lofty human communion. His theology shows
> clearly that the universal Church itself is, first of all, the incarnation not
> only of the commandment of the love of God, but also of love for one's
> neighbor, and is as unthinkable without the second as without the first.
> Without the second commandment there would be no sense in Soloviev's
> teaching about Godmanhood [*Bogochelovechestvo*], because it becomes one
> and organic, the genuine Body of Christ, only when united and brought to
> life by the flow of fraternal love that unites everyone at one Cup and brings
> everyone to partake of Divine Love. Only this commandment makes clear
> Dostoevsky's words about each of us being guilty for all, and each of us an-
> swerable for each other's sins.[20]

While Mother Maria clearly knew of Soloviev, not to mention Khomyakov and Fedotov and other creative Russian theologians, I think that in
many ways her clearest debt is to the vision of Father Bulgakov. One will
not find much if any mention in her writings of the figure of Divine Wisdom, so central for Father Bulgakov's depiction of the relationship of the

divine and the human, nevertheless the grasp of the connection is always there. For Father Bulgakov, the entire divine plan for the redemption of the world could be described as "churching," that is the assembly of the entire cosmos into communion with the Holy Trinity and with each other. And the "one Cup" is the communion with God and each other, the Eucharist, for both Father Bulgakov and Mother Maria the always-present contact with Christ and the kingdom.[21] Mother Maria's distinctive expression of this was to see the love of God and love of the neighbor as indissoluble, indistinguishable:

> We are called to embody in life the principles of *sobornost'* and Godmanhood, which are at the foundation of our Orthodox Church; we are called to oppose the mystery of authentic human communion to all false relations among people. This is the only path on which Christ's love can live; moreover, this is the only path of life—outside it is death. Death in the fire and ashes of various hatreds that corrode modern mankind, class, national and racial hatreds, the godless and gift less death of cool, uncreative, imitative, essentially secular democracy. To all forms of mystical totalitarianism we oppose only one thing: the person, the image of God in man. And to all forms of passively collectivist mentality in democracy we oppose *sobornost'*. . . . We simply want to live as we are taught by the second commandment of Christ, which determines everything in man's relation to this earthly life, and we want to live this life in such a way that all those who are outside it can see and feel the unique, saving, unsurpassable beauty, the indisputable truth of precisely this Christian path.[22]

THE HUMANITY OF GOD AND
THE DIVINITY OF HUMANITY

Fundamental to Mother Maria's writing and her work is her understanding of human nature as the image and likeness of God in the human person. St. Irenaeus of Lyons, a very early church father, grasped this in his saying that "the glory of God is a person fully alive."[23] This human image and likeness is distorted by sin but redeemed, refashioned by Christ's death and resurrection. This divine imprint and the constant action of God within the lives of people is a good definition of the Eastern Church idea of "the humanity of God" (*Bogocheloveschestvo*) and of theosis, of each person being "divinized" by God's grace. Society, culture, politics, and law are human creations, but are themselves the image and likeness of God. God made all things. God loves all things. God, in Christ, has entered into all things. God wishes to draw all things back to himself, to restore the original communion. All of human making stands under both the judgment and great compassion of God. As Father Bulgakov argues, if in the resurrection Christ has triumphed over evil and death and ascended to the Father, carrying all of creation with him, filling all things, then how can evil ever finally imprison anyone? Would this not mean that the Son of God's victory was less than complete? Has not God united all to himself, both in his creation and redemption?[24] This vision, however, did not make of Mother Maria a sentimental dreamer about the harsher realities of both the human person and social life.

> We get from the world and from man what we count on getting from them. We may get a disturbing neighbor in the same apartment, or an all-too-merry drinking companion or a capricious and slow-witted student, or obnoxious ladies, or seedy old codgers, and so on, and relations with them will only weary us physically, annoy us inwardly, deaden us spiritually. But, through Christ's image in man, we may partake of the Body of Christ. If our approach to the world is correct and spiritual, we will not have only to give to it from our spiritual poverty, but we will receive infinitely more from the face of Christ that lives in it, from our communion with Christ, from the consciousness of being a part of Christ's body. . . . Social endeavor should be just as much of a liturgy outside the church as any communion with man in the name of Christ. . . . Everything in the world can be Christian, but only if it is pervaded by the authentic awe of communion with God, which is also possible on the path of authentic communion with man. But outside this chief thing, there is no authentic Christianity. . . . He who rejects the sorrowful face of Christ in the name of the joys of life believes in those joys, but tragedy is born at the moment when he discovers that those joys are not joyful. Forced, mechanized labor gives us no joy; entertainment, more or less monotonous . . . gives us no joy; the whole of this bitter life gives us no joy. Without Christ the world attains the maximum of bitterness, because it attains the maximum of meaninglessness. Christianity is Paschal joy. Christianity is collaboration with God, an obligation newly undertaken by mankind to cultivate the Lord's paradise, once rejected in the Fall; and in the thicket of this paradise, overgrown with the weeds of many centuries of sin and the thorns of our dry and loveless life, Christianity commands us to root up, weed, plow, sow, and harvest.[25]

The basis for Mother Maria's vision, as that of Father Bulgakov, is the hope of the Incarnation and Resurrection; with an optimism grounded in these, she had no difficulty in recognizing the result of evil, the ever-present neighbor's suffering. It seems that Mother Maria's great sensitivity to human suffering was the portal through which her theological development and understanding passed. Already profoundly moved by suffering and death in her family, in the revolution and forced emigration of which she was a part, she was to encounter both the ultimate pain and ultimate presence of God, in the death of her children. Years later, in a moving essay called "Birth and Death," she recalled these experiences, though not in explicit detail.

Having made the difficult trip from the Black Sea to Georgia then on to Istanbul and Belgrade to Paris, she and her family squeezed out a living. Daniel Skobtsov was a teacher and taxi driver; Elisabeth designed silk scarves, made dolls, and sewed clothes. On March 7, 1926, after a prolonged hospital stay, four-year-old Nastia died of meningitis, her mother helplessly watching her dying. Beside herself, Elisabeth nevertheless came away from this horror of horrors, the premature loss of a child, with the gift of God's presence and love. Her spiritual father, Fr. Sergei Bulgakov, likewise years before had had to endure the painful death of his son from nephritis and in the worst of sorrows found God once more there, in love. Fr. Sergei Hackel provides some of the reflections Elisabeth put down at this time:

> At Nastia's side I feel that my soul has meandered down back alleys all my life. And now I want an authentic and purified road, not out of faith in life, but in order to justify, understand and accept death. . . . No amount of thought will ever result in any greater formulation than these three words: "Love one another," so long as it [love] is to the end and without exceptions. And then the whole of life is illumined, otherwise an abomination and a burden. . . . People call this a visitation of the Lord. A visitation which brings what? Grief? No, more than grief; for he suddenly reveals the true nature of things. And on the one hand we perceive the dead remains of one who was alive . . . the mortality of all creation, while on the other, we simultaneously perceive the life-giving, fiery, all-penetrating and all-consuming Comforter, the Spirit.[26]

In June 1936, word came from Russia of the death of her eldest child, Gaiana, who was only twenty-two. She had decided the previous year to return there. Those who attended the memorial service recounted how Elisabeth lay prostrate in prayer and grief on the floor of the St. Sergius Institute chapel throughout. Poems were a kind of journal for release and reflection for Elisabeth all through her life, and many of them deal with the death of her daughters. She later wrote one of the most powerful of her essays on love of one's neighbor as the imitation of the Mother of God, who watched as her own son died in great pain. In 1931, in Toulouse, she had seen a fresco by Marcel Lenoir of the coronation of the Virgin Mary, as Helene Arjakovsky-Klepinine points out. In it, the Mother of God holds on to her son, not as the King of Kings but as the Man of Sorrows, crucified. This was to be the last icon Mother Maria ever made, embroidering it out of threads supplied her by fellow camp inmates from their work assignments. It could well be an icon of Mother Maria herself, an image neither of grief nor despair but of love, in the face of death and loss.

TWO LOVES, YET ONE: OF GOD AND THE NEIGHBOR

For Mother Maria, both the dignity and freedom of the human person are signs of the life of God breathing within. One therefore, cannot separate love of God and love of the neighbor, despite efforts to do so in theological writing and churchly practice. The Mother of God is an image of both how God loves and how we are to love each other.

> If a man is not only the image of God but also the image of the Mother of God, then he should also be able to see the image of God and the image of the Mother of God in every other man. In man's God-motherly soul not only is the birth of the Son of God announced and Christ born, but there also develops the keen perception of Christ's image in other souls. And in this sense, the God-motherly part of the human soul begins to see other people as its children; it adopts them for itself. . . . The human heart should also be pierced by the two-edged swords, the soul-cutting weapons, of other people's crosses. Our neighbor's cross should be a sword that pierces our soul. . . . To my mind, it is here that the authentic mystical bases of human communion lie.[27]

Woven throughout Mother Maria's writings, I believe, is the theme of love's centrality, and I also believe, her battling with love in her own life. Both Sophie Koloumzine and Elisabeth Behr-Sigel, who knew her years ago, have remarked on the strain in Mother Maria's life between the love for her own children and family and the enormous expenditure of herself and time in caring for those she found in need and suffering. It could be easy to say that she neglected her own in favor of others. As already noted, Mother Maria's efforts, as remarkable and heroic as they were, did not evoke support or even compassion from some of her peers. In part of one of her longest and most insightful meditations on love of God and of the neighbor, Mother Maria actually considers maternal love not just as a love of giving but also very much as a love of taking. There may in fact be much of the ego in all the self-sacrifice and forgetting of oneself for one's children, a loving of one's own reflection, of one's own "I" in these small egos, the desire to shape them in certain ways, the need to see how successful and happy they will eventually be.[28]

In the "natural" view, according to not only what our families, our teachers, and our culture but also even the church appears to say, charity begins at home. Mother Maria's challenge, however was, must it end there?

As noted, fundamental to her thinking about love was the equivalence of the love of God and the love of the neighbor.

> Christ gave us two commandments: to love God and to love our fellow man. Everything else . . . is merely an elaboration of these commandments, which contain within themselves the totality of Christ's "Good news." . . . their truth is found only in their conjunction. Love for man alone leads us into the blind alley of an anti-Christian humanism, out of which the only exit is, at times, the rejection of the individual human being and love for him in the name of all mankind. Love for God without love for human beings, however, is condemned: "You hypocrite, how can you love God whom you have not seen, if you hate your brother whom you have seen?" (1 Jn 4:20)[29]

Not to love the person before us is not to love God, whose images he or she is, is not to love God who comes to us only through human beings, words, gestures. Not to love the brother or sister is furthermore not to love myself.[30] Yet, we cannot really love the neighbor before us unless we also love God, for in so doing, we not only love the image of God that each person is, but we also love in the power of God, with God's grace. Mother Maria's anthropology presumes the creation, redemption, and constant presence of God in each person. Furthermore, it is Christ-centered, incarnational, for the life of the God-become-human has forever transformed humanity, just as the Incarnation has forever transformed God. In Christ, in "God's humanity," we see the prototype, the image of what human life should be. In the Christ who completely gave of himself, Mother Maria emphasizes a christology dear to the Russian tradition, that of *kenosis*, of the God who stoops down, empties himself, in his absurd love (*eros manikos*) for us.[31] Here she again recalls "nonpossession" of poverty as the charism not just of monastic life but also of all Christian existence. The hymn to the Son of God in the letter to the Philippians (2:6–12) who took on the form of a servant for us is the prototype. Yet, this sacrificial love runs counter to ordinary human rules and perceptions.

Why is it that the wisdom of this world not only opposes this commandment of Christ but simply fails to understand it? Because the world has at all times lived by accommodating itself to the laws of material nature and is inclined to carry these laws over into the realm of spiritual nature. According to the laws of matter, I must accept that if I give away a piece of bread, then I become poorer by one piece of bread. If I give away a certain sum of money, then I reduce my funds by that amount. Extending this law, the world thinks that if I give my love, I am impoverished by that amount of love, and if I give up my soul, then I am utterly ruined, for there is nothing left of me to save.

In this area however, the laws of spiritual life are the exact opposite of the laws of the material world. According to spiritual law, every spiritual treasure given away not only returns to the giver like a whole and unbroken ruble given to a beggar, but it grows and becomes more valuable. They who give, acquire, and those who become poor, become rich. We give away our human riches and in return we receive much greater gifts from God, while those who give away their human souls, receive in return eternal bliss, the divine gift of possessing the Kingdom of Heaven. How do they receive that gift? By absenting themselves from Christ in an act of the uttermost self-renunciation and love, they offer themselves to others. If this is indeed an act of Christian love . . . then they meet Christ Himself face to face in the one to whom they offer themselves. And in communion with that person they commune with Christ himself. . . . Thus the mystery of union with man becomes the mystery of union with God. What was given away returns, for the love that is poured out never diminishes the sources of that love, for the source of love in our hearts is Love itself. It is Christ.[32]

STUDENT OF LIVING TRADITION, POET OF THE KINGDOM

As an Orthodox Christian, Mother Maria identified as authoritative scripture and the church's "living tradition"—that is, the experience and lives of the saints, in particular the Mother of God, the liturgical texts, and ascetic and theological writings—as the primary sources for our understanding of God, the world, the other person, how we live together in peace and love. Her essays concretize this tradition, showing how the life of God is to be lived out in daily existence, liturgy made incarnate in care for the suffering, in pursuit of justice in society.

Mother Maria's encounter with traditional monasticism is a particularly revealing. Although Father Basil Zenkovsky almost cynically observes that seeking monastic tonsure may not have been a profound or serious response to a vocation, the actual monastic life Mother Maria did lead, as well as her thinking and writing on it, witness otherwise. Monastic life did become an intensely personal way of her living the gospel's demands. Yet as an important institutional part of Christian history, a tradition in its own right much challenged by the events and consciousness of the modern era, monasticism became for her crucial in thinking through how faith must be adapted to new situations and needs.

While her own entrance into monastic life was something of an exception—she had three children and was married twice—she nevertheless tried to acquaint herself with its traditional form and content. Not only did she intensely study the literature and history, but she also visited the few women's monasteries not closed by the revolution, these being in Estonia and Latvia. Her firsthand experience was for the most part negative. In a word, she found the monastics well intentioned but trapped in the past, obsessed with meticulous observation of the rules and ways of the classic monastic tradition. As for the turmoil of twentieth-century life, either the brutal repression in the Soviet Union or the poverty and growing threat of fascism in the West, the monastics were clueless at best or indifferent at worst. Mother Maria could not reconcile the humanity, the sensitivity to the world of the early fathers and mothers of the desert with the staid, distanced mentality of contemporary traditional monastics. In "Types of Religious Lives," she puts it in a most startling, even brutal way.

In fact, we have today two citadels of such an Orthodoxy—traditional, canon-based, patristic and paternal: Athos and Valaam. A world of people removed from our bustle and sins, a world of faithful servants of Christ, a world of knowledge of God and contemplation. And what do you suppose most upsets this world of sanctity? How does it regard the present calamities that are tearing us apart, the new teachings, heresies perhaps, the destitution, the destruction and the persecution of the Church, the martyrs in Russia, the trampling down of belief throughout the whole world, the lack of love? Is this what most alarms the islands of the elect, these pinnacles of the Orthodox spirit? Not at all. What strikes them as most important, the most vital, the most burning issues of the day, is the question of the use of the Old or the New calendars in divine services. It is this that splits them into factions, this that leads them to condemn those who think otherwise than they do, this that defines the measure of things. It is difficult to speak about love against this background, since love somehow falls outside both the New and the Old Calendars. We can, of course, state that the Son of Man was Lord of the Sabbath, and that he violated the Sabbath precisely in the name of love.

But where they do not violate it, where they cannot violate it, this is because there is no "in the name" nor is there love. Strict ritualism reveals itself here to be the slave of the Sabbath and not the way of the Son of Man.... Instead of the Living God, instead of Christ crucified and risen, do we not have here a new idol, a new form of paganism, which is manifest in arguments over calendars, rubrics, rules, and prohibitions—a Sabbath which triumphs over the Son of Man?[33]

Likewise, she considers the ascetic mentality dominant in traditional monasticism, namely the conviction that everything one does is done out of obedience—to God, to the superior, to the monastic rule. The purpose for all of this is the salvation of one's own soul, becoming "perfect even as your Father in heaven." Once more, something is not right in such a vision, for

The whole world, its woes, its suffering, its labors on all levels—this is a kind of huge laboratory, a kind of experimental arena, where I can practice my obedience and humble my will. If obedience demands that I clean out stables, dig for potatoes, look after leprous persons, collect alms for the Church, or preach the teachings of Christ—I must do all these things with the same conscientious and attentive effort, with the same humility and the same dispassion, because all these things are tasks and exercises of my readiness to curb my will, a difficult and rocky road for the soul seeking salvation. I must constantly put virtues into practice and therefore I must perform acts of Christian love. But that love is itself a special form of obedience, for we are called and commanded to love—and we must love.[34]

But where is there any recognition of the other, the neighbor who is being fed, clothed, or visited? Rather than self-renouncing, self-giving love that embraces the other, this "strange and fearsome holiness" pursues all kinds of works of love because it is the rule, because God or the superior orders it, because it is necessary for the salvation of my soul. Unlike the ancient monastics, an Anthony the Great, Syncletica, Pachomius, or Paisius, the world and the other, even when directly before me, evaporates. In a particularly discerning passage, Mother Maria concentrates on some of the particular features of modern life distressing to traditional monasticism and thus necessary to flee or avoid:

There is no doubt as to the inner and outer unhappiness and misery of the world today . . . the threat of impending war, the gradual dying out of the spirit of freedom, the revolutions and dictatorships which are tearing people apart . . . class hatred and a decline in moral principles. It would appear that there are no social ills that have not affected contemporary life. Yet at the same time we are surrounded by crowd of people who are oblivious to the tragedy of our age . . . surrounded by boundless self-satisfaction, a total lack of doubt, by physical and spiritual saturation, by an almost total overdose of all things. But this is no "feast during the plague." . . . Today, in a time of plague, one as a rule counts one's daily earnings and in the evening goes to the cinema. There is no talk of the courage of despair because there is no despair. There is only contentment and spiritual quiescence. The tragic nature of the psychology of contemporary man is self-evident. And every fiery prophet, every preacher will be in a quandary: on which side of the café table should he sit? How can he cast light on the nature of today's stock market gains? How can he break through, trample, and destroy this sticky, gooey mass that surrounds the soul of today's philistines? How can he set the people's hearts on fire with his words?[35]

What has this sociological and spiritual diagnosis of the world, from the year 1937, to do with monastic life? From the hard words just cited, Mother Maria proceeds to delineate an evangelical or gospel type of Christianity. The monastic, however, finds himself or herself for the most part in the midst of this world. Gone are the spacious corridors, expansive properties, and large communities of older endowed monasteries as well as the pilgrims flocking to them. This is even more the case today, almost seventy years later. Monasticism, she argues, is both not needed and needed. Society and culture hardly are interested, but monasticism has much to give to people. It is needed "on the roads of life, in the very thick of it." The real innovation or adaptation, the authentic renewal not only of monastic life but also of the church as a whole is to realize that the place to be and to work is very simply, right there, in the world of "pains, all the wounds, all the sins of life, with drunkenness, depravity, thoughts of suicide" but also" longing for a little material well-being, competition and peaceful, quiet 'everyday' godlessness."[36]

If a monastery is a place of healing, nourishment, air, and light, in the spiritual sense, it is not too much to say that the whole world needs if not wants to be there. Yet, this cannot be. But, for the monastic,

there is more love, more humility, more need in remaining in the world's backyard, in breathing bad air, in hungering after spiritual food—sharing all these burdens and all the world's anguish with others, lightening them for others. Christ, in ascending to heaven, did not take the Church with him; he did not halt the path of human history. Christ left the Church in the world . . . as a small bit of leavening, but this leavening is to leaven all the dough (Gal. 5:9).[37]

At the core of monastic life are community in prayer, work, and possessions in imitation of the primitive church (Acts 2:42–47; 3:32–35). In the Russian monastic tradition, Mother Maria perceptively notes the importance of nonpossession or poverty to such renowned figures as Sergius of Radonezh, Nilus of Sora, Joseph of Volokholamsk, and Seraphim of Sarov. What was crucial for them was not just the absence of private property, but also the love of the neighbor, the heart of generosity—the joyous giving away of food, clothing, shelter, time, and, finally, oneself. Call it coming back full circle. Call it simply a "return to the sources." Call it "living tradition," but in Mother Maria's frequently polemical criticism of her tradition, that of the church and of monasticism, in the end she neither rejects either nor imposes upon them anything alien to their essential character. Rather, she comes back to the two loves that are really but one, of God and the neighbor. Here, in the modern era, can both the church and monasticism be revived and work, "for the life of the world."[38]

SOCIOLOGICAL IMAGINATION, ESCHATOLOGICAL VISION

Very much a woman of the modern era, Mother Maria was a participant in as well as observer of the years of ferment in Russia, beginning in the demonstration and brutal put down of the same on "Bloody Sunday," January 5, 1905, leading up to the civil war and Bolshevik Revolution. She had an acute "sociological imagination," as C. Wright Mills called it, aware of the interactions among the individual and the state, economy, other social institutions, church, and culture.[39] Early on, she recognized the need for profound political, economic, and social change in Russia. Siding with many of the intellectuals of the first decades of the century, she aligned herself with the socialist vision of transformation. Like another former Marxist, Father Bulgakov, she never abandoned her socialist sympathies, though she distanced herself from the ruthless policies of the Bolsheviks. Once an ally of Trotsky, she eventually was part of the group ordered to assassinate him. (She did not.) Yet meeting him years later, in Paris, she was able to turn his gratitude into financial contribution to her hostels. Still later, she attacked the complicity of the Russian Church under the imposed strictures of the Petrine era. She stressed the incompatibility of the state church situation of Orthodoxy under the tsars as incompatible

with the gospel, and this was in turn criticized by more conservative dev-
otees of "Holy Russia."

The Bolshevik Revolution was for her, as for Father Bulgakov and
Berdyaev and many others, a tragedy—but also a true liberation. It forced
Russian Christians to reject the support of monarchy and fashion a new
democratic and pluralistic social order. Here she clashed profoundly
with the conservative monarchist Russians of both the Karlovtsky Synod
(the Russian Orthodox Church Outside Russia) as well as those in Paris
who adhered to the Moscow patriarchate despite state manipulation of
the church. However, Mother Maria also had Peter Berger's "humanistic
perspective," namely, the sense that events and ideologies can both liberate and enslave.[40] Mother Maria's view is that the individual is precious and unique, a child of God, never to be surrendered to the good of
a class or ethnic group or religious tradition. So she rejected not only the
extreme clergy-lay division but also the aristocrat-peasant, class, religious and ethnic prejudices of prerevolutionary Russia as well as the naive and sinister mentality of the Communist Party.

It is all too easy to cast the conflict as one between virtuous traditional
monarchy, the alliance of czar and patriarch, on the one hand, and godless, brutal communism on the other. Such are the extreme views of both
monarchists and Bolsheviks. Thus it cannot be the cross or the cross and
the hammer and sickle. Revolution is cleansed of party perversion, bears
within the seed of true change, reliant on help from without, from God.

> The liberation of life from the dead end it finds itself in can proceed only
> from where there is a power greater than life, only from where there is the
> possibility of a supra-physical, supra-historical resolution of the question.
> Only the Church can liberate and direct our life. The Church must turn to
> the cry of the world, to the social hell, to injustice, crises, unemployment,
> and speak the words given her from all eternity: "Come unto me, all ye that
> labor and are heavy laden, and I will give you rest" (Mt. 11:28). . . . Christ, the
> cross and the Church can in no circumstances go hand in hand with any-
> thing that contains an element of violence and servitude. . . . Christ is free-
> dom: the face of Christ is the affirmation in every person of his own free and
> God-like face; the Church is a free and organic union of the faithful with
> Christ, with Christ's freedom; and Christ calls those who labor and are
> heavy laden to take up his burden, which is light because it is taken up
> freely.[41]

Mother Maria concludes by asserting that though the grace of God is
essential, so too is human work to transform society, to offer help to the

poor and suffering, to oppose what is unjust, and where possible to change the society that creates poverty and misery. She imagines this community of workers as a "kind of monastery," in the world, "a spiritual organism, minor order, brotherhood." For her, the model for such community and common work is the church, not so much the institutional form we know from history but also, and more importantly, "the one great monastery, organism, order, brotherhood."[42]

As we have seen in her thinking about tradition and the necessity of adaptation or renewal, Mother Maria harbored no romantic illusions about the faith, the church, or even the institution of monasticism. For her, the past was not a solid whole to be preserved but a mix of elements, some sound and appropriate for the present, some no longer valid, still others wrongheaded, corrupt and to be abandoned. The authentic Christian tradition, as John Meyendorff, among others, has pointed out, is living, always being modified and capable of further modification, while its essential truths endured.[43] She cannot be accused of otherworldly, out-of-touch piety. Rather, her "sociological imagination" is empirically grounded. While she insists on the presence of God and reliance on his grace, she also sees no alternative to purposeful action and no other arena for action but that of our own social world—neighborhood, city, and country.

When in paraphrasing St. John Chrysostom, she talks about the "sacrament of the brother/sister," she means that to be real, our prayer must be enacted. "We do not just say prayers," as Paul Evdokimov puts it, "we become prayer, prayer incarnate."[44] If we find our religion making us look away from the face of God in those around us, if this religion urges us to insulate ourselves in beautiful churches, liturgical chants, and incense to the extent that we forget the brother or sister next door, we are short, very short indeed of the demands of Christ and his gospel. We will have missed, in the face of the neighbor, the icon of Christ who lives in each person. It should come as no surprise that many others, through the overwhelming experiences of immigration, the Great Depression, the war, should have come to precisely the same conclusions. The "return to the sources" motif—often associated with the likes of Henri de Lubac, Jean Daniélou, Yves Congar, Bernard Botte, M-D. Chenu, Lambert Beaudin, J-J. von Allmen, Joachim Jeremias, and Gregory Dix, among others—was rooted in exactly the same passage through suffering and death to life that their confreres in the other churches made. In the postwar years many of these would gather in various settings, one being the annual week of liturgical study and prayer, organized by Fathers Cyprian Kern and Nicolas Afanasiev and just celebrating its fiftieth anniversary, at St. Sergius Theological Institute in Paris, or in the continuing Fellowship of St. Alban and St. Sergius, over seventy years old, in the United Kingdom. The worker-priest movement, the study that blossomed in the documents of Vatican II, the rediscovery of the priesthood of all the baptized, of the church as eucharistic community, of the ministry as service, of the need for healing division among Christians and religious traditions across the world—all these significant recoveries and more were born in the same experiences as Mother Maria encountered and of which she writes.

TYPES OF RELIGIOUS LIVES: FALSE AND TRUE HOLINESS

For Mother Maria, the vision of her teacher, Father Sergei Bulgakov, was pivotal, but it was augmented by others in the emigration and, of course, deeply rooted in the Christian tradition. Her defense of her philanthropic ministry is explicitly based on New Testament texts, as well as the collection of Eastern Church spiritual writings called the *Philokalia*, or "Love of Beauty."[45] In addition, she draws upon the texts of the Eastern Church liturgy and on the lives of saints. The purpose of law, as of the rest of politics, society, and culture, was to enhance the fullness of human life, not to create a heaven on earth but rather to reveal the paradise, the kingdom of God already present—though not fully. Hers was a "realized eschatology," a vision of the "new age" and possibilities of a "new City," a "new Jerusalem," an eschatological vision of a just and compassionate society such as that of Father Bulgakov in his last books, *The Bride of the Lamb* and *The Apocalypse of St. John*. Christianity was for her the royal road, the gospel the charter, yet not oppressively or imperialistically.

Perhaps there is no better exposition of Mother Maria's critical and constructive thinking about Christianity in our time than "Types of Religious Lives." It was written in 1937 but was not published until 1996, after Antoine Arjakovsky and Helen Arjakovsky-Klepinine discovered it among the papers of her mother, Sophie Pilenko, in the Bakmatiev Archive at Columbia University. In it, Mother Maria looks in considerable detail at five forms or types that religious faith and practice can take. Her types are very specific to Russian Orthodox history, yet there is enough discernment in her analysis for the reader to make connections in many other Christian contexts. A Roman Catholic, Episcopalian, Methodist, or Lutheran, not to mention Baptist, could trace out the variations that would make at least some of the types relevant within each of these confessions.

As with all efforts in typology, as Max Weber pointed out, the construction draws from numerous particular cases, yet it would be hard to find any one individual who would perfectly embody the type. Mother Maria admits this, as well as other limitations such as other varieties of religiosity too diverse to be included. What is more, it is also possible to find elements of one type diffused in other types. Obsession with liturgical rubrics and other details, for example, can be found across several of Mother Maria's type, so prevalent has this been in Russian Orthodoxy.

Nevertheless, enough accurate, defining characteristics are captured if a specific type is effectively rendered. This is certainly the case with Mother Maria's efforts here, even if one does not agree with details of her analysis. The "portraits" she executes of Russian Orthodox piety are both familiar and striking.

The "synodal" type has its origins in the modifications of the church perpetrated under Peter the Great, changes that in turn created a religious consciousness that far outlived his era. Although it is impossible to examine all Mother Maria's types in detail here, it is still possible to get to the heart of each. And the core of this one is the church as "essential, but the motivations for this needs often were of a national rather than ecclesial character."[46] This is the religiosity in which, as Father Alexander Schmemann later described it, one's yearly communion was understood as "an important Russian custom," the most popular service was the memorial rite (*panikihda*) and generally, attendance at church was restricted to several major holidays, religious observance essentially equal to being a "good Russian."[47] Such minimalism was required: by family pressure, school rules, or other forms of regulation. Enormous sums were spent on church construction, decoration, and performance: golden chalices, gospel book and icon-covers, the best voices recruited for deacons and choirs. Even in the destitution of the emigration, churches were created out of garages, sheds, and basements, liturgical objects out of everyday items like upholstery fabric for vestments, tin cans for censers, preserve glasses for candleholders. Artists of all kinds were conscripted. Some the leading iconographers of the twentieth century, such as Leonid Ouspensky, Father Gregory Krug, and Sister Joanna Reitlinger, were exactly such artist-conscripts.[48] Mother Maria was herself a master adaptor in this regard, embroidering vestments, icons, and turning garages and henhouses into chapels. But the point about this type was not the ingenuity just described but the lack of creativity and spontaneity, the absence of commitment, the minimalism, all of which equated church with being and remaining "Russian."

In the "ritual" type, and for that matter in the "aesthetical" and "ascetic" types of piety, Mother Maria turns to a far more passionate, in fact obsessive, attachment to liturgy, texts, the forms of prayer, faith, and religious behavior, although in somewhat different modalities. While there was as early as in the medieval Muscovite era the tendency to freeze Orthodox Christianity brought from Constantinople, the crisis of the "Old Believers" and their schism from the rest of the Russian Church was a profound historical influence on extreme ritualistic conservation. The "Old Believers" are the quintessential ritualists, rejecting as maters of truth and salvation the liturgical reforms of Patriarch Nikon in a fanatic, irrational fashion. They refused, for example to use three fingers rather than two in making the sign of the cross. They insisted on archaic spellings of "Jesus," on double rather than triple repetitions of certain responses. On the other hand, they did preserve the classical icons and style of iconography. In the end, though, many ended up without clergy or sacraments, the icon screen alone attached to the eastern walls of their chapels. But for Mother Maria, the "Old Believers" are hardly the only ritualists, and she identifies many other behaviors as symptomatic of a piety where form is paramount, the heart and soul invested only in the externals. The fasts of the church year must be kept meticulously no matter what means are required and hardships imposed on others. Correct chanting tone and pronunciation and speed are crucial, even though neither the one chanting nor the congregation understands a word. Every detail of the calendar and the rubrics becomes divine, and errors and those erring are subjected to abusive treatment. No lack of zeal or commitment here, yet does such religion have anything to do with Christ, or the person before me, with the realities of everyday life.

> Its very principle, a constant repetition of rules, words and gestures, excludes any possibility of creative tension. From ancient times strict ritualism has been opposed to prophecy and creativity.[49] Its task was to preserve and to repeat and not to tear down and rebuild. . . . The main question . . . is this: how does it respond to Christ's commandments concerning love for God and for other people? Does it have a place for them? . . . Christ, who turned away from scribes and pharisees, Christ, who approached prostitutes, tax collectors and sinner, can hardly be the teacher of those who are afraid to soil their pristine garments, who are completely devoted to the letter of the law, who live only by rules and who govern their whole life according to the rules.[50]

The section on the ritualists concludes with the hard words about the Sabbath replacing the Lord and humankind quoted earlier in Mother Maria's critique of monasticism in the modern era. The ritualist type is only one of the more obsessive forms of piety she examines. As an artist herself in various media, Mother Maria was hardly anti-aesthetic, but in her sketching out of the aesthetic type, she stresses how elitist and egotistic such a type makes a person. It is here not "the letter of the law," the precise observance of rubrics and maintaining of rules but devotion to the fine performance of a choir, a preacher, an iconographer. Rather than encouraging the creativity necessary to finding new forms for our time, new ways of experiencing the beauty of the Lord and his house, in the aesthetic form much is simply lost in the passion for perfection, in enchantment with style. Left behind, too, are the vast majority of people, deemed unable to appreciate the beauty, ignorant of its history, details, too uncouth to have around. "The aesthetically minded custodians of grandeur will preserve that chasm" established between Christ and the crowd of ordinary women and men, "in the name of harmony, rhythm, order and beauty."

> Christ himself departs, quietly and invisibly, from the sanctuary protected by a splendid icon-screen. The singing will continue to resound, clouds of incense will still rise. . . . But Christ will go out onto the church steps and mingle with the crowd: the poor, the lepers, the desperate, the embittered, the holy fools. Christ will go out into the streets, the prisons, the hospitals, the low haunts and dives. . . . The most terrible thing is that it may well be that the guardians of beauty . . . will not comprehend Christ's beauty, and will not let him into the church because behind him there will follow a crowd of people deformed by sin, by ugliness, drunkenness, depravity and hate. Then their chant will fade away in the air, the smell of incense will disperse, and Someone will say to them: "I was hungry and you gave me no food, thirsty and you gave me no drink, a stranger and you did not welcome me."[51]

In an echo of the essay by her opponent Father Cyprian Kern, she regretfully acknowledges that Christ's servants, the clergy, supposedly preachers, healers, and the ministers of his love, have become servants rather of the cult, worried about the rubrics, the cut of the vestments, the quality of the voice for chanting.[52]

The last type Mother Maria serves up for analysis is the ascetic. The pages she devotes to this form are moving, lyrical, and we have already heard some of these passages in discussing her ideas about renewal of monasticism.[53] As there, here too the problem is the spiritual egocentrism of the ascetic fixation. All these fasting rules, all the distasteful tasks I do under obedience, all the things I deny myself—these in the end are all about me. Even when doing something good for the neighbor, I am doing it to save myself. The neighbor just happens to be the target of my good deeds. No real communion is established between myself and the other and thus, little or no real communion with God. Real asceticism has as its goal clearing out the debris, opening one to God and the neighbor.

However, the pseudo-asceticism here described achieves exactly the opposite, closing me up in myself, turning me back constantly inward.

The final type Mother Maria presents is the one she unreservedly celebrates and recommends as authentically Christian, of the gospel, evangelical though not in our contemporary denominational sense of this term. In fact, she explicitly distinguishes this type from a sectarianism that turns the Bible into a list of moral precepts, and a sectarian mentality that ridicules other Christians, their worship and life, claiming a biblical self-righteousness in so doing. And by now, the features of this type are no mystery to us for we have come upon them at many other places in Mother Maria's writings and especially in her life.

Rather than use the term "churching of life," so preferred by others in the Russian emigration, she coins another as descriptive of the chief aim of this type:

> "Christification" ... is based on the words, "It is no longer I who live, but Christ who lives in me." (Gal 2:20) The image of God, the icon of Christ, which truly is my real and authentic essence or being, is the only measure of all things, the only path or way which is given to me. Each movement of my soul, each approach to God, to other people, to the world, is determined by the suitability of that act for reflecting the image of God which is within me.[54]

Love for humanity alone or in general, while an ideal of the Enlightenment and of the modern era, leads us into the blind alley, as she calls it of a humanism that is at once anti-Christian, impersonal, theoretical, and, in the end, not humane. But equally, as we have also seen, the flight into religiosity of various forms, the attempt to place the love for God above that for the neighbor, to play Martha off against Mary, destroys love, both for God and for the neighbor.

The two loves are but one love. To attempt to "Christify" the world is not impose upon it something external, but to deal with it in its own terms—as God's creation, out of love, as the constant object of God's love, God's becoming part of it, living in it, dying and rising—"for the life of the world." To "Christify" means to be the world's beloved, the *philanthropos* or "Lover of mankind," as the Eastern Church liturgy repeatedly names God. As scripture scholar James Kugel points out, an image of God we have lost is that of a God who does not so much sit on his throne in his heavens, waiting for our obeisance, but the God who descends and walks among us, often completely unnoticed, seeking us out in love.[55] One cannot grasp Mother Maria's thinking here without recognizing deep within, a quite different image of God and correspondingly, of the human person than those we employ in everyday discourse. There is in her theology and anthropology Father Bulgakov's most intimate relationship between God and humankind, the reciprocity he meant to connote by his constant reference to Sophia, but for which he also employed Soloviev's idea of "God's humanity." For Mother Maria, God is pure, his love for his creation is complete. He makes himself into that creation, pursues us with a passion—and wishes that we would "go and do likewise." At the Last Judgment, Mother Maria reasons, when the master of all, who is the servant of all, says that he was the one who was hungry, thirsty, naked, without a home, it is not a question of fulfilling obligations, performing rituals, but being love, being holy fools like the most foolish of lovers, God. If we find ourselves having followed only the politically, socially "correct" ways, we will find that there is no one but ourselves to blame. It is "our loveless hearts, our stingy souls, our ineffective will, our lack of faith in Christ's help" that will judge us. But it will be God who nevertheless welcomes us in to dine with him (Rev. 3:20).

It is simply not possible to accuse Mother Maria of abandoning the church, prayer, the liturgy, or sacraments in her vision of the love of God and the neighbor. This sort of criticism, often leveled at movements such as liberation theology and the Social Gospel, do not apply. At the conclusion of the "Types" essay, within the gospel or evangelical type, she produces several of the most eloquent pages in contemporary Christian writing on the Eucharist as the "Church's most valuable treasure, its primary activity in the world," as "the mystery of sacrificial love."[56] There is no contradiction in her writings as in her own existence, between prayer and action, between liturgy and life. Christianity was nothing less than an eternal offering, not only of the divine liturgy inside but also beyond the church walls.

> It means that we must offer the bloodless sacrifice, the sacrifice of self-surrendering love not only in a specific place, upon the altar of a particular temple; the whole world becomes the single altar of a single temple, and for this universal liturgy we must offer our hearts, like bread and wine, in order that they may be transformed into Christ's love, that he may be born in them, that they may become "divine-human" hearts and that he may give these hearts of ours as food for the world, that he may bring the whole world into communion with these hearts of ours that have been offered up. . . . Then truly in all ways Christ will be all in all.[57]

MOTHER MARIA'S INFLUENCE AND LEGACY

We do not receive a systematic theology from Mother Maria. Neither is it the focused academic sort. If, however, in this volume one hopes to hear from a modern Christian thinker important insights on the person, on life in the social and political worlds, amid the laws and institutions of our time, then we have heard much. But the one word, and the core theme is that of the life-giving love of God for us and likewise, the liberating, transforming love we in turn have for the neighbor who is always before us. As a Kierkegaard scholar, I am much taken by the correspondence of Mother Maria's essential thinking here with Kierkegaard's very important *Works of Love*, a volume only very recently receiving attention for its proclamation of Christian life and ethics. For Mother Maria, as for Kierkegaard, love is the hidden "sprout in the grain," always able to presume love in the other, always cooperating with God in his work of loving.[58]

Mother Maria was not the type to have disciples. As noted, even the two other nuns who came to live with her in the "monasteries in the world" at Villa de Saxe, rue de Lourmel, and Noisy-le-Grand, Mothers Evdokia and Blandina, had difficulties with the turmoil of trying to observe the daily cycle of services and care for so many people. The more traditional monastery they established still exists in Bussey-en-Othe. Her chaplain, Father Cyprian Kern, continued his work teaching at St. Sergius Institute after he left the church at rue de Lourmel. He mentored the young priest and teacher, Father Alexander Schmemann, who became the leading Orthodox voice in liturgical and spiritual renewal in America. Father Lev Gillet, another chaplain and close friend of Mother Maria, went to work in England, and it remained his base for the rest of his life. Father Bulgakov died in 1944, during the occupation, after a stroke and a long coma.

Mother Maria founded neither a "school" of theological reflection nor a religious order. The hostels she established are now all gone, though one remained as a parish until the 1970s and another as a retreat house until the late 1980s. The wonderful icon screen that iconographer Father Gregory Krug created for the chapel at Noisy-le-Grand in her memory now adorns the monastery church at Marcenat.[59] There is no shrine to Mother Maria in Paris or elsewhere. The veneration of her, though widespread, is completely private and unofficial. As noted, the process for her official recognition—"glorification" as canonization is called in the Eastern Church—seems to have been placed on hold. She always had her critics and detractors as recent rejections of her thinking by Father Valentin Asmus and others in Russia witness.[60] Yet I would argue that her life, person, and thinking have been appropriated, most often without explicit acknowledgment by a number of fellow Orthodox Christians. Some, like her, experienced the new freedom of the emigration as well as its hardships, and in it they also discovered the fresh, radical character of the gospel life of prayer and service to which she witnessed.

Surely one striking example would be the ninety-seven-year-old lay theologian Elisabeth Behr-Sigel, who knew Mother Maria and whose life and work echo Mother Maria's own fearless commitment to freedom in Christian life.[61] Close to Father Bulgakov, Father Lev Gillet, Paul Evdokimov, and many others of the Paris emigration as well as to Mother Maria, she has taught and written on the nineteenth-century Russian theologian Alexander Bukharev, on the kenotic Christ in Russian spirituality, and, more recently, on the place of women in the Orthodox Church, in particular the question of the ordination of women.[62] Painstaking and scholarly, her writing on the last subjects is never polemical, always historically insightful and theologically challenging. Both Metropolitan Anthony Bloom and Bishop Kallistos Ware have supported her keeping open dialogue and encouraging study and debate on the question of women in the Orthodox Church generally and the more difficult and specific issue of deaconesses and other orders in the past and the possibility of the restoration of these and possibly other blessed and ordained orders in the future. Active in the Resistance during World War II, Elisabeth Behr-Sigel has continued her involvement in the movement to assist victims of torture, the Christian Association for the Abolition of Torture. In her overview of the spirituality of the Eastern Church, she demonstrates that openness to the world to characteristic of the Russian thinkers just noted. But the unambiguous connection between prayer and service to others, between church and society, between liturgy and life is clear throughout her writings and her own life.

Another who also dedicated himself to care of the suffering was a colleague of Mother Maria's from days in the Russian Christian Students Movement, its first general secretary, also a member of the first graduating class of the St. Sergius Theological Institute, the lay theologian Paul Evdokimov (1901–69). Mother Maria's vision of serving God and the neighbor was expressed in his writings and activities.[63] Also active in the Resistance, he directed several hostels for refugees in the postwar era. Despite his degrees from the Sorbonne and St. Sergius Institute and a doctorate from the University at Aix-en-Provence, he remained in service work. He was an authentic lay pastor, exercising, as he said, his baptismal priesthood. He counseled the refugees, displaced persons, troubled individuals, and Third World students who found the hostels not only an affordable place to live but also a true community in both spiritual and human terms. In the late 1950s he defended a second dissertation and began teaching on his alma mater, St. Sergius's faculty, also teaching in the World Council of Churches Ecumenical Institute at Bossey and the Catholic Institute of Theology in Paris, among other places. His publications included a masterful overview of Orthodox theology, a study of the theology of the icon, as well as studies of the history of contemporary Russian theology and the state of debate on the place and role of the Holy Spirit. The strong emphasis on the priesthood and hence daily ministry of all the baptized along with his sensitivity toward service of the suffering are the echoes of Mother Maria in both his writing and life.

Mother Maria, along with her colleagues in the Paris Russian emigration, left an important legacy not only to their Orthodox Church but also to the Western churches. Clearly, those closest to Mother Maria, such as Fathers Bulgakov and Gillet, exemplified her passionate commitment to the suffering neighbor as the love of God. Others put into practice her zeal for the love of the neighbor by emphasizing the need for the church to reach out to the world in love, in service and mission. Fathers Alexander Schmemann and John Meyendorff and another contemporary martyr, Father Alexander Men, not only wrote about this but also lived it.[64]

In his reflections on holiness in our time, Paul Evdokimov, like Simone Weil, notes that we need a new type of sanctity.[65] Although we need to respect the models of holiness from the past, we need to not imprison ourselves in these but rather to find those shapes that better correspond to our world, our time and our lives.[66] Like Mother Maria, Evdokimov realized that holiness in our time would have its heroic, unusual patterns. But for the most part, the loving of God and of the neighbor would be everyday, so ordinary and usual as to be "hidden." Routine and unnoticed, unlike the great feats of traditional sanctity, such a holiness of our time will not be so easily acknowledged, but its presence is universal.

POSTSCRIPT

In a document dated January 16, 2004, almost sixty years after the death of Mother Maria, and after petitions were submitted to church authorities over the past decades, the holy synod of the Ecumenical Patriarchate recognized her and several of her associates as saints.

The Holy Church of Christ knows to honor and celebrate forever in all piety and in hymns and praises those who in the present life conduct themselves in a holy and pious manner, and who exert themselves in word and deed in the service and in the love of God and of the neighbor, and who, after their departure for the beyond, through signs and miracles have been confirmed by God, and to invoke their intercession, which is acceptable to God, for the remission of sins and the healing of the sick.

Along with Mother Maria, Father Dimitri Klepinine, chaplain of the hostel at rue de Lourmel, her son Yuri Skobtsov, and treasurer Ilya Fondaminsky were canonized, all of them having also died in Nazi prison camps. A faithful and holy priest who served in the poor mining town of Ugine, Father Alexis Medvedkov, was also included.

The act of canonization affirmed,

> by the dignity of their lives and their good example, they contributed to the edification of the souls of the faithful; several of them, during the Second World War, suffered greatly from evils and were subjected to torments, which they bore with fortitude. In consequence, we have decided, following the usual practice of the Church, to accord to these very holy people the honor which is due to them. This is why we have decreed and ordered in Synod, and recommended in the Holy Spirit, that the Archpriest Alexis Medvedkov, the Priest Dimitri Klepinine, the nun Maria Skobtsova and her son Yuri Skobtsov and Ilya Fondaminsky, who ended their life in sanctity and, certainly, in martyrdom, be counted among the blessed martyrs and saints of the Church and be honored by the faithful and celebrated in hymns of praise.

Canonization, through an official ecclesiastical act, does not make a saint. Holiness consists in living out the gospel, loving God and neighbor, in words and actions. As with so many others, we may also say of Mother Maria that long before she was canonized her sanctity was enacted in the lives of those around her and known by many more. Now she is recognized among the saints of our time.

NOTES

1. Several good biographical essays on Mother Maria exist in addition to T. Stratton Smith's *Rebel Nun* (Springfield, Ill.: Templegate, 1965). The most recent is Jim Forest, "Mother Maria of Paris," in *Mother Maria Skobtsova: Essential Writings*, trans. Richard Pevear and Larissa Volokhonsky (Maryknoll, N.Y.: Orbis Books, 2003), 13–44; Michael Plekon, *Living Icons: Persons of Faith in the Eastern Church* (Notre Dame, Ind.: University of Notre Dame Press, 2002), 59–80. Particularly rich is Hélène Arjakovsky-Klepinine, "La joie du don," in *Le sacrement du frère*, ed. Helene Arjakovsky-Klepinine, Françoise Lhoest, and Claire Vajou, 15–69 (Paris: Éditions du Cerf, 2001), 15–69, and the essay by Elisabeth Behr-Sigel, who knew her, "Mother Maria Skobtsova 1891–1945," in *Discerning the Signs of the Times: The Vision of Elisabeth Behr-Sigel*, ed. Michael

Plekon and Sarah E. Hinlicky, 41–54 (Crestwood, N.Y.: St. Vladimir's Seminary Press, 2001). Metropolitan Anthony Bloom's memories of Mother Maria in the May 2001 *Cathedral Newsletter* can be found at http://www.sourozh.org. I am indebted to conversation with two remarkable women of the Orthodox Church who knew Mother Maria in their youth and were willing to share some of their memories of her. These are the late Sophie Koloumzine, teacher and founder of religious education among the Orthodox in America and the incomparable Elisabeth Behr-Sigel, who at ninety-six was still active as a lay theologian, and who is regarded as the "mother" of the Orthodox Church in France. I am also grateful to Helen Arjakovsky-Klepinine, daughter of Father Dimitri Klepinine, and one who has preserved Mother Maria's memory and translated her writings, bringing them to a wide range of readers in Europe. Another helpful biographical effort is that of Laurence Varaut, *Mère Marie: Saint-Pétersbourg-Paris-Ravensbrück, 1891–1945* (Paris: Perrin, 2001). The classic is Sergei Hackel, *Pearl of Great Price: The Life of Mother Maria Skobtsova, 1891–1945* (Crestwood, N.Y.: St. Vladimir's Seminary Press, 1982). Last, I am indebted to Father Alvian Smirensky for sharing with me his translations of the memoirs of Father Basil Zenkovsky, *My Encounters with Prominent People*, published by the Association of Russian Scholars in America.

2. *La chemin de ma vie* (Paris: Presses Saint-Serge, 2003). Openness and freedom are the traits emphasized by Father Basil Zenkovsky in his memoir of Metropolitan Evlogy.

3. Many of these remarkable members of the Russian community in Paris are examined in Nicolas Zernov, *The Russian Religious Renaissance of the Twentieth Century* (New York: Harper & Row, 1963). Also see Marc Raeff, *Russia Abroad* (New York: Oxford University Press, 1990), and Nikita Struve, *Soixante-dix ans de l'émigration russe, 1919–1989* (Paris: Fayard, 1996).

4. The cited volumes by Antoine Arjakovsky, Sergei Hackel, Helene Arjakovsky-Klepinine, and Laurence Varaut contain these photos. Until recently there was a Paris-based Web site with many photos of Mother Maria, but it was discontinued. See also Orthodox Peace Fellowship, "Mother Maria," *In Communion*, http://incommunion.org/contents/mother-maria.

5. Antoine Arjakovsky, *Histoire de la pensée orthodoxe contemporaine: La génération des penseurs religieux de l'émigration russe-La revue La Voie (Put') 1925–1940* (Paris: L'Esprit et la Lettre, 2002); Paul Valliere, *Modern Russian Theology: Soloviev, Bukharev, Bulgakov* (Grand Rapids, Mich.: Eerdmans, 2000); Rowan Williams, *Sergii Bulgakov: Towards A Russian Political Theology* (Edinburgh: T & T Clark, 1999); Anastassy Brandon Gallaher, "Bulgakov's Ecumenical Thought," *Sobornost/Eastern Churches Review* 24, no. 1 (2002): 24–55; Gallaher, "Bulgakov and Intercommunion," ibid., 9–28; Gallaher, "Catholic Action: Ecclesiology, the Eucharist and the Question of Intercommunion in the Ecumenism of Sergii Bulgakov" (M.Div. thesis, St. Vladimir's Orthodox Theological Seminary, 2003).

6. Varaut, *Mère Marie*, 149–154; Hackel, *Pearl of Great Price*, 123–149.

7. See the report of this and the talk given by Bishop Gabriel (de Vylder) in *Service Orthodoxe de Presse* 276 (March 2003): "A la haine ils répondaient par l'amour, a l'indifférence par la charité" (They responded to hatred with love, to indifference with charity).

8. Hackel, *Pearl of Great Price*, xi–xii.

9. Arjakovsky, *Histoire de la pensée orthodoxe contemporaine*, 233–235, 257–258, 323, 474–475.

10. This essay is in *Essential Writings*, 156–165. On the debate between Father Chetverikov and Mother Maria in both *Put'* and *Messenger of the Russian Christian Students' Movement*, see Arjakovsky, *Histoire de la pensée orthodoxe contemporaine*, 471–474.

11. Ion Bria, "The Liturgy after the Liturgy," in *Baptism and Eucharist: Ecumenical Convergence in Celebration*, ed. Max Thurian and Geoffrey Wainwrights (Grand Rapids, Mich.: Eerdmans, 1983), 213–218.

12. *Essential Writings*, 80–81.

13. Thomas Merton, *The Asian Journal of Thomas Merton*, ed. Naomi Burton, Brother Patrick Hart, and James Laughlin (New York: New Directions, 1975), 338.

14. Both essays are included in Michael Plekon, ed., *Tradition Alive: On the Church and the Christian Life in Our Time* (Lanham, Md.: Sheed & Ward, 2003), 83–106.

15. "The Cross and the Hammer and Sickle" and "Under the Sign of Our Time," in *Essential Writings*, 84–89, 107–115.

16. "Birth and Death," in Plekon, *Tradition Alive*, 195–202.

17. See the studies cited in note 5 above. Biographical material appears in all of these; in Nicolas Zernov and James Pain, eds., *A Bulgakov Anthology* (Philadelphia: Westminster Press, 1976), ix–27; and in Plekon, *Living Icons*, 29–58.

18. See Zernov and Pain, *A Bulgakov Anthology*, 15–21, for some of his provocative remarks on the episcopate.

19. See the concluding volume of Father Bulgakov's great trilogy on the humanity of God, dealing with eschatology and the Church: Sergei Bulgakov, *The Bride of the Lamb*, trans. Boris Jakim (Grand Rapids, Mich.: Eerdmans, 2001); see also Bulgakov, *The Orthodox Church*, trans. Lydia Kesich (Crestwood, N.Y.: St. Vladimir's Seminary Press, 1988). Most of Bulgakov's major works have been translated into French by his student Constantine Andronikof.

20. *Essential Writings*, 58–59.

21. See Sergius Bulgakov, *The Holy Grail and The Eucharist*, trans. Boris Jakim (Hudson, N.Y.: Lindisfarne Books, 1997), as well as Gallaher, "Catholic Action."

22. *Essential Writings*, 60.

23. *Against the Heresies*, 4, 7, 20.

24. See *The Bride of the Lamb*, 379–526; and *Apocatastasis and Transfiguration*, trans. Boris Jakim (New Haven, Conn.: Variable Press, 1995).

25. *Essential Writings*, 81–83.

26. Hackel, *Pearl of Great Price*, 4–5.

27. *Essential Writings*, 70–71.

28. Ibid., 177.

29. Ibid., 175–176.

30. Ibid., 176.

31. See Nadia Gorodetsky, *The Humiliated Christ in Modern Russian Thought* (London: Macmillan, 1938); Elisabeth Behr-Sigel, "The Kenotic, the Humble Christ," in *Discerning the Signs of the Times*, 29–40; Paul Evdokimov, "God's Absurd Love and the Mystery of His Silence," in *In the World, of the Church: A Paul Evdokimov Reader*, ed. and trans. Michael Plekon and Alexis Vinogradov (Crestwood, N.Y.: St. Vladimir's Seminary Press, 2001).

32. *Essential Writings*, 182–183.

33. Ibid., 154–155.

34. Ibid., 167–168.

35. Ibid., 170–171. The translators of this anthology note, "*The Feast During the Plague* is the title of a play by Alexander Pushkin (1799–1837) and it is a poem of his, 'The Prophets,' which ends: 'and sets the hearts of men on fire with your Word.'"

36. *Essential Writings*, 94.

37. Ibid., 95.

38. I have not been able to find any significant references to Mother Maria in his writings, nevertheless the strong sense of the liturgy, the Church's "mission," of being "for the life of the world," is present in the person and the efforts of Father Alexander Schmemann (1921–1983). See "Alexander Schmemann: Teacher of Freedom and Joy, in the World as Sacrament," in *Living Icons*, 178–202.

39. C. Wright Mills, *The Sociological Imagination* (New York: Grove Press, 1961).

40. Peter L. Berger, *Invitation to Sociology: A Humanistic Perspective* (New York: Doubleday, 1963).

41. *Essential Writings*, 85, 87.

42. Ibid., 89.

43. *Living Tradition* (Crestwood, N.Y.: St. Vladimir's Seminary Press, 1978), 13–26.

44. Paul Evdokimov, *The Sacrament of Love*, trans. Anthony P. Gythiel and Victoria Steadman (Crestwood, N.Y.: St. Vladimir's Seminary Press, 1985), 62.

45. See further discussion of this source in chapter 5, this volume.

46. *Essential Writings*, 143.

47. See Alexander Schmemann, *Introduction to Liturgical Theology*, trans. Ashleigh Moorhouse (Crestwood, N.Y.: St. Vladimir's Seminary Press, 1966), 19–25, as well as many passages in *The Journals of Fr. Alexander Schmemann 1973–1983*, ed. and trans. Juliana Schmemann (Crestwood, N.Y.: St. Vladimir's Seminary Press, 2000). See also part of his statement at the oral defense of this study as his doctoral dissertation in *Living Icons*, 188–189.

48. See Jean-Claude Marcadé, ed., *Un peintre d'icônes: Le père Gregoire Krug* (Paris: Institut d'Études Slaves, 2001); Fr. Barsanuphius, ed., *Le père Gregoire,*

moine iconographe du skit du Saint-Esprit, 1908–1969 (Domerac: Monastery of Korsun, 1999); and Emilie van Taack, Anne Philippenko-Bogenhardt, and B. Pardo-Zacariel, L'iconographie de l'église des Trois Saints Hiérarques et l'oeuvre de Léonide A. Ouspensky et moine Gregoire Krug (Paris: Paroisse des Trois Saints Hiérarques, 2001).

49. Though by no means a supporter of Mother Maria, one of her former chaplains, Father Cyprian Kern, wrote a provocative essay about just this loss of the prophetic, published in the collection Zhivoe predanie (Living Tradition) in 1937, "Two Models of the Pastorate: Levitical and Prophetic," translated and included in the anthology Tradition Alive, 109–120.

50. Essential Writings, 154.

51. Ibid., 160–161.

52. Ibid., 162.

53. Ibid., 163–173.

54. Ibid., 174.

55. James L. Kugel, The God of Old: Inside the Lost World of the Bible (New York: Free Press, 2003).

56. Essential Writings, 183–185.

57. Ibid., 185.

58. Michael Plekon, "Kierkegaard the Theologian: The Roots of His Theology in Works of Love," in Foundations of Kierkegaard's Vision of Community: Religion, Ethics and Politics in Kierkegaard, ed. Stephen C. Evans and George Connell, 2–17 (New York: Humanities Press, 1991).

59. Fr. Barsanuphius, ed., Icônes et fresques du père Gregoire Krug (Marcenat: Monastery of Zanamenie, 1999).

60. Valentin Asmus, "Propochoskii golos Nikity Struve i Mat' Mariia (Skobtsova)," Radonezh 17 (November 1999). Also Nikita Struve, "Novye svedeniia o poslednikh dniakh Materi Marii." and " Mat' Mariia i Otsenke Prot. V. Asmus," Vestnik Studencheskogo Russkogo Khristianskogo Dvizheniia/La Messager, 178.

61. See her The Ministry of Women in the Church, trans. Steven Bigham (Crestwood, N.Y.: St. Vladimir's Seminary Press, 1991), and with Bishop Kallistos Ware, The Ordination of Women in the Orthodox Church (Geneva: World Council of Churches, 2000) and Discerning the Signs of the Times, especially the essay on Mother Maria, 41–53.

62. See the anthologies' notes as well as Alexandre Boukharev: un théologien de l'église orthodoxe russe en dialogue avec le monde moderne (Paris: Beauchesne, 1977) and the anthology in honor of Elisabeth Behr-Sigel's ninety-sixth birthday: Toi, suis-moi: Mélanges offerts en hommage à Élisabeth Behr-Sigel (Iasi, Romania: Editura Trinitas, 2003).

63. See Evdokimov, Ages of the Spiritual Life; In the World, of the Church; and The Sacrament of Love. He is profiled in Olivier Clément, Orient-Occident: Deux Passeurs, Vladimir Lossky, Paul Evdokimov (Geneva: Labor et Fides, 1985) and in Plekon, Living Icons, 102–127.

64. Ibid., 178–260.

65. *The Sacrament of Love*, 92; Simone Weil, *Waiting for God*, trans. Emma Crau-furd (New York: Harper & Row, 1973), 98–99.

66. See *Ages of the Spiritual Life*, 77–82, 193–258, as well as "Holiness in the Tradition of the Orthodox Church," *In the World, of the Church*, 95–154.

ORIGINAL SOURCE MATERIALS

THE SECOND GOSPEL COMMANDMENT

... An absolute majority of them [daily morning and evening prayers] are addressed to God from *us* and not from *me*. ...

... What is most personal ... most intimate in an Orthodox person's life, is thoroughly pervaded by this sense of being united with everyone ... the principle of *sobornost'*,[1] characteristic of the Orthodox Church. ...

If this is so in a person's private prayer, there is no need to speak of prayer in the church. A priest cannot even celebrate the liturgy if he is alone; for that he must have at least one person who symbolizes the people. And the eucharistic mystery itself is precisely the common work of the Church, accomplished on behalf of all and for all.

... In the Orthodox Church man is not alone and his path to salvation is not solitary; he is a member of the Body of Christ, he shares the fate of his brothers in Christ, he is justified by the righteous and bears responsibility for the sins of the sinners. ... And that is not something invented by theologians and philosophers, but a precise teaching of the Gospel, brought to life through the centuries of existence of the Church's body. ...

... For the fulfillment of love for one's neighbor, Christ demanded that we lay down our soul for our friends. Here there is no sense in paraphrasing this demand and saying that it has to do not with the soul but with life. ...

Equally irrefutable is Christ's teaching about how we should deal with our neighbor, in His words about the Last Judgment [Mt 25:31–45], when man will be asked not how he saved his soul by solitary endeavor but precisely how he dealt with his neighbor, whether he visited him in prison, whether he fed him when he was hungry, comforted him—in short, whether he loved his fellow man, whether this love stood before him as an immutable commandment of Christ. And here we cannot excuse ourselves from active love, from the selfless giving of our soul for our friends.

But even if we set aside the separate and particular Gospel teachings in this regard and turn to the whole activity of Christ on earth, it is here that we find the highest degree of the laying down of one's soul for others, the highest measure of sacrificial love and self-giving that mankind has known. "For God so loved the world that He gave His only-begotten Son" [Jn 3:16], calling us, too, to the same love. There is not and there cannot be any following in the steps of Christ without taking upon ourselves a certain share, small as it may be, of participation in this sacrificial deed of love. Anyone who loves the world, anyone who lays down his soul for others, anyone who is ready, at the price of being separated from Christ, to gain salvation for his brothers—is a disciple and follower of Christ. . . .

. . . Here we cannot reason like this: Christ gave us the firm and true teaching that we meet Him in every poor and unhappy man. Let us take that into consideration and give this poor and unhappy man our love, because he only seems poor and unhappy to us, but in fact he is the King of Heaven, and with Him our gifts will not go for nothing, but will return to us a hundredfold. No, the poor and unhappy man is indeed poor and unhappy, and in him Christ is indeed present in a humiliated way, and we receive him in the name of the love of Christ, not because we will be rewarded, but because we are aflame with this sacrificial love of Christ and in it we are united with Him, with His suffering on the Cross, and we suffer not for the sake of our purification and salvation, but for the sake of this poor and unhappy man whose suffering is alleviated by ours. One cannot love sacrificially in one's own name, but only in the name of Christ, in the name of the image of God that is revealed to us in man.

A person should have a more attentive attitude toward his brother's flesh than toward his own. Christian love teaches us to give our brother not only material but also spiritual gifts. We must give him our last shirt and our last crust of bread. Here personal charity is as necessary and justified as the broadest social work. In this sense there is no doubt that the Christian is called to social work. He is called to organize a better life for the workers, to provide for the old, to build hospitals, care for children, fight against exploitation, injustice, want, lawlessness. In principle the value is completely the same, whether he acts on an individual or a social level; what matters is that his social work be based on love for his neighbor and not have any latent career or material purposes. For the rest it is always justified—from personal aid to working on a national scale, from concrete attention to an individual person to an understanding of abstract systems for the correct organization of social life. . . .

. . . In turning his spiritual world toward the spiritual world of another, a man encounters the terrible, inspiring mystery of the authentic knowledge of God, because what he encounters is not flesh and blood, not feelings and moods, but the authentic image of God in man, the very incarnate icon of God in the world, a glimmer of the mystery of the Incarnation and Godmanhood. . . . [2]

ON THE IMITATION OF THE MOTHER OF GOD

... We must be convinced that the question of an authentic and profound religious attitude toward man is precisely the meeting point of all questions of the Christian and the godless world, and that even this godless world is waiting for a word from Christianity, the only word capable of healing and restoring all, and perhaps sometimes even of raising what is dead.

If we decide responsibly and seriously to make the Gospel truth the ultimate standard for our human souls, we will have no doubts about how to act in any particular case of our lives: we should renounce everything we have, take up our cross, and follow Him. . . .

... That is the exhaustive meaning of all Christian morality. And however differently various peoples in various ages understand the meaning of this imitation, all ascetic teachings in Christianity finally boil down to it. . . .

The meaning and significance of the cross are inexhaustible. The cross of Christ is the eternal tree of life, the invincible force, the union of heaven and earth, the instrument of a shameful death. But what is the cross in our path of the imitation of Christ; how should our crosses resemble the one cross of the Son of Man? For even on Golgotha there stood not one but three crosses: the cross of the God-man and the crosses of the two thieves. Are these two crosses not symbols, as it were, of all human crosses, and does it not depend on us which one we choose? . . .

What is most essential, most determining in the image of the cross is the necessity of freely and voluntarily accepting it and taking it up. Christ freely, voluntarily took upon Himself the sins of the world, and raised them up on the cross, and thereby redeemed them and defeated hell and death. . . .

In taking the cross on his shoulders, man renounces everything— and that means that he ceases to be part of this whole natural world. . . . Natural laws not only free one from responsibility, they also deprive one of freedom. . . .

And so the Son of Man showed his brothers in the flesh a supranatural—and in this sense not a human but a God-manly—path of freedom and responsibility. He told them that the image of God in them also makes them into God-men beings and calls them to be deified, to indeed become Sons of God, freely and responsibly taking their crosses on their shoulders.

The free path to Golgotha—that is the true imitation of Christ.

... According to the Gospel, the sword is a symbol of suffering endured passively, not voluntarily chosen but inevitable—a weapon that pierces the soul. The cross of the Son of Man, accepted voluntarily, becomes a two-edged sword that pierces the soul of the Mother, not because she voluntarily chooses it, but because she cannot help suffering the sufferings of her Son.

And this two-edged sword is not uniquely and unrepeatably bound up with the destiny of the Mother of God[3] alone—it teaches all of us something and obliges us to something. To understand that, we need to feel the Mother of God's earthly path, to see all that is both exceptional and universal in it.

... She is not only the suffering Mother at the cross of her crucified Son, she is also the Queen of Heaven, "more honorable than the cherubim and more glorious beyond compare than the seraphim." Orthodox consciousness understands her, the Virgin of the tribe of Judah, the daughter of David, as the Mother of all that lives, as the living and personal incarnation of the Church, as the human Body of Christ. The veil of the Mother of God protects the world, and she is also the "moist mother earth."[4] This last image acquires new strength in connection with thoughts of the cross that becomes a two-edged sword. The earth of Golgotha with the cross set up on it, piercing it, the earth of Golgotha red with blood—is it not a mother's heart pierced by a sword? The cross of Golgotha, like a sword, pierces the soul of Mother-earth.

And if we turn away from what is revealed to us in the glorified image of the Mother of God, if we take her only in her earthly path, that is, where it is possible to speak of "imitating" her, that is quite enough to enable a Christian soul to understand some of the special possibilities opened up to it. It is precisely on this path of God-motherhood that we must seek the justification and substantiation of our hopes, and find the religious and mystical meaning of true human communion, which otherwise somehow escapes us.

And here the most important thing is to feel what the Son's Golgotha is for the Mother.

He endures His voluntary suffering on the cross—she involuntarily *co*-suffers with Him. He bears the sins of the world—she *co*llaborates with him, she *co*-participates, she *co*-feels, *co*-experiences. His flesh is crucified—she is *co*-crucified.

... On Golgotha she is the handmaid of her suffering God-Son, the handmaid of His sufferings. It is the same obedience as on the day of the Good News, the same *co*-participation in the Divine economy, but then it was the path toward the Nativity, toward *co*-participation in the angelic song: "Glory to God in the highest, and on earth peace, good will toward men" (Lk 2:14), while now it is participation in the suffering of Golgotha, the *kenosis* of God, inevitable from all eternity. . . .

There is much in this maternal suffering that we can perceive and learn today, drawing conclusions with regard to our own human suffering.

First and foremost, we see Christ's humanity, the Church of Christ, the Body of Christ, of which the Mother of God is also the Mother. . . . And if so, then what she felt in relation to her Son is as eternally alive in relation to the Church. As the Mother of Godmanhood—the Church—she is pierced even now by the suffering of this Body of Christ, the suffering of each member of this Body. In other words, all the countless crosses that mankind takes on its shoulders to follow Christ also become countless swords eternally piercing her maternal heart. She continues to *co*-participate, *co*-feel, *co*-suffer with each human soul, as then on Golgotha.

. . . She always walks with us on our own way of the cross, she is always there beside us, each of our crosses is a sword for her.

But there is another thing, no less essential. Every man is not only the image of God, the icon of the Divinity, not only a brother in the flesh of the God-man, deified by Him, and honored by His cross, and in this sense a son of the Mother of God. Every man is also the image of the Mother of God, who bears Christ in herself through the Holy Spirit. In this sense, every man deep inside is this bi-une icon of the Mother of God with the Child, the revelation of this bi-une mystery of Godmanhood. . . . In this sense we can speak of the physical participation of mankind—and therefore of every separate man—in the birth of the Son of God. But of this we can and must speak at the deepest, most mystical level of human souls. And, finally, an analysis of the verbal equation "Son of God—Son of Man" gives proof of the God-bearing of man.

Thus the human soul unites in itself two images—the image of the Son of God and the image of the Mother of God—and thereby should participate not only in the destiny of the Son, but also in her destiny. Both the Son of God and His Mother are age-old archetypes, symbols by which the soul orients itself on its religious paths. In this sense it should imitate not only Christ but also the Mother of God. This means it should accept and take up not only its freely chosen cross; it should also know the mystery of the cross that becomes a sword. First of all, the cross of the Son of Man on Golgotha should pierce every Christian soul like a sword, should be experienced by it as a co-participation, a co-suffering with Him. Besides that, it should also accept the swords of its brothers' crosses.

If a man is not only the image of God but also the image of the Mother of God, then he should also be able to see the image of God and the image of the Mother of God in every other man.... The God-motherly part of the human soul begins to see other people as its children; it adopts them for itself.... So we must also perceive God and the Son in every man. God, because he is the image and likeness of God; the Son, because as it gives birth to Christ within itself, the human soul thereby adopts the whole Body of Christ for itself, the whole of Godmanhood, and every man individually.

The first founder of the deed of love teaches us the humble acceptance of these other crosses. She calls every Christian soul to repeat tirelessly after her: "Behold the handmaid of the Lord," even to shedding one's blood, even to feeling as if a sword has pierced one's heart.

This is the measure of love, this is the limit to which the human soul should aspire. We can even say that this is the only proper relation of one person to another. Only when one's soul takes up another person's cross, his doubts, his grief, his temptations, falls, sins—only then is it possible to speak of a proper relation to another.

THE MYSTICISM OF HUMAN COMMUNION

... All the trends of social Christianity known to us are based on a certain rationalistic humanism, apply only the principle of Christian morality to "this world," and do not seek a spiritual and mystical basis for their constructions.[5]

To make social Christianity not only more Christian-like but truly Christian, it is necessary to find one more dimension for it, to bring it out of flat soulfulness and two-dimensional moralism into the depths of multidimensional spirituality....

... Worldly people are essentially separated from the world by an impenetrable wall. However much they give themselves to the joys of the world, whatever bustle they live in, there is always an impassable abyss in their consciousness: "I" and the world, which serves me, amuses me, grieves me, wearies me, and so on. The more egoistic a man is, that is, the more he belongs to the world, the more alienated he is from the authentic life of the world, the more the world is some sort of an inanimate comfort for him, or ... inanimate torture, to which his uniquely animate "I" is opposed. If he loves the world, science, art, nature, family, friends, politics, it is with what may be called lustful love—"my family," "my art," "my nature," "my politics." ... In this relation to the world there exist insuperable, high walls that separate man from man, nature, and God.

... In Christianity, where two God-given commandments—about the love of God and the love of man—should resound, we often run into the same separation from man and from the world. ...

... When hermits wove mats and fashioned clay pots, it was a job. When we peel potatoes, mend underwear, do the accounts, ride the subway, that is also a job. But when the monks of old, by way of obedience, buried the dead, looked after lepers, preached to fallen women, denounced the unrighteous life, gave alms—that was not a job. And when we act in our modern life, visiting the sick, feeding the unemployed, teaching children, keeping company with all kinds of human grief and failure, dealing with drunkards, criminals, madmen, the dejected, the gone-to-seed, with all the spiritual leprosy of our life, it is not a job and not only a tribute to obedience that has its limits within our chief endeavor—it is that very inner endeavor itself, an inseparable part of our main task. The more we go out into the world, the more we give ourselves to the world, the less we are of the world, because what is of the world does not give itself to the world.

... The great and only first founder of worldly endeavor was Christ, the Son of God, who descended into the world, became incarnate in the world, totally, entirely, without holding any reserve, as it were, for His Divinity. ...

In His worldly obedience He emptied Himself, and His emptying is the only example for our path ... when and at what moment did His example teach us about inner walls that separate us from the world? He was in the world with all His Godmanhood, not with some secondary properties. ... In the sacrament of the eucharist, Christ gave Himself, His God-man's Body, to the world, or rather, He united the world with Himself in the communion with his God-man's Body. He made it into Godmanhood. ... Christ's love does not know how to measure and divide, does not know how to spare itself. Neither did Christ teach the apostles to be sparing and cautious in love. ... Here we need only learn and draw conclusions. ...

I think that the fullest understanding of Christ's giving Himself to the world, creating the one Body of Christ, Godmanhood, is contained in the Orthodox idea of *sobornost'*.[6] And *sobornost'* is not only some abstraction, on the one hand, nor is it ... a higher reality having no inner connection with the individual human persons who constitute it: it is a higher reality because each of its members is a member of the Body of Christ, full-grown and full-fledged, because he is that "soul" which is worth the whole world. ... He is indeed the image of God, the image of

Christ, the icon of Christ. Who, after that, can differentiate the worldly from the heavenly in the human soul, who can tell where the image of God ends and the heaviness of human flesh begins! In communing with the world in the person of each individual human being, we know that we are communing with the image of God, and, contemplating that image, we touch the Archetype—we commune with God.

There is an authentic, and truly Orthodox, mysticism not only of communion with God, but also of communion with man. And communion with man in this sense is simply another form of communion with God. In communing with people we commune not only with like-minded people, friends, co-religionists, subordinates, superiors—not only, finally, with material for our exercises in obedience and love; we commune with Christ Himself, and only a peculiar materialism with regard to Christ's appearing and abiding in the world can explain our inability to meet Him within the bustle, in the very depth of the human fall. . . . He foresaw our rationalistic and proud lack of faith when He prophesied that, to his accusation, people would ask in perplexity: "Lord, when did we not visit you in the hospital or in prison, when did we refuse you a cup of water?" If they could believe that in every beggar and in every criminal Christ Himself addresses us, they would treat people differently. . . .

And it seems to me that this mysticism of human communion is the only authentic basis for any external Christian activity, for social Christianity, which in this sense has not been born yet. . . . Everything in the world can be Christian, but only if it is pervaded by the authentic awe of communion with God, which is also possible on the path of authentic communion with man. But outside this chief thing, there is no authentic Christianity.

THE CROSS AND THE HAMMER-AND-SICKLE

. . . The world now needs, and needs urgently, an authentic idea of the hammer and the sickle purified of communist perversion.[7] What's more, not only the world but also the cross needs that this authentic idea of the hammer and sickle be realized. . . .

. . . Only in Christ's name can we do the one thing that needs to be done to the world—lead it out of the dead end of contemporary godless fruitlessness and giftlessness. By the name of Christ, by the cross of Christ, the hammer-and-sickle can be given their authentic meaning; by the cross labor can be sanctified and blessed. . . .

Christ is freedom: the face of Christ is the affirmation in every person of his own free and God-like face; the Church is a free and organic union of the faithful with Christ, with Christ's freedom; and Christ calls those who labor and are heavy laden to take up His burden, which is light because it is taken up freely. Thus Christ and coercion are incompatible. . . .

How easy and simple it is to prove with very convincing arguments the possibility of free labor and of the free construction of society on the principle of labor! In fact, mankind has enough experience of the two opposite systems of coercion and violence. The old coercion of the capitalist regime, which destroys the right to life and leaves one only with the right to labor, has recently begun to deprive people of that right as well. Forced crisis, forced unemployment, forced labor, joyless and with no inner justification—enough of all that. But try going to the opposite system. It turns out to be the system of communist enforcement: the same joyless labor under the rod, well-organized slavery, violence, hunger—enough of that, too. It is clear to everybody that we must seek a path to free, purposeful, and expedient labor, that we must take the world as a sort of garden that it is incumbent upon us to cultivate. Who doubts that?

Christ, in giving us His free path and His freely chosen burden, thereby confirmed, as it were, the possibility of a belief in human freedom and in the divine dignity of the human face.

. . . Do we believe in that freedom? Do we believe in that dignity? Not only in someone else, but in ourselves, each in himself? . . .

What am I talking about? About the most terrible thing that exists in earthly life, in the historical process, in the throbbing of modernity: that no one, no one wants in a voluntary and friendly, free and brotherly fashion to build an authentic, laboring, free, and loving Christian life. If they do build, they build something different, and if there is something that is not different, it is not in the building of life, but always in words and theories, sometimes quite remarkable, but only words and theories.

As a pianist or singer must play or sing the simplest scales every day as exercise [and otherwise will be unable to do anything complicated], as a craftsman needs certain muscular habits, as a wrestler needs training—so in the Christian deed of transfiguring the world a small everyday life should be freely created.

Why speak of the brotherhood of the people, if we do not live with our roommate in brotherly fashion?

Why speak of freedom, if we are unable to freely combine our creative efforts?

Why speak of a Christian attitude toward labor, if we work under the rod or do not work at all?

Free laboring—that is the basis of our path in Christ. And this basis should pervade our everyday and routine life. . . .

. . . Our efforts should make of every common deed a sort of monastery, a sort of spiritual organism, a sort of minor order, a sort of brother-hood. . . .

Great is the joy of those who do not doubt that free laboring can be realized in people's lives. And woe to those who shake that faith.

TOWARDS A NEW MONASTICISM

One often hears mention of "the new monasticism."[8] Some people endow these words with a positive meaning: it's about time, they say. Others think that "new monasticism" means all but "no monasticism," and that there is a lie and a temptation hidden here. And yet I do think that even granted this negative attitude, everyone understands that the new monasticism is something that really exists.

. . . But there are other ways for the "new" to emerge.

For instance, there existed an ancient tradition, based on a Gospel text, of standing in church at the Palm Sunday vigil holding palm branches. This tradition was observed in Byzantium, and that without any difficulty, since it was easy for them to find palm branches. But imagine a Palm Sunday vigil in Moscow or even in Kiev. Where will they get palm branches? The tradition has to be changed. People start cutting pussywillow branches.[9] Probably warily at first, afraid of leading people into temptation—it's a matter of a clear deviation from the Gospel text. Later nothing was left of the temptation, the new thing became a tradition, and so much so that many would probably be tempted now if they were offered fir or birch branches instead of pussywillows. Now there are probably Russian people in Africa, where palm branches are easily obtained, who think: "How's that? 'Pussywillow Sunday' without pussywillows?" In the same way, probably, Byzantine dried figs and olives during the Great Lent were replaced in the Russian north by pickled cabbage. No Greek Typikon[10] makes any mention of this pickled cabbage, but imagine Russian lenten tradition without it! These are all little everyday things, you may say. Let them be little; they show the essence of the matter more easily, because the same things happen on a serious level as well.

There is thus a "new" that is not invented by the idle human mind, but that follows inevitably from the conditions of life. Every attempt to preserve the old on such occasions is either impossible (like palm branches in the north), or does not correspond to the spirit of the old tradition: in Constantinople the simplest food was olives, and so they were prescribed during Lent, while in Moscow an insistence on olives would not be the simplest thing—olives are a rarity there, a delicacy. The simple thing would be cabbage. . . .

It is undoubtedly not monasticism but only the monastic life that has been going through a crisis for a long time now, perhaps more than a century. . . .

. . . The old tradition (now corresponding infinitely less to the needs of life) was still being lived out, though no directive for it came from the surrounding life. . . . A tradition remains, if it does remain, only as such, as a certain petrified rite, whose performers gradually forget the reason for it. Even with the sharpest hatred of novelty and the most ardent striving to preserve the old, it is simply physically impossible to remain outside the new conditions. There are only two possible attitudes toward them, as it actually happens: either to deny the new needs of the time without understanding them—as purposeless, unthinking, unwitting innovations—or, taking this new life into consideration, to innovate according to a plan, in a creative way—more than that, to innovate so as to create a new tradition. In this alone lies the difference between contemporary traditionalists and innovators.

Traditionalists, having no physical possibility of preserving the old, also do not create a new life. Innovators, not trying to preserve the unpreservable, organically create a new life and a new tradition. Thus the roles here are essentially changed.

What are the new conditions of life to which this slowly created future tradition should correspond?

. . . We can put it like this: innovation is determined by the fact that the modern monk, *whether he likes it or not*, finds himself not behind strong monastery walls, within defined, ossified traditions, but on all the roads and crossroads of the world, with no opportunity of orienting himself by old traditions, with no hint of new traditions. And woe to him who dislikes these worldly roads and crossroads: he will neither preserve the old, nor create the new. In other words: today's monasticism must fight for its very core, for its very soul, disregarding all external forms, creating new forms.

Let us imagine a person who not only strives toward the core, toward the soul of monasticism, but who also does not want to embody his monasticism in the forms of the old tradition. . . . There is no monastery, no skete, no seclusion. Instead, there are the wide roads of life, a parish, maybe even in some backwater, and in the parish all the pains, all the wounds, all the sins of life, with drunkenness, depravity, thoughts of suicide. And, on the other hand, there is the longing for a little material well-being, there is competition, there is peaceful and quiet "everyday" godlessness—all that he saw in the world and that he wanted to leave behind, and did not leave behind, because he had *nowhere to go.* Nowhere, because as a monk he is not needed, or perhaps monasticism is not needed?

Absolutely wrong. He is both needed and not needed, precisely he, as a monk, because monasticism in general is needed, but it is needed mainly on the roads of life, in the very thick of it. Today there is only one monastery for a monk—the whole world. This he must inevitably understand very soon, and in this lies the force of his *innovation.* Here many must become innovators against their will. This is the meaning, the cause, and the justification of the new monasticism!

The new here is not characterized mainly by its newness, but by its being *inevitable.* . . .

. . . It would be incorrect to think that monasticism cannot exist outside this historical framework, and that we are now called at all costs to recreate what existed earlier—and, if the life conditions for it are not there, to create at least an external stage set, to restore the historically accurate costumes, so to speak, of the old monasticism.

Monasticism is determined not by a way of life, not by the monastery, not by the desert; monasticism is determined by the vows made during the rite of tonsuring. The rest is a historical covering, which can and must change, and which has only relative value: it is valuable as long as it contributes to the fulfillment of the vows.

[These vows are three:] obedience, chastity, and nonpossession. . . .

The vow of chastity has always been understood with perfect clarity, and historical conditions, of course, cannot introduce any changes in it. . . .

. . . The vow of nonpossession, meanwhile, was simplified to an elementary renunciation of the love of money or, at best, of one's own material property. . . .

Obedience as such remains unchanged, but its meaning becomes different. A monk should be obedient to the work of the Church to which he is assigned; he should give his will and all his creative powers entirely to this work. Obedience becomes service. . . . The Church herself becomes his *starets,* and also judges him, while the obedience requested is the responsible fulfillment of what the Church has charged him to do.

Is this an innovation? Perhaps so, but here life itself is the innovator. It does not ask us whether we want to understand the vow of obedience we have made in this or some other way. It tells us that in contemporary conditions it cannot be understood in any other way. . . .

The question here is simple: we need not to restore the old but to try responsibly to accept the new, to comprehend it, to make out precisely what it demands of us.

And, finally, the third vow: nonpossession . . . is in need of greater comprehension and deepening.

. . . It cannot be limited to a material understanding. . . .

. . . The principle of nonpossession can be expressed in any relationship. The subtler the egocentrism, the higher the limits of the human spirit it reaches, the more repulsive it is. . . .

Poverty of spirit is not, of course, the renunciation of any intellectual interests; it is not a sort of spiritual idiocy. It is the renunciation of one's spiritual exclusiveness, it is the giving of one's spirit to the service of God's work on earth, and it is the only path for common life in the one *sobornal* organism of the Church.

A monk should find the strength in himself to say together with Christ: "Into thy hands I commend my spirit" (Lk 23:46). He should consciously want to become the fulfiller of God's work on earth—and nothing else. He should be a conductor of divine love and a co-participant in divine sacrifice.

Nonpossession should not be merely passive—they don't ask, so I don't give. Nonpossession should be active: a monk should seek where to place the gifts given him by God precisely for that end.

It goes without saying that this point of view implies the necessity of monastic activity in the outside world. But it should be remembered that all its forms—social work, charity, spiritual aid—are the result of an intense desire to give one's strength to the activity of Christ, to the humanity of Christ, not to possess but to spend it for the glory of God.

It seems to me that this new understanding of the vow of nonpossession should determine the path of the modern monk. In practice, he may acquire some new and unaccustomed appearance because of it, but that is an external thing. In reality, he will stand on the foundation of the ancient vows that determine the very essence of his monastic effort.

THE POOR IN SPIRIT

. . . We know that Christ taught us to lay down our soul for our friends. This laying down of the soul, this giving of oneself, is what makes a person poor in spirit. It is the opposite in everyday life; even with the most negative attitude toward material possession, we are used to regarding the spiritual holding back of ourselves as something positive. . . .

Christ did not know measure in His love for people. And in this love He reduced His Divinity to the point of incarnation and took upon Himself the suffering of the universe. In this sense His example teaches us not measure in love but the absolute and boundless giving of ourselves, determined by the laying down of our soul for our friends.

Without striving for such giving of oneself, there is no following the path of Christ.

... People's care for their spiritual peace, their locking themselves away, leads before our eyes to self-poisoning, demoralization, loss of joy; they become unbearable to themselves, turn neurasthenic. In a most paradoxical way, they become poor from holding on to themselves, because their eternal self-attention and self-admiration transform them. The poor hold on to their rags and do not know that the only way not only to preserve them but also to make them precious is to give them with joy and love to those who need them.

And why?

These rags are the corruptible riches of the kingdom of this world. By giving them away, by giving himself away entirely, with his whole inner world, laying down his soul, a man becomes poor in spirit, one of the blessed, because his is the Kingdom of Heaven, according to our Savior's promise, because he becomes the owner of the incorruptible and eternal riches of that Kingdom, becomes it at once, here on earth, acquiring the joy of unmeasured, self-giving, and sacrificial love, the lightness and freedom of nonpossession.

... We know that in the time of the Russian civil war, choice implied death, imprisonment, exile, the total crippling of one's life.... And still more we know what it means to confess one's faith where it is persecuted, where the whole force of the state is raised against it... how people would be deprived of their crust of bread for the baptismal cross on their neck, how they would be sent to the camps for a book of religious content, and so on.

Now we've become émigrés. What does that mean? First of all it means freedom....

... We should understand the providential meaning of the freedom given us. We must receive it as a weighty gift, and not only relate to it externally, but let it penetrate to the very depths of our spirit, rethink and test in its light all our usual and habitual opinions and bases....

... While we have lost our earthly motherland, we have not lost our heavenly motherland, that the Church is with us, in our midst—the whole Orthodox Church in her entirety, not divided into any sub-churches ....

Let us look at the Church's work from the point of view of our freedom.... Not long ago I happened to speak on this subject in a certain magazine. My article provoked a response that came as a total surprise to me. The mere observation of the fact of our extraordinary freedom, compared with the situation of the Church in all the time of her existence, made certain people suppose for some reason that I consider only the life of our émigré Church authentic, and that I throw away, cross out, count as nothing the two thousand years of Church history. Beyond that, the conclusion was drawn that I deny the righteousness and holiness of the Church in the time of her state captivity. It is hard to refute such arbitrary and totally unfounded conclusions drawn from one's own precise words. Perhaps the thing to do is not refute them, but simply repeat the same thoughts in different words until they finally become comprehensible. The history of the Church in all times contains pages devoted to authentic holiness. Privation of freedom in no case diminishes the possibility of holiness; what's more, it may be precisely in periods of the maximum privation of freedom that the most obvious, most unquestionable holiness blossoms. . . .

But the Church's destiny need not only be considered from the point of view of the increase of holiness. . . . And no one who says that the Church was not free is thereby saying that there was no holiness in her, or that she was torn apart by heresies, or anything else except one thing—that she was not free. . . .

Freedom obliges, freedom calls for sacrificial self-giving, freedom determines one's honesty and strictness with oneself and one's path. And if we want to be strict and honest, worthy of the freedom given us, we must first of all test our own attitude toward our spiritual world. We have no right to wax tenderhearted over all our past indiscriminately—much of that past is far loftier and purer than we are, but much of it is sinful and criminal. . . . We cannot stylize everything as some sweet ringing of Moscow bells—religion dies of stylization. We cannot cultivate dead customs—only authentic spiritual fire has weight in religious life. We cannot freeze a living soul with rules and orders—once, in their own time, they were the expression of other living souls, but new souls demand a corresponding expression. We cannot see the Church as a sort of aesthetic perfection and limit ourselves to aesthetic swooning—our God-given freedom calls us to activity and struggle. And it would be a great lie to tell searching souls: "Go to church, because there you will find peace." The opposite is true. She tells those who are at peace and asleep: "Go to church, because there you will feel real alarm about your sins, about your perdition, about the world's sins and perdition. There you will feel an unappeasable hunger for Christ's truth. There, instead of lukewarm you will become ardent, instead of pacified you will become alarmed, instead of learning the wisdom of this world you will become foolish in Christ."

It is to this foolishness, this folly in Christ that our freedom calls us. Freedom calls us, contrary to the whole world, contrary not only to the pagans but to many who style themselves Christians, to undertake the Church's work in what is precisely the most difficult way.

And we will become fools in Christ, because we know not only the difficulty of this path but also the immense happiness of feeling God's hand upon what we do.[11]

A JUSTIFICATION OF PHARASAISM

Long ages go by when the scribes, doctors of the law, and pharisees safeguard the law bequeathed them by their fathers, when everything is calm in this eternal, universal Israel, the prophets are silent, sacrifices are offered in the temple, the pharisee beats his breast and thanks God that he is not like this publican.[12] Then fire breaks out in the world. Again and again comes the Forerunner's call to repentance, again and again settled life is broken up, and the fishermen abandon their nets, and people leave their dead unburied to follow Him. And the eternal prophecy is fulfilled: the house is left empty, the sun goes out, the earth is shattered—and man has no refuge.

Golgotha grows, becomes the whole world. There is nothing left but the Cross.

Amidst the people of God . . . the guardians of their truth, of their election, the keepers of the law, of every letter of the law, the scribes, the doctors of the law, the pharisees towered up like sturdy oaks, like invincible fortresses. Man betrays, but the law will not betray. Man's soul is perverse, but the letter is fixed. And therefore the letter is higher than the soul, the sabbath is higher than man.

. . . These are the rules for the whole nation; these are also the commandments for each separate human soul. Fulfill what is written, offer the prescribed sacrifice, give to the temple what you ought to give. Keep the fasts. Do not defile yourself by communing with the unclean—and you will get your reward, or if not you then your son will get it, but you already have it, too, because you have observed the law, every letter of it, because you are righteous, because you are not like this publican.

No doubt everyone feels this stiff-necked pharisaic truth, and can make no objection to it before the time comes. And no doubt even the contemporary human soul, every human soul, passes through this pharisaic truth, through the parched and fruitless desert of waiting, perhaps saving a last sip of water: I won't drink it, because there will be no new water.

Yes, in the desert of the spirit, in a time of terrible spiritual drought, the pharisee is justified; he alone is reasonable and thrifty, watchful and sober.

And it is not for the spendthrift, not for the one who, in the time of the great exodus, stuffs himself with manna and game, and drinks too much pure water, and dances before golden calves—it is not for him to denounce the stern thriftiness of the doctor of the law, who fasts even amidst universal famine and fulfills everything as he should. He will preserve the tables of the Covenant in the tabernacle; he will lead the souls of the people into the promised land.

How many times does the stern guardian of traditions and laws in each of our souls curse the unfaithful crowd of seducers, the violators of the law! The struggle goes on in each of us for the purity of the prescribed, for the Typikon,[13] for the letter of the law, for that which is connected with what is to come—only what is to come—the not yet incarnate promise.

When prophecy is silent in us, when our spirit is not molten, who will keep it from being dispersed and wasted if not the guardian of the law, who always stands on watch. He, too, is justified in our soul.

... There is something that displaces these laws of the natural world, that annihilates all the righteousness of the pharisees and all the faithfulness of the doctors of the law and all the wisdom of the scribes. And this something is fire.

Fire came down into the world. The word of God became flesh. God became man. Not for nothing and not by chance was this wonder, this fulfillment of the promised and the looked-for, opposed precisely by those who were guardians of the promised, looked-for covenant. A struggle began between the doctors of the law and that which was higher than the law of the sabbath, with the Son of Man. He who ate and drank with publicans and sinners, He who healed on the sabbath, He who spoke of rebuilding the destroyed temple in three days—was He not bound to appear to them as the most terrible violator of the prescribed, of the traditional, of the habitually saving? And they rose against Him in the name of their age-old truth. ...

Fire came down into the world. Human hearts melted. The cross of Golgotha stood on the path of the Resurrection. It would seem that those who crucified Him, those who betrayed Him, remained on the other side, in the old, decrepit, yielding, and receding covenant. And on this side, with Him, remained those of the new covenant, the fiery ones, who took the cross on their shoulders, sanctified and transfigured by the mystery of the Resurrection—forever, until the end of the world, the members of His Church, which Hell cannot prevail against, participants in eternal life here in their earthly days.

But in fact Christianity preserved all the forces that were active in the Old Testament. The same stiff-necked, indifferent, inconstant crowd, the same guardians of the law (now His new law), Christian scribes, pharisees, doctors of the law—and also the same prophets to be stoned, the same holy fools, bearers of grace who do not fit into the framework of the law, lawless for those who are under the law.

Properly speaking, the entire history of Christianity is the history of the extinguishing and new igniting of the fire. History develops that way in each separate soul, and it has developed that way in the world. We know the coldness and deadness of whole epochs of Christianity, we know the flaring up and spreading of the flames of authentic Christian evangelization, we know how scribes and pharisees alternate with the initiators of new paths, and their time with broad waves of suffering, asceticism, witness, repentance, and purification.

And once again we must say in all fairness that the role of the pharisees in Christianity is not exhausted only with the extinguishing of the fire, the freezing and killing of all that is alive and ardent. They do actually and authentically watch over, keep, preserve, and bear the coffer of Christian treasures through the narrow passes of dead and self-satisfied epochs. . . . They faithfully defend Christianity against the paganism that abides eternally in the world, against the cult of petty passions, prejudices, the cult of various idols, calves made of various metals—the iron calf of state power, the golden calf of economic prosperity, and so on.

But along with that they try to protect the Church against authentic Christian fervor, against all fire in general; they only preserve what is sacred to them and keep others from being nourished by it. The evaluation of pharisaism's significance and usefulness for the Church depends largely on the epoch in which the pharisees live. That evaluation therefore varies greatly and is subject to very marked fluctuations.

We stand now at the beginning of a new epoch in the Church. Much in its character is already clear. From this clarity we may judge what the Church needs at the given moment, what will contribute to her growth and ardor, and what, on the contrary, is harmful for her.

. . . This gives us the possibility of seeing what new things the Church now demands of us and what we must now free ourselves from so as not to harm her with what is old and even antiquated.

INSIGHT IN WARTIME

. . . War.

Do we accept it? Do we not accept it? Is war heroic? Is war organized crime? Is a warrior a martyr, a "passion-bearer"? Was the warrior in ancient times denied communion? Are there wars that are just, that are almost righteous? So many questions, questions which show all the contradictoriness in the very nature of war. . . .[14]

I think that, in our notions of war, the definitions of attacking and defending sides are not sufficiently detailed. These notions are put in place at the beginning of a conflict with the aim of using them at the end for diplomatic, political, and economic purposes. But in fact the real moral or even religious distinction has not been made. If a robber breaks into a house and the one who lives in it defends himself, then later on, when the trial takes place, regardless of whether or not the robber carried out his crime, or even if the attacked one overcame him, it is still the robber who will be in the dock. And it is not that, while the robber was actually the first to attack, everything then became confused in the general fight, and it no longer even matters who began it, but what matters is who won. . . .

I think that Christian consciousness can never be guided by the motivation of the robber; that is, to take an aggressive part in war is never acceptable for it. Much more complicated is the question of enduring war, of passive participation, of war in defense. And here I am approaching the main thing that defines the Christian attitude toward war. The strength is not in war, but in what is beyond it.

There is something in war that makes people listen—not all, but many—and suddenly, amidst the roar of cannons, the rattle of machine guns, the groaning of the wounded, they hear something else, they hear the distant, warning trumpet of the archangel.

There is also, in a sense, a more terrible phenomenon, which cannot be accounted for by statistics: it is the brutalization of nations, the lowering of the cultural level, the loss of creative ability—the decadence of souls. Every war throws the whole of mankind back. . . .

The war demands of us, more than ever, that we mobilize absolutely all our spiritual powers and abilities. . . . In our time Christ and the life-giving Holy Spirit demand the whole person. The only difference from state mobilization is that the state enforces mobilization, while our faith waits for volunteers. And, in my view, the destiny of mankind depends on whether these volunteers exist and, if they do, how great their energy is, how ready they are for sacrifice.

And, finally . . . I know with all my being, with all my faith, with all the spiritual force granted to the human soul, that at this moment God is visiting His world. And the world can receive that visit, open its heart— "ready, ready is my heart"—and then in an instant our temporary and fallen life will unite with the depths of eternity, then our human cross will become the likeness of the God-man's cross, then within our deathly affliction itself we will see the white garments of the angel who will announce to us: "He who was dead is no longer in the tomb." Then mankind will enter into the paschal joy of the Resurrection.

Or else . . . Maybe it will not even be worse than before, but merely the same as before. Once again—and how often has it been?—we will have fallen, we will not have accepted, we will not have found the path to transfiguration.

TYPES OF RELIGIOUS LIFE

I will now move on to characterize the evangelical type of spiritual life, which is as eternal as is the proclamation of the Good News, always alive within the bosom of the Church, shining for us in the faces of saints and at times lighting with the reflection of its fire even righteous people outside the Church. . . [15]

Christ gave us two commandments: to love God and to love our fellow man. Everything else, even the commandments contained in the Beatitudes, is merely an elaboration of these two commandments, which contain within themselves the totality of Christ's "Good News." Furthermore, Christ's earthly life is nothing other than the revelation of the mystery of love of God and love of man. These are, in sum, not only the true but the only measure of all things. And it is remarkable that their truth is found only in their conjunction. Love for man alone leads us into the blind alley of an anti-Christian humanism, out of which the only exit is, at times, the rejection of the individual human being and love for him in the name of all mankind. Love for God without love for human beings, however, is condemned: "You hypocrite, how can you love God whom you have not seen, if you hate your brother whom you have seen" (1 Jn. 4:20). Their conjunction is not simply a conjunction of two great truths taken from two spiritual worlds. It is the conjunction of two parts of a single whole.

. . . In fact, if you take away love for man then you destroy man (because by not loving him you reject him, you reduce him to nonbeing) and no longer have a path toward the knowledge of God. God then becomes truly apophatic, having only negative attributes, and even these can be expressed only in the human language that you have rejected. God becomes inaccessible to your human soul because, in rejecting man, you have also rejected humanity, you have also rejected what is human in your own soul, though your humanity was the image of God within you and your only way to see the Prototype as well. This is to say nothing of the fact that a human being taught you in his own human language, describing God's truth in human words, nor of the fact that God reveals Himself through human concepts. By not loving, by not having contact with humanity we condemn ourselves to a kind of a deaf-mute blindness with respect to the divine as well. In this sense, not only did the Logos-Word-Son of God assume human nature to complete His work of redemption and by this sanctified it once and for all, destining it for deification, but the Word of God, as the "Good News," as the Gospel, as revelation and enlightenment likewise needed to become incarnate in the flesh of insignificant human words. For it is with words that people express their feelings, their doubts, their thoughts, their good deeds and their sins. . . .

On the other hand, one cannot truly love man without loving God. As a matter of fact, what can we love in a man if we do not discern God's image in him? Without that image, on what is such love based? It becomes some kind of peculiar, monstrous, towering egoism in which every "other" becomes only a particular facet of my own self. I love that in the other which is compatible with me, which enriches me, which explains me—and at times simply entertains and charms me. If, however, this is not the case, if indeed there is desire for a selfless but nonreligious love for man, then it will move inevitably from a specific person of flesh and blood and turn toward the abstract man, toward humanity, even to the idea of humanity, and will almost always result in the sacrifice of the concrete individual upon the altar of this abstract idea—the common good, an earthly paradise, etc.

In this world there are two kinds of love: one that takes and one that gives. This is common to all types of love—not only love for man. One can love a friend, one's family, children, scholarship, art, the motherland, one's own ideas, oneself—and even God—from either of these two points of view. Even those forms of love that by common consent are the highest can exhibit this dual character.

What was Christ's love like? Did it withhold anything? . . . Christ's divinity was incarnate fully and to the end in his spit-upon, battered, humiliated, and crucified humanity. The cross—an instrument of shameful death—has become for the world a symbol of self-denying love. . . .

We are not speaking here about good deeds, nor about that love which measures and parcels out its various possibilities, which gives away the interest but keeps hold of the capital. Here we are speaking about a genuine emptying, in partial imitation of Christ's self-emptying when He became incarnate in mankind. In the same way we must empty ourselves completely, becoming incarnate, so to speak, in another human soul, offering to it the full strength of the divine image which is contained within ourselves.

... There is not, nor can there be, any doubt but that in giving ourselves to another in love—to the poor, the sick, the prisoner—we will encounter in that person Christ Himself, face to face. He told us about this Himself when He spoke of the Last Judgment: how He will call some to eternal life because they showed Him love in the person of each unfortunate and miserable individual, while others He will send away from Himself because their hearts were without love, because they did not help Him in the person of his suffering human brethren in whom He revealed Himself to them. If we harbor doubts about this on the basis of our unsuccessful everyday experience, then we ourselves are the only reason for these doubts: our loveless hearts, our stingy souls, our ineffective will, our lack of faith in Christ's help. One must really be a fool for Christ in order to travel this path to its end—and at its end, again and again, encounter Christ. ...

And this, I believe, is the evangelical way of piety. It would be incorrect, however, to think that this has been revealed to us once and for all in the four Gospels and clarified in the Epistles. It is continually being revealed and is a constant presence in the world. It is also continually being accomplished in the world, and the form of its accomplishment is the Eucharist, the Church's most valuable treasure, its primary activity in the world. The Eucharist is the mystery of sacrificial love. Therein lies its whole meaning, all its symbolism, all its power. ... Again and again the sins of the world are raised by Him upon the cross. And He gives Himself—his Body and Blood—for the salvation of the world. By offering Himself as food for the world, by giving to the world communion in His Body and Blood, Christ not only saves the world by His sacrifice, but makes each person a "christ," and unites him to His own self-sacrificing love for the world. He takes flesh from the world, He deifies this human flesh, He gives it up for the salvation of the world and then unites the world again to this sacrificed flesh—both for its salvation and for its participation in this sacrificial offering. ... He raises the world as well upon the cross, making it a participant in His death and in His glory.

... The Eucharist here is the Gospel in action ... the eternally existing and eternally accomplished sacrifice of Christ and of Christlike human beings for the sins of the world. ... The Eucharist is true communion with the divine. And is it not strange that in it the path to communion with the divine is so closely bound up with our communion with each other? It assumes consent to the exclamation: "Let us love one another, that with one mind we may confess Father, Son, and Holy Spirit: the Trinity, one in essence and undivided."

The Eucharist needs the flesh of this world as the "matter" of the mystery. It reveals to us Christ's sacrifice as a sacrifice on behalf of mankind, that is, as His union with mankind. It makes us into "christs," repeating again and again the great mystery of God meeting man, again and again making God incarnate in human flesh. And all this is accomplished in the name of sacrificial love for mankind.

. . . It is possible to speak of the whole of Christianity as an eternal offering of the divine liturgy beyond church walls. . . . It means that we must offer the bloodless sacrifice, the sacrifice of self-surrendering love not only in a specific place, upon the altar of a particular temple; the whole world becomes the single altar of a single temple, and for this universal Liturgy we must offer our hearts, like bread and wine, in order that they may be transformed into Christ's love, that He may be born in them, that they may become "God-manly" hearts, and that He may give these hearts of ours as food for the world, that He may bring the whole world into communion with these hearts of ours that have been offered up, so that in this way we may be one with Him, not so that we should live anew but so that Christ should live in us. . . . Then truly in all ways Christ will be in all.[16]

NOTES

1. [*Sobornost'* is derived from the Russian word *sobor*, "council," which also became the word for "cathedral." It means "conciliarity" or "catholicity," the coming together of many to form a whole, a communion among free persons.]

2. [Translators' note:] Soloviev coined this description of the Incarnation, God's taking on humanity (*Bogocheloveschestvo*), and it has been commonly translated as "Godmanhood." Paul Valliere has argued that a better rendering is "the humanity of God" (*Modern Russian Theology* [Grand Rapids, Mich.: Eerdmans, 2001]). Nevertheless the more familiar expression is used here.

3. [The Mother of God is the image of our suffering with our neighbor in love. We learn more about how to give of ourselves and to love the neighbor from this essay.]

4. [Translator's note:] *Mat' syra zemlia*, literally "mother moist earth" in Russian, is a name given to the bountiful, nourishing earth in Russian folk tales. It was sometimes extended in the folk imagination to the Virgin Mary. An old peasant woman in Dostoevsky's *Demons*, when asked who the Mother of God is, replies: "The Mother of God is our great mother the moist earth, and therein lies a great joy for man."

5. [There is only one basis for loving the neighbor, for Christian social work in the world: teaching, providing shelter, food, clothing, medical care and other necessities. It is God's love for us and God's desire that we love God in return—in the sister or brother, the neighbor before us.]

6. [See note 2.]

7. [Mother Maria reflects on the deeper meaning of revolution. She never lost her revolutionary fervor. She found once more its real source: the freedom of Christ and his gospel.]

8. [Metropolitan Evlogy said Mother Maria's monastery would be in the desert of suffering people's hearts. Her following the gospel would not be in the traditional monasteries of the past but in the heart of the world, in the center of the city. And this is precisely where she lived out her monastic profession, at several different locations in Paris and its suburbs. In this essay she examines what this means.]

9. [Translator's note:] Russians traditionally use pussywillow branches in place of palms on Palm Sunday, which is popularly known as "Pussywillow Sunday." In Europe, boxwood branches are commonly used.

10. [Translator's note:] The Typikon is the collection of rules and canons governing the liturgical and ascetic life of the Church.

11. [Mother Maria cared for all kinds of needy people in her hostels, many being refugees, émigrés like herself, uprooted by a brutal revolution in Russia. Mother Maria nevertheless recognized God's hand in this as the gift of freedom as the following passages indicate.]

12. [This essay is a debate on the past and the present Church and world.]

13. [See note 10.]

14. [Mother Maria deals with many aspects of armed conflict. Preemptive or unilateral attack is unequivocally condemned by Christianity in her view. But in our time, the individual Christian or even the churches and other faith traditions often cannot stop states from war. Then spiritual mobilization is essential.]

15. [Mother Maria evaluates forms of piety in the recent history of her own Russian Church. While culturally specific and very particularly Orthodox, nonetheless those of other traditions can find the analogies to their own pieties. These selections are from the last form, for her that which most authentically conforms to the New Testament and Christ's preaching, what she called "evangelical" or Gospel Christianity.]

16. [All selections in this chapter come from *Mother Maria Skobtsova: Essential Writings*, trans. Richard Revear and Larissa Volokhonsky (Maryknoll, N.Y.: Orbis Books, 2003), 46, 47–49, 54, 57, 62, 63, 64–65, 67, 68, 69–70, 71, 75–76, 77–80, 82, 85, 86, 87, 88, 89, 91–95, 97–98, 100–101, 102–103, 105–106, 108–109, 112, 113–115, 117, 121–124, 135–137, 138, 139, 173, 175–177, 179, 183–185.]

[CHAPTER 5]

Dumitru Stăniloae (1903–1993)

COMMENTARY

LUCIAN TURCESCU

The youngest of five children, Dumitru Stăniloae was born on November 16, 1903, in the village of Vladeni in Transylvania, then a region of the Austro-Hungarian Empire, absorbed into Romania at the end of World War I. Partly because of his rural upbringing, partly because of Romanian intellectual and cultural movements that exalted the peasant, Stăniloae loved peasant culture and reflected it in his writings. Stăniloae's parents were both devout Orthodox Christians; his father was a church chanter. Both parents exerted a lasting influence on him and on his choice of an ecclesiastical and theological career.

From 1922 to 1927, Stăniloae studied theology at the Faculty of Theology in Cernauti, now in the Ukraine, receiving some financial support from Nicolae Balan, Orthodox Metropolitan of Transylvania (1920–55). Several of his professors in Cernauti were locally prominent theologians. Dumitru, however, did not like the Westernized style of academic theology that prevailed throughout the Orthodox world at the time, with its characteristic scholasticism and nineteenth-century religious rationalism. In 1927, he went to Athens for a few months of research, again with the financial support of Metropolitan Balan.

In 1928, Stăniloae returned to Cernauti and hastily completed and defended a very brief doctoral dissertation in church history entitled "The Life and Work of Patriarch Dositheos of Jerusalem and his Relations with the Romanian Lands." In this work, he presented the Romanian lands as a meeting place between the Greek and Slav worlds, and as a guardian of the Byzantine heritage. He has also emphasized his country's special position within the world as the only predominantly Orthodox country that used Latin.

For another full year after obtaining his doctorate in theology, Stăniloae traveled to Munich, Berlin, and Paris for additional study and research. He was drawn especially to the dialogical theology of Martin Buber and the French personalists, as well as the theology of Gregory Palamas (1296–1359), the main promoter of Hesychasm, a doctrine and practice of prayer of the heart and contemplation of God. These were formative experiences for Stăniloae's later development of a deeply personalistic theology that wove together, in a creative and rather coherent whole, modern personalism, patristic views, Hesychasm, and Orthodox spirituality.

In September 1929, Stăniloae started teaching theology. He first taught at the Theological Academy in the Transylvanian city of Sibiu (1929–46) and served as rector there (1936–46). He then taught at the Faculty of Orthodox Theology in Romania's capital, Bucharest (1947–58, 1965–73). Shortly after being appointed to teach in Sibiu, he married and was ordained as a priest in the Romanian Orthodox Church. He and his wife had three children. Two of his children died at a young age. The surviving daughter, Lidia, a Romanian-language writer and poet, lives in Germany today with her son Dumitras.

While continuing to teach dogmatic, apologetic, and pastoral theology, Stăniloae embarked on an extensive program of research, translation, and publication. In 1930, he published a Romanian translation of the then standard Greek textbook of dogmatic theology by Christos Androutsos— "an example of the basically Latinizing scholastic approach to theology," as John Meyendorff notes.[1] Some of Stăniloae's first books were collections of articles previously published in Romanian theological and cultural journals and diocesan newspapers. Yet several of these early books, notably *The Life and Teaching of St. Gregory Palamas* (1938) and *Jesus Christ, or the Restoration of Man* (1943), already distinguished him as a very original theological thinker. The former book was a groundbreaking study in Palamite scholarship. It gave a very different picture of Palamism than the very negative picture then presented in the West by the Roman Catholic scholar Martin Jugie. Stăniloae, together with such other Orthodox scholars as Basil Krivocheine, Vladimir Lossky, and John Meyendorff, used Palamism to revive and transform Orthodoxy. They also influenced the development of a more scholarly and objective treatment of Palamism by Roman Catholic scholars such as André de Halleux, Jacques Lison, and Robert Sinkewicz, and have made it an important theological alternative to Westerners.

Stăniloae still considered his second book, *Jesus Christ, or the Restoration of Man*, as one of his major works when I spoke to him two years before his death. In this work, for the first time in Romanian theology,

Stăniloae emphasized the ontological aspect of salvation, which he found present abundantly in the Greek church fathers. In this work, he also engaged in dialogue with some of the best Western theologians and philosophers at the time.

During his Sibiu period, Stăniloae also began compiling and translating single-handedly the Romanian version of the *Philokalia*, twelve volumes of which were published between 1946 and 1991. Although based on the Venice edition of the *Philokalia of the Holy Ascetics* (1782), a collection of texts compiled by Nikodemos of the Holy Mountain and Makarios Notaras, Stăniloae's *Philokalia* differs from it in several important ways. Stăniloae substantially supplemented the texts of the original *Philokalia*, adding, among many other sections, an appendix entitled "Hesychasm and the Jesus Prayer in the Romanian Orthodox Tradition" in volume 8. He also provided his own introductions for the modern reader and accompanied the texts with very rich commentaries and footnotes.[2]

In the Sibiu period, Stăniloae also published articles on the relationship between Orthodoxy and Romanianism, a theme that he revived after the fall of Communism in 1989 and published as *Reflections on the Spirituality of the Romanian People* (1992). Greater Romania was the state formed in 1918 by the three formerly independent principalities of Wallachia, Moldova, and Transylvania (the first two had become one unit in 1859) as well as several other smaller regions. Between the world wars, Romanianism was held up as an imagined shared ethnic identity allegedly superseding Moldovan, Wallachian, and Transylvanian allegiances. The philosopher, poet, and theologian Nichifor Crainic and the philosopher and poet Lucian Blaga, together with a number of other intellectuals, were advocating Romanianism following the formation of Greater Romania. They stressed the characteristics that bound together the inhabitants of the new state (religion, language, customs, and traditions), while differentiating them from ethnic minorities and neighboring peoples. The discussion continued in Romania during the Communist period, and indeed continues to this day.

Stăniloae joined Crainic's cause, though he was more moderate than Crainic, who tried to make Orthodoxy a touchstone for the identification of the "Romanian soul."[3] Between 1935 and 1944, Stăniloae wrote seventeen articles in *Gândirea* (*Thought*), one of the most notorious magazines of Romanian nationalism, directed by Crainic at the time. Stăniloae published other articles on the subject in the diocesan newspaper *Telegraful Român* (*Romanian Telegraph*), whose directorship he held between 1934 and 1946. Stăniloae's articles were then collected in the volumes *Orthodoxy and Romanianism* (1939) and *The Position of Mr. Lucian Blaga vis-à-vis*

Christianity and Orthodoxy (1942). These texts probably figured promi-
nently in substantiating the charges against Stăniloae in his trial of
1958.

Crainic referred to Stăniloae as the "great religious thinker from Sibiu,"
and considered him the promoter of a new, original phase in the evolution
of Romanian theology.[4] Crainic was the foremost exponent of Gândirism,
a form of nationalism, autochthonism, and neo-Orthodoxy associated
with *Gândirea* magazine. He was also a leader of the Iron Guard, the Romanian fascist, anti-Semitic movement. For those reasons and for his anticommunist stance, Crainic was arrested in 1947. At the time, Communism
was establishing more permanent roots in Romania, having been exported
into the country by the Soviets following the Yalta Treaty of 1945, which
gave the Soviet Union full control of Romania.

Romania's newly acquired freedom following the 1989 collapse of the
Communist regime of President Nicolae Ceausescu paved the way for access to documentary materials previously unavailable (including *Gândirea* and various archives) and the possibility to comment publicly on
those materials. As a result, several researchers have started piecing together a portrait of Stăniloae and his relationship with Crainic. According
to Orthodox Church historian Mircea Pacurariu, the first Communist
prime minister, Petru Groza, wrote several times to Metropolitan Balan
threatening him with "grave consequences" if he did not distance himself
from Stăniloae (who was still Balan's protégé at the time). Due to his activities and views, as well as his relations with Crainic, Stăniloae was eventually forced to resign his post as director of the *Telegraful Român* in May
1945 and his position as rector of the Theological Academy in February
1946.[5]

Stăniloae did write some anticommunist articles before 1945 and even
wrote a eulogy for Ion Mota and Vasile Marin, two leaders of the Iron
Guard, who died in 1937 in Spain fighting on Franco's side.[6] He also revealed his admiration for Mota and Marin in an article in the new Iron
Guard publication, *Gazeta de Vest*, in 1993.[7] It is worth noting, however,
that, while contemporary Iron Guardists acknowledge Crainic as one of
their leaders, they do not consider Stăniloae as one of their members and
do not mention him on their Web sites.[8]

In January 1947 Stăniloae moved to Bucharest, where he replaced
Crainic and began teaching ascetics and mystics in the Faculty of Orthodox Theology. That Stăniloae replaced Crainic likely raised suspicion in
the minds of Communist officials. In 1948, as part of a general crackdown
on religion, officials placed the Faculty of Orthodox Theology outside the
state University of Bucharest and recognized it as a separate university-

level institution. This move gave Communist officials more leverage and control over the faculty. The law on religious denominations, adopted on August 4, 1948, in accordance with Article 27 of the Constitution of April 1948 concerning the freedom of conscience, allowed only denominations officially recognized by the Communist authorities to continue their activity, and it established the state's firm control over churches. On July 17, 1948, the authorities abrogated the Concordat between Romania and the Vatican that had been signed in pre-Communist times. In October 1948 they also disbanded the Greek Catholic Church in Romania and forced Catholics to "reintegrate" with the mother Orthodox Church, which received all Greek Catholic property in exchange for its compliance with state religious policies.

Despite the hardships created by the government's crackdown on things "spiritual" and "mystical" during the first years of the Communist regime, Stăniloae collaborated on two volumes of theology, *A Manual of Christian Orthodox Teachings* (1952) and *Dogmatic and Symbolic Theology for Theological Institutes* (1958). The second work, however, does not bear his name, because he was arrested before it went to press.

After Stăniloae moved to Bucharest, the Communist secret police began secretly following him. They also repeatedly warned him about his associations with the wrong people. In the 1950s, he became involved with a spirituality group, "The Burning Bush," which included monks, intellectuals, and students. Some members, such as Benedict Ghius and Constantin Joja, were Iron Guardists. Others, though genuinely concerned with spirituality, were sent to prison for conspiring to overthrow the Communist regime, as part of the regime's wider antireligious and anticlerical campaign.

Stăniloae, too, was imprisoned in 1958 and was not released until January 1963. His release came at a time when Romania was starting to move from the Soviet form of totalitarian Communism to its own form of national Communism, which had a limited degree of openness and freedom. On his release, however, Stăniloae was not allowed to return to the Faculty of Theology in Bucharest until 1965, and even then he was only to teach doctoral courses and supervise doctoral dissertations. These restrictions greatly limited the number of his students. After his retirement in 1973, he continued to serve as supervisor for doctoral dissertations until the early 1980s.

The Communist prison experience was a terrible ordeal for Stăniloae, as it was for others, many of whom did not survive. Following his release, Stăniloae spoke very little about it and refused to name some of the most ferocious prison guards and secret police officers who tortured him. He maintained his silence even after Romania embraced freedom of speech in 1989. His daughter Lidia wrote recently that "the extreme suffering [my father] underwent was an experience that brought him even closer to God. He bore it all with the same patience with which he bore many other difficulties. He never held a grudge against those who made him suffer or against those who—even if they owed him much—turned their back on him."[9] To French Orthodox theologian Olivier Clement, Stăniloae remarked that it was only in jail that he could practice the Jesus prayer with amazing power.

In 1978, at the age of seventy-five, Stăniloae published his magnum opus, the three-volume, 1,347-page *Orthodox Dogmatic Theology*. Like all of his works, he wrote his *Dogmatics* in Romanian. But the work is now partly available in French and English, and entirely available in German translation.[10] The English translation came out as *The Experience of God*, but the two volumes published to date represent only the first volume of the Romanian edition. According to Bishop Kallistos Ware of Diokleia, who wrote the foreword to the first volume of *The Experience of God*, the work "embodies the mature fruits of [Stăniloae's] theological reflection after more than half a century of teaching and writing."[11] As Bishop Kallistos explains, the word "dogmatic" was removed from the title of the English translation for fear that it might be taken to mean obligatory teaching, imposed from above by an external authority. This, however, was not at all what Stăniloae meant by dogmatic theology, as it was not the case for, say, Karl Barth in titling his *Church Dogmatics*.

In *Dogmatics*, Stăniloae tried to blend in a very creative fashion patristic insights with contemporary theology, both Western and Eastern. A keen sense of the importance of the personal, as well as of the complementarity between apophatic and kataphatic theology, pervades Stăniloae's *Dogmatics* and his theology in general. The *Dogmatics* is somewhat similar in structure to his earlier *Dogmatic and Symbolic Theology for Theological Institutes*. In the 1978 *Dogmatics*, though, Stăniloae used the church fathers more heavily than in the earlier edition and, of course, he felt more at ease providing his own reflections based on his dialogue with the tradition and modernity, including contemporary ecumenism.

Several other significant works by Stăniloae published in Romanian include *Spirituality and Communion in the Orthodox Liturgy* (1986), *The Eternal Image of God* (1987), *Studies in Orthodox Dogmatic Theology* (1991), *The Evangelical Image of Jesus Christ* (1992), and *Commentary on the Gospel According to John* (1993). To these one should add numerous other Romanian translations from various church fathers and hundreds of journal and newspaper articles.

REVELATION AND THE LAW

Stăniloae's *Experience of God* opens with the statement, "The Orthodox Church makes no separation between natural and supernatural revelation."[12] This is often understood to mean that there is no separation between the sacred and the profane in the Orthodox tradition. A statement such as Stăniloae's would perhaps baffle a Westerner, but not necessarily an aboriginal shaman or a Hasidic Jew, for example, for whom the sacred is present in the daily life and in every single gesture he or she makes. Yet "separation" does not mean "distinction." The Orthodox Church does distinguish between natural and supernatural revelation, but does not necessarily separate them for purposes other than to understand them. It does not separate them in its daily preaching (the Greek *kerygma*), thus trying to show the essential continuity between them.

The first two chapters in *The Experience of God* deal with natural and supernatural revelation and their relationship. The relationship between the two types of revelation is important in the context of law and human nature, because it is in the Law that God gave to Moses at Mount Sinai that Stăniloae sees the supernatural revelation expressed in a concentrated form. To be sure, Stăniloae is reluctant to use the word "law." He does mention the Law given to Moses and cites Romans 2:14–15, where Paul speaks about the distinction between the natural law and the revealed law, but he seems unwilling to elaborate his theology along legal lines. Instead, Stăniloae talks a lot more about human knowledge of God and the dialogue a person has with God. This is not unlike what one sees in the works of other Orthodox theologians included in this volume. With few exceptions, Orthodox theologians tend to avoid talking about the law, a topic the modern Orthodox tradition has perceived as principally of Catholic and Protestant inspiration, although the Bible clearly discusses it.[13]

Contemporary biblical scholarship acknowledges that Paul's most frequently used image of salvation in Christ, namely, "justification" (*dikaiosune*), is drawn from Paul's Jewish law background and denotes a societal or judicial relationship, either ethical or forensic—that is, it is related to law courts, as in Deuteronomy 25:1. The righteous or upright person (*dikaios*) came to refer usually to one who stood acquitted or vindicated before a judge's tribunal (Exodus 23:7; 1 Kings 8:32). Jews also tried to achieve the status of "righteousness" or "uprightness" in the sight of Yahweh the Judge by observing the rules and regulations of Mosaic law (see Psalms 7:9–12). When Paul says that Christ has "justified" humans, he means that Christ has made it possible for them to stand before God's tribunal as acquitted or innocent. The characteristically Pauline contribution to the notion of justification is his affirmation of the gratuitous and unmerited character of this justification of all humanity in Romans 3:20–26.[14]

Though he does not speak directly on the subject, Stăniloae says a good deal about law and human nature in an indirect way. Human beings and the cosmos constitute the natural revelation of God from the point of view of knowledge.

> The cosmos is organized in a way that corresponds to our capacity for knowing. The cosmos—and human nature as intimately connected with the cosmos—are stamped with rationality, while man (God's creature) is further endowed with a reason capable of knowing consciously the rationality of the cosmos and of his own nature. . . . We consider that the rationality of the cosmos attests to the fact that the cosmos is the product of a rational being, since rationality, as an aspect of a reality which is destined to be known, has no explanation apart from a conscious Reason which knows it from the time it creates it or even before that time, and knows it continually so long as that same Reason preserves its being.[15]

Words such as "rational," "reason," "consciousness," and "knowledge," rather than "law," recur repeatedly in Stăniloae's writings. Without explicitly referring to it, Stăniloae seems to have embraced the anthropic principle, according to which a rational God created the rational cosmos whose rationality and meaning the humans—as the crown of this creation—are meant to understand.

Like other Orthodox theologians, Stăniloae uses the biblical and patristic view of humans created in the image of God (Genesis 1:26–27). To be created in the image of God is to be a rational being. Using their reason and capacity to reflect and understand their surroundings and themselves, and storing this awareness in their complex psyche, is what distinguishes humans from the rest of the created visible world. At this point, despite his attempts to be true to the patristic understanding of the human person, Stăniloae collapses together, in an otherwise creative way, patristic and modern insights about the person.[16] Their rationality and consciousness make humans personal beings and, as such, they are capable of communicating with, and knowing, other persons, including divine persons. In their attempt to know the one God in three persons and to achieve "eternal perfection in God and [be] strengthened in communion with him even while on earth," humans get their information from the surrounding world and from themselves; this is what constitutes natural revelation. Yet humans get only partial information about God from natural revelation, especially in our current postlapsarian state.[17] Therefore, supernatural revelation is necessary, that is, the revelation that comes from God's own initiative, constitutes God's self-disclosure, and is contained in the Bible. This is the line along which Stăniloae prefers to develop his understanding of revelation.

Stăniloae's source of inspiration for the view that natural and supernatural revelations are not to be separated is Maximus the Confessor. Stăniloae paraphrases Maximus as follows: "Natural revelation has the same value as supernatural revelation [for the saints], that is, for those raised to a vision of God [it is] similar to that of supernatural revelation. For the saints, the written law is nothing other than the law of nature seen in the personal types of those who have fulfilled it, while the law of nature is nothing other than the written law seen in its spiritual meanings beyond these types."[18] What Stăniloae says is that the lack of a separation between natural and supernatural revelation is evident to the saints, but unfortunately not to ordinary Christians.[19] This view represents an emphasis on the spirit, rather than the letter, of the law, and it leads Stăniloae to deemphasize law.

While Stăniloae does not value the law in itself too much—except perhaps as a transitory step toward something higher—he is concerned about justice in light of Orthodox soteriology. Human beings are persons and as such they do not lead individual lives but are in relationship with other persons. This relationality is present in everyday life, but also when it comes to salvation: One cannot be saved in isolation, but one needs to be helped by others and has to help others in return.[20] Christ helped us to become saved, and, therefore, we, too, have to help our fellow humans. "Let us commend ourselves and each other and our whole life to Christ our God," sing the faithful at the Orthodox liturgy. "Salvation is communion in Christ (*koinonia*) and therefore the obligation of Christians to strive to maintain and develop their ecclesial unity through love is plain: 'For the love of Christ gathers us together' (2 Corinthians 5:14)."[21]

This concern with helping others does not apply only to other Christians, but to the whole world, including non-Christians, again in imitation of Jesus. Helping people sometimes leads to reconciliation between them. In speaking about reconciliation among humans, Stăniloae does not equate it with a "purely formal peace, a mere coexistence and lack of aggression covering over profound disagreements." A lasting reconciliation is a combination of love, equality, and justice among humans and nations. Genuine reconciliation is possible only in light of the reconciliation performed by God who, after having regarded humankind as an enemy because of the sin, reconciled humanity to himself and allowed humans to partake of all good things in Christ.[22]

Christians should not only help other individuals, Stăniloae insisted, but should also be concerned about promoting justice at the national, and even global levels. An elasticity in the social structures—which was not present in the past—makes that type of justice increasingly possible today.[23] This is one of the aspects of globalization, if we are to think only of the International Tribunal at The Hague, which tries to administer justice at an international level. Stăniloae was somewhat of a visionary in this regard, having argued for global justice already in 1972. It is also worth noting that he saw the effort for global justice as "the effect [of] Christ's activity guiding the world towards the Kingdom of Heaven, in spite of the fact that this is a goal which in its final form cannot be reached in this world, given the corruptible nature of matter and all its attendant ills."[24] The lack of justice in the world provides a justification for eternal death, which means eternal separation from God who is justice itself. But "the removal of injustice deprives eternal death of any such justification."[25]

FALLEN HUMAN NATURE AND THE LAW

Like every other Orthodox theologian, Stăniloae addresses the Fall of the first humans, as recorded symbolically in the story of Adam and Eve's eating from the tree of the knowledge of good and evil. Chapter 6 of the second volume of *The Experience of God* is suggestively entitled "The Fall." While the first volume deals with revelation and knowledge of the triune God, the second volume, subtitled *The World: Creation and Deification*, is devoted to the created world. It is important to understand the way in which Stăniloae views the Fall, its consequences for the human nature, and the law's role as a temporary corrective.

Stăniloae begins by noting that human beings did not consolidate their obedience to God or grow in the knowledge of him, because otherwise the Fall would not have occurred at all or at least not so easily. Stăniloae provides the reader with a long quote from Maximus the Confessor, and then complements it with similar quotes from Nicetas Stethatos and Gregory Palamas. The Maximian view defines Stăniloae's understanding of the Fall: "Perhaps the creation of visible things was called the tree of the knowledge of good and evil because it has both spiritual reasons that nourish the mind and a natural power that charms the senses and yet perverts the mind. Therefore, when spiritually contemplated, it offers the knowledge of the good, while when received bodily it offers the knowledge of evil."[26] Maximus's speculative thoughts on the matter are indicated by the word "perhaps," but his explanation captures Stăniloae's attention almost entirely, as we shall see shortly. What Maximus says is that the created world is good, because God made it so. Nevertheless, it depends on how we human beings, endowed with freedom, see and use this good creation. It is like money, a human creation, which in itself is as neutral as other material things, but which can become good when given to charities or bad when used to pay for carnal pleasures or to pay a hit man.

The Fall occurred, according to Maximus and Stăniloae, because humans hurried to taste God's creation through the senses. This move brought evil upon them. Humans, not yet strengthened in the good contemplation of the created world, needed to persist longer in their obedience to God in order for them to be able to see the created world as God sees it and not to have the mind perverted by it.[27] The "primordial state," the condition of the first human parents when they came into existence, was a very short-lived condition. In it, humans were supposed to remain and grow, but Stăniloae, following Basil of Caesarea, cannot help but notice the "rapidity" with which humans decided in favor of disobedience.[28]

It is a pity that Stăniloae, given modern paleontological data available to him, did not ask the question why God left such an important decision for the human race to the first, undeveloped humans, who probably were troglodytes. Later in the same chapter, he seems to hint at this question, without providing an answer: "There can be no denying, however, that knowledge of the rationality of nature through the mediation of human reason represents in its own way a development of the human spirit. Thus, here, too, we have an ambiguity, a simultaneous growth and reduction of our powers symbolized by the tree of the knowledge of good and evil."[29] This is a regrettable feature of many modern Orthodox theologians, who rely on the church fathers but tend not to engage current learning. In embracing the church fathers without bringing some modern insights into play, one always faces the danger of not addressing one's contemporaries.

In refusing to try to exercise their freedom in obedience and growth to know God and the created world as God knows it, the first humans had become slaves to "the easy pleasure afforded by the senses."[30] Basil of Caesarea, whom Stăniloae quotes again, names the cause of the Fall: it is lack of wisdom, thoughtlessness, or even laziness of the will (*aboulia*) on the part of the first humans. "By commanding man not to eat from the tree of consciousness before he was guided by freedom of the spirit, God, in fact, commanded him to be strong, to remain free, and to grow in spirit, that is, in freedom. This commandment made appeal to man's freedom."[31] In connection with the tree of the knowledge of good and evil, Stăniloae uses the words "consciousness" and "freedom." It is worth noting that he identifies the tree itself with the consciousness that Adam was supposed to develop. Let us remember that consciousness is an important part of the person— both divine and human. In fact, Stăniloae defines a person as a center of consciousness, but warns that consciousness in endless self-replacing succession is meaningless if each member of this succession is not carried into eternity, but disappears for good once the body dies.[32]

Stăniloae offered further reflections on human freedom. In not responding to God by loving obedience, he argues, humans thought they were affirming their freedom.

> In fact, it was this act that marked the beginning of the human's selfish confinement within himself. This was how he enslaved himself to himself. Reckoning on becoming his own lord, he became his own slave. The human person is free only if he is free also from himself for the sake of others, in love, and if he is free for God who is the source of freedom because he is the source of love. But disobedience used as an occasion the commandment not to taste from the tree of the knowledge of good and evil.[33]

Stăniloae does not elaborate on why freedom is not necessarily freedom of choice. But he hints that that type of freedom is present in humans as well. Stăniloae understands freedom as that by which a willing subject always chooses the good. Adam and Eve were created free in the sense of being expected always to choose the good, to choose to obey God, the supreme good. Instead, they opted out of their relationship with God.

The English language does not have two words for these concepts, but uses only "freedom." In Greek, however, where these fine distinctions were first developed, there are two words to explain the difference. The Greek philosopher Plotinus spoke of the will to choose (*prohairesis*) and the will to be what one wishes to be (*boulesis*). The Greek church father Gregory of Nyssa picked up this distinction and applied it to the Christian God. Gregory presented God as one who always chooses the good and wishes to be what he is because he is the supreme good. In speaking of Christ as the son of God, Gregory says that, unlike humans, he does not change from an inferior to a superior state. Nor does he need another son to bestow adoption upon him. Accordingly, Gregory maintains that the only-begotten is properly called the Son of God because he is the Son of God by nature.[34] The distinction between "by nature" and "by choice" is very important in Gregory's view, and he emphasizes it several times. Yet the case of the son of God is very different from the case of human sons:

God, being one good, in a simple and uncompounded nature, looks ever the same way, and is never changed by the impulses of choice (*prohairesis*), but always wishes (*bouletai*) what he is, and is, assuredly, what he wishes (*bouletai*). So that he is in both respects properly and truly called Son of God, since his nature contains the good, and his choice (*prohairesis*) also is never severed from that which is more excellent, so that this word [son] is employed without inexactness, as his name.[35]

These are powerful statements, informed by Plotinianism. They are powerful because in the divine case, sonship-by-nature and sonship-by-will converge in the same direction of the good. There is no contradiction between the goodness of the divine nature and the good (or, rather, the supremely good) choice the Son of God makes. They are Plotinian because Plotinus, in referring to the One God about a hundred years before Gregory, made an almost identical statement: the One God is "all power, really master of itself, being what it wills to be."[36] The son is thus a "willing" subject. However, his will appears as both the will to choose (*prohairesis*), which is always directed toward choosing the good, and the will to be what he wishes to be (*boulesis*), which is an ontological will.

It is the latter type of will that Stăniloae has in mind when dealing with the human Fall, especially since he mentioned Basil's *aboulia* as the main cause of the fall. It is this immature *boulesis* in Adam and Eve that leads them to the Fall by making them reject what they should have been.

Misused freedom is the cause of the Fall of Adam and Eve, Stăniloae insists. In believing that they exercised their freedom, the first humans fell into slavery to sin. This is how the patristic tradition tended to view the Fall. Shortly after that, God expelled Adam and Eve from paradise in order to prevent them from having access to the tree of life, and to live eternally in this fallen condition. Again appealing to the church fathers, Stăniloae says that the two trees are in fact the same tree, the visible world already mentioned. "Viewed through a mind moved by spirit, that world is the tree of life that puts us in relationship with God; but viewed and made use of through a consciousness that has been detached from the mind moved by spirit, it represents the tree of the knowledge of good and evil which severs man from God."[37]

According to Genesis, Adam and Eve did not sin on their own, untempted initiative. The serpent was present, tempting Eve. Christian theology has seen the serpent as the symbol of evil or the devil, Satan himself. Stăniloae notices at this point that evil in itself, in its nakedness, is unattractive to many people. Therefore, it has to "deck itself in the colors of some good by which it lures those who are deceived into desiring it."[38] Evil

was thus fascinating to both Eve and Adam, who eventually became capti-
vated by it. Yet, they were still afraid of the consequences their trespass of
the divine commandment could have. According to Stăniloae, that is
where the devil intervened, trying to calm the human soul by telling Eve
the consequences were not too dramatic, but that God wanted to deceive
the first humans out of envy.[39]

After the Fall, such consequences have become apparent in all manner
of ways. These included a person's estrangement from God, a proclivity to
passionate impulse as a result of mixing sensuality and the sensible aspect
of the world, a more complex understanding of the sad knowledge of good
and evil, pride, reduced knowledge of God's creation, domination, satisfaction of bodily needs and pleasures, now become passions, corruption,
and eventually death.[40] Stăniloae notes: "Neither corruptibility nor
death . . . are punishments from God; they are instead consequences of
our alienation from the source of life."[41] He reminds the reader that, according to the Orthodox understanding, although the consequences of
sin have been very serious, they have not made human knowledge totally
and fatally opaque, conforming it to a similarly opaque world. "Humans
can penetrate this opacity in part by means of another kind of knowledge,
and indeed, they often manage to do this, but they cannot wholly overcome this opacity and the knowledge that conforms to it."[42] The withdrawal of the divine Spirit from the world immediately after the Fall
weakened the character the world had as a transparent medium between
God and humans and among humans themselves.

"Even in the state of sin," Stăniloae tells us, "it is providence that preserves and directs the world."[43] However, God does not work alone in this
endeavor and certainly does not work against the human will. God collabo-
rates with the human will in what the Orthodox tradition calls "synergy."[44]
"Synergy" is a sinner's movement toward higher goals and perfection, a
movement implying newness for the sinner.

Stăniloae includes reflections on law in elaborating his doctrine of
"synergy." He picks up and develops the theme of newness from the book
of Revelation: "Behold, I make all things new" (21:5). He complements this
with quotes from St. Paul (Eph. 4:24; 2 Cor. 5:17; Gal. 6:15). What catches
Stăniloae's attention is that St. Paul opposed the "newness of spirit" to
the oldness of the letter or the law as he opposed the life of the resurrection to abiding in death. In Stăniloae's view, the law is identified with the
law of the Old Covenant and represents a sign that sin still reigns.[45]
Again, this is in line with St. Paul who wrote to the Corinthians: "The
sting of death is sin, and the power of sin is the law" (1 Cor. 15:56). The end
of the law is Christ. Stăniloae argues that, when people do not draw that

conclusion, per Romans 10:4, 13:10, "then the law is the power of sin that leads to death."

Stăniloae does not have nice words to say about the law, and for some reason, he seems to condemn together Old Testament law and the laws of modern states. He opposes law to love, as if they are two opposites and cannot stand side by side. For reasons I confess not to understand, Stăniloae writes that "the law is repetition, according to an external norm, within the monotonously confined horizon of egoism and death."[46] Love is indeed the fulfilling of the law (Rom. 10:4; 13:10). The "newness of life," which is the love Stăniloae opposes to the law, is inspired by Gregory of Nyssa's theory according to which in the afterlife the souls of the blessed will not be static in the contemplation of God, but will advance infinitely from one stage of beatitude toward the next. Gregory of Nyssa calls each of these stages *epektasis*.[47] Stăniloae, however, does not elaborate Gregory's views. It is not clear how, in his view, human society could survive without the law. Not everybody shows or reaches that dimension of love that Stăniloae champions.

Stăniloae's negative view of the law was not simply a reaction to living under Communism and atheistic laws when he wrote his *Dogmatics*. A similar view of the law comes through years later in *Seven Mornings with Father Stăniloae*, a book of interviews by Sorin Dumitrescu, a famous Romanian religious painter and intellectual. Dumitrescu asked Stăniloae to explain why in the West human relations were better regulated and more disciplined than in the East, where during Communist times there were practices such as excessive gossiping and informing on one's neighbor to the secret police.[48] Stăniloae answered that the supposedly better regulation of human relations in the West has brought something of a distance and a chill among people. Moreover, the laws that "somehow sustain the correctness" in human relations in the West are secular laws. In Romania, by contrast, the import of the same secular laws since the nineteenth century has led to a bizarre mix of hospitality and the various cultural excesses that Dumitrescu listed. Stăniloae betrays ample anti-Westernism and antilegalism in this and other interviews. He begins one interview by saying:

> Without Christ everything is monotonous, legalistic, everything unfolds in a forced way. We do not get rid of these miseries by moving toward powerless old age, sickness and final death. . . . Through sin, the world fell into monotony, in the prison of invariable laws and causal determinism. Through the Incarnation, God himself has brought the world back to what he intended it to be when he created it. It was brought back to the advance in the infinity of the divine goodness.[49]

Again, Stăniloae presents law as monotonous and completely negative in contrast with the love, freedom, and newness brought about by Christ and the Spirit.

COMMUNISM, THE CHURCH, AND COLLABORATION

One issue that has dominated the political scene of postcommunist Eastern Europe and the former Soviet Union is that of "transitional justice." Since 1989 most countries of the former Communist bloc have passed laws regulating access to the files of the former secret police and banning former Communists and secret police officers from participating in postcommunist politics. These laws, however, have passed more easily in some countries than others. Romania was among the last countries to adopt such laws, and only after many years of bickering and with enormous opposition that continues to this day.[50] Some Orthodox Church leaders and priests have vehemently opposed the opening of the secret police archives, no doubt fearing that they contain incriminating evidence about their collaboration with the dreaded political police, the Securitate.

Stăniloae offered his reflections on this issue and on the role of the Orthodox Church in reconciling postcommunist Romanian society in a series of interviews by Sorin Dumitrescu in March and April 1992. This was at a time when the debate about collaboration was still in its early stages in Romania. While the eighty-nine-year-old Stăniloae proved to be remarkably vivid, the interview showed that after forty-five years of Communist repression, Stăniloae was unable to distinguish Christian love from Christian justice and to realize the necessity not only of the former but also of the latter.

Dumitrescu invited Stăniloae to reflect on the church's role in the new democracy, particularly in the society's search for the truth. Dumitrescu started by asking whether the church, as a moral institution, should not try to distinguish between the executioners, who collaborated with the Communist regime and benefited from the collaboration, and the victims, who were discriminated against, lost their jobs, were imprisoned, tortured, and even killed in Communist prisons because of their opposition to the regime.[51] Instead of distinguishing between executioners and victims, thus helping to restore decent, if not cordial, relations in society, the church remained silent and allowed executioners and victims to live side by side in postcommunist Romania. Dumitrescu asked Stăniloae whether the time had not come for a moral, respectable institution such as the

Romanian Orthodox Church to help to sort things out and to separate light from darkness.

Stăniloae answered, on the strength of his theology of personhood and communion, that it is the church's mission to preach Christ, not to assign guilt especially in the public sphere. Clerics must not separate themselves from bad people, but try to persuade them to change their lives "by personal example, help and words of consolation." Party politics is not for priests, bishops, and monks, Stăniloae argued, though he recognized that they not always lived up to these expectations because they themselves are humans and can err.[52]

Dumitrescu then asked whether the Christian theme of forgiveness of sins was not being used by postcommunist Romanian politicians (some of whom publicly declared themselves to be atheists) to cover up their own guilt and the guilt of the executioners.[53] He drew a parallel between Hitler's officers and soldiers, who claimed exoneration because they were merely following orders, and Communist-era executioners who were now claiming exoneration because they deserved Christian forgiveness. Is this not a pretextual, and indeed sinful, use of Christian forgiveness, Dumitrescu pressed Stăniloae.

Stăniloae again insisted that the church cannot publicly condemn anybody, because the church uses other methods to deal with malefactors. One such method is the Orthodox practice of individual confession of the penitent to a confessor, who can be either a priest or a bishop. Like its Roman Catholic counterpart, the Orthodox sacrament of confession may not be used to extract information that could incriminate someone publicly. The confessor father is under a vow of secrecy not to divulge the secret of the confession even in very grave cases. The confessor can assign penance to the believer who confesses his or her sins, including the harsh punishment of banning a confessed sinner from communion.[54]

This answer, however, assumes that a sinner is also a believer and genuinely comes to confess his or her sins. But what is Romania to do with those executioners who are not believers, who are not even Christians and cannot receive the sacrament of penance and reconciliation? What should be done with the large group of people who want some justice done in order for them and the society to be reconciled? And what should be done with the priests who disregarded the secrecy of confession and passed information on to the Securitate? Stăniloae did not say.

Instead, Stăniloae held up the gospel story of the adulterous woman who was brought to Jesus by her accusers who wanted to stone her. All of her accusers dropped their stones and left when Jesus said, "He who is without sin cast the first stone" (John 8:7). Using this story, Stăniloae insisted that all of us are guilty and deserving of punishment. Moreover, as a confessor father himself, he could not betray the vow of secrecy and divulge information, for that would invite harsh punishment on the accused.[55]

Dumitrescu challenged Stăniloae, however, to look beyond the sacrament of penance: "Excuse me, but what you say refers to the personal relationship of the penitent and the confessing father.... Do you not think the Church, without naming names, should take a public stand and say that its teachings are misused? Because, you see, the Church does not want to homogenize guilt by [indiscriminate] forgiveness; the Church can be intransigent if it wants to."[56] Stăniloae simply could not make this leap from individual forgiveness to the forgiveness required at a larger level, that of the society. He did not seem to understand why another type of forgiveness might be necessary.

Part of Stăniloae's reluctance to address such issues of social justice and reconciliation might well have been a function of his environment. These themes were simply not an issue that the church faced in Communist times. A greater part of his reluctance might well have been Stăniloae's long-time preoccupation with the *Philokalia*, which mainly addressed monastic and ascetic themes and readers. Its focus was on Christian ascetic withdrawal, on the individual's path to spiritual perfection, rather than on what is good and just for the society. This attitude is present in some of his other works as well.

It is evident from his questions that Dumitrescu wanted Stăniloae to say that the church's teachings are being manipulated by the postcommunist Romanian political actors in order for them to save face and to be excused for their collaboration with the Communist regime.[57] He expected him to say that the church must not dispense indiscriminate forgiveness by declaring that either nobody is guilty or everybody is guilty. Instead, it should point to degrees of guilt and start the civic healing process from there. But Stăniloae said none of this. Only after much prodding did he acknowledge grudgingly that the Romanian Orthodox Church itself shares some degree of culpability, and that this prevents it from proclaiming more loudly that justice is needed in Romania today. In his words, "What can we do? There is a long road from teaching to practice. Nobody is perfect in this world. Nor are the churchmen. We plead for the good, we seek to win the others to our cause, but few of us are perfect supporters of the Christian teachings in their own lives."[58]

Stăniloae, however, did not acknowledge that the sacrament of penance and reconciliation is about both love and justice. Dumitrescu reminded him that Jesus forgave, but he also entered the temple with a whip, chasing out the moneychangers who had desecrated his father's house. Stăniloae mentioned in passing that the church does "whip" the society at times, but he did not elaborate. As for whether it should support various political actors, policies, and ideologies, Stăniloae insisted that the church as a whole is apolitical these days, and those clerics who give opportunistic support to different political parties do not represent the church in all their actions.[59]

Stăniloae's views on this vexed subject have proved rather typical among current Romanian Orthodox leaders. The end of Communism ushered in a new era for the Orthodox Church and a chance for it to redefine the new Romanian democracy.[60] After 1989, however, the Orthodox Church and its head, Patriarch Teoctist Arapasu, were strongly criticized for supporting the Communist regime to its very end. The Church Synod responded on January 10, 1990, apologizing for those "who did not always have the courage of the martyrs," and expressed regret that it had been "necessary to pay the tribute of obligatory and artificial praises addressed to the dictator" to ensure certain liberties.[61] The synod also annulled all the ecclesiastical sanctions previously imposed on some clergymen for political reasons. Faced with increasing criticism, Patriarch Teoctist resigned his office on January 18, 1990, only to return three months later at the insistence of the synod. Some 136 religious and cultural leaders protested his reappointment, but the synod opted for continuity in face of political change and acknowledged the views of the other Orthodox churches that recognized Teoctist as patriarch.

Since 1989, the Orthodox Church as an institution has avoided any moral self-examination and has never openly admitted to its collaboration with the Communist authorities or the Securitate. Romanian Metropolitan Nicolae Corneanu was among the very few Orthodox clergy to acknowledge his efforts on behalf of the Communist authorities to infiltrate Romanian communities in Western Europe and North America, and to defrock five priests who denounced "the Church's prostitution with the communist power, and its hierarchy's involvement with Ceausescu's politics."[62] In 1997, Corneanu revealed the extent of the church's collaboration, and he named Metropolitan Plamadeala among the most active promoters of Ceausescu's antireligious and anti-Orthodox policies.[63]

For many Orthodox Romanians, however, Patriarch Teoctist's short retreat to a monastery and the synod's partial apology for collaboration with the Communists was contrition enough. With a few notable exceptions, every Romanian was open to criticism regarding her or his compliance with the Communist regime. Because of this, most Romanians have been willing to overlook the Orthodox Church's past political compromises.[64]

Stăniloae's instruction and example on this vexed subject are now regrettably commonplace.

ORTHODOXY AND NATIONALISM

In chapter 3 of this volume, Mikhail Kulakov demonstrates that Vladimir Lossky regarded nationalism as a disease and paid the price for his view by being marginalized by the Russian Orthodox diaspora community. By rejecting nationalism, Lossky was rather an exceptional figure in the Orthodox world. Many theologians both in Orthodox countries and in the diaspora have fallen prey to the disease of nationalism. They have also fallen prey to what the 1872 Synod of Constantinople called the heresy of phyletism, the view that makes race or culture the cornerstone of church unity.

Many Orthodox theologians, including Stăniloae, have tried to justify their nationalism theologically. They usually refer to Apostolic Canon 34, which reads:

> The bishops of every nation (*ethnos*) must acknowledge him who is first among them and account him as their head, and do nothing of consequence without his consent; but each may do those things only which concern his own parish, and the country places which belong to it. But neither let him (who is the first) do anything without the consent of all; for so there will be unanimity, and God will be glorified through the Lord in the Holy Spirit.[65]

The Greek word *ethnos* is the key to understanding this stipulation. Canon 34 was issued in the fourth century. It is thus closer to the New Testament time than to ours. The biblical meaning of *ethnos* is reflected in the passage where Jesus tells his apostles to "go and make disciples of all the nations (*ethnos*)" (Matt. 28:19; Mark 16:15–16). There *ethnos* referred to Gentiles (Hebrew, *goyim*), that is, Christians of non-Jewish descent living together regardless of their ethnic origins.[66] This understanding of *ethnos* meshes well with the modern definition of a civic state, a community, usually ethnically diverse, that is bound together by allegiance to a set of common institutions and practices.

Most Romanian Orthodox today, however, define *ethnos* as an ethnic group defined by a common language, history, race, and religion. Romanian canon lawyer Ioan Floca, for example, believes that in Canon 34, *ethnos* can only mean an ethnic group (*neam*) and cannot refer to all inhabitants of a "province" or "land."[67] For Stăniloae, too, an *ethnos* or nation is built along ethnic not civic lines, and nationalism and patriotism are interchangeable. "Nationalism is the consciousness of belonging to a certain ethnic group, the love for that group and the enacting of that love for the well-being of the group."[68]

To the above understanding of "nation" (*natiune* or *popor* in Romanian), one should add the meaning of *neam*. *Neam* represents a people centered on an ethnic group (Romanians, in this case) with alleged stability and long-established historical roots, like the Romanian people in the view of the Orthodox Church. In one of his early writings, Stăniloae contends:

> The Romanian nation (*neam*) is a biological-spiritual synthesis of a number of elements. The most important of them are the Dacian element, the Latin element, and the Christian Orthodox element. . . . The synthesis is new, it has its own individuality, and a principle of unity which differs from the partial components. The highest law of our nation (*neam*), the law which expresses what the nation is in the most appropriate way, is the one that the whole experiences, not the ones experienced by the parts. The parts are stamped with a new, unifying, and individualizing stamp which is Romanianhood (*românitatea*). Therefore, we can say that the highest law for our nation (*neam*) is Romanianhood. Not Romanity, not Dacianism, but Romanianhood with all it includes is the highest law by which we live and fulfill our mission. . . . Which is the Romanian way of communion with the transcendental spiritual order? History and the current life of our people tell us that it is Orthodoxy. Orthodoxy is the eye through which Romanians gaze at heavens and then, enlightened by the heavenly light, they turn their eye toward the world while continuing to attune their behavior to it. We also know that this is the only eye that is correct and healthy. . . . Certainly, in theory it is hard to understand how it is possible for Orthodoxy to interpenetrate with Romanianism without either of them to have to suffer. Yet, the bi-millennial life of our nation (*neam*) shows that in practice this is fully possible. . . . Orthodoxy is an essential and vital function of Romanianism. The permanent national ideal of our nation can only be conceived in relation with Orthodoxy.[69]

Stăniloae grounded his ethnic nationalism in the Augustinian theory of *rationes aeternae*, and developed something very similar to what modern anthropologists call an "imagined community."[70] According to St. Augustine, eternal reasons (*rationes aeternae*) are the divine archetypes or patterns of all created species and individuals; they are much like Plato's ideas or forms, placed in the mind of God.[71] For Stăniloae, ethnic nations are something God desired and even planned. Since God's creation is good and since God created nations, nations are good and so is nationalism.

In approaching the topic this way, there are signs that Stăniloae was reacting to the modern critique of nationalism. He certainly wanted to ask the deeper, still unanswered question "why are there multiple languages and plural ethnic groups?" And he certainly wanted to bring God into play in creating them as something good. Yet in the 1930s and 1940s when he reflected on the topic, Stăniloae did not have the conceptual instruments necessary to explain the existence of a diversity of languages and of ethnic groups. He writes:

Concerning man in particular, God created Adam and Eve in the beginning. In them were virtually present all nations. These are revelations in time of the images which have existed eternally in God. Every nation has an eternal divine archetype that it has to bring about more fully. . . . There is one instance when nations may not be from God and we would have to fight against them: when human diversification into nations would be a consequence of sin and a deviation from the way in which God wanted to develop humanity. In that case, the duty of every Christian would be to get humanity out of that sinful state and to fuse all nations into one.

Is diversification of humanity a sin or a consequence of sin? We could reject that presupposition by the mere universal law of fauna and flora. . . . But the answer can be given differently also: sin or evil is of a different order than unity or diversity. Sin means a deformity, a disfiguration of a given thing. . . . Is national specificity a deformity of humanity, a decay of the human being? This would be the case when national specificity would be something vicious, petty, and without heights of purity and thought. . . . The removal of humanity from the sinful state is being done not through the annulment of the national features, but by the straightening of human nature in general. If there were something sinful in national specificity, then one could not distinguish between good and evil people within a nation, but all would be evil. . . . We should note that there is no a-national person. Adam himself was not a-national, but he spoke a language, had a certain mentality, a certain psychic and bodily structure. A pure human, uncolored nationally, without national determinants, is an abstraction.[72]

All of these opinions have to be viewed in their proper context, that of post–World War I Romania, when there was a wide debate about the true meaning of Romanianism.

CONCLUSION

As other contributors to the Orthodox volume of this series have noted, Orthodox theologians tend to talk a lot about human nature, but much less about law, politics, and society. Stăniloae was no exception. Compared to Lossky, Berdyaev, and Soloviev, he said even less explicitly and directly about law. Nevertheless, several important points about law, politics, and human nature are reflected in his works. He saw law as a necessary result of the Fall into sin of the first humans, Adam and Eve. For him, the law given to Moses on Mount Sinai expresses the concentrated form of the will of God. It is God's supernatural revelation, but it is meant only as a transitory step toward something higher that comes through Christ. In line with Apostle Paul and the book of Revelation, Stăniloae opposed the "newness of the spirit" to the "oldness of the law" and contended instead that as long as there is law there is sin and that the law was given to remove humanity's sinful state. But eventually love has to take the place of the law.

Sinfulness is connected with freedom. Misused freedom is the cause of the fall from grace of Adam and Eve, according to Stăniloae. In believing that they exercised their freedom, the first humans fell into slavery to sin. This is how the patristic tradition tended to view the Fall. Shortly after that, God expelled Adam and Eve from paradise in order to prevent them from having access to the tree of life, and to live eternally in this fallen condition. Stăniloae understood freedom as that by which a willing subject always chooses the good. Adam and Eve were created free in the sense of being expected always to choose the good, to choose to obey God, the supreme good. Instead, they opted out of their relationship with God.

According to Stăniloae, the church's role in postcommunist societies is to preach Christ, not to assign guilt, especially in the public sphere. The church cannot publicly condemn anybody, because the church uses other methods to deal with malefactors. The most important such method is the sacrament of confession. This traditional role of the church, however, poses some problems in postcommunist times, as it assumes that most members of society are (Orthodox) Christian and that they will come forward to confess their sins and receive forgiveness. In short, it assumes some sort of a Christian state. But this is hardly the case, and the issue of civic justice and reconciliation in Romania remains unsolved. In this regard, it would have been helpful for Stăniloae to reflect more fully than he did on the relationship between church law and secular law.

In Romania, Stăniloae's work has been very influential, although he himself recognizes that there are yet to appear local theologians able to emulate him. Older Orthodox theology professors, such as Ion Bria, Dumitru Popescu, and Dumitru Radu, did their doctoral studies with Stăniloae, and their own ecclesiologies were influenced by his ecclesiology. Younger theologians, including Evangelical Protestants connected with the Emmanuel Bible Institute in Oradea, have written doctoral dissertations on various aspects of Stăniloae's theology under the guidance of both Orthodox and non-Orthodox professors in the United Kingdom. They seem to have taken a particular interest in Stăniloae's theology, and their writings meet Western standards of scholarship.

Outside of Romania, Stăniloae's theology has attracted attention in all the main branches of Christianity. Some Roman Catholics (such Ronald Roberson and Maciej Bielawski) have written doctoral dissertations on his theology, while others (such as Robert Barringer) studied with him and learned Romanian in order to translate some of his works into English. Various Anglican theologians have written books (Charles Miller) or articles (A. M. Allchin) on Stăniloae, while the Lutheran Romanian theologian Hermann Pitters translated his *Dogmatics* into German. In the French-speaking world, Stăniloae has exerted considerable influence on Orthodox theologians such as Olivier Clement and Marc-Antoine Costa de Beauregard, while attracting the admiration of Russian and Greek Orthodox. The potential for Stăniloae's further influence continues to grow given that his works are increasingly available to Western readerships and that Romanians are currently taking a keen interest in his thought.

In Romania, no one was allowed to engage in any type of political activity other than in support of the Communist Party between 1947 and 1989. That period covered almost half of Stăniloae's life. He refused to engage in Communist politics, and indeed he had to suffer five years of political imprisonment for his political convictions that bordered in some cases on the extreme right. Stăniloae published his views on Romanian nationalism in both pre–World War II and postcommunist writings. But he did not develop much original political thought, and he appeared incapable of dealing with some of the hard political issues facing postcommunist Romania. These included issues of how Orthodox clergy and laity were to deal with prior collaborators with the Communist secret police, the Securitate, and how to heal Romanian society following the collapse of Communism in Eastern Europe and the Soviet Union.

NOTES

1. John Meyendorff, foreword to Dumitru Stăniloae, *Theology and the Church*, trans. Robert Barringer (Crestwood, N.Y.: St. Vladimir's Seminary Press, 1980), 8.

2. For a fine presentation, see Maciej Bielawski, "Dumitru Stăniloae and his Philokalia," in *Dumitru Stăniloae: Tradition and Modernity in Theology*, ed. Lucian Turcescu (Iasi, Romania: Center for Romanian Studies, 2002), 25–52; Maciej Bielawski, *The Philocalical Vision of the World in the Theology of Dumitru Stăniloae* (Bydgoszcz, Poland: Homini, 1997).

3. Zigu Ornea, *Anii treizeci: Extrema dreaptă românească* (The 1930s: The Romanian Extreme Right Wing) (Bucharest: Editura Fundatiei Culturale Romane, 1995), 113–115.

4. See Mircea Pacurariu, "Preotul Profesor si Academician Dumitru Stăniloae," in *Persoană şi comuniune: Prinos de cinstire Preotului Profesor Academician Dumitru Stăniloae la împlinirea vârstei de 90 ani* (Person and Communion: Festschrift for Stăniloae on his Ninetieth Birthday), ed. Mircea Pacurariu and Ioan I. Ica Jr. (Sibiu, Romania: Editura Arhiepiscopiei ortodoxe Sibiu, 1993), 6.

5. Pacurariu, "Preotul Profesor Stăniloae," 7.

6. Gheorghe F. Anghelescu, "Bibliografie sistematica a Parintelui Prof. Acad. Dumitru Stăniloae," in Pacurariu and Ica, *Persoană şi comuniune*, 2:4.

7. Dumitru Stăniloae, "Ofranda adusa lui Dumnezeu de poporul roman," *Gazeta de Vest* 18 (February 1993): 18. See also Olivier Gillet, *Religion et nationalisme: L'idéologie de l'église orthodoxe roumaine sous le regime communiste* (Brussels: Editions de l'Université de Bruxelles, 1997), 136–139.

8. For contemporary Iron Guard doctrines, see http://www.miscarea-legionara .org and http://www.miscarea.com and affiliates.

9. Lidia Stăniloae, "Remembering My Father," trans. R. Roberson, in Turcescu, *Dumitru Stăniloae*, 21.

10. See Andrew Louth, "Review Essay: *The Orthodox Dogmatic Theology* of Dumitru Stăniloae," *Modern Theology* 13, no. 2 (April 1997): 253–267; reprinted in Turcescu, *Dumitru Stăniloae*, 53–70.

11. Bishop Kallistos [Ware] of Diokleia, foreword to Dumitru Stăniloae, *The Experience of God*, trans. Ioan Ioniţă and Robert Barringer, 2 vols. (Brookline, Mass.: Holy Cross Orthodox Press, 1994), 1:xiii.

12. Stăniloae, *The Experience of God*, 1:1.

13. See Lucian Turcescu, "Soteriological Issues in the 1999 Lutheran-Catholic Joint Declaration on Justification: An Orthodox Perspective," *Journal of Ecumenical Studies* 28, no. 1 (Winter 2001): 64–72.

14. Joseph A. Fitzmyer, "Pauline Theology," in *The New Jerome Biblical Commentary*, ed. Raymond E. Brown et al. (London: G. Chapman, 1990), 1397.

15. Stăniloae, *The Experience of God*, 1:2.
16. The church fathers did not have the modern Cartesian-Lockean concept of the person understood as a center of consciousness. Lucian Turcescu, *Gregory of Nyssa and the Concept of Divine Persons* (New York: Oxford University Press, 2005); Sarah Coakley, ed., *Rethinking Gregory of Nyssa* (Oxford: Blackwell, 2003).
17. Stăniloae, *The Experience of God*, 1:16.
18. Maximus the Confessor, *The Ambigua*, in *Patrologia Graeca* 91.1149C–1152B, 1176BC, paraphrased by Stăniloae in *The Experience of God*, 1:16–17.
19. This high-brow theology has caused some to label Stăniloae as elitist. Emil Bartos, "The Dynamics of Deification in the Theology of Dumitru Stăniloae," in Turcescu, *Dumitru Stăniloae*, 246.
20. Dumitru Stăniloae, *Theology and the Church*, trans. Robert Barringer (Crestwood, N.Y.: St. Vladimir's Seminary Press, 1980), 204.
21. Ibid.
22. Ibid., 210.
23. Ibid.
24. Ibid., 211.
25. Ibid.
26. Maximus the Confessor, *To Thalassius: On Various Questions*, in *Patrologia Graeca* 90.257C–260A; Stăniloae, *The Experience of God*, 2:163.
27. Ibid., 163–164.
28. Ibid., 164–165.
29. Ibid., 175.
30. Ibid., 166.
31. Ibid.
32. Ibid., 1:6.
33. Ibid., 2:166.
34. Gregory of Nyssa, *Contra Eunomium* III, 1, 123ff.; *Select Writings and Letters of Gregory, Bishop of Nyssa, Nicene and Post-Nicene Fathers*, 2d ser. (New York: Christian Literature Co., 1893), 5:149. *Contra Eunomium Libri* in *Gregorii Nysseni Opera*, vols. 1–2, ed. Werner Jaeger (Leiden: Brill, 1960). An English translation of the whole work predating Jaeger's critical edition can be found in *Select Writings*, 5:33–315.
35. Gregory of Nyssa, *Contra Eunomium* III, 1, 125.
36. Plotinus, *Enneads* VI.8.9.45–46, in *Enneads*, 7 vols., trans. A.H. Armstrong. (Cambridge, Mass.: Harvard University Press, 1966–1988). For Gregory's knowledge of Plotinus, see Turcescu, *Gregory of Nyssa*.
37. Stăniloae, *The Experience of God*, 2:166–167.
38. Ibid., 166.
39. Ibid., 168–169.
40. Ibid., 170–172.
41. Ibid., 187.
42. Ibid., 172.

43. Ibid., 191.

44. This is the topic of the last chapter of Stăniloae's second volume of *Experience of God*, entitled "Providence and the Deification of the World."

45. Stăniloae, *The Experience of God*, 2:194–195.

46. Ibid., 195.

47. Gregory of Nyssa, *Homilies on the Song of Songs* 6, in *Patrologia Graeca* 44.999A; see Stăniloae, *The Experience of God*, 2:195 nn. 173 and 175.

48. Sorin Dumitrescu, *Şapte dimineţi cu Parintele Stăniloae* (Seven Mornings with Father Stăniloae) (Bucharest: Anastasia, 1992), 97. English translations for the present volume are mine.

49. Ibid., 165–166.

50. See Lavinia Stan, "Moral Cleansing Romanian Style," *Problems of Post-Communism* 49, no. 4 (July–August 2002): 52–62; Stan, "Access to Securitate Files: The Trials and Tribulations of a Romanian Law," *Eastern European Politics and Society* 16, no. 1 (2002): 55–90.

51. Dumitrescu, *Şapte dimineţi*, 53–54.

52. Ibid., 54.

53. Ibid., 55.

54. Ibid., 55.

55. Ibid., 56.

56. Ibid., 57.

57. Following the December 1989 Romanian revolution, political power was transferred from dictator Nicolae Ceausescu and his tight circle of friends and relatives to a group of second-echelon officials led by the new President Ion Iliescu, a one-time close collaborator of the dictator, and Premier Petre Roman, the son of a high-ranking Communist official.

58. Dumitrescu, *Şapte dimineţi*, 58.

59. Ibid., 60.

60. See Lavinia Stan and Lucian Turcescu, "The Romanian Orthodox Church and Post-Communist Democratization," *Europe-Asia Studies* 52, no. 8 (December 2000): 1467–1488.

61. Rompress (January 12, 1990), http://www.rompres.ro.

62. *Romania libera* (March 10, 1997), http://www.romanialibera.com, citing a 1981 letter sent to Patriarch Justin Moisescu.

63. In 1986 Plamadeala defended Ceausescu's massive church demolition program by contending that "city urbanization and modernization is a general and inevitable phenomenon [which] unfortunately requires, as everywhere, sacrifices." See Alexander Webster, *The Price of Prophecy: Orthodox Churches on Peace, Freedom, and Security*, 2d ed. (Washington, D.C.: Ethics and Public Policy Center, 1995), 114.

64. Stan and Turcescu, "The Romanian Church and Democratisation," 1471.

65. *The Seven Ecumenical Councils of the Undivided Church: Their Canons and Dogmatic Decrees*, ed. and trans. Henry Percival, *Nicene and Post-Nicene Fathers*, 2d ser. (New York: Scribner's, 1900), 14:596.

66. Gillet, *Religion et nationalisme*, 93. See also Maximus of Sardis, *Le patriarcat oecumenique dans l'église orthodoxe: Etude historique et canonique* (Paris: n.p. 1975), 377–387.

67. Ioan N. Floca, *Canoanele Bisericii Ortodoxe, Note si Comentarii* (The Canons of the Orthodox Church with Notes and Commentaries) (Sibiu, Romania: Polsib, 1992), 27.

68. "Nationalismul sub aspect moral" (The moral aspect of nationalism), trans. Lucian Turcescu, *Telegraful Român*, 85, no. 47 (1937): 1.

69. Dumitru Stăniloae, "Idealul national permanent" (The permanent national ideal), trans. Lucian Turcescu, *Telegraful Român* 88, no. 4 (1940): 1–2, and 88, no. 5 (1940): 1.

70. Benedict R. Anderson, *Imagined Communities: Reflections on the Origin and Spread of Nationalism*, 2d ed. (London: Verso, 1991).

71. Augustine, *Eighty-three Different Questions*, q. 46, 1–2, in *The Essential Augustine*, ed. Vernon J. Bourke (Indianapolis: Hackett, 1974), 62–63.

72. Dumitru Stăniloae, "Scurta interpretare teologica a natiunii" (A Brief Theological Interpretation of the Nation), *Telegraful Român* 82 (1934): 15.

ORIGINAL SOURCE MATERIALS

NATURAL REVELATION

The Orthodox Church makes no separation between natural and supernatural revelation. Natural revelation is known and understood fully in the light of supernatural revelation, or we might say that natural revelation is given and maintained by God continuously through his own divine act which is above nature. That is why Saint Maximos the Confessor does not posit an essential distinction between natural revelation and the supernatural or biblical one. According to him, this latter is only the embodying of the former in historical persons and actions.[1]

This affirmation of Maximos must probably be taken more in the sense that the two revelations are not divorced from one another. Supernatural revelation unfolds and brings forth its fruit within the framework of natural revelation, like a kind of casting of the work of God into bolder relief, a guiding of the physical and historical world toward that goal for which it was created in accordance with a plan laid down from all ages. Supernatural revelation merely restores direction to and provides a more determined support for that inner movement maintained within the world by God through natural revelation. At the beginning, moreover, in that state of the world which was fully normal, natural revelation was not separated from a revelation that was supernatural. Consequently, supernatural revelation places natural revelation itself in a clearer light.

It is possible, however, to speak both of a natural revelation and of a supernatural one, since, within the framework of natural revelation, the work of God is not emphasized in the same way nor is it as evident as it is in supernatural revelation.

Speaking more concretely and in accordance with our faith, the content of natural revelation is the cosmos and man who is endowed with reason, with conscience, and with freedom. But man is not only an object that can be known within this revelation; he is also one who is a subject of the knowledge of revelation. Both man and the cosmos are equally the product of a creative act of God which is above nature, and both are maintained in existence by God through an act of conservation which has, likewise, a supernatural character. To the acts of conserving and leading the world towards its own proper end, there corresponds within the cosmos and within man both a power and a tendency of self-conservation and of right development. From this point of view, man and the cosmos can themselves be taken as a kind of natural revelation.

But man and the cosmos constitute a natural revelation also from the point of view of knowledge. The cosmos is organized in a way that corresponds to our capacity for knowing. The cosmos—and human nature as intimately connected with the cosmos—are stamped with rationality, while man (God's creature) is further endowed with a reason capable of knowing consciously the rationality of the cosmos and of his own nature. Nevertheless, according to Christian doctrine, this rationality of the cosmos and this human reason of ours which enables us to know are, on the other hand, the product of the creative act of God. Thus, natural revelation is not something purely natural from this point of view either.

We consider that the rationality of the cosmos attests to the fact that the cosmos is the product of a rational being, since rationality, as an aspect of a reality which is destined to be known, has no explanation apart from a conscious Reason which knows it from the time it creates it or even before that time, and knows it continually so long as that same Reason preserves its being. On the other hand, the cosmos itself would be meaningless along with its rationality if there were no human reason that might come to know the cosmos because of its rational character. In our faith, the rationality of the cosmos has a meaning only if it is known in the thought of an intelligent creative being before its creation and in the whole time of its continuing in being, having been first brought into existence precisely that it might be known by a being for whom it was created, and that a dialogue between itself and this created rational being might thus be brought about through its mediation. This fact constitutes the content of natural revelation.

Christian supernatural revelation asserts the same thing when it teaches that, to God's original creative and conserving position vis-à-vis the world, there corresponds, on a lower plane which is by nature dependent, our own position as a being made in the image of God and able to know and to transform nature. In this position of man, it can be seen that the world must have its origin in a Being which intended through the creation of the world—and through its preservation continues to intend—that man should come to a knowledge of the world through itself and to a knowledge of that Being.

We appear as the only being which, while belonging to the visible world and stamped with rationality, is conscious both of the rationality it possesses and, simultaneously, of itself. As the only being in the world conscious of itself, we are, at the same time, the consciousness of the world; we are also that factor able to assert the rationality of the world, and to transform the world consciously to our own advantage, and able, through this very act, to transform ourselves consciously by our own act. We cannot be aware of ourselves without being conscious of the world and of the things in it. The better we know the world, or the more aware we are of it, the more conscious we are of ourselves. But the world, by contributing in this passive manner to our formation and to the deepening of our self-consciousness, does not itself become—through this contribution—conscious of itself. This means that we are not for the sake of the world, but the world is for us, although man does also need the world. The point of the world is to be found in man, not vice versa. Even the fact that we are aware that we need the world shows man's superior position vis-à-vis the world. For the world is not able to feel our need for it. The world, existing as an unconscious object, exists for man. It is subordinated to man, even though he did not create it.[2]

THE ORTHODOX DOCTRINE OF SALVATION

Christ did not bring us salvation so that we might continue to live in isolation, but that we might strive towards a greater and ever more profound unity which has as its culmination the eternal Kingdom of God.

We see this reflected in the fact that we cannot gain salvation if we remain in isolation, caring only for ourselves. There is no doubt that each man must personally accept salvation and make it his own, but he cannot do so nor can he persevere and progress in the way of salvation unless he is helped by others and helps them himself in return, that is, unless the manner of our salvation is communal. To be saved means to be pulled out of our isolation and to be united with Christ and the rest of men. "Let us commend ourselves and each other and our whole life to Christ our God," sing the faithful at the Orthodox liturgy. Salvation is communion in Christ (*koinonia*) and therefore the obligation of Christians to strive to maintain and develop their ecclesial unity through love is plain: "For the love of Christ gathers us together." (2 Cor 5:14)

Inasmuch however as Christ has accomplished the work of salvation and continuously offers its fruits in order to bring all men together into the Kingdom of God, Christians, as servants of Christ obliged to strive for the union of all men in that Kingdom of perfect love, also have certain obligations towards those who are not Christians. In what follows a brief attempt will be made to set forth these obligations, or, more precisely, the motives which lie behind them. . . .

6. Reconciliation therefore does not consist of a purely formal peace, a mere coexistence and lack of aggression, covering over profound disagreements. Lasting reconciliation is inseparable from the kind of love which strives to secure equality and justice among men and nations, and to

promote continuous mutual exchange animated by love. It is the result of a true understanding of the meaning of reconciliation with God who unites himself to man and causes him to partake of all good things in Christ. Through such a reconciliation God adopts us as his sons and divinizes us according to his grace.

7. Christians can make no fruitful contribution to this profound reconciliation between men and nations if they are concerned solely with service to individual men and therefore neglect to promote just and equitable relations on a broader social and international scale. If Christians in the past often limited their acts of service to needy individuals because social structures tended to remain static, today, when social structures are more elastic because of the powerful influence of those who are aware of their own solidarity as victims of injustice and who confidently believe that they can produce more satisfactory forms of social life, Christians must make the kind of contribution which will favour the continuous adaptation of these structures to meet contemporary aspirations for greater justice, equality, and fraternity in man's relation to man. It has become more obvious today that the whole world is being moved to seek more just and fraternal human relations, and it is our belief as Christians that we can see in this movement the effect of Christ's activity guiding the world towards the Kingdom of Heaven, in spite of the fact that this is a goal which in its final form cannot be reached in this world, given the corruptible nature of matter and all its attendant ills.

Any reconciliation not founded on true universal justice and equality among men will always be threatened with collapse, and the absence of a lasting peace will threaten the life of every human being. Christians therefore must labour on behalf of such a lasting peace in order to assure to every man the chance to prepare for his own resurrection. Seen in this light, war presents as many risks to those who are killed as it does to those who do the killing. Though it may seem that the same risk sometimes attaches to a premature natural death, we can be sure that this happens according to the will of God and that God has his reasons. The Christian has a duty, therefore, to fight on behalf of justice because the presence of injustice can appear to provide a justification for eternal death, while the removal of injustice deprives eternal death of any such justification. One who struggles to end injustice follows in the path of Christ who was the first to use justice as a means to deprive death of its justification. Moreover, Christ gives us the power to do the same because our own struggle for justice depends on his power.[3]

8. Justice, equality, brotherhood and lasting peace cannot be realized if we have no interest in the material universe. The material universe,

like mankind itself, is destined for transfiguration through the power of the risen body of Christ, and through the spiritual power of his love which urges us to restore the material universe to its original role of manifesting our mutual love, not, as is now the case, of serving as a means of separation and strife. We must demonstrate increasingly in practice the meaning of material goods as gifts, as the means of mutual exchange between men. The universe belongs to Christ; it is mysteriously attached to his crucified and risen body. Yet it also belongs to men, to Christians and non-Christians alike who suffer and advance towards salvation. Nicholas Cabasilas says: "That blood flowing from his wounds has extinguished the light of the sun and caused the earth to quake. It has made holy the air and cleansed the whole cosmos from the stain of sin."[4]

Only if all men are united can they transform the world and respond to the call to treat the world as a gift, as the means of mutual exchange. When we share in the material goods of the universe we must be conscious that we are moving in the sphere of Christ, and that it is by making use of these material things as gifts for the benefit of one another that we progress in our union with Christ and with our neighbour. We must also be aware that when the material world becomes the means whereby we communicate in love, then we are communicating in Christ. Thus, the universe is called to become the eschatological paradise through the agency of fraternal love. It is our duty to free the universe from the vanity of the blind and selfish use we make of it as sinners, and to see that it shares in the glory of the sons of God (Rom 8:21), the glory which is an inseparable part of our union as brothers.[5]

THE TREE OF THE KNOWLEDGE OF GOOD AND EVIL

We do not know how long the human being remained in the primordial state. In any case, he did not undertake to consolidate his own obedience to God or to grow in the knowledge of him, for had he done so, the Fall would not have come about so easily, or it would not have come about at all. St. Maximus the Confessor said:

> Perhaps the creation of visible things was called the tree of the knowledge of good and evil because it has both spiritual reasons that nourish the mind and a natural power that charms the senses and yet perverts the mind. Therefore, when spiritually contemplated, it offers the knowledge of the good, while when received bodily it offers the knowledge of evil. For to those

who partake of it in the body, it becomes a teacher of passions, leading them to forget about divine things. Maybe that is why God had forbidden man the knowledge of good and evil, postponing for a while the partaking of it so that first of all, as was right—man knowing his own cause by communing with it in grace, and through this communion, changing the immortality given him by grace into freedom from passions and unchangeability, like one already becomes a god through deification—he, together with God, should gaze harmlessly and fearlessly on God's creatures and receive knowledge of them as God, not as man, possessing by grace and with wisdom the same understanding of things as God, thanks to the transfiguring of the mind and senses through deification.[6]

Likewise, Nicetas Stethatos, developing this idea, declared that the tree of the knowledge of good and evil is sensation applied to the sensible world or to the body. The human being was able to contemplate sensible things without danger by means of the sense faculties under the guidance of the mind. To behold sensible things through sense faculties not yet under the guidance of such a strengthened mind was, however, dangerous. Thus, the human being needed to grow first until he was capable of beholding the world with his sense faculties under direction from a mind that had become spiritual.[7]

The same opinion was expressed by St. Gregory Palamas, who is even more precise:

> Therefore, while they lived in that sacred land, it was to the profit of our ancestors and it was incumbent upon them never to have forgotten God, to have become still more practiced and, as it were, schooled in the simple, true realities of goodness and to have become accomplished in the habit of contemplation. But experience of things pleasant to the sense is of no profit to those who are still imperfect, those who are in mid-course and who, compared with the strength of the experienced, are easily displaced toward good or its opposite.[8]

We might infer that the primordial state lasted only a very short while, for in this state halfway between obedience and disobedience, our first parents were obliged from the very beginning to show themselves either as obedient or as disobedient. Had they shown themselves obedient over a period of time, they would have begun to be habituated to good, and so the Fall would have become a more difficult thing. It would seem, therefore, that they let themselves be overcome at once by the temptation to disobedience.

The expression "primordial state" thus points to that condition of our first parents when they came into existence through the creative act of God, and in which, as in their normal state, they were called to remain and to grow. St. Basil the Great spoke directly of the "rapidity" with which Adam decided in favour of disobedience, but he, too, affirmed the real existence of a short period of time prior to this decision for evil. He helps us to understand that, strictly speaking, the primordial state means that the human being did not come forth as intrinsically evil from the creative act of God, but that evil was chosen by the human being. Hence he had a short period of time in which to make up his mind before choosing. God could not create the human being evil, but he wanted man to strengthen himself in the good through his own cooperation as well. St. Basil even spoke of a certain complacency in the human being that came from his having everything. For the human being, all things lay too much ready at hand before he had grown spiritually by his efforts to win these things for himself. Instead of deciding to expend that effort required if he was to persist and advance in his participation in things that were good but less sensible, he preferred rather to choose enjoyment, without effort, of those good things more easily grasped. The fact that nature, too, was beautiful and rich in a way corresponding to the beauty of the intelligible meanings and realities constituted a further temptation for man to enjoy what was at hand rather than what demanded effort if he was to know and enjoy it.

> Adam was above, not spatially, but by the will, when, recently given (*arti*) soul and looking towards heaven, he rejoiced at what he had seen, loving the Benefactor who granted him the enjoyment of eternal life, rested upon him the pleasures of paradise, gave him mastery like that of the angels, and an existence like that of the archangels, and made him a hearer of the heavenly voice. Protected in all these matters by God and enjoying His good things, he was soon (*tachu*) satiated with everything and became somehow insolent in his repletion, preferring the delight appearing before the eyes of the flesh to intelligible beauty and placing a full belly above spiritual enjoyments. At once he was outside paradise, outside that happy way of life, not evil from necessity, but from lack of wisdom (*aboulia*). Thus he sinned because of a wicked choice and died because of sin.[9]

The *aboulia* of which St. Basil spoke partly means imprudence and partly lack of will, or laziness of the will. The human being had fallen because of imprudence and laziness in expending the effort to make use of his freedom. God wanted man to grow in freedom through his own effort. Freedom, as a sign of spiritual power, is more than just a gift; it is also a result of effort. From the beginning man refused that effort and so has fallen into the slavery of the easy pleasure afforded by the senses. God breathed spirit into man, but the spirit breathed into him was in great part a potency that man needed to make pass into act. By commanding man not to eat from the tree of consciousness before he was guided by freedom of the spirit, God, in fact, commanded him to be strong, to remain free, and to grow in spirit, that is, in freedom. This very commandment made appeal to man's freedom.

The human fall away from God consisted formally in an act of disobedience. Through that very act the human being detached himself interiorly from God and from positive dialogue with him. He no longer responded to God, believing that he was thereby affirming his freedom, and autonomy. In fact, it was this act that marked the beginning of the human's selfish confinement within himself. This was how he enslaved himself to himself. Reckoning on becoming his own lord, he became his own slave. The human person is free only if he is free also from himself for the sake of others, in love, and if he is free for God who is the source of freedom because he is the source of love. But disobedience used as an occasion the commandment not to taste from the tree of the knowledge of good and evil.

The fathers cited above imply that by the two trees we are to understand one and the same world: viewed through a mind moved by spirit, that world is the tree of life that puts us in relationship with God; but viewed and made use of through a consciousness that has been detached from the mind moved by spirit, it represents the tree of the knowledge of good and evil which severs man from God.

St. Gregory of Nyssa asserted this in his own way when he analyzed the ambiguous character of the tree of the knowledge of good and evil. The permitted tree of life is everything, or rather every instance of knowledge and experience, through which man advances in real goodness. The forbidden tree of the knowledge of good and evil is likewise every thing, or every instance of knowledge and experience of which man partakes, but in this case when he is led astray by the idea that it is good, when in reality it is evil ". . . for surely it is clear to all who are at all keen-sighted what that 'every' tree is whose fruit is life, and what again that mixed tree is whose end is death: for he who presents ungrudgingly the enjoyment of 'every' tree, surely by same reason and forethought keeps man from participating in those which are of doubtful kind."[10]

Like the fathers mentioned above, St. Gregory of Nyssa saw the tree of the knowledge especially in the sensible aspect of the world, but he put particular stress on the fact that this aspect may give rise to evil in the human person because it is grasped in an exclusive manner through his senses. In itself the sensible aspect of the world is by no means evil but can become quite dangerous for the human person because the senses, before they are spiritually strengthened, can be easily inflamed by the sensible beauty of the world. Accordingly, it is better for the human person to concentrate his attention on the spiritual meanings of the world until he himself is strengthened in spirit.[11] The danger in concentrating the powers of sensation on the sensible aspect of things comes, according to St. Gregory of Nyssa, from the possibility that due to the human bodily kinship with animal nature, the passions will be brought to birth in him.[12] Hence, the sensible aspect of the world acquires its characterization as the tree of the knowledge of good and evil, and through its encounter with the human powers of sensation, is mixed together with the sensible aspect of things, apart from any guidance by a mind moved by spirit. To this Satan, too, in the form of the serpent, symbol of all cunning insinuations, makes his contribution. ". . . and that fruit is combined of opposite qualities, which has the serpent to commend it, it may be for this reason that the evil is not exposed in its nakedness, itself appearing in its own proper nature . . ."[13] Evil would be ineffective if it did not deck itself in the colors of some good by which it lures those who are deceived into desiring it,

> but now the nature of evil is in a manner mixed; keeping destruction like some snare concealed in its depths and displaying some phantom of good in the deceitfulness of its exterior. The beauty of the substance [silver] seems good to those who love money: yet "the love of money is a root of all evil" . . . so, too, [with] the other sins. . . . It speaks of it [the fruit] . . . not as a thing absolutely evil (because it is decked with good), nor as a thing purely good (because evil is latent in it) . . . [Thus] the serpent points out the evil fruit of sin, not showing the evil manifestly in its own nature (for man would not have been deceived by manifest evil), but giving to what the woman beheld the glamour of a certain beauty . . . he appeared to speak to her convincingly . . . "and she took of the fruit thereof and did eat," and that eating became the mother of death to men.[14]

Evil cannot captivate by itself but decks itself with flowers taken from the good. The human person preserves an indelible remnant of the good within himself and must deceive himself by thinking that the sin he is committing has some justification through good. In its inability to stand on its own, evil is ambiguous, hence the perversity—presenting evil as good—to which any tempter must resort if he is to persuade someone to commit the evil he puts forward. Certainly, one who allows himself to be deceived retains in his deception a certain amount of insincerity. He consents to being deceived and is aware that he is deceived. Yet even this need to deceive himself represents a minimum of good left in him like a flimsy bridge by which evil gets in. Without this, evil cannot enter into him.

Evil offers an initial sweetness or good but in the end shows its destructive effect. In regard to the beginning of evil, the devil has no great need of deceiving man, for evil captivates on its own. It is from the human being's fear of the end, that is, of the consequences of an evil deed, that the devil must calm the human soul. As long as the voice of God, which resounded in the depths of the woman's sincere conscience, was telling her: "If you eat from the, tree, you shall die" (Gen 2: 17), it set this fear over against the tempting whisper of the serpent who was deceiving her with the words: "Of course you will not die, but you will be like God" (Gen 3: 4–5). Afterwards, however, this reassurance regarding the end of her evil deed grew stronger in the display of its initial sweetness.

St. Basil the Great interpreted the good and the evil connected with the fruit of this tree in a different way. His interpretation opened up an optimistic perspective toward the future and completed rather than contradicted that of St. Gregory of Nyssa. For St. Basil, the good and the evil committed by Adam are to be seen in the fact that by eating from the tree, Adam committed an act of disobedience on the one hand, while on the other hand, he was led to the knowledge of his own nakedness and hence to the knowledge of shame. Thus—and here St. Basil's approach is the reverse of St. Gregory's—if the beginning is evil, the end is good; or rather, after the evil end, or as he comes to encounter evil, repentance is born in man. In Adam's case, it was through his eating that the idea came to him of making clothes for himself so as to curb his fleshly impulses. In general, the temptation of the serpent served to alert the first humans to the battle to protect themselves against his temptations and to the struggle necessary to vanquish Satan. It was God himself who placed in man this impulse to fight against Satan, and in the Son of Man, Christ, this impulse led to the breaking of Satan's power. In Christ the ultimate end of the battle is found. "I will put enmity between you and the woman, and between your seed and her seed; he shall bruise your head, and you shall bruise his heel" (Gen 3:15). Even the beauty of the tree has served for the human person as an occasion to fight against temptations. By himself the human person will certainly not be able to conquer the evil that was introduced within him, but neither will the evil do away entirely with the good in the human person. The human person will remain in an ambivalent state. Emphasizing this struggle on behalf of the good in the human person and against the evil likewise present within him, St. Basil the

Great said: "That is why there was planted a tree bearing beautiful fruits, so that by abstaining from its sweetness and displaying the good of abstinence, we might justly be deemed worthy of the crown of patience. For not only disobedience followed upon the eating, but also the knowledge of nakedness."[15]

According to the interpretations of the fathers, the knowledge of good and evil, acquired when the activity of the senses unites with the sensible aspect of the world, consists in a knowledge of the passions born in the human person, while according to the special interpretation of St. Basil, it consists also in the fight against these passions. From the patristic interpretations we see that on account of the Fall, the human person was left with the knowledge of evil in himself but overwhelmed by it. He continued to be opposed to evil but could not succeed in bringing his struggle to a victorious conclusion.

From the fact that the state of disobedience as estrangement from God is reciprocally involved with the passionate impulse that takes its birth from the weaving together of sensuality and the sensible aspect of the world, a more complex understanding of this sad knowledge of good and evil results, that is, of the fall of man.

Disobedience, pride, and our own selfish appetite arise as a weakening of the spirit. These, moreover, produce a restriction on the knowledge of God's creation; the human person looks to what he can dominate and to what can satisfy his bodily needs and pleasures, now become passions. The bodily passions, in turn, will feed the pride in the human person that satisfies them. His exclusively material needs and passions will be a source of pride justified by his proud claim to be autonomous.

We should note, that in our description of this restricted knowledge of creation, we have already passed on to the consequences of sin, inasmuch as this restricted image of the world in a particular way, but in part, too, this restricted knowledge (which both hold sway within man against his will) are no longer produced by an actual sin.

This restricted knowledge is adapted to an understanding of the world as ultimate reality, but as a reality characterized as object and destined to satisfy exclusively the bodily needs—now become passions—of rational creatures. It conforms to the human passions and pride under whose power it has fallen, and it sees creation as a vast, opaque, and ultimate object possessed of no transparence or mystery that transcends it. This knowledge took its origin from a spiritually undeveloped human person, and it has remained at his measure, arresting his spiritual growth in relation to the horizon that lies beyond the sensible world. It is a knowledge that veils what is most essential in creation, hence a knowledge in the ironic sense that God uses to speak of in Genesis 3:22. It is a knowledge that will never know the ultimate meaning and purpose of reality.

The difficulty of coming to know the transparent character of creation and of person itself, characters that open their infinite meanings, derives also from the fact that creation and the human person can no longer put a stop to the process of corruption that leads each human person toward death. Had Adam not sinned, the conscious creature would have advanced toward a kind of "stable" motion within a greater and greater convergence and unification of the parts of creation, of the human person in himself and of humans among themselves and with God, within a movement of universal love whereby creation is overwhelmed by the divine Spirit. Instead, through the Fall, a motion toward divergence and decomposition entered creation. It is only through Christ, as God incarnate, that the parts of creation have begun to recompose themselves so as to make possible its future transfiguration, for from Christ the unifying and eternally living Spirit is poured out over creation.

We note that in the Orthodox view, the world after the Fall did not take on a totally and fatally opaque image, nor was human knowledge wholly restricted to a knowledge that conformed to an opaque, untransparent image of the world. Humans can penetrate this opacity in part by means of another kind of knowledge, and indeed, they often manage to do this, but they cannot wholly overcome this opacity and the knowledge that conforms to it. These remain dominant structures.[16]

PROVIDENCE AND THE DEIFICATION OF THE WORLD

A good part of more recent theology puts the idea of hope in the forefront. "Any idea of God that cements the existing social order is abandoned. Today it makes sense to speak about God only if he opens a future and has a function of transforming the world."[17] That is, only if, as God leads the human being toward himself and toward salvation, he is leading him to higher levels.

This work of God is bound up *par excellence* with the category of the "new": "Behold, I make all things new" (Rev 21:5). This is the final perspective opened for us by God. But in the view of this final newness, humans must become new from now onwards (Eph 4:24; 2 Cor 5:17; Gal 6:15). Not at the end alone will all things be made new; it is true from the first coming of Christ (2 Cor 5:17). And this newness is not one that grows old, but one in which we must unceasingly be walking and growing: "[so that] . . . we too might walk in newness of life . . . so that we might serve not under the old written code but in the newness of spirit" (Rom 6:4, 7:6). To walk in "newness of life" or "newness of spirit" means to be always open to "the new." For the "spirit" is always alive, that is, spirit does not remain within the same things. This is that "stability" within the movement of ascent described by St. Gregory of Nyssa, a stability that is simultaneously motion and without which the human being no longer remains within continuous newness but as a consequence, falls.[18] Moreover, God is life. St. Gregory of Nyssa said: "True being is true life . . . It is not in the nature of what is not life to be the cause of life. This truly is the vision of God: never to be satisfied in the desire to see him."[19]

St. Paul the apostle opposed the "newness of spirit" to the oldness of the letter or the law as he opposed the life of the resurrection to abiding in death. Now where the law is, there is found a sign that sin reigns. "The sting of death is sin, and the power of sin is the law" said St. Paul (1 Cor 15:56). When the law does not prepare men to go beyond the level it has helped them to attain, that is, when man does not draw the conclusion as a kind of constant newness, that Christ is "the end of the law" or that "love is the fulfilling of the law" (Rom 10:4, 13: 10), then the law is the power of sin that leads to death. Moreover, sin is the sign of the survival of the old man. To remain always within the identical forms is an expression of the survival of sin, of staying within the limits of the self. The genuinely "new" does not represent growth in self-centeredness, but rather continual surpassing of the self, advancement beyond the self; it is not the extension of one's own dominion in order to provide even greater security for the ego.

The law is repetition, according to an external norm, within the monotonously confined horizon of egoism and death. To walk in "newness of life" means to live beyond repetition as love or knowledge or the good passes by degrees from one stage to another, from *epektasis* to *epektasis,* as St. Gregory of Nyssa put it.[20] God makes any state already attained, any result already achieved, a relative thing only. Every such state only represents a step leading to another and higher one. The "reign of freedom" transcends any level that is attainable, and it is toward such liberty that we are advancing, always unhindered by any level we might have reached already.

God reveals himself in this way as the factor that forms a humanity that is being raised higher and higher, and as the force that is leading us toward a future that is never closed back in on itself. This factor shows itself in the form of a love for humans that is continuously bestowing more upon them and wanting them to be more and more loving toward one another. Thus, love for God, or more strictly, thought taken for God, represents a continuous contribution toward keeping the world in move-ment toward more and more authentically human relations among hu-mans. God resists making any structure or condition humans have achieved among themselves into an absolute reality. He shows his effec-tiveness in two ways: first, by keeping the human person's spiritual hori-zon free when it is confronted with any degree or form of this kind of absolute structure or relationship; second, by bestowing upon our nature the impulse to find paths that lead toward ever more improved relations among humans and to the goal of a humanity elevated to the highest pos-sible degree, a degree that cannot be defined beforehand. St. Maximus the Confessor expressed this vision through evaluating movement in time in a positive manner, that is, as movement toward the ultimate goal of rest in loving union with God who has no limits and who, at the same time, is not identical with our own "I." "For necessarily the free movement of all things in desire around anything else will cease when the ultimate goal, which is wished and participated in, appears, the goal that will fill to overflowing, so to speak, those who will participate in it according to their capacity. For it is toward it that every way of life and every thought of what is elevated tends and in it all desire rests and is by no means carried beyond it."[21]

SEVEN MORNINGS WITH FATHER STĂNILOAE

Sorin Dumitrescu [SD]: I would like to ask you whether it is not the time for the Church, out of respect for history and society, to make some dis-tinctions to help renew the civil society or to bring about at least an imaginary consensus in [the Romanian] society? Today we [Romanians] have a country in which executioners and victims live side by side, mixed up deliberately to the point of being indistinguishable from each other.

Dumitru Stăniloae [Fr. DS]: As I said earlier, as social beings humans need other humans. Nevertheless, I cannot say that I exist up to this point and from thence there is someone else. I have to be in a relationship with both good and bad people, always having the consciousness of a [Chris-tian] mission. I mean to say that churchmen—first bishops, priests, monks—and lay people should not separate themselves from the other members of the society. Churchmen should not imitate the others, but help them to improve themselves by personal example, help, and words of consolation. Churchmen should always be dynamic and efficacious exam-ples in society. I do not get involved in politics and will not say, "I belong to such and such party, let's get rid of the other party, or I want such and such ministers. . . ."

SD: That is politics. However, do you not think the Church should deliver a speech on guilt? Should it not theologize a little on guilt also?

Fr. DS: Not on the guilt of certain persons, because the Church always preaches on how people ought to be. Churchmen—priests, monks, bishops—should be an example in realizing the behavior proposed by writings such as the *Philokalia*.[22] Yet we have to realize that they themselves are humans and that they cannot always be perfect examples. . . .

SD: My question is a little different though. The political leadership tries to use the Christian theme of forgiveness as an electoral slogan, imposing a homogenization of guilt. Today everybody says he or she is not guilty. Those who shot dead young people [protesting against the communist regime of Nicolae Ceausescu in December 1989] say they obeyed orders, while the others, of course, say they are right. The political leadership says, "Look, we are the real Christians, because we do not punish anybody." In this case, should not the Church intervene more decisively?

Fr. DS: The Church cannot publicly condemn anybody, because confession is an intimate matter. Where would hatred stop if one were to say, "This one is guilty, and that one too, and so on and so forth"? These are intimate issues. The Church teaches, it does not condemn publicly. If someone comes to confession saying, "I am wrong, I stole, I killed," the Church tells that person "You cannot have communion with the Lord." Do you think that is an easy thing?

SD: But I do not mean the condemnation of a certain person, but the Church should draw attention—if the matter is real—that God, nevertheless, has two arms: one for forgiveness and love, the other for justice. Can we live only with love? Because the political leadership says now "We love you, nobody is guilty; it's good we got rid of the demon Ceausescu; other than that, calm down because nobody is guilty."

Fr. DS: The Church lives through love, but also by certain goodness. When real believers come to the Church [to confess their sins], the Church tells them simply that they have to change. You are forgiven but you have to promise you will not sin again. When the adulterous woman was brought to Jesus, he said that those without sin should throw the first stone. All her accusers put their stones down and left, while Jesus said to her, "I forgive you, too, but sin no more." He cannot say, "I do not forgive you; I condemn you for what you did." So does the priest: I forgive you, but sin no more. There is goodness mixed with intransigence, as you see. I do not like the sin, but I do not condemn someone definitively either. . . . I

repeat, the Church does not condemn. . . .The Church does not prevent
the State from making its own laws required by history. State laws condemn the perpetrator if necessary. If an executioner . . . comes to a priest,
the latter cannot say, "I will hand you over and let you be killed." If you
repent, stop doing what you have been doing, start leading a very different life, we shall see. For now, you do not receive communion for the next
ten years. After ten years, if you changed, you receive communion. . . . I
cannot hand him over to the police. Jesus forgave the repenting thief. I
have to see real repentance, and this is one way of correcting people.

SD: Excuse me, but what you say refers to the personal relationship between the penitent and the confessing father. . . . Do you not think the
Church, without naming names, should take a public stand and say that
its teachings are misused? Because, you see, the Church does not want to
homogenize guilt by [indiscriminate] forgiveness; the Church can be intransigent if it wants to.

Fr. DS: So, you suggest the Church should prevent the State from using
its laws.

SD: No, to the contrary. The Church should tell the State to use its
laws. We have set free all those who for 45 years have mocked the people.
Everybody is now acquitted; the executioners ride with the victims on
the same buses, applaud together at the same shows. Do you think that is
normal?

Fr. DS: Can the Church say, "Kill the executioners"?

SD: No, it cannot say that. Nevertheless, it can say, "Justice is needed."

Fr. DS: Well, that is what it says all the time.

SD: Still, the Church did not say it loud enough, because the Church itself is culpable.

Fr. DS: What can we do? There is a long road from teaching to practice.
Nobody is perfect in this world. Nor are the churchmen. We plead for the
good, we seek to win the others to our cause, but few of us are perfect supporters of the Christian teachings in their own lives. That is how we are,
as St. Apostle Paul said it, "we are sinners and I am the first among them."
I could not punish. I was in jail myself and I do not even remember well
those who tortured me. Nevertheless, if I knew them, I would not ask for
their punishment.

SD: Yes, but you cannot ask the same from a whole nation, can you? You
keep forgetting that there is a whole crowd of people out there who want
to know who shot the young people dead in 1989. This crowd wants a trial,
regardless of whether they end up forgiving or condemning the executioners. Yet, they want to discern truth from lie. Do you consider this an
unchristian wish?

Fr. DS: I do not know if Christians, priests, the Church could ask for the punishment of those people.

SD: What about discerning who is guilty and who is not?

Fr. DS: Of course, the Church together with others [the State] can discern. If the others [the State] do not do it, should the Church be harsher and say "Kill them, punish them"? Did Jesus say this thing? Did he instigate the people against those who judged him, Pharisees and priests?

SD: Yet he entered the temple with a whip.

Fr. DS: That is true, but he did not ask for the death of the moneychangers. The Church does whip at times. There was a time until the fourth century when public confession was practiced—people confessed their sins in public. That was not a good idea. The Church cannot instigate the society to proceed with punishment. . . .

SD: . . . According to the tradition of the church, penance always accompanies the confession of guilt, that is, so and so comes, confesses his or her sins, and then receives a penance. The Church should propose this model to the political leadership and the civil society. Do you agree with this?

Fr. DS: The Church would have to ask each government to recognize its guilt and thus it would meddle too much in politics.

SD: No, just to suggest it.

Fr. DS: The Church did suggest it, but it cannot do this publicly by saying, "This or that government or party is sinful." There is no perfect party. The Church has another method: it works with people, not with political forces. The Church wants to avoid becoming a force in history itself, in order to avoid critique such as, "Why do you say that, are you better?"

SD: Do you think that one of the Church's methods is to validate immediately a newly installed government who usurped the power? Would it not be wise for the Church to wait a little?

Fr. DS: That is something else. I should not show immediately that I am on their side.

SD: The Romanian Orthodox Church did the exact opposite.

Fr. DS: Well, just a minute. Did all of us do it? There are people and people in the Church. Such and such metropolitan gave opportunistic speeches, approving of the new political power. That was his business, but the Church did not do it. The Church is something else: it is the general consciousness of the Christians. The Church as such, I think, does not approve of what is happening. Orthodoxy, in fact, keeps itself at a distance from these kinds of things.[23]

THE MORAL ASPECT OF NATIONALISM

"Nationalism is the consciousness of belonging to a certain ethnic group, the love for that group and the enacting of that love for the well-being of the group."[24]

THE PERMANENT NATIONAL IDEAL

"The Romanian nation (*neam*) is a biological-spiritual synthesis of a number of elements. The most important of them are the Dacian element, the Latin element, and the Christian Orthodox element. . . . The synthesis is new, it has its own individuality, and a principle of unity which differs from the partial components. The highest law of our nation (*neam*), the law which expresses what the nation is in the most appropriate way, is the one that the whole experiences, not the ones experienced by the parts. The parts are stamped with a new, unifying, and individualizing stamp which is Romanianhood (*românitatea*). Therefore, we can say that the highest law for our nation (*neam*) is Romanianhood. Not Romanity, not Dacianism, but Romanianhood with all it includes is the highest law by which we live and fulfill our mission. . . . Which is the Romanian way of communion with the transcendental spiritual order? History and the current life of our people tell us that: it is Orthodoxy. Orthodoxy is the eye through which Romanians gaze at heavens and then, enlightened by the heavenly light, they turn their eye toward the world while continuing to attune their behavior to it. We also know that this is the only eye that is correct and healthy. . . . Certainly, in theory it is hard to understand how it is possible for Orthodoxy to interpenetrate with Romanianism without either of them to have to suffer. Yet, the bi-millennial life of our nation (*neam*) shows that in practice this is fully possible. . . . Orthodoxy is an essential and vital function of Romanianism. The permanent national ideal of our nation can only be conceived in relation with Orthodoxy."[25]

BRIEF THEOLOGICAL INTERPRETATION OF THE NATION

"Concerning man in particular, God created Adam and Eve in the beginning. In them were virtually present all nations. These are revelations in time of the images which have existed eternally in God. Every nation has an eternal divine archetype that it has to bring about more fully. . . . There is one instance when nations may not be from God and we would have to fight against them: when human diversification into nations would be a consequence of sin and a deviation from the way in which God wanted to develop humanity. In that case, the duty of every Christian would be to get humanity out of that sinful state and to fuse all nations into one.

Is diversification of humanity a sin or a consequence of sin? We could reject that presupposition by the mere universal law of fauna and flora. . . . Nevertheless, the answer can be given differently also: sin or evil is of a different order than unity or diversity. Sin means a deformity, a disfiguration of a given thing. . . . Is national specificity a deformity of humanity, a decay of the human being? This would be the case when national specificity would be something vicious, petty, and without heights of purity and thought. . . . The removal of humanity from the sinful state is being done not through the annulment of the national features, but by the straightening of human nature in general. If there were something sinful in national specificity, then one could not distinguish between good and evil people within a nation, but all would be evil. . . . We should note that there is no a-national person. Adam himself was not a-national, but he spoke a language, had a certain mentality, a certain psychic and bodily structure. A pure human, un-colored nationally, without national determinants, is an abstraction."[26]

NOTES

1. Cf. *The Ambigua*, PG 91.1128D–1133A, 1160B–D.
2. [Dumitru Stăniloae, *The Experience of God*, trans. Ioan Ioniță and Robert Barringer (Brookline, Mass.: Holy Cross Orthodox Press, 1994), 1:1–3.]
3. I have taken this idea from a work found in the Athanasian corpus, *Sermo in Sanctum Pascha*, PG 28,1077A–C.
4. *De Vita in Christo* 4, PG 150, 592A.
5. [Dumitru Stăniloae, "The Orthodox Doctrine of Salvation and its Implications for Christian Diakonia in the World," in *Theology and the Church*, trans. Robert Barringer (Crestwood, N.Y.: St. Vladimir Seminary Press, 1980), 204, 210–212.]
6. *To Thalassius: On Various Questions*, Introduction, PG 90.257C-260A.
7. *Vision of Paradise* 15–17, ed. Darrouzes, SChr81, pp. 170–172.
8. *The One Hundred and Fifty Chapters* 50.1–7, ed. Sinkewicz, 142; ET = Sinkewicz, 143.
9. *God is Not the Author of Evil* 7, PG 31.344C-345A.
10. *The Making of Man* 19.3, PG 44.197A; ET = Wilson, 409.
11. St. Basil the Great considered, however, that the tree of the knowledge of good and evil as a particular tree, but it was not evil in itself, even though it was

tempting because of its beauty and the sweetness of its fruits, hence, as representing the beauty and sensible sweetness of creation. Cf. *God is Not the Author of Evil* 8, PG 31.348C–D.

12. Cf. *The Making of Man* 18.1–9, PG 44.192A–196B.

13. *The Making of Man* 20.2, PG 44.200A; ET = Wilson, 410.

14. *The Making of Man* 20.2–4, PG 44.200A–D; ET = Wilson, 410.

15. *God is Not the Author of Evil* 8, PG31.348D.

16. [Dumitru Stăniloae, *The Experience of God*, trans. Ioan Ioniță and Robert Barringer (Brookline, Mass.: Holy Cross Orthodox Press, 2000), 2:163–172.]

17. Gotthold Hasenhüttl, "Die Gottesfrage heute," in *Gott, Mensch, Universum. Der Christ vor den Fragen der Zeit*, ed. I Hüttenbügel (Graz, 1974), 545–573, 563–564.

18. *The Life of Moses* 2.243–244, PG 44.405C-D; ET = Abraham J. Malherbe/Everett Ferguson, *Gregory of Nyssa. The Life of Moses*, NY etc. 1978, 117–118.

19. *The Life of Moses* 2.235 [233], 239, PG 44.40IB [A], D; ET = Malherbe/Ferguson, 115–116.

20. Cf. *Homilies on the Song of Songs* 6, PG. 44.888A; ET = McCambley, 128, and *The Life of Moses* 2.238–239, PG 44.404C–405A; ET = Malherbe/Ferguson, 116.

21. *The Ambigua*, PG 91.1076C–D. [Stăniloae, *The Experience of God*, 2:194–196.]

22. [*Philokalia* is a collection of Eastern Orthodox spiritual writings. Stăniloae single-handedly produced a monumental twelve-volume Romanian translation between 1946 and 1991.]

23. [Sorin Dumitrescu, *Seven Mornings with Fr. Stăniloae* (Bucharest, Romania: Anastasia, 1992), 53–60. Translated by Lucian Turcescu.]

24. [Dumitru Stăniloae, "The Moral Aspect of Nationalism," *Telegraful Roman* 85, no. 47 (1937): 1. Translated by Lucian Turcescu.]

25. [Dumitru Stăniloae, "The Permanent National Ideal," *Telegraful Roman* 88, no. 4 (1940): 1–2. Translated by Lucian Turcescu.]

26. [Dumitru Stăniloae, "Brief Theological Interpretations of the Nation," *Telegraful Roman* 82, no. 15 (1934): 2. Translated by Lucian Turcescu.]

Copyright Information

Index to Biblical Citations

Index